MW00962840

Come Holy Spirit, Heal and Reconcile !

Called in Christ to be Reconciling and Healing Communities

Report of the WCC Conference on World Mission and Evangelism, Athens, Greece

May 9 - 16, 2005

Jacques Matthey, Editor

COME HOLY SPIRIT, HEAL AND RECONCILE !

Cover design : Graphi4

ISBN 2-8254-1497-2

© 2008, WCC Publications, World Council of Churches
P.O. Box 2100, 150 route de Ferney
1211 Geneva 2, Switzerland

Website : http://www.oikoumene.org

Printed in France, by Graphi4

Table of Contents

Editor's Note

This book documents the preparations and the proceedings of a conference which took place in May 2005. Except where specifically mentioned or where obvious, information and references, including biographical notes and bibliography, correspond to the situation at the time of the conference or when the papers were originally produced. They have not been updated and therefore may not match the present reality or personal situation of the authors or participants whose names appear. The present volume is dedicated respectfully to all who participated in planning and realizing the Athens mission conference, and especially to the memory of those who have died in the months since that event.

As this volume went to press, the world learned of the death of Archbishop Christodoulos, primate of the Greek Orthodox Church and a generous host to the 2005 Conference on World Mission and Evangelism. Without his vision, his theological contribution to the proceedings and the hospitality shown for this first such gathering in a predominately Eastern Orthodox setting, the conference would have been diminished.

This book does not pretend to be a scientific or academic publication. Some of the guidelines and reports of sessions arrived unaccompanied by clear bibliographical references; attempts have been made to provide and check citations. In many cases, this printed publication follows texts as they appear on the WCC website.

Except where specifically stated, opinions expressed in this book and at the conference are not agreed positions of the World Council of Churches nor of the Commission on World Mission and Evangelism, nor of conference organizers and participants. The Athens conference aimed at creating a space for dialogue and debate, and did not produce official statements.

In closing, I wish to extend my gratitude to all those who have helped to prepare the text of this report for publication, and especially to Marlise Freidig, Lindsay Ann Cox, Theodore Gill and Hugh McCullum.

Jacques Matthey

COME HOLY SPIRIT, HEAL AND RECONCILE !

INTRODUCTION

As moderator of the Sixth Conference on World Mission and Evangelism of the World Council of Churches (WCC) meeting in Athens in May 2005, and of its Commission from 1999-2006, it is my pleasure to introduce this report to you.

One of the aims of the Conference always was that the participants would go back to their contexts newly challenged in their engagement in the mission of God by the meeting, debate, prayer and reflection. The influence of such "living letters" is hard to quantify, but I dare to believe from what people were saying as they left the conference that this has been happening in many ways and places. Nonetheless, it is important to have this book with its record of key features of the conference, the plenary papers, reflections and other documents in order to continue to inform and inspire the whole ecumenical movement as we engage faithfully in the mission of God.

Not that the writing of this report has been without challenges. The deliberately different nature of the Conference with its varied "synaxeis" and limited time in debate in plenary, together with increasing use of "power-point" presentations rather than written and read papers, makes the documenting of the Conference difficult. For those who were present, we hope this volume will act as an aide-mémoire; for those who were not present, we hope it gives something of the flavour of the Conference and its content; for those who ask of the ecumenical movement where it is in its thinking about mission, we hope it provides a snapshot.

Much thinking, praying and planning went into preparations for the Conference. The thematic focus was chosen back in August 2001. Little did we know how pertinent it would be; the world remains a place where there is conflict and terror; as churches, too often we are still divided in our witness to the good news; globalization continues to impact communities around the world... to highlight but a few issues. Into such a world God comes, sending his Son, who in turn sends us empowered by the Spirit, so we dare pray, "Come Holy Spirit! Heal and reconcile."

For me, one of the great gifts and joys of the Conference was that by the grace of God the Spirit built community amongst the participants over our days together. Given the wide range of people represented, with a Roman Catholic delegation fully participating as well as those from Pentecostal and evangelical churches and movements not necessarily in membership of the World Council of Churches, this in itself was significant.

In recent years. through its affirmation of a "Common Understanding and Vision", the WCC has invited its member churches to renew their commitment to both deepen and broaden the fellowship. Coming a year before the Ninth WCC Assembly in Porto Alegre, Brazil and after the reporting and implementing of changes following the Special Commission on Orthodox Participation in the

WCC,[1] the Conference was watched by many to see if dreams and commitments could be realized in practice. I believe they were, and foundations were laid for the on-going journey.

I suggest, too, that the themes of reconciliation and healing, which have most often been seen as part of the justice agenda of the churches, found new relevance as they were explored from a missiological perspective. Coming as it did, at the mid-point of the Decade to Overcome Violence (DOV), the Conference reminds us again of the one ecumenical movement and the one holistic mission of God, a confluence in which each stream is as important as the other.

The prayer of the Conference, and the whole liturgical flow of each day, it seems to me, prefigured the decision of the Porto Alegre Assembly to bring Faith and Order, Mission and Evangelism and explorations of spirituality into new relationships of programmatic work in the next cycle of the Council's life. Our being and our doing belong together.

One of the most abiding memories I have of the Conference is scurrying through the pine trees of the Aghios Andreas campus, late as ever because of moderatorial responsibilities, for my home group and the time of biblical reflection. As I made my way I would hear in turn the different groups beginning their time together singing the prayer theme of the conference, "Come Holy Spirit, heal and reconcile." As one group ceased, another would take up the harmony. The prayer, the song, still rises in my heart: as I watch the television news of new situations of violence and atrocities committed, as I live and work in community with those affected by alcohol and drug addiction, mental illness and homelessness, as churches still seem to compete with one another rather than commit to cooperation. For this participant at least, the theme of the Conference continues to resonate, to inform and inspire. I hope it will for you, too, as you read this report.

Shalom

Rev. Ruth Bottoms

The Rev. (Ms) Ruth Bottoms is the moderator of the Commission on World Mission and Evangelism and of the 2005 Conference on World Mission and Evangelism. She has also moderated the Conference Planning Committee. She is a member of the WCC Central Committee and is chairperson of the Council of the Baptist Union in Great Britain. She lives in an ecumenical community (Pilsdon, Bridgeport, UK), working with homeless, recovering addicts, mentally ill (see also the Synaxis on page 234).

---

[1] "Towards a Common Understanding and Vision of the World Council of Churches" (CUV) is a policy document adopted by the WCC Central Committee in 1997 and received after a plenary discussion at the 1998 Harare Assembly. At that same assembly, it was decided to set up a Special Commission to study the full range of issues "related to the participation of Orthodox churches in the WCC and to present proposals about changes in structure, working style and ethos to the central committee for decision" (Diane Kessler, ed., *Together on the Way, Official Report of the Eighth Assembly of the WCC*, Geneva, WCC, 1999, p. 152). The Special Commission submitted its report to the central committee in 2002, with specific recommendations concerning the prayer life and decision-making of WCC meetings as well as the meaning of membership in the Council.

PREPARING FOR ATHENS
2000-2005

Introduction

The Athens conference was organized and led by the Commission on World Mission and Evangelism (CWME), acting on behalf of the World Council of Churches (WCC). It is a conference to be counted among the world mission conferences organized first by the International Missionary Council (IMC) from 1921 to 1961, then, following the merger of the IMC with the WCC, by the CWME. The seminal inspiring event which gave birth to the contemporary ecumenical and missionary movement was the world mission conference at Edinburgh in 1910. Usually one counts the following conferences as the official list of IMC and WCC world mission conferences, beginning with Edinburgh in 1910, Jerusalem,1928; Tambaram, 1938; Whitby, 1947; Willingen, 1952; Accra, 1958, and New Delhi 1961 (the assembly accomplishing the merger between IMC and WCC); Mexico City, 1963; Bangkok, 1973; Melbourne, 1980; San Antonio, 1989; Salvador da Bahía, 1996; and Athens 2005.[1]

Since the integration of the IMC and the WCC, matters related to mission and evangelism are dealt with at three levels. The Conferences on World Mission and Evangelism (CWME) are the largest mission gatherings of the WCC. Usually they take place between general assemblies of the WCC and count between 600 and 800 participants. Specific by-laws of the WCC give guidance for their composition and aim. The version of these by-laws adopted by the central committee of the WCC in 1999 is reproduced in the appendix. The WCC world mission conferences (usually called CWME Conferences) are prepared and led by the Commission on World Mission and Evangelism, an advisory body to the central committee of the WCC. Since the Harare assembly of the WCC (1998), the second level consists of a 30-person commission that is composed of three categories of members:

a) members delegated by the CWME affiliated bodies (mission councils, national councils of churches, church communities or groupings for mission, which are affiliated to the CWME Conference). Some of these represent churches and mission groups not otherwise related to WCC;
b) members delegated by WCC member churches; and
c) members delegated by churches which are not members of the WCC, such as the Roman Catholic Church as well as Pentecostal or evangelical churches or mission bodies.

---

[1] The list explains why there are various ways to count the total number. It all depends whether one includes Edinburgh and New Delhi, or not. If the count includes both, Athens was the 13th world mission conference in that series.

The inclusion of the third category (c) after Harare allowed for representatives of the Roman Catholic Church and of Pentecostal or evangelical non-member churches to have a seat in the CWME commission with the right to participate in decision-making. The CWME commission is newly elected by the central committee after each assembly of the WCC.

The third "level" are the staff of the WCC working on mission and evangelism[2] under the leadership of the general secretary and the central committee.

The Start in 2000

The newly elected CWME commission met for the first time in late March and early April, 2000 at Morges, Switzerland, under the leadership of the Reverend Ruth Bottoms of the UK. It was during that meeting that the decision to propose holding a CWME conference in the coming years, before the next WCC assembly, was agreed upon. Commissioners did not yet have a precise idea of a possible programme or theme. The provisional biblical text chosen as a key word for the coming months was John 10:10 "I have come that they may have life, life in abundance", and a thematic area was formulated as "Global Christian mission witnessing to a gospel of love and life in a globalized world".

The commission adopted the study document "Mission and Evangelism in Unity Today" published later as Conference preparatory paper No 1. The Commission clearly intended that statement to be used for the preparation of the future conference.[3]

The proposal to hold a world mission conference was forwarded to the WCC central committee which confirmed it in February 2001 in Potsdam, Germany.

A Decisive Hour – the Commission Meeting in Techny Towers, Chicago, Ill., August 2001

When the CWME commission met next, it could draw on work done in the years 2000 and 2001, in particular on the healing ministry and on ecclesiology and mission as well as on the results of a brain-storming consultation organized at Cartigny, Switzerland, in March 2001 in cooperation with the Council for World Mission (London, UK), the Cevaa – Community of churches in mission (Montpellier, France), and the United Evangelical Mission (Wuppertal, Germany). Some 15 missiologists had discerned and chosen key issues as potential emphases for a future ecumenical reflection on mission. Several of the persons who participated in these early meetings became important contributors to the preparatory process for Athens.

The commission worked in groups to discern future trends in mission and evangelism. The process allowed for building a consensus that healing and reconciliation were

---

[2] In the preparatory time for the Athens conference, staff worked first in the "Mission and Evangelism team", then, following a change of structure in the WCC, in the "Mission and Ecumenical Formation team".

[3] The statement has been published on the Conference website (www.mission2005.org) and in the book *"You are the light of the world" – Statements on Mission by the WCC 1980 – 2005*, Geneva, WCC, 2005.

the most appropriate focus for Christian witness in a time of globalization, post-modernity, struggles for identity and rising violence. The commission thus decided to propose to the central committee that the next world mission conference be held in early 2005 with the following thematic focus as its theme:

CALLED IN CHRIST TO BE RECONCILING AND HEALING COMMUNITIES

Explanation of the theme

Introduction:
In a time of globalization with increasing violence, fragmentation and exclusion, the mission of the church is to receive, celebrate, proclaim and work for the fullness of life in Christ.

Called:
At this time in a globalized context, God entrusts and commissions us with a message of healing and reconciliation and sends us out in mission. This demonstrates that there is already a relationship between God and us, we rejoice that we are reconciled to God in Christ.

In Christ:
Through the Holy Spirit, God in Christ continues as healer and reconciler in the world. The crucified and resurrected Christ invites us to participate in healing and reconciliation.

To be:
Our being, and our way of being together, needs to reflect our vision of reconciliation.

Reconciling and healing:

Repairing the broken relationships:	*God - human beings*
	People - people
	Churches - churches
	Nation - nation
	Humanity - creation
Health, balance, wholeness of life:	*for individuals*
	for whole communities
	for humanity

Communities:
Reconciling and healing need to be experienced within communities (member to member), between communities where brokenness exists and in humanity's relationship with creation.[4]

---

[4] Reproduced from commission document CWME 01-13, the basis for the report on the plans for a world mission conference in 2005 to the central committee. Cf. also Conference Preparatory Paper No 3, reproduced in this book.

In 2001, the CWME commission took several other key decisions which launched the preparatory process. In particular it set up a conference planning committee with the specific mandate to act on behalf of the commission on major matters related to the conference. It was also decided to plan for another style of conference, not aiming at producing long section reports, but more focused on sharing and a process allowing for some experience of the theme among participants within a liturgical setting during the conference itself.

The commissioners didn't know that the USA and the world would face the 9/11 tragedy just following the end of their meeting. It proved, if proof had been needed, the importance in such a violent world of the gospel message of healing and reconciliation.

From then on, major preparatory work was done by the conference planning committee which was composed of roughly a third of the whole commission.

Further Stages in Preparations

At its meeting in August-September 2002, the central committee approved the thematic emphasis proposed by the CWME commission, as well as the aim of the conference and the guidelines for participation, both in terms of numbers and composition. This meant that the WCC as a whole approved the idea that the composition of the world mission conference would match the composition of the commission itself, with 25 percent participation from affiliated bodies to the Conference, 50 percent participation from WCC member churches, and 25 percent seats offered to representatives of the so-called "wider constituency", principally the Roman Catholic Church and evangelical or Pentecostal churches and mission bodies. In terms of numbers, the CWME was to aim at a total of 500 official participants, to which would be added staff, stewards, observers, press etc. Some of the main decisions taken are reproduced in their final form in the Conference preparatory paper No 3.[5]

When the commission met for its third meeting in Chavannes-de-Bogis, Switzerland at the beginning of April 2003, it received extensive reports on work done by the planning committee, which provided the basis for further major decisions. The full title of the Athens conference would from now on be composed of a slogan "Come, Holy Spirit, heal and reconcile", accompanied by the thematic focus already mentioned: "Called in Christ to be reconciling and healing communities". It was also in Chavannes that the commission sang for the first time the "Athens song" with the melody composed by one of the commissioners, Sister Céline Monteiro, from the Franciscan Missionaries of Mary (FMM). Discussions on the venue had lasted for quite some time, and several options remained open, in particular because CWME had wished to wait until the WCC had decided where its

---

[5] That document refers to so-called signposts on the journey towards the conference. These signposts have played an important role in the early stage of the planning, and at some point the commission began to use them to structure the conference programme itself (in particular with a view to the workshops). That idea was however abandoned, in order not to divide in an artificial manner the various missiological approaches to the theme of reconciliation and healing.

next assembly should meet. Now that the central committee had approved Brazil as the assembly venue, the CWME decided to hold its next conference in Athens, Greece, responding to a gracious invitation by the Church of Greece. An Athens local arrangements committee with representatives of all WCC member churches in Greece would be set up as soon as possible. Dates in May 2005 were chosen as the best possible option.

The commission worked hard on details of conference participation, and invested much time and effort in reflecting on the programme structure and the spiritual life, in particular, by using for it own devotions during the meeting the *lectio divina* approach to Bible meditation in home groups. It decided to set up a spiritual life committee (SLC) which would have the overall responsibility for all aspects of the programme and events at the conference having to do with spirituality, thus not just for prayers and worship. It received the worksheet on reconciliation, later published as Conference preparatory paper No 2, and urged staff to pursue the search for a conference organizer, delayed due to restructuring and reorganization within the WCC.

The Conference Organizer Joined the Staff Team

From August 2003 on, Beate Fagerli from Norway joined the staff team preparing the conference, as the long-expected conference organizer. Adèle Djomo-Ngomedje, from Cameroon, joined the team as intern, graciously seconded by the Presbyterian Church (USA) for administrative tasks related to the preparation and organization of the conference.

From then on, the rhythm of preparations at all levels increased, with meetings of both the conference planning committee and the spiritual life committee, in addition to thematic or regional preparatory meetings and the continuation of the major study processes. These are not referred to in detail here. The results and relevant documents have been published either in the issues of the *International Review of Mission* of the years 2000 to 2005, or as *Conference Preparatory Papers* (many of them reproduced in this book) and in book form. A list is attached.

The last meeting of the commission prior to the Athens conference took place in Matanzas, Cuba in October 2004. Commissioners worked on mission theology through debate and discussion, both in plenary sessions and in groups, on the paper on reconciliation which had been published as Conference preparatory paper No. 4, now submitted to the commission, together with the reactions received to the document from various partners all over the world. Based on the commission's work, a small drafting committee revised the text which became preparatory paper No. 10 (Mission as ministry of reconciliation). Together with No. 11 on the healing mission of the church, this paper may be considered the major content input into the Athens conference, and the result of the study process.

Most of the necessary decisions having been taken by the conference planning committee, the commission concentrated on lessons to be drawn for future conferences and potential revisions of the by-laws, and in particular evoked perspectives on the celebration of the centennial of the Edinburgh world mission conference in 2010.

Main Thematic Emphases

In general, the preparatory process was organized along several thematic lines:

Faith, health and healing, starting from a main consultation in Hamburg in 2000, leading to the drafting of the theological paper on the healing mission of the church (preparatory paper No. 12). This track included major dialogues with and contributions by Pentecostal scholars, with intensive cooperation with the worldwide networks of the former Christian Medical Commission of the WCC. Related to this, but somewhat independent of it, was the ongoing important work on HIV and AIDS. The conference preparatory process also gained much insight from the theological reflection and experience of the WCC Ecumenical Disability Advocates Network (EDAN) based in Nairobi, Kenya.

Specific work on *mission and reconciliation* started with the Cartigny consultation and the commissions' deliberations, both in 2001. It could build on reflection and experience gained over many years both within and outside WCC, in particular on social and political processes. This track could benefit from contributions by several missiological associations linked to the International Association for Mission Studies and from the Urban Rural Mission (URM) network (from the latter, in particular, on the link between reconciliation and justice, cf. preparatory paper No. 9). The final result was the theological document adopted by the commission on "Mission as ministry of reconciliation" (preparatory paper No. 11). That reflection can be considered CWME's contribution to the Decade to Overcome Violence (DOV).

A third general line of reflection had started with the work on the paper "Mission and Evangelism in Unity Today" and the common consultation organized by the teams and commissions on Faith and Order and Mission and Evangelism on *ecclesiology and mission*, both in 2000. Specific work continued on ecclesiology in general (in particular by Faith and Order), on the role of missional churches in postmodern contexts, on ecumenical perspectives on evangelism, on the growing importance of multicultural ministry and on revisiting the *missio Dei* theology. Care was taken to acknowledge the important role of the church in God's mission while remaining aware of the wide horizon of God's presence and action in the world and a holistic interpretation of mission.

Further inter-team cooperation led to the update of WCC's work on *Christian self-understanding and religious plurality*. Three teams and advisory bodies of the WCC were involved: Faith and Order, CWME and Inter-religious relations and dialogue. The study process led to the interim statement published as preparatory paper No. 13, which later became a background paper for the WCC assembly.

Many more matters were addressed either by groups or by individual scholars. Cooperation with the women's desk of the Justice, Peace and Creation team allowed for a renewed reflection on *women and mission*. Also in cooperation with the Ecumenical Institute in Bossey, a seminar could be held on "*mission and youth* in the context of globalization", producing a statement which nurtured the reflection of young people for the pre-conference and for workshops.

Pneumatology and mission were considered in most of the above-mentioned tracks, in an attempt to take up again a major area of reflection begun following the CWME conference in San Antonio (1989) and in preparations for the WCC Canberra assembly (1991).

Among the last, but not least, preparatory events for the conference were the *young missiologists'* consultation held in Rome in January 2005, documented in preparatory paper No. 8 and a consultation of and for *Orthodox participants* in Athens in March 2005. The *Roman Catholic delegation* held several meetings to prepare itself to make a very meaningful contribution to the conference. In all of these, the above-mentioned matters were addressed, so as to give the last touch, before the start of the Conference, to reflection on a contemporary theology of mission.

List of Materials

The commission had decided at a very early stage, in 2001, that the main content papers would be prepared prior to the conference, and that the conference itself was not to produce and adopt major theological documents or any kinds of section reports. Therefore, it seems essential to include the major preparatory papers in a book on Athens. Not all the documents are reproduced in this book, for reasons of space, but mainly those documents which had not yet been published by other organizations and the main texts prepared by CWME itself for the conference. A list of preparatory documents and books is added. It refers to materials published by the WCC or with specific WCC support, in English and particularly designed as a contribution to the preparation of the conference. The list does not contain documents and books which were part of specific preparatory processes by member churches or mission boards, whether in English or other languages. Nor does it refer to the material published by the WCC on HIV and AIDS in the years 2000–2005 despite their link with Athens preoccupations. The picture given by this chapter on the preparatory process remains a partial one, but nevertheless gives a good idea of the reflection which took place prior to the world mission conference.

Preparatory Documents Published by the WCC or with WCC Support

Conference Preparatory Papers, First Published on the Conference Website

1. Mission and Evangelism in Unity Today
2. Worksheet on social reconciliation
3. Theme, thematic area and signposts on the journey towards the Athens Conference
4. Statement on Mission as Reconciliation (first version)
5. UEM study on the charismatic movement and healing (United Evangelical Mission, Wuppertal, Germany)
6. Documentation on EMS consultations on reconciliation (Evangelisches Missionswerk in Südwestdeutschland, Association of Churches and Missions in South-Western Germany, Stuttgart, Germany)
7. Summary of lectures: Mission in the 21st century, United Church of Zambia Theological College, March 2004
8. Young missiologists' consultation, Rome, January 19-25, 2005: "Come, Holy Spirit – heal and reconcile"
9. "Mission from the Perspective of People in Struggle". Report of the URM Global Mission Conference Abokobi, Accra, Ghana, 1-7 May 2004 (Urban Rural Mission)
10. Mission as Ministry of Reconciliation (revised version of paper 4)
11. The Healing Mission of the Church
12. Healing - Empowering, Transforming and Reconciling Act of God
13. Religious plurality and Christian self-understanding

These preparatory papers were published on the website, in English, French, Spanish and German

International Review of Mission (IRM)

The following is not the full list of issues of IRM published in the years prior to Athens, but a reference to those clearly linked to processes leading to the Conference, i.e. mainly thematic issues.

Health, Faith and Healing	January/April,2001 (double issue)
Ecclesiology and Mission (I)	July, 2001
Ecclesiology and Mission (II)	October, 2001
Towards the Fullness of Life	October, 2002
Mission in secular and postmodern contexts (I)	January 2003
Mission in secular and postmodern contexts (II)	April 2003
Missio Dei revisited - Willingen 1952-2002	October 2003
Women and Mission	January 2004
Divine Healing, Pentecostalism and Mission	July/October 2004 (double issue)
Come, Holy Spirit – heal and reconcile	January 2005

Books and Pamphlets

(Not including the conference publications for delegates such as handbook and worship book)

"You are the light of the world" Statements on Mission by the WCC 1980 – 2005. Geneva, WCC, 2005, 162 p.

"By grace you have been saved" Bible studies on healing and reconciliation. Geneva, WCC, 2005, 194 p.

(Also published in French, Spanish and German)

Colville and Seongja Crowe (eds.) *Second International Network Forum on Multicultural Ministry. 7 – 10 May 2002, Pattaya, Thailand.* Sydney, INFORM, 2002, 220 p.

Id. (eds) Third International Network Forum – Multicultural Ministry. 15-19 February 2005, Pattaya, Thailand. Sydney, INFORM, 2005, 40 p.

Usha Jesudasan and Gert Rüppell: *Healing as Empowerment. Discovering grace in community.* Geneva, WCC, 2005, 92 p.

Kirsteen Kim (ed.): *Reconciling Mission. The ministry of healing and reconciliation in the church worldwide.* Delhi, SPCK, and Birmingham, United College of the Ascension, 2005, 219 p.

J. Poling and B. Ruiz (eds): *Healing and Reconciliation. Pastoral Counselling Across Christian Traditions and Cultures.* Geneva, WCC, 2005, 65 p.

Erika Schuchardt: *Why me? Learning to live in crises.* Geneva, WCC, 2005, 144 p. Translated from German.

Preparatory Paper No 2

Worksheet on Social Reconciliation

Introduction

This worksheet is intended to be a **tool** to reflect and/or prepare a discussion on reconciliation and in particular social reconciliation and its relevance for churches in mission.

It is based mainly on reflections taken from Robert Schreiter's book *The Ministry of Reconciliation. Spirituality and Strategies*. Maryknoll, Orbis, 1998, pp. 105 ff., and the experience of WCC colleagues – in particular Guillermo Kerber Mas of the WCC team on International Affairs, Peace and Human Security.

Preamble

Tackling reconciliation at social and political levels is crucial in the present times. The ministry of reconciliation and healing which the churches are called to cannot deal only with inter-personal relations. The churches are challenged to exercise their prophetic ministry in situations that require discernment, wisdom and experience in community processes. They need however to be aware of the necessary distinction between individual reconciliation and social reconciliation, in the sense that the processes are not necessarily the same in each case.

Many times, churches have themselves been responsible for major crimes against humanity (participation of churches in Latin American dictatorships or in the genocide in Rwanda). Church leaders have also played key roles in reconciliation processes in different countries (Archbishop Tutu in South Africa, Cardinal Arns in Brazil, for instance, among others). Too often however, churches and church leaders are reluctant to involve themselves and the churches in reconciliation processes at a social or national level.

Reconciliation should be seen as a broader approach to justice than political or judicial approaches. Peace agreements, judiciary decisions don't achieve full justice for societies. A deeper process including healing of memories, dealing with forgiveness, going beyond the division between victim and victimizer is needed. This is what is meant by a reconciliation process.

Reconciliation Questionnaire

> "Defining reconciliation in a given context is an important
> part of the initial stage of the reconciliation process itself"
> (Schreiter, 1998, p. 106)

The first question to be asked is **what and who needs reconciliation**. Wrongdoers and victims will have different answers to that question. Should reconciliation aim at addressing the most obvious wrongdoings (human right abuses e.g.) or deeper causes (e.g. land ownership, identity questions)? Is a reconciliation process the best way to address the problem or are other means better adapted, such as legal action?

The second question is **Why?** – Why is reconciliation needed in a concrete circumstance? What were the means used to overcome a conflict at a political and judicial levels? How did people react to these means? Is there any feeling of something missing?

The third question is about **appropriate means** for reconciliation. This can raise cultural questions, request reflections about resources which are available (e.g., existence or non-existence of legally trained people), and an analysis of hindrances (powers with responsibility in wrongdoing might still be in place or capable of influence).

Fourthly, a dialogue is needed about what the **reconciled stage** will look like. What is the goal here? It might not be possible to know it in advance, but a discussion on this is needed.

Then reflection is needed about the **actors** and their agenda and role in a reconciliation process (cf. Schreiter, 1998, p. 108-110).

Victims and survivors
Wrongdoers
Bystanders (tacitly complicit with what happened, not directly involved, but not having done anything to stop wrongdoing)
People who have been both victims and wrongdoers (people sometimes forced to do violence to others)
Dead
Future generations
Neighbours (in neighbouring countries)
God

Some **burning issues** that should be addressed while reflecting on reconciliation in general:

1. Issues of **forgiveness**. Is forgiveness possible? How? How do we relate forgiveness to justice? Sometimes Christian understanding of reconciliation is seen as undermining justice procedures. How can this be addressed?
2. Issues of **reparation**. What reparation is foreseen, or has been granted? Many times the discussion is focused on economic reparation, but in talking with victims one realizes that symbolic reparation is as important as economic. Church knowledge of the symbolic dimension of life can be an important contribution in dealing with these issues.
3. Issues of **accountability and responsibility**. Shifting from individual to social level implies to understand responsibility differently. Community and society cannot be seen as innocent or neutral actors. The shift to the social also

implies that victims and perpetrators are not only or mainly individuals but collective and social actors. The collective meaning of "sin" (in Adam) and "redemption" (in Christ) in St Paul's letters could have something to say at this level. The constant need of **conversion** is addressed to Christians as individuals but also to the church as community.

4. Issues of **interreligious dimension** of reconciliation. Many times conflict is seen as involving religions, a factor which is highlighted in the media. However, existing interreligious efforts for reconciliation should also be stressed.

Editor's Additional Note:

This sheet addresses in particular questions related to reconciliation in the socio-political realm and the church's ministry in society. As you work with this sheet, you may however also want to apply it to questions of church unity and mission in unity, and discern how to move towards healing of memories and reconciliation in old or new conflicts involving churches and Christians:

As examples, let us mention local or national conflicts between individual churches, old or new conflicts between denominations or church families, between foreign missionaries or mission bodies and local churches, between churches in economically rich countries and churches in economically poor countries, between conflicting mission movements or between churches or Christian mission bodies and Indigenous Peoples.

Please share with the CWME Conference Office your experiences, reactions, your reflections on such processes and also suggestions for improving this tool.

CWME Conference Office
WCC
150 route de Ferney
CH-1211 Genève 2
Switzerland

Cwme@wcc-coe.org

You will find a first choice of bibliographical references on reconciliation on the "CWME Conference" and "Decade to Overcome Violence (DOV)" Webpages, which you can both access through the WCC website (www.oikoumene.org)

July 2003

Preparatory Paper No 3

Theme, Thematic Area and Signposts on the Journey towards the Athens Conference

The formulations used in this paper have to be understood as incentives for study, reflection and sharing, and not as adopted statements of faith. A certain amount of deliberate ambiguity is contained in the wordings. This reflects the diversity of approaches amongst members of the WCC Commission on World Mission and Evangelism (CWME Commission), responsible for the preparation of the Conference. While drawing on the work and on papers adopted by the CWME Commission or its Conference Planning Committee (CPC), this third bulletin has been prepared by staff.[1]

In a time of globalization with increasing violence, fragmentation and exclusion, the mission of the church is to receive, celebrate, proclaim and work for reconciliation, healing and fullness of life in Christ.

Come, Holy Spirit, heal and reconcile

Calling on the Spirit, we confess that mission is not ours.
Mission is the mission of the triune God, the creator of heaven and earth, whose purpose is that all may have fullness of life.
In Jesus Christ, God laid the basis for real reconciliation and healing, overcoming all enmity and evil.
God the Holy Spirit is continually present and active as healer and reconciler in church and world.

So we believe that God makes it possible to:

* Repair broken relationships between	God and human beings
	People and people
	Churches and churches
	Nations and nations
	Humanity and creation

---

[1] In this text, the term **"we"** participates in the mentioned ambiguity. Depending on the source on which staff depended for the formulation of the paragraphs, "we" may refer to members of the CWME Commission, or of the Conference Planning Committee. "We" can however also mean all Christians who accept these formulations, commitments and hopes. We - who prepared this text - invite you who read it to feel included if you so wish.
We use the terms **"mission"** and **"evangelism"** in the sense in which they have been defined in the recent study document adopted by the CWME Commission. "Mission and Evangelism in Unity Today" has been published also as CWME 2005 Conference Preparatory Paper # 1:
"Mission" carries a holistic understanding: the proclamation and sharing of the good news of the gospel by word (kerygma), deed (diakonia), prayer and worship (leiturgia) and the everyday witness of the Christian life (martyria); teaching as building up and strengthening people in their relationship with God and each other; and healing as wholeness and reconciliation into koinonia — communion with God, communion with people, and communion with creation as a whole.
"Evangelism", while not excluding the different dimensions of mission, focuses on explicit and intentional voicing of the gospel, including the invitation to personal conversion to a new life in Christ and to discipleship.

* Overcome enmity and violence

We hope to see many signs of:

Health, balance and wholeness of life: for individuals
for whole communities
for humanity
for creation

> **We call on God the Spirit:** heal and reconcile, empower us, so that as persons and communities, we may receive, become and share signs of forgiveness, peace, justice and unity, and renounce sin, enmity, violence, injustice and divisions.

Called in Christ to be reconciling and healing communities

At this time in a globalized context, God entrusts and commissions us with a message of healing and reconciliation. The crucified and resurrected Christ invites us to participate in God's mission. It is **our mission** to form healing communities in celebration, witness, mutual love, forgiveness and respect, and to intervene in peace-building, reconciliation processes and healing of memories in society, overcoming violence wherever we can.

Our being, and our way of being together, needs to reflect our vision of reconciliation.

We are called
to create and multiply safe spaces, hospitable to those who are stigmatized, lost, searching for meaning, solidarity and community,

and to journey as and with victims of violence and sin towards reconciliation and justice.

Reconciliation and healing need to be experienced within communities (member to member), between communities where brokenness exists, and in humanity's relationship with creation.

By using the term "communities" (instead of "Community" as referring to the Church) we want to affirm the plurality and the diverse nature of the communities in which we live.

Aim and Objectives of the Conference

The aim and objectives of the Conference have been adopted by the CWME

Commission and received by the WCC central committee.

AIM

To empower participants to continue in their call to be in mission together and work towards reconciliation and healing in Christ, in God's world today.

OBJECTIVES

- To enthuse participants with new vision, energy, tools and skills to bring the holistic mission imperative alive again.
- To enable the conference to be a living community of reconciliation and healing.
- To experience healing and reconciliation that leads to the transformation of persons.
- To ensure safe/sacred spaces where reflections, theory and stories can be heard and dialogue can take place.
- To strive to be a sign of reconciliation and healing among the churches.
- To celebrate our unity in Christ and our God given diversity.
- To enable participants to commit themselves to be agents/multipliers of reconciliation and healing in their own churches, communities and contexts.

Style of the Conference

The aim and objectives make it clear that this Conference will have a **different style** to that of its predecessors.[2] There will be no section work (as has been the case in almost all earlier mission conferences) and no preparation of long reports intended to be received or adopted by the Conference plenary. The main emphasis will be put on creating spaces for sharing, dialogue, debate, listening, presenting experiences and case studies or theological reflections. Participants will be free to choose to which offer of workshop, prayer and healing service, Bible study, creative encounter, they want to contribute and/or participate.

The Conference will also meet in plenary for prayer, celebration and specific inputs.

A major role will be assigned to what the CWME Commission calls the **"home groups"** consisting of approximately 10-12 persons. These will be a place for biblical meditation, silence, prayer and mutual pastoral support, based on personal sharing, story telling and reflection. These groups will meet at least once each day.

---

[2] A summary overview over the previous world mission conferences, first of the International Missionary Council, then of the World Council of Churches can be found on the WCC webpage (see: www.oikoumene.org, search Programmes — Unity, Mission, Evangelism and Spirituality — Mission and Unity).

Throughout the Conference it will be important to maintain the sacredness of the spaces that are provided for sharing and dialogue. Plans include setting up a **meditation centre** where people could spend time in quiet, and a "pastoral team" of facilitators, of people with communication and counseling skills.

The Conference will have a **liturgical flow**, with elements of liturgy finding a place in the day to day activities of the meetings, as well as offering a framework to the overall flow of the conference. Such liturgical elements need not follow any rigid pattern, but could happen simultaneously in different places, and as the Spirit leads. There could be planned elements that will be for the whole Conference like celebration, confession, affirmation of faith etc, but the smaller groups too may experience the elements of such a liturgical flow as they go through the day.

> Suggested liturgical elements:
>
> Get to know each other, welcome and celebration
> Repentance/ forgiveness
> Glory to God
> Listening to the Word of God, Bible study and reflection
> Offering of our experience in healing and reconciliation
> Intercessions
> Moment of peace
> Sending out or commissioning
> Affirmation of faith

The major **outcome** of the Conference will be persons, who are transformed through their experience, energized and empowered for mission in their local churches, communities and contexts.

A short evocative **message** from the participants, which could be sent to churches and mission bodies, will share an immediate perspective from the Conference and also hold the participants themselves to accountability.

The production of a **book** or CD with texts, speeches, case-studies, prayers, stories, etc. linked to the Conference is planned to document the event. It will include materials related to the Conference and to its preparation as well as appropriate forms of missiological evaluations of the event.

Preparatory Process

The preparatory processes for the Conference will draw on the reflection and experience of churches, mission bodies, networks and congregations who are already involved in and reflect on reconciliation and healing.

a) Internet

A web page created within the WCC website is a main instrument for collecting and sharing information and documentation. Questions, stories, ideas, theories, but also poetry, worship resources, prayers, can be posted and discussion can take place. The CWME constituency are to be asked to consider a link from any websites of their own to the Conference webpage and /or the inclusion of reference to the thematic area and the Conference on their own sites.

b) Regional/National Meetings

National councils and CWME affiliated bodies[3] are invited to organize specific national or regional meetings to discuss the theme and the signposts and to share experiences and reflections. Under certain conditions, it might be recommended to use existing and already planned meetings and consultations to include contributions towards the Conference.

c) Major Church Events

Several important international meetings have recently undertaken work on the themes of reconciliation and healing.[4] As seems appropriate, insights and challenges will be fed into the CWME preparatory process.

d) Publications

This document is part of a series of CWME 2005 Preparatory Papers, published on the Web and as hard copies. In addition, articles of more academic nature appear in the International Review of Mission, story, case study and experience sharing takes place also through the Ecumenical Letter on Evangelism and Contact, both available online.

Themes and Interest Areas which Seem Key for Reconciliation and Healing in Mission

As we have started our journey towards the 2005 world mission conference, we want to explore what reconciliation and healing mean for contemporary mission theory and practice. This will be CWME's contribution to the *Decade to Overcome Violence*[5]. In the following paragraphs, we present a very brief overview of the

---

[3] The "CWME affiliated bodies" are mission or church councils affiliated to the CWME Conference according to its By-Laws. There are more than 50 now, in many countries and continents of the North and the South. Many of these bodies were originally member councils of the International Missionary Council until its merger with the WCC in 1961. New affiliations are regularly accepted by the CWME Commission.

[4] Conference of European Churches (CEC), June 25 – July 2, 2003, Trondheim, Norway: *Jesus Christ heals and reconciles: Our witness in Europe*. Lutheran World Federation (LWF), July 21-31, 2003, Winnipeg, Canada: *For the healing of the world*. World Alliance of Reformed Churches (WARC), July 30-August 14, 2004, Accra, Ghana: *That all may have life in fullness*.

[5] The "Decade to Overcome Violence – churches seeking reconciliation and peace" was decided at the Harare assembly of the WCC in 1998 and officially launched in Berlin in 2001. Four main themes have been identified as major concerns: the spirit and logic of violence; the use, abuse and misuse of power; issues of justice; religious identity and plurality. Cf. the special Website: www.wcc-coe.org/dov
Suffice here to refer to the following resource materials:
* *Why Violence? Why not peace? A study guide to help individuals and groups in the churches to reflect and act in the Decade to Overcome Violence*. Geneva, WCC, 2002.
* *Margot Kässmann: Overcoming Violence. The challenge to the churches in all places*. WCC, 2000 (rev.ed.)

current missiological context, followed by introductions to four "signposts", themes or interest areas which seem key for a reflection on mission as led by the Spirit. It is obvious that these signposts overlap and thus must not be treated as separate items.[6]

Summary Overview of Current Missiological Context

After the cold war era, the world order has moved towards a unified market, which, accompanied by social and cultural phenomena, is usually referred to by the term globalization. The bipolar political economic ideology has become a monopolar neo-liberal one, in which the market becomes the main reference all over the world and the measure for judging values, social achievements and even human beings and communities themselves. Partly in reaction to the risk of cultural leveling by the leading market forces and the media, new conflict areas emerged, among and within nations, often with a cultural, ethnic or religious background. These developments modify local and regional political alliances and tend to reinforce the control of the power centres of Western societies over the world.

In this context, missiology needs to focus anew intentionally on Christ's life-affirming ministry as an alternative and a means of resistance to political, economic and religious trends and forces leading to oppression, alienation and death. Witnessing to the fullness of life in Christ leads Christians and churches to consider the whole of creation as the horizon of mission. The basis and framework of Christian mission must be consistently trinitarian, based on and related to the work of God, Father, Son and Holy Spirit, from the beginning of creation to the end of time. There is particular urgency to better understand the role of the Spirit in church and world and to work out the consequences for mission in practice.

Reconciliation appears to be a central term, describing God's forgiveness given in Christ, the intention of God's own presence and action in the world, and the vision of the final aim of God's mission (*missio Dei*). Authentic reconciliation is costly and cannot easily be reached if separated from justice, truth about responsibilities, love for enemies and forgiveness. It has personal, community, social and ecological dimensions. It implies healing from past and present wounds, from injustices and guilt, at personal, community and social levels.

Signposts

1. Concerns of identity amidst Multi-faceted and Changing Contexts

The way cultural and religious identities are formed and experienced change rapidly. Due to migration and the new information society, identities mix and overlap, are shaped by new content or by search for security in conservative

---

[6] As already mentioned, this will not lead to four thematic sections at the conference itself. All "signposts" enable reflection and sharing of experiences on the theme of the conference.

forms. This is not a new factor, however the speed of change seems to grow dramatically, particularly in cultures influenced by secularization and the trends towards postmodernity. Postmodernity, both a challenge and an opportunity, no longer understands culture as being a homogeneous cluster of traditions, social forms and world-views. Culture is often seen as a complex process in which human beings and communities seek to establish and maintain their identity anew, in constant relationship with other influences. Most contexts are increasingly multicultural and multireligious. Churches in mission thus need to affirm the need for multicultural ministry and for increased cooperation with people of other faiths wherever possible. This will require a reformulation of the understanding of the role of Christianity vis-à-vis religion in general and calls for a witness which keeps a creative tension between faithfulness to Christ and openness to others and to the Spirit. Wherever identities are in violent conflict, there is a particular urgency for the ministry of reconciliation.[7]

2. Healing and Reconciling Ministries in a Violent World

There is need to focus on the multifaceted aspects of a contemporary vision of the healing and reconciling ministry.

Particular care is needed to recover the church's calling to be a **healing community** and an open and secure space for vulnerable people. This calling includes the traditional healing ministry of the church which has been carried out through two different ways
- pastoral visiting, prayer, anointing, special healing liturgies and sacraments
- through the medical profession and medical institutions.
Sometimes these seem to be in conflict.

There is a difference between cure and healing. All people including those involved in "faith healing" look for cure. But it is possible to be healed even if there is no cure. The question of the meaning of life in fullness is raised by terminal or chronic illnesses, as e.g. also by HIV/AIDS.

---

[7] Each paragraph will be accompanied by a short list of selected resources published by the WCC. A fuller bibliography is available on the Conference webpage. See www.mission2005.org)
Overall introduction: "Toward the Fullness of Life". Special issue of the *International Review of Mission (IRM)*, October 2002. Contains papers on identity and plurality, on healing and HIV/AIDS and on intercontinental partnerships.
Gospel and Cultures:
* Christopher Duraisingh (ed.): *Called to One Hope. The Gospel in Diverse Cultures.* Geneva, WCC 1998. Contains all relevant documents from the 1996 world mission conference in Salvador de Bahía.
* Series of "Gospel and Cultures pamphlets" published before the Salvador conference.
* "Mission in secular and postmodern contexts" I and II, *IRM* January and April 2003.
Multicultural Ministry:
* Seongja Yoo-Crowe and Colville Crowe (eds.): *Reports from the First and the Second International Network Forum on Multicultural Ministry.* Sydney, Uniting Church and INFORM, 2000 and 2002.
* "Open Space: African Christian Diaspora in Europe and the Quest for Human Community" special issue of *IRM*, July 2000. *Religious plurality and interreligious relations;*
* *Ecumenical Considerations for Dialogue and Relations with People of other Religions. Taking stock of 30 years of dialogue and revisiting the 1979 Guidelines.* Geneva, WCC, 2003.

Can people who may not have hope for cure and are physically ill have fullness of life? Is there possibility of healing when someone is dying? How can the church be a presence for those who suffer and how does it challenge the medical profession?

At the same time, traditional churches need to receive the challenge posed by healing practices of Pentecostal and charismatic mission churches which experience charisms which were known in the earliest times of Christian mission.

Theologically speaking, we also need to dialogue on the respective understandings of the healing presence of the Spirit, on the nature of the link between healing and salvation and resume the necessary intercultural dialogue on what "health" means as well as a thorough reflection on the biblical meaning of reconciliation.

Reconciling ministry in a violent world

Particular emphasis needs to be put on the churches' role in conflict situations, addressing questions such as repentance, forgiveness, restitution, and healing of memories. A critical evaluation of the challenges put to mission by the role of Christians and churches in recent ethnic conflicts still has to be undertaken[8].

3. Seeking Alternative Communities in a Globalized World

The struggle for alternative communities expresses the Christian hope that another world is possible. It is a movement of resistance against the commodification of all aspects of life (including the creation, culture and religion), the struggle to open up and enlarge, or keep at least, some spaces for just and sustainable human relations.

The term "alternative" is essential and refers to alternative values, relations and identities. According to the market rules it is the better, the stronger, the more imaginative, who wins. The gospel however draws its priorities from God's grace and values those who seem to "lose", the small, humble, excluded, poor. To speak of "alternative" means thus that there is something wrong with the world, that there is a judgement on the world. If we want to emphasize what "alternative" means, we should also speak of inclusiveness. The essence of the gospel of reconciliation

---

[8] Selected resources published by the WCC include:
* *Healing:*
* "Health, Faith and Healing". Double issue of the *International Review of Mission* (IRM), Jan. /April 2001.
* *Facing AIDS. The challenge, the churches' response.* A WCC study document. Geneva, WCC, 1997.
* Karin Granberg-Michaelson: *Healing Community.* WCC, 1991.
* *Healing and Wholeness. The churches' role in health.* Report of a study by the Christian Medical Commission. Geneva, WCC, 1990
Many other documents are available in particular on AIDS. Check the WCC Website or ask the WCC health desk as well as the coordination office of the Ecumenical HIV/AIDS Initiative in Africa.
Reconciliation:
* CWME Conference Preparatory Paper No 2: worksheet on reconciliation processes.
* Geneviève Jacques: *Beyond Impunity. An Ecumenical Approach to Truth, Justice and Reconciliation.* Geneva, WCC, 2000.
* Philip Lee (ed.): *Communication & Reconciliation. Challenges facing the 21st century.* Geneva, WCC, 1991.

is about communities that do not exclude, either for racial, economic, spiritual or other reasons.

There are several traditions which lie behind the use of the word "alternative": it's the Christian base communities, monastic or monastic-type communities (such as Iona), many local congregations, the Gospel and Cultures networks, Roman Catholic missionary congregations, the Urban Rural Mission networks and, among others, also the experiences of shared partnership in mission structures.

Speaking of reconciliation and healing implies to find constantly new and increased ways to be in solidarity with alternative communities, in particular those among the poor and victims of the actual economic system. This will give a testimony to our hope and vision of another world .[9]

4. Being a Missional and Evangelizing Church

The message of reconciliation in Christ must also be shared widely (II Cor. 5:18-20). The CWME should be able to affirm the importance of sharing the gospel in an appropriate way with all people, in particular with those who have not yet heard it. If however the churches are not being reconciled among themselves, they fail to respond to their calling (John 17: 20-23) and their witness loses its credibility. The longing and search for unity is at the core of an ecumenical vision of mission. There is need to reinforce efforts towards common witness as first steps towards reconciliation. Trends towards confessionalisation and aggressive competition (proselytism) must be resisted and the primacy of the local church in mission recognized.

There is an urgent need to come to a clearer ecumenical stand on the place and role of evangelism within a holistic mission theology. This requests a positive appreciation of the rich diversity in theologies and practices of evangelism. Many historical churches lost the passion of sharing the gospel in a fresh way relevant and meaningful to the societies in which they serve, in particular in postmodern situations. Churches which should have a pro-active approach have a reactive one, when they feel threatened by aggressive evangelists. Pentecostal and evangelical churches, among the most dynamic mission forces, are often perceived more as a challenge than as an opportunity for spiritual renewal. Such spiritual renewal is however essential, since people yearn for spirituality in many contexts. Perhaps a way forward is to revisit the "ecumenical strategy for congregational evangelism" proposed by Raymond Fung with its three pillars: partnership, worship and discipleship. Local Christians and church communities are called to get involved

---

[9] Selected resources published by the WCC include:
* *A Church of All and For All.* An interim statement prepared by the Ecumenical Disabilities' Advocates' Network (EDAN) in cooperation with Faith and Order and received by the WCC Central Committee. WCC 2003.
* Ian M. Fraser: *Many Cells, One Body. Stories from small Christian Communities.* Geneva, WCC, 2003.
* Jim Forest: *The Resurrection of the Church in Albania. Voices of Orthodox Christians.* WCC 2002.
* Lothar Bauerochse: *Learning to Live Together. Interchurch partnerships as ecumenical communities of learning.* WCC 2001
* Hugh Lewin: *A Community of Clowns. Testimonies of people in Urban Rural Mission.* WCC 1987.

with neighbouring communities on issues of life in dignity and justice, to nurture the struggle with regular worship life and to issue personal invitations to discipleship whenever this seems appropriate. Such a strategy attempts to overcome the division between the struggle for social justice and the concern for evangelism and bases evangelistic witness upon the life and practice of a healing and reconciling community.[10]

October 2003

---

[10] Selected resources published by the WCC include:

* Raymond Fung: *The Isaiah Vision. An Ecumenical Strategy for Congregational Evangelism.* WCC, (1992) reprinted 2002.

* *Towards Common Witness. A call to adopt responsible relationships in mission and to renounce proselytism.* A document commended to the churches by the Central Committee of the WCC. 1997.

* Raymond Fung and Georges Lemopoulos (eds): *Not A Solitary Way. Evangelism stories from around the World.* WCC, 1992

* Raymond Fung (ed.) *Evangelistically Yours. Ecumenical Letters on Contemporary Evangelism.* WCC 1992.

Preparatory Paper No 7

Summary of Lectures: Mission in the 21st Century United Church of Zambia Theological College March 2004

The Conference **"Mission in the 21st Century. Mission as Evangelism in Tension with Mission as Development"**, was held from 25 March to 1 April 2004 and was organized by the United Theological College of Zambia (UTCZ).

The **purpose** of the Conference was to explore and examine the commonalities and tensions between mission as evangelism and mission as development as it has been, and is being, experienced in many of the once politically colonized and the presently economically colonized countries of the south.

The **goals** were to understand and appreciate the gift of mission as evangelism and the gift of mission as development from a variety of contexts; to identify, and begin to understand and grapple with the complexities of the issues that we face as a world church; to hear from each of the continents, and begin to understand their focus for mission as evangelism, as we discern the relevance of this understanding for our own work and to interact with a wide variety of people and understandings of mission as evangelism.

The gathering also included preparation work for the 2005 Conference on World Mission and Evangelism (CWME), to be held in Athens, Greece. In order to accomplish this, information was provided to the participants in lectures and through panels, which focused on the previous conferences, and in particular on the Athens conference. The following document, prepared by one of the lecturers (Prof. Michael Kinnamon, from Eden Theological Seminary) summarizes the lectures, focusing specifically on reconciliation and healing, the thematic focus of the 2005 Conference, as a contribution to its preparation process.

(Note: since the document refers to the authors of the paper, there is a list of participants at the end).

Carlos E. Ham
Mission and Ecumenical Formation Team Co-coordinator

Summary of Lectures

I.   **Shared understandings and affirmations**
      A.   Common analysis of the contemporary world situation
            1.   The U.S. is now an Empire, seeking to impose a Pax Americana, with negative implications for all of the countries represented at the conference.
            2.   We face massive threats to the human future, including growing disparity between rich and poor, ecological destruction and militarization (Joy).
            3.   Women are still subordinated, especially in the more traditional cultures.
            4.   Fundamentalism, understood as "escapist spirituality" without ethical content that creates dependence by promising security (Gebara) is spreading worldwide. Many of the rapidly-growing Christian communities in Africa are proclaiming a "prosperity gospel" that reduces mission to numerical increase and reinforces the often-oppressive status quo by focusing on personal salvation while ignoring economic and political injustice.
            5.   Most of the nations discussed are marked by increasing religious and cultural pluralism.

      B.   Common understanding of the gospel, e.g.,
            1.   "God is at work in the hearts and history of all people to overcome empires, break bondage and free people" (Ferguson).
            2.   Christianity is heavily implicated in colonialism, racism and sexism, but the gospel encourages the struggle for liberation and a self-critical church (Phiri).
            3.   The Bible has been and is used to oppress, but, properly understood, it is liberative – individually and socially. Jesus established a social movement that had, as its goal, the political economic, social and religious renewal of Israel (Wanamaker). Paul also affirms struggle in this world if we reject de-historicized readings of him and, instead, locate him in the context of the Roman Empire (Tamez).

      C.   Common approach to mission
            1.   We properly speak of God's mission (*missio Dei*), a mission of *tikkun olam* (justice for God's creatures and healing for God's creation) in which the whole church is called to participate.
            2.   Historically, Christian mission has often been understood as bringing truth for civilizing alien cultures (Legge). We now see these parts of mission history as an arm of imperialism that confused the gospel with western culture.
            3.   Participation in God's mission must be "holistic" in the sense that it seeks to overcome dualism and spiritualization of

the Good News (Tamez). Mission is incarnation, witness, liberation (A. Ham); formation, proclamation, healing (C. Ham); salvation and humanization (Selvanayagam, drawing on M. M. Thomas).

4. Participation in God's mission includes the healing of our own communities through solidarity with others and a willingness to be self-critical.

5. The kingdom (Dominion) of God is the proper context and goal of the church's proclamation.

6. These changes in the theology of mission have, to a large extent, not affected local congregations (the church doesn't practice what it preaches – Mombo) and are now being challenged by fundamentalist forms of Christianity (Gebara).

7. In the West, many development workers appear to believe in development rather than the gospel (Plant). The mission work of the church needs a strong theological foundation.

II.   **Key Issues/Dialectics**

A.   Evangelism and Development

This, of course, was a thematic focus for the conference. The general approach, perhaps best summarized by Tamez, is that we need to overcome the dualism, not just "maintain the tension." The church must share the gospel, witnessing in word and deed; and it must work to enable a better life for those who live in poverty and fear, including the poor in western countries (Ross). Both words have been corrupted – "evangelism" by being equated with coercive or manipulative forms of proclamation, "development" by being identified with practices that perpetuate patterns of dependency. Properly understood, however, they are both essential to holistic mission.

B.   Healing and Reconciliation

These terms will figure prominently in next year's world mission conference in Athens; and, again, both are problematic. Healing is often associated with magical cures, while reconciliation sounds to some ears like compromise with oppressors. At our meeting, however, "healing" was frequently used to define mission (e.g., Gnanadason), to signal the link between evangelism and development. Similarly, "reconciliation" was affirmed so long as it involves "not only listening to the suffering caused but evidence that it has been heard, the wrong-doing acknowledged, and steps of repentance and redress taken" (Legge). Both terms are prominent in contemporary African theology: reconciliation in the aftermath of apartheid, healing as a practice common in African religion (as well as Christian scripture).

C.   Gospel and Culture

This dialectic was central to the last world mission conference (Salvador, 1996). Now, as then, speakers from the North (West) see the issues differently from those in the South. The former understandably call for the church to be a counter-cultural voice or presence in the midst of idolatrous societies; the latter understandably call for the church to be more at home in their various settings, working, for example, to ensure fair elections or to promote AIDS education.

D.   Dialogue and Witness

The same kind of tension, though with somewhat different partners, surfaced over the issue of interfaith relations. Presenters from Europe, North America, and Asia (home to great religious plurality) tended to rail against the idolatry of their cultures but to affirm that God can and does speak through other faith traditions. Presenters from Africa, in particular, tended to affirm that God speaks through various cultures but to be more cautious about making such claims for other religions. (Nearly every speaker was more suspicious of right-wing Christians than of persons of other faiths.) If we had pressed for a theological consensus, it might have echoed the 1989 mission conference in San Antonio (as quoted by C. Ham): "We cannot point to any other salvation than Jesus Christ; at the same time, we cannot set limits on the saving power of God."

E.   Solidarity and Diversity

There was broad agreement that the church should be marked by global partnership but should reject the promotion (let alone imposition) of a single theology or culture. We need, in the words of Musa Dube (as quoted by Legge), a "liberating interdependence," a "dialogical sharing among all the diverse experiences and expressions of the love of God in Christ" (Gnanadason), as an alternative to destructive forms of globalization. An obvious example of needed solidarity would be for western churches to press for affordable drugs to combat AIDS in Africa. The discussion got far more difficult, however, when the rights of homosexuals was added to the justice agenda by speakers from North America! The question of the limits of diversity (when solidarity breaks down) was left unanswered.

G.   Unity and Mission

Many of the conference speakers came from churches formed by the union of confessional traditions (e.g., the United Church of Zambia, the Church of South India, and the United Church of Canada). As a result, there was some discussion of how our divisions serve the purposes of empire (Ferguson) and of the need for churches in the South, for the sake of mission, to repudiate divisions recycled from the West (Selvanayagam). Christianity, as Gebara put it, has become a source of fragmentation when its role should be to gather those whose community has been fragmented by the world.

F.   Contextual and Universal
This is really another formulation of the previous dialectic. There was a great deal of talk about the importance of contextual theology and contextualized mission emphases. The conference agenda reinforced the significance of contextuality by inviting speakers to address the mission situation in their own particular settings. At the same time, however, the papers are filled with universal claims about God's will for justice, healing, reconciliation and unity. This may argue in favour of what the South African mission scholar, David Bosch (referred to in several papers), called "bold humility" – bold in our witness to God's truth made known in Christ, humble in our recognition that our perceptions of that truth are necessarily limited by history and culture.

H.   Hope and Realism
While the speakers realistically assessed the state of the world, the dominant theme of the conference was hope. Several speakers cited the World Social Forum's call "to believe that another world is possible" and/or defined mission as hope in action (Ferguson). Conversely, they noted the wide-spread lack of hope (A. Ham), saw the prosperity gospel as "cheap hope" (Phiri), and pointed out that much mission work is shaped by secular eschatologies rather than by scripture's vision of God's promised future (Plant).

Michael Kinnamon
Eden Theological Seminary
Saint Louis, Missouri, USA

The Speakers of the Conference Included:
-     Elizabeth Joy from CWM
-     Abraham Berinyuu from EDAN
-     Charles Wanamaker from South Africa
-     Elsa Tamez from Costa Rica (sent her paper)
-     Carlos Ham from Cuba with WCC
-     Peter Henriot, Jesuit from Zambia
-     Israel Selvanayagam from India working in Cambridge
-     Aruna Gnanadason from India with WCC
-     Charles Thomas from Mindolo
-     Michael Kinnamon from the USA
-     Maake Masango from South Africa
-     Esther Mombo from Kenya
-     Edwin Zulo from South Africa

- Lucy Kasanga from Zambia
- Ivone Gebara from Brazil
- Adolfo Ham from Cuba
- Jacques Thomson from Scotland
- Ernst Conradie from South Africa
- Stephen Plant from England
- Ken Ross from Scotland
- John Kafwanka from Zambia
- Caroline Wickens from England serving in Kenya
- Marilyn Legge from Canada
- Chris Ferguson from Canada
- Musonda Bwalya from Zambia
- Muimui Sinyama from Zambia
- Tobias Brandner from Switzerland serving in Hong Kong
- M Mahlangu-Ngeobo from South Africa serving in the USA
- Garth Mundle from Canada
- Isabel Phiri from Malawi serving in South Africa
- Japhet Ndhlovu from Zambia.

Preparatory Paper No 8

Young Missiologists' Consultation
Centro Internazionale Animazione Missionaria C.I.A.M.
Rome, Italy - January 19 – 25, 2005
"Come, Holy Spirit – heal and reconcile"

1 - Introductory Remarks

The "young missiologists consultation" was organized by the Mission and Ecumenical Formation Team of the World Council of Churches, on behalf of the Commission on World Mission and Evangelism, following a suggestion formulated during a session of the Central Committee of the WCC. 32 young theologians, coming from seven regions, many denominations and interested in missiology, learnt to know each other and worked on themes related to the forthcoming world mission conference in Athens (May 9-16, 2005). Whereas the result of the consultation is being shared as a valuable contribution to the preparations for the Athens conference, the consultation had its own identity and purpose, i.e. to provide a space for a dialogue on important issues in missiology between young missiologists.

The consultation was hosted at the CIAM, a centre for missionary spirituality meetings located on the campus of the Pontifical Urbaniana University, immediately adjacent to Vatican City. The WCC expresses its gratitude to the Pontifical Council for Promoting Christian Unity for its support in organizing the consultation as well as to the staff of CIAM, in particular its director, Father Romeo Ballan, for their invaluable hospitality.

Three introductory theological presentations were made:
"The missionary significance of the Holy Spirit as God's empowering, healing and reconciling presence" (Anastasia Vassiliadou, Orthodox, Greece);
"Mission and reconciliation processes" (Puleng LenkaBula, Protestant, South Africa);
"Healing ministries and healing communities" (Baard Knapstad, Pentecostal, Norway).

The major part of the consultation was spent in four thematic groups.
The present document reproduces the reports of the discussions in the groups (chapter 2) and a summary of the debates at the end of the consultation (chapter 3: discussion of group reports, chapter 4: general recommendations). None of these texts was adopted by the consultation. They provide some insight into the debates.

The participants in the consultation could visit the archives of the Congregation for the evangelization of peoples, just behind the CIAM. Opportunities were provided for dialogue with Dr Renato Maiocchi, Executive Secretary of the Federation of Protestant Churches in Italy, and Msgr John Mutiso-Mbinda, Pontifical Council for Promoting Christian Unity.

2 - Reports Presented by the Four Groups on their Discussions

It is important to remember that these reports were not adopted and are a description of part of the discussion which took place in the groups. Recommendations contained in these reports also represent exclusively the discussion in the groups themselves. They were not adopted by the consultation.

2 a - Group on Reconciliation

REPORT ON GROUP DISCUSSION

Four themes:
1. Reconciliation as the nature of the church (its identity)
   This nature or identity comes from Scripture, wherein we affirm that God has reconciled and continues to reconcile us to himself/Godself (2 Corinthians 5:18-19). In this we affirm our responsibility (the church's responsibility) to the ministry of reconciliation. We also affirm the ambiguity of human and social agency in the ministry of reconciliation, where sometimes we are agents of conflict and sometimes we are agents of reconciliation.
   a. to be the church is to be a body of reconciliation
   b. Christians should not forget to reconcile within themselves
   c. there are different levels of reconciliation, i.e. personal or familial, social or communal, and structural.

2. Timing within processes of reconciliation
   We raise the question of when is the proper time to begin a process of reconciliation. We clarify also that "being aware of history" (a phrase used below) means being aware of past wounds and offences, as well as the continuous effects of these wounds and offences.
   a. necessity of being aware of history in the process of reconciliation
   1. inherited sin
   2. memory
   3. timing
   b. reconciliation as continuous action (ongoing work)

3. How forgiveness is incorporated into processes of reconciliation
   We clarify that forgiveness is a fundamental part of the ministry of reconciliation, however it is not a pre-requisite.
   a. reconciliation requires the changing of viewpoints *(metanoia)*
   b. how parties involved must acknowledge their wrongs (accountability and repentance)
   NB: when people are unable or unwilling to acknowledge their participation in wrongdoing, reconciliation cannot happen. We note here the difference between direct and indirect participation in wrongdoing and injustice.

4. Relationship of justice to reconciliation
   We recognize the connection here to *metanoia* and how a change in one part of a system or life necessitates change in other areas of the system or life.

    a. Economic justice, Luke 19 and the story of Zacchaeus.
    1. Zacchaeus commits to giving half of his wealth to the poor.
    2. Matthew 6:24, serving God and mammon.
    b. Restorative justice
    1. Luke 15:11-31, the story of the prodigal son

How does reconciliation imply a change of culture (changes in culture)?
To what extent?

Question of gender violence and the ministry of reconciliation at a personal level.
Is it a question of intimacy and friendliness? Are these signs of reconciliation?

The qualities of the ministry of reconciliation (2 Corinthians 6)
v.4	through great endurance
v.6	by purity, knowledge, patience, kindness, holiness of spirit, genuine love
v.7	truthful speech, and the power of God with the weapons of righteousness
v.8 – 10	treated as impostors, and yet true ....as unknown, and yet are well known ....as sorrowful, yet always rejoicing ....as poor, yet making many rich ....as having nothing, yet possessing everything

The fruit of the Spirit may be (are) signs of reconciliation (Galatians 5:22)
- love, joy, peace, patience, kindness, generosity, faithfulness, gentleness, self-control

Metanoia affects everything. It's a change of heart, of attitude.
(Come, Holy Spirit, change our hearts)

PROPOSALS FOR MOVING FORWARD

Concrete ways to facilitate the churches ministry of reconciliation:
- use case studies, i.e. the bishop in Europe[1]
- biblical analysis (bible study)

Doing another consultation on more specific themes, for instance the connection between ecological justice and reconciliation. We believe this is one of many critical matters that face the church today.
Another critical matter is looking at the elements that inhibit reconciliation. Perhaps this could be a thematic focus of a follow-up consultation?

We represent a variety of Christian traditions and communions.

---

[1] A story told in and to the group. Cf. the report on the plenary discussion in 3a, below.

2 b - Group on the Healing Ministry in Churches

Report on the discussions in the group

Introduction

The definition of healing as introduced in the preparatory papers of the WCC conference, "Called in Christ to be reconciling and healing communities," covers a great number of issues, such as "well-being of the individual and society, of physical, mental, spiritual, economic, political and social well-being – of being in harmony with each other, with the material environment and with God".[2] Although we value such a general definition of healing, our group considered it important to emphasize the "personal aspect of healing"[3]. The decision to emphasize this aspect of healing was caused by the impression that until now, WCC has not paid sufficient attention to the question of healing on the personal level. Members of the group also want to emphasize that in this case it is important to operate with the holistic understanding of a person, namely, the understanding that includes physical, spiritual, emotional, mental as well as social aspects of being human. The group also intends to draw attention to the reality of miraculous healing that appears frequently in the ministries and life of churches.

Our discussions on the topic of healing were concentrated on four main points:
1. Impact of worldviews on our understanding of healing;
2. Relation between healing and power, and healing and faith;
3. Practices of healing;
4. Healing with a consideration for those who are not healed.

1. Impact of worldviews on our understanding of healing

Discussions on the question of worldviews revealed how different backgrounds impact theological understanding of healing. The question of the spiritual realm as an essential aspect of reality and understanding of the cause of illness seemed to be a problem, mainly for those coming from church traditions deeply influenced by the post-Enlightenment paradigm. It seems as if WCC has favoured the post-Enlightenment worldview over and against other worldviews. In relation to that a question was raised whether worldview should be understood in cultural or theological terms. Still an agreement was found concerning the need to challenge the post-Enlightenment worldview which is based on a belief that everything needs a scientific proof and explanation. This belief is particularly devastating for the understanding of healing because it excludes the spiritual realm as well as the reality of miracles.

2. Relation between healing and power, and healing and faith

Different denominational and cultural backgrounds of the members of the group

---

[2] The definition is to be found in: *Healing and Wholeness. The Churches Role in Health. A report by the Christian Medical Commission.* Geneva, WCC, 1990, p. 6
[3] By the term "personal aspect of healing" we understand healing that involves physical, spiritual, emotional and/or mental healing of an individual.

played a significant role also in the second part of the discussion of healing: the emphasis of the discussion was put on two different problems according to the cultural background of the members. Some churches have difficulties acknowledging the possibility of miraculous healing. Other churches struggled with the question how to discern between Christian and non-Christian healing practices. However, we were able to reach a certain level of agreement concerning the nature of healing; i.e., it must be performed in the name of the triune God and it also must point to Christ. The churches must be careful in discerning the healings performed by other spiritual powers and should always stress the power of God as the source of healing. Healing must also be followed by incorporating the healed person in the body of Christ, thus providing him/her the possibility to grow in faith.

3. Practice of healing

The group had a greater level of agreement concerning this part of the discussion. A conviction was shared that churches must rediscover the tradition of healing and the experience of the early church. Here the interdenominational dialogue is very important for sharing the experience of existing healing traditions (liturgical, etc.) as well as helping to rediscover the forgotten ones. Some members acknowledge the recent influence of the Pentecostal/Charismatic churches as a valuable contribution to the healing practices of the churches in the world. There should also be a space for the variety of healing practices without disregarding medical ways of treatment. The members of the group were also engaged in discussion of who could exercise the ministry of healing. Everybody agreed that the ministry of healing should not be narrowed down only to the responsibility of the priest/pastor. Members of the group wished that churches should provide the structural space for gifts of healing to be cultivated. People should be taught about healing as spiritual gift; and the ones who have it should be encouraged to use it. The ones who use it should, however, be guided by more experienced Christians in order to avoid misusage of this spiritual gift. The image of the crucified Christ, empting himself for others, should be a model for using the power of healing. The group also pointed out a need for a space in the liturgy and the church's life for witnessing and sharing the experience of healing.

4. Healing with a consideration for those who are not healed

In the discussion of this particular aspect of healing, the group decided not to discuss the causes of the illnesses in general, considering this question to be too broad. We also agreed that a distinction must be drawn between the notion of healing and that of curing. A person can remain physically ill but still be healed in his/her heart and be a full-bodied part of community. The community bears much responsibility to incorporate ill or handicapped persons. We also considered it important that God's freedom to heal or not to heal must be regarded in one's search for healing: suffering or illness can be a path to Christ in the same way as the healing can. Still the ones that do not get healed, and their communities, should be encouraged to believe that God's love is the same for the healed and sick ones. Cases when a person does not get healed should not discourage churches from the healing practices: practices of healing must not be driven by the presuppositions of the post-Enlightenment paradigm that demands that every action should have a result in order to be validated.

Recommendations

- The group recommends the WCC to pay more attention to the personal level of healing, including miraculous healing.
- We also like to stress a need for the WCC to work on a language that would provide a space for serious consideration for miraculous healings as a part of our worldview.
- We consider it important to include the subject of miraculous healing as a part of theological education in general.
- We wish to encourage the interdenominational dialogue concerning the ministries of healing in order to exchange the experience of existing practices of healing as well as support and encourage the churches that wish to develop the ministries of healing.
- The WCC should encourage the member churches to cultivate the education and reflection of the spiritual gift of healing among their members. Moreover, those engaged in the ministry of healing should be provided with encouragement, support and guidance from the churches.
- Some members of the group want to emphasize that the modern ecumenical movement should acknowledge, and engage in dialogue with, the growing Pentecostal/Charismatic influence in the world today, especially in regard to their healing ministries.

2 c - Report on the Discussions of the Group on Dialogue

Preamble

We met as a group of people that had different needs for dialogue and different attitudes towards it. But there was a general sense that dialogue is important. The group proved that dialogue was possible and shared the different necessities among diverse participants. Dialogue can originate out of situations of tension. Creative tensions could lead to new insights and deeper reflections.

Our group on dialogue was diverse. Our group is comprised of 8 "young" theologians. We come from different backgrounds: one from South Africa, two from Greece, one from Germany, one from the USA, one from Switzerland, one from Syria and one from the Netherlands. We are five women and three men. We are three Orthodox, one Pentecostal, one Lutheran, three Presbyterian/Reformed. Our backgrounds reflect the concerns and issues we brought to (the) dialogue.

In the report below you will find the subjects we have shared with each other. In the report we do not aim to streamline the topics: there are tensions and incongruences, and we agreed to let those come through.

Introduction

Has "dialogue" replaced Christian mission? This is the question we explored throughout our discussions of the last three days. We recognized the legacy of colonialism and mission. Examples mentioned were the Crusades and the violent colonization of Latin America and Africa. Due to this negative connotation of "mission," we explored the positive qualities of dialogue. One positive example of dialogue was liturgy which will be expounded upon later. Whereas mission can imply a one way direction, dialogue necessarily involves an exchange. We understood in our conversations that dialogue could replace mission, yet we discussed dialogue as a form of mission. We recognized there was a tension between dialogue as an aim and dialogue as having an aim, namely unity between churches. To some group members, unity was a clear aim; for others, this unity was abstract.

Coming from different backgrounds our pre-occupations were with different kinds of dialogue: dialogue rises from a need of people, communities and churches to come to understanding and a way of living together. This meant that our respective interests were with interreligious, inter-denominational, inter-cultural dialogue and dialogue with secular society. In our report we do not necessarily define dialogue every single time to one of these particular types; where needed, we will be specific.

Whereas we disagreed on the aim of dialogue, we were more united on the attitudes that participants need to bring to the dialogue. Humans have been given reason and free will: dialogue needs to be enjoyed as a tool to express God's love by listening, openness and acceptance. Dialogue is a way of witness to our faith. The Holy Spirit is at work in and between us in our dialogues with God and with each other.

We agreed that dialogue is a space where perceptions and misperceptions can be shared, with the purpose of working towards unity. All engaged in dialogue bring their social location with them to the table. Openness towards others means that we realize we are more complete together than individually. Both parties are transformed as a result of engaging in the mutual learning process of dialogue. Dialogue depends on balanced power relations. We addressed [that there are] inequalities between people and communities: our gender, ethnicity, geo-political situation and our age could be either to our advantage or our disadvantage.

We recognized that a focus on denominational growth – aggressive evangelization of and competition among Christians – is an obstacle to inter-church dialogue. We rejected the idea of "franchise mission" (Ray Bakke/Urban missiologist), i.e. different churches *selling* a similar product competing over *consumers*. Mission in dialogue means to move beyond competition to co-operation. Instead of being self-sufficient, churches need to learn from each other through dynamic mutual exchanges. This includes that all participate: not only North to South and West to East but multi-directional in partnership. We recognized that the churches in the global south ("Two-Thirds World") are growing, and that there is a lively interest in mission, despite the negative experiences of the past.

Up to now, most of our observations have focused on inter-denominational dialogue. In our group, we did address dialogue with people who have no religious beliefs – as is the experience in parts of Europe. Yet, we did not come to conclusions if this dialogue is different from engaging in dialogue with people of different faiths.

We discerned various approaches to the *interreligious dialogue* from a Christian point of view. On the one side we find the opinion that all religions are equally true. On the other side we find the conviction that there is no salvation outside Christianity. None in our group identified with these extreme positions. We would like to enter the exchange with people of other faiths with the same attitude as described above for inter-denominational dialogue. We give witness to our faith and receive the other in order to live in peace, harmony and respect in our societies. As an example of interreligious dialogue in the Middle East, the Christian-Muslim dialogue was mentioned. Each religion considers itself to be the source of absolute truth. However, the experience of living together – with all its positive and negative aspects – leads to the discovery of the importance of moving beyond exclusivism to mutual respect and understanding.

We have different theological understandings of mission and how dialogue functions within it. Below we will mention some of the approaches mentioned.

- Liturgy as dialogue: For the Orthodox, the eucharist constitutes a fundamental act of mission (as an initiative and as the content of missionary activity and dialogue between the different churches and cultures). The eucharist (that in the Orthodox context is called Divine Liturgy) manifests the very essence of the Church as an eschatological Kingdom of God, the reality of communion (koinonia) and of unity. The gathering together into one (synaxis), for communication with each other (horizontally) and with God (vertically) is, at the same time, the going forth for mission. It is through the eucharist that church dialogues with the entire world, assuming it and transforming it. Therefore it is the transformation of the world and of the humanity that the Church proposes.
- In the Bible we have an example of dialogues: between God and people and among people. This dialogue is not simple nor unambiguous. Our contexts are a part of the ongoing dialogue with/in the biblical texts.
- Dialogue reflects back on the self: we need to evaluate ourselves and the other to validate the dialogue. This leads to transformation, which does not signify that we lose our ecclesial or religious identity.
- The role of the minister can facilitate the dialogue between the congregation and God and represent the people before God.
- Dialogue may have an aim in unity, but this needs to be translated in social action.

As we reflected on dialogue under the perspective of **mission** we were influenced by various different backgrounds
A. We have to admit that mission is often regarded as a term with a strict positive or negative connotation
   - From a positive connotation mission is the basic character/ essence of the church.
   - From a negative connotation it is still an expression of colonization and proselytism.

Concluding this, we could say that **Mission** splits.

B. We should admit that **Dialogue** is often or mostly regarded as a term with a strict positive notion. **Dialogue** seems to combine
    - For some people it has a certain aim (unity),
    - For some others it is a dynamic process with an open end. So the general idea was that it could be helpful to come up with concrete suggestions for future plans. The nature of our dialogue was completely diverse as a result of our diversity.

Recommendations

1. The clarification of definitions must be a priority and we have to understand those definitions respecting their contextuality. Dialogue is also a matter of terms. The language of dialogue is a theme of great importance. Dialogue is full of confusion because of the difficulty to understand the language.

2. Mission academics, practitioners/scholars and church leaders could collect, refine, disseminate information in ways that are accessible both to academic and grass-roots level. Dialogue has often lacked an adequate public dimension. Instead it has focused on individual or ecclesial concerns. Participation in public forums, politics, social movements and citizenship should be considered as a basis for creative dialogue.

3. Community Bible studies can be developed which highlight issues of dialogue between culture, context, religion, gender and class. Develop and encourage the use of contextual-narrative paradigm as a dynamic form of dialogue.

4. The conference in Athens could also develop a participant accountability plan, i.e. time table for regional reports.

5. Initiative research projects concerning youth perceptions on inter-church dialogue and church unity. This research should be qualitative with the option for the development of and critique of contemporary themes regarding the issues above.

6. Analyse denominational constitutions, policies and statutes that cause exclusion and division in the body of Christ.

7. Encourage and facilitate "glocal" dialogue to create awareness of different world view; i.e., North-South, first and two-thirds world.

Conclusion

The process of dialoguing on dialogue has been intensive and transforming for us as a group: the trust and openness among us, with all our differences have been a gift for which we are grateful. This has been a challenging process that we would like to continue. Hopefully it will be received and continued by other young theologians/missiologists. We will carry this enriching experience with us from here, back to our countries, churches, congregations and studies.

2 d - Pneumatology Group: Report of Discussion

Our group affirmed the growing interest in the theology of the Holy Spirit as a helpful way of understanding and even changing the way we live mission.

We identified several important topics for consideration if we want to understand more about the Holy Spirit in connection with various aspects of mission:

- Reconciliation as the work of the Spirit in the Church so that we can be reconciling and healing communities in the world.

- Participation in the Spirit's work of healing, restoration and renewal.

- Recognition of the work of the Spirit in other faiths, which can change the nature of interreligious dialogue.

- Participation with the Spirit, as Christians are formed into the Body of Christ precisely through diversity, variety and multiplicity.

- Invitation through the Spirit to let our identity be shaped as being Christ's and agents of the new reality of the kingdom.

- Focus on the presence of the Holy Spirit in all creation, which calls us to an ecclesial understanding of nature; our responsibility comes from our ecclesial self-understanding.

Although our lives should be lived as mission, "Christian living" does not always incorporate such an understanding. This is because we find it necessary to go outside our usual contexts for living and cross boundaries into the contexts of others- this is a major part of what constitutes mission, and we are able to do it only through the power of the Holy Spirit. In this sense, we can suggest that mission consists of the fruit and gifts of the Holy Spirit. Our Christian identity consists of being open to and be led by the Spirit, so that we can be agents of this mission.

A major challenge our group identified is that of discerning or characterizing the nature of the Holy Spirit. This led us to formulate several key questions:

- How, if at all, can we discern that the work of the Church is in fact the work of the Spirit?
- Can we discern a difference between experience of the Holy Spirit and other spiritual experiences?
- What is the purpose, if any, of describing the nature of the Holy Spirit?
- How do we perceive and appreciate the different manifestations of the fruit and gifts of the Spirit that we observe in Christian traditions in various contexts?

- How can we understand the relations between the persons of the Trinity as a way of being *ad intra* and how this relation *(perichoresis)* is lived *ad extra*, as the way of how God is manifesting Himself?
- Is there any relation between Christ's *oikonomia* and Spirit's *oikonomia* and mission of Christ and mission of Spirit?

We can identify an aspect of contemporary ecumenical mission as the need for open encounter with Christians from diverse communities in order to learn from each other. Within the Church we recognize different types and expressions of spirituality, which are present in diverse traditions in various contexts. Each of these expressions may add to our understanding of the Holy Spirit, although they cannot be said in sum to complete it. Trying to discern the Holy Spirit in this way contributes to Christian unity.

Finally, an emphasis on the Holy Spirit is also powerful in that it directs us to a focus on relevance to this world when we talk about mission. This focus no longer rests so much on a specific message that can be preached but on a radically transformative understanding of experiencing the Kingdom of God here and now, not just in the *eschaton*. Being transformed by the Spirit leads us to become agents of the Kingdom in our communities and in the global community. Therefore, mission becomes the work we do to realize the Kingdom every day, in every place.

(The group added here some thoughts and observations about the consultation in general which were taken up in the evaluation session.)

3 - Summary of Discussion Points Raised when the Plenary Received the Group Reports

The following notes have a personal character and reflect the way the final sessions have been understood and noted by the two co-moderators. Theses are not official minutes of the discussion, nor an adopted aide-mémoire.

Where needed and possible, this document refers to quotes from the group report in italics.

3 a - Discussion on Report of Reconciliation Group

1. The question of *inherited* sin mentioned in the report is based on a story told in the group about a bishop of a European country who first refused to apologize for sins committed by his church against the Roma during the second world war, on the basis that any church representative of today could not be considered responsible for wrong actions of the past ("We did not do this ourselves"). This raises the question of the collective responsibility of communities, which often are called to apologize for wrongs committed by earlier generations. Should present church authorities or governing bodies confess such sins and, if so, how and on behalf of whom? In other terms: if for reconciliation there is a need to correct past wrongs, who is called to take responsibility for it?

There was no controversial discussion on this in the consultation, but the story itself was a story of high controversy.

2. *Forgiveness is not a prerequisite*. Challenged on this formulation, the group explained its text. Forgiveness is essential to any process of reconciliation, as is the desire by the perpetrators to seek for forgiveness, there is no doubt about it. However, the group didn't want to fix a strict chronological sequence and acknowledged that, yes, the "perpetrators" must be hold accountable and become aware of what they did, but that could come at any point during a reconciliation process. It didn't have to be the condition for starting it. Not everybody agreed with the explanation. For some, without forgiveness at the very start, one finds oneself in a logic of revenge.

3. *"Metanoia"*: During the discussion, it was felt that the liturgical aspect of reconciliation was missing (e.g., the sacrament of confession or reconciliation). The group acknowledged, but had never intended to be complete in the description of reconciliation processes.

4. Critique was expressed that the report did not mention the importance of punitive or retributive justice. It hadn't come up in the group's discussions, was the answer.

5. Some missed the personal aspect of reconciliation with God and the need of every human being to be reconciled with God. The group pointed out it wanted to emphasize humanity's response to God's reconciliation. The fact of being reconciled was, for them, the point of departure (not a matter of discussion). It has to do with Christian identity (that's why the text affirms in its § 1 that the identity of the church *comes from scripture*). It is an implicit point. However, they all do recognize that there is no reconciliation without the fruit of the Spirit, and so that reconciliation is linked to pneumatology.

3 b - Discussion on Report of Healing Group

The report was not read, but summarized in plenary.

Both general agreement and (more often) fundamental disagreement were expressed as to the way this report describes elements of the healing ministry and criticizes the post-Enlightenment worldview (the term being not very helpful, if it refers to the rational scientific approach which is precisely the one of the Enlightenment). "I am in deep agreement with this group on post-Enlightenment" "Important – we have a lack of talking about healing and the Holy Spirit" – " I don't find this fits my context and my church" - "I agree with the critique"- "I don't find that this reflects my background".
Some of the critical points raised could be summarized as follows:

1. The insistence on the *"miraculous"* was challenged. According to the temptation story, in the desert, Jesus rejected the use of the miraculous to manifest the kingdom. He chose the way of powerlessness, the theology of the cross. Others

would have preferred terms such as "deeply spiritual" instead of "miraculous". Some were of the opinion that space had to be opened for miracles, but questioned the weight put on it in the text.

2. The critique of the Enlightenment approach was considered too one-sided by most speakers, with the exceptions of people who thought that was necessary, since the ethos of the Enlightenment had frustrated so many Christians. More care was expected from the treatment of the Enlightenment world-view, and the understanding of the sacred and the uncreated energies of God.

3. The lack of a wider perspective was criticized. Even within the Enlightenment paradigm, there are forms of personal healing, there is pastoral care and approach, and much which psychotherapy could contribute to such a discussion and which is totally missing in the group's report. The plenary pleaded for integrating various traditions on the personal healing aspect. There was also criticism expressed because the social levels of the healing ministry had not been addressed (a fact acknowledged in the group report).

4. Questions were raised as to the relation between faith and healing. What was priority: faith in Christ or in miraculous healing? One should also clarify the goal of healing. Basically, healing was based on redemption and restores people to redemption. In other terms, what is the nature and purpose of healing, what are the goals of healing?

5. A specific question was raised as to what was meant by *the more experienced Christians* who should guide those with spiritual gifts (in § 3 Practice of healing). To this, the response was that spontaneous healing has to be controlled from outside, i.e. the community, so that it remains within Christianity. The group didn't want to speak of church magisterium, but wanted to insist on accountability.

In the responses coming from the group, it was clear that there had been internal discussions as well. However, it was stated that the capacity to heal was one of the gifts of the Spirit and could not be disregarded, because of its serious biblical grounding. It is part of the ministry of the church (I Cor. 12, Mark 16). There needs to be a distinction between the miracles Jesus refuses in the temptation story, and his practice of healing, well attested in the New Testament. However, one must be aware that for every biblical "original", there was a "duplicate" in the world, and so there are miracles done by others. The relation between faith and healing is not so simple, since it may imply the faith of the person that is the healer and/or the faith of the person healed. At times faith is significant in healing stories, at times not. However, faith is what makes people well.

The group was aware of the limitations of its report. It had decided to use that lens for approaching the healing ministry, because that had not often been debated in ecumenical circles. It was aware that it neglected other aspects. There was general agreement in challenging the excessive use of "should" language in the report. It was clear that this report was a starting point for discussion, not a concluding paper on the question.

3 c – Discussion on Report of Dialogue Group

Following the presentation of the report by the dialogue group, there was also a lively discussion. Debates and comments addressed the following matters:

1. *No salvation outside Christianity .... extreme position?*
Can one say that a position affirming that there is no salvation outside Christianity is an "extreme" position? If some religions are more true than others and yet there is salvation outside Christianity, a question was asked, does this mean that in the group's opinion, absolute truth is not necessary for salvation? "To live in peace, does that mean one has to deny what we believe?" Some participants for whom mission is a priority affirmed that salvation is in Christ and there is no salvation outside faith in Christ. They didn't feel it correct to have such a position qualified as extreme. They would not however affirm that salvation was possible only in Christianity. Reference was made in the discussion to people from Muslim background having received the revelation of Christ without having links with a church or institutionalized Christianity.

The group acknowledged it had only been able to start exploring the question. They explained that it in the discussions, they had not denied salvation in Christ. The text is to be understood as following: in interreligious dialogue, there are different theories and positions. Some affirm that all religions are true. Others say that only Christianity is the true religion. "We found ourselves in the middle" was the oral summary of the group's position on this question. The word "extreme" in the text means the two ends of a line of possibilities. By "Christianity" is meant: "institutionalized Christianity".

This answer provoked a follow-up question: "Can I take with me into a dialogue the conviction that there is no salvation outside faith in Jesus Christ?". The answer from the group was: yes. The group said it had tried to convey the fact that in a dialogue (e.g. between Christians and Muslims) both will continue to believe in the respective message of their religion, but will be more open. The group wanted to distance itself from exclusivist positions. On church and salvation, one participant remarked that it was necessary and important to distinguish between the canonical and the charismatic limits of the church.

2. During the discussion, several persons shared thoughts about how they perceived *truth* as related to mission and dialogue. This was not a structured discussion on truth and theology, however. "We do not own truth, we're part of the truth" said one of the participants. For another, defending an Orthodox point of view, as churches we are the truth, we are not part of the truth. If you don't have the feeling you are the truth, if you think you are not the truth, then no dialogue is possible.

3. There was some debate on the use of the terms *mission* and *dialogue*, and their relation in the text. Did dialogue replace mission or should it be seen as a part of mission? What was the aim of dialogue? The group explained that they had realized how mission had very different significations in the variety of contexts

represented in its discussions. They thought that the term was difficult. The group discussed dialogue as a description of God's love and urged to adopt with people of other religions the same attitude as in ecumenical relations. But there was no final conclusion to the terminology debate in the group nor in plenary.

4. Several other items were addressed briefly. One difficult question could not find an answer in that meeting: What are the next steps for Christians living in a situation of religious intolerance, after they have tried as much as possible to dialogue, without receiving a satisfactory answer?

The paragraph on "liturgy as dialogue" received appreciation in the discussion. Mission should not only be considered as "going outside".

5. What is the significance of dialogue or mission in a fully *secularized world* (with a classical scientific worldview) in which people have no religious beliefs whatsoever? In such contexts, mission has a very negative connotation. What about interreligious dialogue then, was asked. "We can dialogue also with an atheist. To be Christian is a possibility to see in the other the face of Jesus Christ. We can thus not limit dialogue to those having a specific understanding of truth".

3 d – Discussion on Report of Pneumatology Group

"What is in the report on our discussions contains 10% of what we discussed....."

In the plenary discussion, the following themes were highlighted:

1. *Focus on the presence of the Holy Spirit in all creation*
It was not clear what was exactly referred to. If the Holy Spirit is present everywhere, what then is the significance of baptism? Does the group refer to environment questions or to the presence of the Spirit in other religions?
The response emphasized that one should think of stages of the presence of the Spirit. The Holy Spirit is present in different ways, in eucharist, the word, human beings, animals, the environment. It is not true to affirm that the Holy Spirit was not present before Pentecost. The Spirit was at work since creation, which does not mean we "naturalize" the Spirit nor disregard Pentecost. Everything which comes to life does so through the Holy Spirit, nothing has life because of itself. How, would one say, does an animal worship God? Through its own existence. God is not only the creator (in the beginning), but continuously sustains everything.

2. There is a special sense in which the church is "pentecostal", but it was difficult to describe it, said the group in answer to a question. The sentence "participation with the Spirit, as Christians are formed into the body of Christ precisely through diversity, variety and multiplicity" tries to convey something of the discussion in the group.

3. Some persons in the plenary needed explanation on the meaning of *perichoresis*.[4] In their response, group members reminded that all starts from

---

[4] A Greek term referring to the mutual giving and receiving among the three persons of the Trinity, and their interpenetration.

God being relational in Godself. The question is how that is lived in the church. When we speak about the Holy Spirit in the world, we mean manifestations of God in the world, which are not separate from God's own life. The term *perichoresis* defines what is meant by the inner-trinitarian relations (reference to an image of joining hands).

4. The group responded to a question on the significance of the proposal to move away from the classical (ecumenical) paradigm based on God's mission (*missio Dei*). The proposed greater emphasis on the role of the Holy Spirit obliges to take seriously the fact that God is a God in relation. It will also emphasize the relational aspect of human life (*I–Thou* relationship in philosophy) and of Christian witness. It can open new ways for an understanding and practice of dialogue.

5. A question was raised – independently of the text of the group report - about the meaning of the reference in Matt. 12:31-32 to the unforgivable sin (blasphemy against the Spirit). One member of the group answered that they had discussed the question, and acknowledged the difficulty and seriousness of the matter. That verse had silenced conversation on the Holy Spirit in many places. No final answer could be given: There is blasphemy when one disregards the witness of the Holy Spirit. E.g.: If the Spirit is present/at work in all creation, blasphemy would be to disregard this.

6. Remarks came from the plenary to the link between the Holy Spirit and mission. One said that as Christians we go out because we received the Spirit. It's God's mission which leads us to do so. Mission is a direct consequence of the Spirit's presence and empowerment (reference to Acts 1:8). Another intervention mentioned the importance of Christ's incarnation (Phil 2) as focus on mission in his particular context, as more important than an exclusive emphasis on the Spirit.

Several members of the group responded. Christian incarnation is indeed the model of mission. But one has to see that it's the Holy Spirit who gives identity to Jesus (when Jesus is baptized), then Jesus crosses boundaries and preaches. The Spirit gives the dynamics and pulls persons out of their own situation. Mission is to be understood basically as living out Christian life. But it has something to do with crossing boundaries, going out of one's "ego". To go out to the end of the earth and love people is only possible through the Spirit.

4 - Common Recommendations

The plenary did not want to own all recommendations coming from the groups as such. They remain group recommendations. There was however on the last evening of the consultation a time dedicated to a plenary exchange on follow-up. The present notes are not to be considered as adopted minutes of that discussion, but summarize matters (not formulations) on which we seemed to have reached some consensus.

* The experience of such a work with and among young missiologists must continue

and the WCC/CWME must take the responsibility to facilitate the organization of further consultations such as that held in Rome.

* As much as possible, continue with the same persons, enlarging the group however with persons from denominations or regions not enough represented. It was felt important to build now on relationships which had been established, instead of starting with a totally new group. If the age became a problem, they said, then call this group "forever young missiologists".

* Facilitate the creation of a network of young missiologists through a database or an internet directory.

* The *International Review of Mission* is asked to make space to the young missiologists, and perhaps even dedicate a special issue to their research and writings, drawing on persons from this group to form an editorial committee for that.

The following **themes** for future common work and consultations were mentioned in the discussion:
Reconciliation and ecological justice
Reconciliation and healing in broken communities[5]
Liturgical aspects of the themes discussed (rituals of healing, of reconciliation, sharing of wealth of liturgical resources)
Mission (crossing boundaries, dialogue with other people) in the wide sense of the term.

Notes offered by the two co-moderators of the Rome consultation, Beate Fagerli who moderated the final sessions, and Jacques Matthey who took notes.

Geneva, February 7, 2005

---

[5] The world mission conference in Athens was encouraged to include the miraculous when talking about healing.

Preparatory Paper No 9

"Mission from the Perspective of People in Struggle" Report of the URM Global Mission Conference Abokobi, Accra, Ghana, 1-7 May 2004

Part 1: Introduction and Core Reflections

Introduction

The Urban Rural Mission conference on "Mission from the Perspective of People in Struggle" was the culmination of a two-and-a-half year process of grassroots missiological reflection initiated by the URM Global Working Group in its meeting in Jacerei, Sao Paolo, Brazil, February/March 2002. It was carried out by the regional networks of URM in Africa, Asia, Europe, Latin America, Middle East and North America. In most cases reflection was done at the local community level, the national level and the regional level. In all cases reports were produced that summarized the key insights of the reflections.

The conference at Abokobi in Accra gathered more than eighty participants from 36 countries and seven of the eight regions of the WCC. There were no participants from the Pacific.

Both the conference and the preparatory process leading to it were designed to achieve two main goals. One was to articulate a vision for mission, from the perspective of people in struggle, that would shape the work and perspective of URM for the years ahead. The other was to bring forward an articulation of that vision of mission to the WCC World Mission Conference in Athens in 2005. This two-pronged concern shaped the discussions and focus of our conference.

The conference was designed to allow these two goals to inform an open-ended process that would allow the conference participants to shape the conversation and also let ideas and concerns inform the discussion as they arose. In order to facilitate this process a series of smaller group discussions were scheduled that would require reporting back to plenary, and were guided by the insights of an appointed group of listeners. This group, chaired by Rev. Dr George Mathew, consisted of representatives from each of the regions. The other members were Mr Mario Gonzales Figueroa (Latin America, with translation assistance from Ms Maria Bentancur Paez), Ms Helena Hooper (Africa), Ms Anna Marsiana (Asia), Rev. Garnet Parris (Europe), Dr Daniel Scott (North America) and Mr Gamal Zekrie (Middle East). The task of the Listeners Group was

- to listen and note the issues and concerns being raised during the events of the conference,

- to summarize and reflect on the content of the discussion as a guide to the next steps in the process, and
- to help gather the insights and results of the discussions.

This report is a synthesis of the core reflections of the Accra conference. It is compiled and prepared from the common report of the group of listeners/reflectors at the conference and some of the common threads from the reports of the regional processes.

Core Reflections

a) URM, The Church, and Mission
A clear element in the evolution of the WCC-URM programme is the development of a network that has come to understand itself as a global movement of people, rooted in the Christian faith, who are called, along with others, to the mission of God in a particular way. It has understood this as a call to participate in the struggles of the exploited, the marginalized and the oppressed, for the building of a new community based on justice and inclusiveness, in the perspective of the reign of God.

In light of this self-understanding, URM finds itself faced with some complex and difficult questions and realities regarding its experience of "the church" as institution and its relationship with that institution. URM acknowledges that this relationship has often been characterized by a certain "discomfort" that seems to have become a permanent though not altogether unhealthy aspect of the relationship.

From the midst of struggles there have been different experiences of the institutional manifestation of the "church". In history there have been positive experiences of "the church" standing side by side with the oppressed and the excluded. However, the predominant experience has been of a church that has either ignored or co-operated in the exclusion of the wounded and marginalized.

URM understands that the church as the "body of Christ" is called to be "in the midst" – a living presence of God among all of God's people. Often this means that the church must live and witness in the complex reality of a multicultural and multi-religious world and face a multiplicity of choices and options in keeping faith with Christ. From the perspectives of the marginalized, however, this is above all a call to a life-giving and life-transforming presence among and alongside people in struggle and in pain. It is a call for participation in their struggle to overthrow the structures and systems that fragment human community, making some oppressors and keeping others oppressed.

URM interprets its own mission in the light of this understanding and thus often finds itself confronting and criticizing the churches for not clearly taking sides in favour of the weak. In this way URM finds its own place "in between" the churches and the poor, working *in and on behalf* of the churches as well as of the poor - a prophetic voice of the one to the other. It is clearly not a position of neutrality, but one of mediation and commitment to those on the margins. This makes for a relationship that is both complementary and contradictory, characterized by solidarity and critique. URM acknowledges that its mission is not without the church even if it sometimes has to work outside the structures of the churches. However, from time to time it has to challenge the churches to be with the people in struggle and not to abandon the people in the face of pressure, political interference or other forces opposed to life.

We were aware in raising these issues that we would need to struggle with what we mean by "church" and to acknowledge that local and regional circumstances and experiences will shape our understanding and relationships. And finally we acknowledged that in some regions this dialogue is one that must be inter-faith as much as it is ecumenical.

In its relationship with the churches as "institutions", URM sees its role as educative. This is understood as a process of keeping the churches informed and aware of the concerns and perspectives of the poor and marginalized and their struggles for life with dignity, as well as of the issues that debilitate peoples and communities. In this concern to give voice to the perspectives of the excluded, URM has often been critical of the hierarchical structures of the church, challenging the churches to widen their understanding and practice of mission. URM, however, sees itself as acting in a positive way to support and encourage the churches to pay attention to the missiological and evangelical dimensions of issues of justice, poverty and human dignity. Its goal is to influence the churches towards a vision of mission that includes greater solidarity with the poor and a willingness to be with them in the midst of their struggle.

It must also be said that in many traditions, evangelism and spirituality have been stripped of their essential prophetic character and dimension, as they are often opposed to the struggles of people for justice and life with dignity. The separation of the churches' work for justice from that of proclamation introduces a certain hierarchy of values that in itself often becomes a cause for division in churches and congregations. From the perspectives of people in struggle, this dichotomy promotes a false spirituality that enables evangelism to serve the interests of power and maintain the *status quo*. For them, the integrity of the gospel as "good news to the poor" is what is at stake. True evangelism is the preaching of a gospel that identifies the church with the poor and downtrodden, a gospel that tears down the barriers which divide and separate humanity from God, from each other and from the rest of creation. This calls for a need to refocus evangelism on the reconciling mission of God which denounces all that separate, marginalize and oppress, as exemplified in the life and teaching of Christ. This also means a need to re-place the church's work for social justice within the framework of the proclamation of this reconciling mission of God.

As people involved with this mission, we see ourselves working with the churches in a partnership in which there is mutual need to enable the gospel to find expression in many forms. We see the role of URM as a voice calling the church to prophetic evangelism and to a spirituality of resistance to dehumanization. This means being alert and ready to address issues that affect the most marginalized: migrants and refugees, victims of all forms of discrimination, oppression, conflict and other forms of violence, and all those whose rights and freedom are at risk or are being violated, as well as issues relating to the concern for and care of the whole earth and all its creatures and resources. We see URM as a prophetic instrument of the church that calls the church to see, understand and stand alongside peoples in struggle. The churches need to be constantly reminded of this call and we need the support of the churches to continue to be in the world in the midst of people's struggles. As URM serves to be the church with people in struggle it also serves as a means for the voices of the poor to be heard and acknowledged in the church. Our tradition of story telling is part of making known the realities of poverty and marginalization. It is also one of our methods of building and developing inclusive communities. Our hope is that the voices of the poor will be heard and the practice and thinking of mission will be shaped by their insights.

In the face of globalization we recognize that there are more poor and marginalized than ever before. The gap between the rich and the poor is growing and we feel it is urgent for the church to devote more of its mission resources to accompanying and supporting the poor in their struggle. Resources are needed for training and community mobilization, and for community building and development. There is a need to build new alliances across ecumenical and inter-faith lines. We need to acknowledge that this work will take many forms in response to local circumstances and realities and that it can only be effective when it is rooted in the particular of local situations, addressing local concerns and reflecting the call of Isaiah 58.

It is recommended that the process that URM follows in dealing with communities and the problems they face be in a continuous state of reforming and refocusing. This includes increased sensitivity in exposure visits and giving space for actions arising from such visits rather than being focused on diagnosing the problems witnessed. We have to continually seek ways to give more space to the grassroots to be much more active in the process of taking decisions and dealing with problems, including giving them a role in both the meetings and activities of URM and the larger church communities.

b) Violence and Violation and the URM Response

It was clear that a concern for "mission from the perspective of people in struggle" will require a response to the various forms of violence and violation that are part of the experience of people in struggle. Mission as we in URM understand it, as a practice of accompaniment, demands a thoughtful response to the challenges posed by the reality of globalized violence that reduces people to hopelessness. This response must address particularly the issue of mission to the victims of violence and violation in a way that is consistent with the gospel of Christ who brings life in all its fullness to all. Among other concerns, the following need to be addressed:

–   In the discussions of the church being "in between" there are also questions about mission in relation to the perpetrators of violence, and our role in the work for justice, but also in healing and reconciliation. How is this mission to be carried out?

– To address violence in its many forms and help devise "strategies of resistance" requires a thoughtful and critical analysis of contexts and circumstances. It also requires spiritual discernment and a reliance on the guidance of the Holy Spirit so that accompaniment is not misplaced or misdirected as in the case of Job's comforters.

– Finally, we heard a concern to address violation as one of the many forms that violence can take and that can persist in the lives of the marginalized. This also calls for standing with and alongside those who are struggling and those who are marginalized.

In responding to these concerns and challenges we want to strongly affirm the need to do mission "in between" without being misled into a position of neutrality or indifference. We see the church's mission as a call to "accompaniment" and not "neutral observation". We have to make sure we are first and always on the side of the victims, but when it is possible we have to be able to work with the perpetrators/violators in order to bring about justice and reconciliation. Violence is a persistent challenge to the church and the gospel, and must not be ignored, dismissed or minimalized.

We acknowledge that in our work for social justice, it is important that we move from the purely juridical and political understanding of justice and reconciliation that has often been associated with peoples' struggles. We believe that for URM and the church the work of reconciliation cannot be merely to heal the past. It must include the necessary prevention of the repetition of the same wrongs in the future. Repentance requires a change of direction: a turning away. While our priority is to accompany the victims of violence and injustice, perpetrators who are willing to change can become companions in the dialogue and search for reconciliation. We must maintain this hope. In taking sides we want to be clear that we are calling the churches to take the side of justice and of the weak, in the understanding and conviction that the social and political problems that must be addressed have deep theological, ethical and therefore evangelical dimensions. We must be wise to avoid entanglement in political games and hold on to a prophetic role that challenges political, social, economic as well as religious structures that compromise the fullness of life in the perspective of the "good news" of Christ.

There is a persistent temptation to speak on behalf of the victim. URM must be clear that our role is more to create spaces and possibilities for the victims to speak on their own behalf. Consequently we strongly recommend that the WCC provide such an opportunity and create spaces at the world mission conference for the people in struggle, the victims of violence, the marginalized and afflicted to be and speak for themselves.

From the beginning URM has included people of other faiths within the movement which has presented some challenges to our sense of Christian identity, making it seem less clear. We believe that we are called to be the salt that preserves and gives taste, and that we are not losing our Christian identity but finding our true identity in giving life to others. We insist on the spiritual power of our mission and the hope present in building communities and linking peoples of different backgrounds, especially in contexts where dialogue across traditions is critical for reconciliation, justice and peace building. We see this capacity as nourishing others and ourselves and encourage URM to continue in this spirit.

We are also concerned that URM examine its practices of exposure visits and be aware of the potential of an exposed community being viewed and not engaged. It is important that any visit to a community be an act of solidarity and that any visit has an objective for that visit. We encourage a shift from exposure to immersion so that the visit achieves bonding, understanding and provides exchanges of stories and experiences.

c) Restorative Justice, Healing and Reconciliation

Authentic reconciliation must be based on justice and truth that deals with the root causes of conflict, violence and violation. Among people in struggle, there is serious concern that the discourse on healing and reconciliation would not take seriously the concerns for justice. This is because the powerful and the perpetrators of injustices often talk about reconciliation and not about justice. For people in struggle, "restorative justice" remains one of the critical tasks – the unfinished business – for mission. This raises the question: What is the nature of the restorative justice that we seek and what are the necessary steps in moving to and beyond it to true healing and reconciliation?

The call for the churches to become reconciling and healing communities is also a call for them to recognize the brokenness of the world in which they are called to witness and minister. It is a call to recognize that the world is broken and continues to be broken through a persistent abuse of power, the marginalization and oppression of the weak and the de-humanization of the other. Human history is replete with instances of genocide and other crimes against humanity. Some of these have caused the disappearance of whole peoples and cultures. Those of the last and present centuries are sombre reminders of this reality. Impunity and regimes and rules of terror are a part of our recent memory. We continue to witness violent civil, ethnic and religious conflicts. Violent dispossessions, transplantations, occupations, old and new forms of economic and social marginalization and victimization, and the kind of violent resistance that these have elicited have thrown the world into a new era of polarization that all sides see as a threat to their way of life. In dealing with this threat, the concerns for national and international security have shaped policy and response. Thus the powerful have seized the opportunity to entrench their self-interest. In this approach, there seems to be a blurring, on both sides, of the distinction between might and right, between self-defence and aggression, between resistance and terrorism, justice and the terror of "counter-terrorism."

These have all continued to contribute to the fragmentation of human communities creating a broken world full of people with shattered self-worth. It is this human condition itself that most needs healing. In this condition should be seen the real challenges to the gospel as "good news" to all, and it is in this perspective that "repentance", "restitution", "forgiveness" and "the healing of memories" become critical to mission as it works for humanity and creation reconciled to itself and to God.

We need to recognize the de-humanization of the human condition in these acts of human beings against one another, but we also need to understand that de-humanization is a two-edged sword, a two-way process in which both the victim and the perpetrator are de-humanized. Our work for restorative justice is thus work towards re-humanization. While there cannot be restoration to a kind of primordial perfection, there can be a restoration of humanity through the recognition of one's humanity in the other. This also requires repentance and a change of attitudes.

Here we caution against a purely anthropomorphic understanding of humanization. We affirm that it is the image of God in each that makes a human being. Our de-humanization of each other is our refusal to see this image in each other. It also is our deliberate attempt to deny the others their potential to see God's image in themselves and to attain that potential. It is important that our work for humanization has this spiritual dimension that moves us beyond an anthropocentric humanity to a God-filled one - to *theosis* or deification. This is a never-ending process of becoming, of growing in and into God.

We assert that such kind of restoration is essential for true healing, as no healing or reconciliation can take place if the injustices of marginalization, discrimination, exploitation and abuse of power persist. Justice and reconciliation must be seen to be complimentary in God's mission. It is God who heals and reconciles us to each other and to Godself in Christ. In him we are reconciled to God in the re-creative power of the Holy Spirit. We are reminded that this also is a never-ending process that requires spiritual vigilance. The prophetic voice of the church must be raised at all times against all tendencies to dehumanize or perpetuate human brokenness, if she is truly to participate in this mission of God.

There needs to be a critical assessment of recent more juridical approaches to restorative justice that have focussed on material restitution. Does this form of restorative justice lead to healing and reconciliation? This is important because restorative justice cannot be an end in itself. It must lead to healing, the healing of people and communities.

In our reflections on healing and reconciliation we realize again that we are called to take the side of the victim, even as we work for a community based approach. Thus we must take care that the work to restore and heal the brokenness and fragmentation of community does not hurt or victimize the victims any further, or create more victims for that matter.

d) Globalization and the Commodification of Life

The stories of peoples' struggles highlighted a concern about globalization and the capacity of its ideology and accompanying legal practices to turn all things — resources, water, human beings — into commodities to be bought, sold, seized or exchanged for the benefit and profit of a limited few. The churches have not grasped the importance of this ideology and the challenges that its claims pose to the gospel that we are commissioned to proclaim. It is important that URM engages the churches to reflect on and articulate a theological response to the ideology of commodification that drives globalization. It is essential that the churches are enabled to engage both their rich and poor to understand and challenge the idolatry of this ideology, and resist its ability to fragment and destroy life, including all forms of human community and the natural order.

URM believes that its mission is to denounce this trend and its effects on the lives of people and communities, but also to encourage the development of alternatives at the concrete level of community building. Also in the face of the disappearance of the ideological debate, the world seems caught between the neo-liberal theses that drives a global mono-culture, and a growing exclusivist nationalistic and ethnicist vision. URM asserts the need for a counter-ideology discourse, and the need to be proactive in this regard.

In the creation stories of Genesis and the cosmologies of other religious and cultural traditions, we recognize that the Spirit works to create life in every circumstance. God's breath/spirit turns dust into being and the same Spirit creates order out of chaos. The coming of Christ is God's response to humanity leading creation back into brokenness, into chaos, through its death dealing acts of disobedience and de-humanization. In Christ God calls us out of this brokenness into wholeness; through Christ's death and resurrection, God calls us out of death into life, restoring us, in the power of the Spirit, to a humanity centred once again in God. We therefore see our call to participate in this mission of God as an invitation to the feast of life in which all people are being re-humanized, in which order is being re-created and life is being restored to its fullness and its wholeness. We see the commodification of life as the perpetuation of de-humanization and of creation's brokenness - a denial of God's saving act and power in Christ. And we call the churches to resist this.

We assert that the poor, especially, should have easy access to the essentials of life such as land, food and water, and to the services that support life, such as education and health care, as basic human rights, and we condemn the commodification of these and other life-related human activities such as culture and the environment. Thus we believe that there is need to defend some of the social achievements of the past and for resistance against the total dismantling of those social security systems that have resulted from peoples' struggles.

Instead of the survival of the fittest, we affirm, in response to the call of the gospel, a spirituality of commitment to the most vulnerable, to "the least of [those] who are members of [God's] family" (Matt. 25: 40). Instead of the sacredness of wealth, we affirm the sacredness of God-given life, characterized by grace, gratuity, generosity and hospitality. We call for resistance to the deification of money. We confess God as the only source of all life and being, and affirm the goal of mission as the deification (*theosis*) of humanity, empowered by the Holy Spirit to participate in Christ and in Christ's mission of salvation and reconciliation to God and to one another. We affirm the sharing of material goods and spiritual gifts and potential, as an essential aspect of this mission, as portrayed in Matthew 25. We believe that values based on the gospel must inspire state regulations to limit the absoluteness of the free market, and that this is an important part of the prophetic mission of the church.

Globalization, however, must not be seen only for its economic impact on the poor and on human community. There is serious concern that new forms of identity, relationships and relatedness are, in this era of globalization, being forced on whole populations and peoples. This is being done both in people's own traditional contexts, through a systematic and intentional process of cultural imperialism or, in new contexts where people have been uprooted, through policies and processes of assimilation. These tend to perpetuate and reinforce the cultural genocide that has now so clearly been identified as one of the negative consequences of the way in which mission was done in the past. This trend towards an imposed global mono-culture and a singular or "melting-pot" identity that allows little diversity poses as much a threat as any to the integrity of God's creation, and a challenge to mission. This is not new either. Throughout human history, and especially in the past half millennium, the arrogance of one civilization or another has led to the genocide of others and significant losses to humanity. True reconciliation requires facing and challenging such tendencies, be they in policies or people's behaviour. It requires new ways of preaching and living the gospel today that enable people to recover value in themselves and in their own identities, as these interact with others and grow.

Therefore:

1. We will need to articulate a theology of wealth that respects the spiritual disciplines and practices of Isaiah 58 so that we can maintain our hope for abundant life while being able to critique a theology of prosperity. We recommend this a task for the mission conference, and to future mission work in the ecumenical movement.

2. Our work in mission will also require us to call the rich to repentance and admission of culpability. The rich are all those who have responsibility, who use/abuse resources for their own ends, who have power over others. We will need to consider limits to wealth.

3. We are concerned for the need to reclaim words, concepts and ideas that have been hijacked to serve ends other than justice. We see the basis of justice as the work of the Spirit.

4. Our work, if we are to move ahead, will require us to create alternatives of several kinds:

— Sharing and communicating practical alternatives for community building and development and economic and social practices that respect peoples' legitimate identities, and the participation and well-being of all peoples.

— In our work of accompaniment opening spaces for cooperative discourse on ideology, including the possible creation, in the future, of a "URM Institute for Alternative Ideologies".

e) Concluding Statement

Isaiah 58: 1-11 presents the URM movement with a non-negotiable position in our efforts to fulfil "mission from the perspective of peoples in struggle". We see this as having two complimentary aspects. The movement has stressed the following as its praxis in mission, namely, "mission from below, giving space for the voiceless to be heard, and accompanying the poor and marginalized in their struggles". However, URM is being called to be prophetic in and on behalf of the church which makes its position both complimentary and contradictory.

URM is challenged by a praxis of mission that will lead to healing and reconciliation when this praxis is informed by the challenge of Isaiah 58: 1-11. Our mission will continue to resist seeking our own pleasure and comfort. It will continue to resist oppression of the powerless and the poor and resist neglecting the homeless and the abuse of marginalized communities. Above all else it will resist remaining silent in the face of the silence of the church or her refusal to take the side of the poor and be active in their struggle for re-humanization and a life with dignity.

Conference Communiqué

We are gathered here in Accra, Ghana from all parts of the world; from Africa, Asia and the Middle East, from Europe and from North America, Latin America and the Caribbean. We have come to renew, reaffirm and strengthen our mission in the midst of people in struggle as URM networks. This comes at a time where institutionalized oppression, systematic violence, occupation and militarization, marginalization and socio-economic deprivation and exclusion present new challenges to humanity. We note with deep concern processes of illegal occupation and oppression of sovereign lands and peoples under the guise of the "war on terror", citing especially the situation in the Middle East. We are concerned that policies of hegemony, unilateralism, and neo-colonialism, along with their economic capitalist dimensions, are devastating and fragmenting many parts of the world.

We, as the global URM movement, are part of and work with grassroots communities that are committed to working among those in struggle – of whom we are part – for solidarity, for spiritual empowerment, by providing safe space for their stories of struggle to be heard, for the improving of their quality of life by developing alternatives and by actively resisting the powers of oppression and dehumanization.

We visited Cape Coast and were reminded of the deep historical wounds of slavery that need to heal in Africa and all around the world. We also visited with churches and local communities, hearing their needs, sharing experiences, joys and hopes, and were enriched by the cultural and spiritual heritage of the people of Ghana.

Mission, for us, is the proclamation of the fullness of life. As people from churches, other faith communities, and diverse social movements around the world, as individuals and communities living the struggle, we are called to provide open space through which the voices of pain and suffering are lifted to the church and the community. In story-telling circles we have listened to the stories of communities in struggle and reflected on our social commitment to act on these stories. Through this sharing, we intend to build community in solidarity.

URM mission begins with the stories of the people, stories of liberation from bondage, stories of personal and communal cries of pain, joy and hope, of individual liberation and community emancipation. These story-telling circles were enriched by the wealth of religious and cultural traditions – a richness that is integral to the URM global family.

As we renew our hope for communities that are blessed with "life in abundance", our mission begins with speaking our prophetic voice to expose and condemn the capitalist-led, globalized context and its new geo-political realities that intentionally destroy human community. We specifically examined the effects of violence and its impact on those who are violated; commodification as the catalyst for globalization; injustice and the need for restorative justice, and the mission of URM as the spirituality of resistance to this injustice and oppression. We affirm the call "another world is possible".

In the midst of this global context, we heed the call to be healing and reconciling communities, believing that truth and faithfulness of the memory of the victims must qualify this healing, and that reconciliation in the context of broken communities is a process that must be informed by justice at all levels. We are living and working in communities where killing, enslavement, and oppression are taking place daily, and it is our understanding that forcibly silenced cries of pain cannot be overshadowed by the language of pacification. Just, sustainable and lasting interpersonal and inter-communal healing is built on a spirituality of reconciliation that respects the voice of the victims. We have been inspired by words of Isaiah 58 and Luke 4, indicating that mission will lead to healing and reconciliation when it is characterized by a spiritual discipline that resists egoism and oppression and breaks the yoke of injustice.

Our URM mission is based on spiritual empowerment that is life-giving, fulfilling and is a motivating power towards individual and community emancipation from the shackles of economic servitude, political repression, cultural oppression and social marginalization.
Today, as we come from all around the world, we reaffirm our commitment to working with the poorest of the poor and the most marginalized. We reaffirm our commitment to working with the church and through people's movements in each of our local contexts.

Preparatory Paper No 10

Mission as Ministry of Reconciliation

Introduction

This paper offers reflections on *mission as ministry of reconciliation* from an ecumenical point of view and is shared by the Commission on World Mission and Evangelism (CWME) of the World Council of Churches as a document for reflection and study in preparation for the world mission conference in Athens in May 2005. The present paper is a slightly revised and expanded version of the earlier document published in 2004 as CWME Conference Preparatory Paper No 4. It takes into account suggestions and reactions received from many places, as well as the results of the discussions held at the CWME Commission meeting itself last October. This revised version was elaborated in January 2005 by a small editorial group appointed by the Commission. Together with the document on *the healing mission of the church* (CWME Conference Preparatory paper No 11), it provides a summary of the state of discussion on mission as ministry of reconciliation and healing in the WCC. None of these two papers do however represent an official position of the WCC. They have not been adopted by one of its governing bodies. They are offered as resources for reflection and study on the significance and importance of mission in the beginning of the 21st century. Reactions and contributions to the study process are welcome and can be sent to:

Jacques Matthey
Programme Executive for Mission Study
Mission and Ecumenical Formation Team
WCC

Jacques.Matthey@wcc-coe.org

Geneva, February 2005

Mission as Ministry of Reconciliation

1) Mission and Reconciliation – an Emerging Paradigm

1. Mission is understood in different ways in various times and places, also among actors in the ecumenical movement. From time to time, there is an attempt at a more holistic interpretation of Christian witness. In 1982, the World Council of Churches (WCC) reached such a balanced understanding of mission, in its Ecumenical Affirmation on Mission and Evangelism.[1] Responding to the challenge of the gospel and the request of the time, that declaration combined the focus on sharing the gospel with the concern for the liberation of the poor. It remains until now the basic WCC text on mission and evangelism. Since the late 1980s new aspects emerged and mission has been increasingly connected with reconciliation and healing. The language of reconciliation has come to the fore in many different contexts and catches the imagination of people inside and outside the churches. In this situation we have come to discern anew that reconciliation is at the heart of Christian faith. This takes place both in ecumenical and evangelical mission thinking. The reconciling love of God shown in Jesus Christ is an important biblical theme and a central element in the life and ministry of the church. We affirm thus now that the Holy Spirit calls us to a ministry of reconciliation and to express this in both the spirituality and strategies of our mission and evangelism.

2. There are a number of other reasons why reconciliation has become so prominent in the world today. These are related to the contemporary trends of globalization, post-modernity and fragmentation as identified in the CWME study document "Mission and Evangelism in Unity Today" (2000).[2] Globalization has brought different communities of the world into closer contact than ever before and has highlighted human commonality. At the same time it has exposed the diversity of interests and worldviews among different groups. On the one hand, there are new ways to express unity and cross the boundaries that have divided us. On the other hand, there are also clashes of cultures, religions, economic interests and genders, which leave a legacy of hurt and grievances. The heightened enmity that has resulted from globalization and the imbalance of power in today's world has been strikingly confirmed in the terrorist acts of September 11, 2001 and the subsequent "war on terror". In this context also, a number of initiatives, both by civil society and by churches, have contributed to the reconstruction of societies after conflict through processes of truth and reconciliation. Christian witnesses are called upon to help bring peace with justice in situations of tension, violence and conflict. As the churches seek reconciliation and peace, the World Council of Churches has launched the *Decade to Overcome Violence* (2001-2010).

3. The dominance and pervasiveness of global market forces have led to enormous changes in the way people live and work, yet economic globalization is highly ambiguous. While free trade and competition have led to economic growth and increased prosperity in some countries, particularly in Asia, the economic policies

---

[1] *Mission and Evangelism: An Ecumenical Affirmation.* Geneva, WCC, 1982. Approved by the Central Committee of the WCC.
[2] *Mission and Evangelism in Unity Today.* CWME Conference Preparatory Paper No 1. Statement adopted as a study document by the CWME Commission in the year 2000.

of the richer nations have had tremendous and often highly damaging effects on poorer nations. More are victims rather than beneficiaries. Unfair trade laws protect the richer nations and exclude and exploit the poorer ones. Many of the poorer countries are saddled with debt and its repayment is an intolerable burden. Structural adjustment programmes imposed by global bodies pay little regard to local wisdom and it is the poor who suffer most under them. In this situation, the *Jubilee Debt Campaign* has had a significant effect in raising awareness of trade imbalance and influencing G8 decisions. True reconciliation that involves the repentance of the rich and brings justice for the poor is urgently needed.

4. The network of global communications also brings benefit to some and excludes others. In some respects, by increasing the possibilities of dialogue and cooperation, it is beneficial in widening fellowship and facilitating alternative movements for change. However the mass culture of post-modernity spread in this way is often experienced as a threat to personal and national identities and contributes to the increasing fragmentation of societies. As a result of globalization, many have lost their family and local roots, many have been displaced by migration, and exclusion is widely experienced. Many are longing for the embrace of others and sense a need for belonging and community. In this situation, we are called to be reconciling and healing communities.

5. We look to the Holy Spirit, who in the Bible is related with communion (2 Cor. 13:13), to lead us and all creation in integrity and wholeness towards reconciliation with God and one another. However, exposed to the strength and vicissitudes of global forces, the difficulties of discerning the Holy Spirit among the complexities of the world have never been greater as we are faced with difficult personal and strategic choices in mission. In 1996, at the last WCC conference on mission and evangelism, we were reminded in Salvador, Bahía, Brazil how the perpetrators of economic injustice denied the rights of indigenous populations and plundered resources given by the creator for all. We asked for forgiveness for this and sought reconciliation.[3] Affirming that "the Spirit poured out on the day of Pentecost makes all cultures worthy vehicles of God's love" and "enables a real awakening of the image of God" in persons in oppressed groups, we committed ourselves at Salvador to "the search for alternative models of community, more equitable economic systems, fair trade practices, responsible use of the media and just environmental practice".[4]

6. All over the world, we are experiencing a thirst for spiritual experience, a renewal within religions, a resurgence of fundamentalist forms of religiosity, as well as a proliferation of new religious movements. All this is linked to the influence of globalization and post-modernity. On the one hand, the variety of spiritualities

---

[3] During the Salvador conference, a particularly important and moving celebration took place at the Solar do Unhão dock, the place where the ships loaded with slaves and coming from Africa landed. Representatives from both European and African origin expressed repentance from participation in the sin of slavery and asked for forgiveness. Cf. Jean S. Stromberg, "From Each Culture, with One Voice. Worship at Salvador" in: Christopher Duraisingh (ed.), *Called to One Hope. The Gospel in Diverse Cultures*. Geneva, WCC, 1998, pp. 166-176.
[4] Christopher Duraisingh (ed), *Called to One Hope. op.cit.*, pp. 27 and 28. Acts of commitment of the 1996 world mission conference in Salvador da Bahía, Brazil.

to which we are exposed raises our spiritual awareness, enriches our perception of God's mystery and broadens our horizons. On the other, we also discern increasing tensions between religions which are due to many internal and external factors, in particular religious reinforcement of closed identities, justification of violence and aggressive methods of religious propagation. These trends make it even more urgent for us to seek a reconciliatory spirituality for mission.

7. Within the Christian faith, while some churches continue to decline, many are experiencing rapid numerical growth. The centre of gravity of Christianity has decisively shifted towards the poorer nations of the world and the faith is widely expressed in a Pentecostal-charismatic form. The rapid growth of the Pentecostal and charismatic churches is a noticeable fact of our time. The positive impact of charismatic experience gives great encouragement and hope for the future of Christian faith. It calls our attention to the theology of the Holy Spirit and the way in which the Spirit repeatedly renews the church for its mission in every age. At the same time, the potential for tension and disunity reminds us of the Spirit's close association with reconciliation and peace. It is important that this pneumatological orientation should never take the form of a "pneumatomonism", as in the past when a hidden "christomonism" relegated the Holy Spirit into an ancillary role. In the mission of the church the understanding of Christology should always be conditioned in a constitutive way by pneumatology.

8. Since Pentecost the Holy Spirit has inspired the church to proclaim Jesus Christ as the Lord and Saviour and we continue to be obedient to the command to preach the gospel in all the world. The Holy Spirit anointed the Son of God to "preach good news to the poor, heal the brokenhearted, proclaim liberty to captives, recovery of sight to the blind and set at liberty those who are oppressed" (Luke 4:18). We seek to continue his liberating and healing mission. This involves bold proclamation of the liberating gospel to people bound by sin, a healing ministry to the sick and suffering, and the struggle for justice on the side of the oppressed and marginalized. Recognizing that the Spirit of God has been present in creation since the beginning and goes before us in our mission and evangelism, we have also affirmed the Spirit's creativity expressed in diverse cultures and we have entered into dialogue with people of other faiths. Now, confronted with the world situation we have described, we are rediscovering the ministry of the Spirit to reconcile and to heal.

2) The Triune God, Source and Initiator of Reconciliation: Biblical, Theological and Liturgical Perspectives

9. Reconciliation is the work of the triune God bringing fulfilment to God's eternal purposes of creation and salvation through Jesus Christ: "For in him all the fullness of God was pleased to dwell, and through him to reconcile to himself all things, whether on earth or in heaven, making peace by the blood of his cross ... For in Him the whole fullness of deity dwells bodily" (Col. 1: 19-20; 2:9). In the person of Jesus Christ the divine nature and the human nature were reconciled, united forever. This is the starting point for our reconciliation with God. We have to actualize by God's grace and our efforts, what we already have in Christ, through the Holy Spirit.

The Godhead, the Three-in-One, expresses the very nature of community, the reconciliation we hope for: "The Trinity, the source and image of our existence, shows the importance of diversity, otherness and intrinsic relationships in constituting a community."[5]

Reconciliation from a Biblical Perspective

10. The Bible is full of stories of reconciliation. The Old Testament tells a number of stories of conflict and strife between brothers, family members, peoples; some of these end in reconciliation and others are unresolved. It acknowledges and bemoans the dimension of violence and underlines the need for and the power of reconciliation. The family stories of Jacob and Esau (Gen. 25:19-33:20), or of Joseph and his brothers (Gen. 37-45) are examples for interpersonal – and perhaps also communal – conflicts. They also illustrate the power of reconciling attitudes of people who try to solve strife, enmity, and experiences or perceptions of injustice through negotiations, repentance, forgiveness and searching for a common basis and a shared future. The Old Testament addresses again and again the estrangement between God and God's people and God's desire and urge for reconciliation and restoration of a relationship that was broken and fragmented through human pride and various forms of rebellion against the God of life and justice. Reconciliation is thus very much a theme in the biblical narratives and in the liturgical language of Israel – such as the Psalms, even though the Hebrew language does not know the specific term "reconciliation". In the books of the lament tradition, such as Lamentations and Job, human longing for reconciliation with God is poignantly expressed.

11. Similarly in the New Testament, though the actual term "reconciliation" does not appear very prominently, the matter itself is prevalent throughout. John's Gospel shows a particular concern for truth and peace; in the gospel of Luke salvation is closely linked to the healing ministry of Jesus. The Book of Acts tells how Jews and Gentiles were reconciled in one new community. And throughout his letters, Paul is greatly concerned that those whom Christ has reconciled in his body should not be divided and that community life should be the first expression of God's plan to reconcile all things. He envisages the unity of not only Jew and Gentile but also of slave and free, male and female in Christ (Gal. 3:28).

12. Apart from Matthew 5:24, where it relates to the reconciliation of individuals, we find the terms "reconciliation" and "to reconcile" – the Greek words are *katallage and katallassein* – only in the letters of the Apostle Paul (2 Cor. 5:17-20; Rom. 5:10-11; 11:15; 1 Cor. 7:11, and then Eph. 2:16 and Col. 1:20-22). However, the apostle expresses the theme so forcefully that it emerges as a key notion in the Christian identity as a whole. Paul uses the term reconciliation in exploring the nature of God, to illumine the content of the gospel as good news, and to explain the ministry and mission of the apostle and the church in the world. The term "reconciliation" thus becomes an almost all-embracing term to articulate what is at the heart of the Christian faith.

---

[5] *Mission and Evangelism in Unity Today, op.cit.,* § 39.

There are several features of reconciliation as used by Paul to note briefly:

13. The very notion of reconciliation presupposes the experience of broken communion. This may be in the form of estrangement, separation, enmity, hatred, exclusion, fragmentation, distorted relationships. It usually also encompasses a certain degree of injustice, harm and suffering. Reconciliation, in biblical as well as secular language, is understood as the effort towards and engagement for mending this broken and distorted relationship and building up community and relationships afresh.

14. Paul applies the notion of reconciliation to three different though overlapping realms of brokenness and hostility, in which healing of relationship occur: reconciliation between God and human beings; reconciliation of different groups of human beings; reconciliation of the cosmos.

15. Reconciliation is much more than simply a superficial fixing of distortions, the arrival of a status quo of coexistence. Reconciliation looks at a transformation of the present, a very deep-rooted renewal. The "peace" which Paul speaks about is first and foremost peace with God (cf. Rom. 5:1, 11). It is also in a prominent way the transformation of human relationships and the building of a community: It is the radical new peace between Jews and Gentiles that results from Christ breaking down the wall of hostility (Eph. 2:14). It is even the transformation of the whole creation towards peace as it is expressed in Colossians 1:20, where Paul speaks of Christ as reconciling "all things, whether on earth or in heaven, making peace by the blood of his cross". The last reference indicates that reconciliation indeed envisions a new creation as Paul expresses so vividly in 2 Corinthians 5:17. The category of "new creation" shows that there is even more in view than a mending of brokenness. Reconciliation is a totally new quality of being, as expressed in the hymn celebrating the gathering of all things in Christ (Eph. 1:10).

16. According to Paul, it is God who takes the initiative towards reconciliation. Furthermore, God has already achieved reconciliation for the world: "In Christ God was reconciling the world to himself" (2 Cor. 5:19). Human beings may seek for reconciliation and minister reconciliation but the initiative and the effectiveness of reconciliation lies with God. Human beings are only recipients of the gift of reconciliation. It is therefore essential to affirm that Christian life and attitude is grounded in the experience of reconciliation through Godself. Christians discover what God has already done in Christ.

16. The human predicament that creates the need for reconciliation with God is the alienation from God that is due to human sin, disobedience to and break of communion with God, resulting in guilt and death, both spiritually and physically (Rom. 3:23; Eph. 2:1-3) This enmity between God and human beings was overcome through the death of Jesus on the cross. "When we were enemies we were reconciled to God through the death of his Son" (Rom. 5:10). On the cross the Son of God freely gave his life as an atoning sacrifice for the sins and guilt of the whole world. He is the lamb of God who carries the sins of the world (John 1:29), who himself "bore our sins in his own body on the tree" (1 Pet. 2:24). Through Christ's substitutionary death "for us" (Rom. 5:8; Gal. 1:4), reconciliation

has been achieved once for all leading to forgiveness of sins, communion with God and new life in God's kingdom. This is all by the grace and love of God.

17. The Christian narrative of reconciliation is thus based on and centred in the story of the incarnation, passion, death, resurrection and ascension of Jesus Christ. The messianic ministry of Jesus of Nazareth links his suffering with the suffering of all humanity, and is therefore an expression of the deep solidarity of God with an agonized, fragmented and tortured world. The cross is, at the same time, an expression of the divine protest against this suffering, for Jesus of Nazareth suffered as the innocent victim. He refused to take refuge in violence, he persisted in the love of his enemies and he made love towards God and his fellow-human beings the central concern of his life. The gruesome act of throwing "the one who was just" out of this world is in itself the judgment of a world in which the powerful seem to prevail over the victims. In Christ, through whose wounds we are healed (1 Pet. 2:24), we also experience God seeking to rectify the wrongs of this world through the power of love with which God, in his Son, gave himself up for others, even for the perpetrators of violence and injustice.

18. The cross of Christ, and the obligation of the Christians to participate in the suffering of the people and their struggle for a better life, which results from it, is not the only criterion for the mission of the church. It is through the resurrection that the death of Christ receives its true meaning. The resurrection means that God himself recognized Jesus and his cross; it was a liberating judgement making the cross an instrument of salvation and reconciliation. The resurrection is even more, however, being itself an integral part of God's reconciling work in Christ. For Christians resurrection is not understood as just an historical event of the past, nor just an article of faith, but also a mystically lived present day reality. In missiology, cross and resurrection form an indissoluble unity. The church exists not only because Christ died on the cross, but also and primarily because he is risen from the dead, thus becoming the first fruit of all humanity (cf. 1 Cor. 15:20). The centrality of resurrection in both the N.T. and the life of the church not only gives "the hope that is in us" (1 Pet. 3:15), but it inevitably leads to the primary importance of eschatology.

19. It is through the Holy Spirit that human beings are empowered to share in the narrative of God reconciling the world in Jesus Christ. In Romans 5, where Paul explores the way God reconciles sinners and even God's enemies and the ungodly with Godself, Paul says that the love of God has been poured out into our hearts through the Holy Spirit. In Jesus Christ, who was raised and ascended into heaven, we not only enjoy the gift of reconciliation, we are also sent in service and ministry into the world. This is expressed, for example, in the ethical teaching of Paul where he urged individuals and communities to be signs and expressions of the reconciliation they had experienced (cf. Rom. 12:9-21). It is also expressed in the way Paul talks about his own mission as a "ministry of reconciliation" (2 Cor. 5:18). To share in this ministry of reconciliation – that is to participate in the Holy Spirit's work of reconciliation and communicate God's reconciling activity to all of humanity – is the Christian calling today as much as in Paul's day.

20. This means that God's work of reconciliation with human beings was not finished on the cross and in the resurrection; it goes on through history in the ministry of reconciliation that has been entrusted to the church. Based on the reconciliation effected in Christ's death and resurrection and on God's behalf, the church challenges and invites all people to be reconciled with God. "Now all things are of God, who has reconciled us to himself and given us the ministry of reconciliation" (2 Cor. 5:18-21). This offer of reconciliation is received and becomes a personal reality through faith (Eph. 2:8).

The Holy Spirit and Reconciliation

21. The Holy Spirit empowers the church to participate in this work of reconciliation as the document "Mission and Evangelism in Unity" states: "The mission of God (*missio Dei*) is the source of and basis for the mission of the church, the body of Christ. Through Christ in the Holy Spirit, God indwells the church, empowering and energizing its members."[6] The ministry of the Spirit (2 Cor. 3:8) is a ministry of reconciliation, made possible through Christ and entrusted to us (2 Cor. 5:18-19).

22. In the power of the Spirit, the church as *koinonia* – the communion of the Holy Spirit (2 Cor. 13:13) – continually grows into a healing and reconciling community that shares the joys and sorrows of her members and reaches out to those in need of forgiveness and reconciliation. According to the Book of Acts (2:44-45; 4:32-37), the early church, having been born on the day of Pentecost, shared her goods among her members, pointing to the interrelatedness of "spiritual" and "material" concerns in Christian mission and church life. One aspect of the empowering ministry of the Holy Spirit is to endow Christians and Christian communities with charismatic gifts, which include healing (1 Cor. 12:9; Acts 3).

23. The church herself is in need of continuing renewal by the Spirit to be able to discern the mind of Christ as well as be convicted by the Spirit of division and sin within (John 16:8-11). This repentance within the church of Christ is itself part of the ministry and witness of reconciliation to the world.

24. The Holy Spirit blows where the Spirit wills (cf. John 3:8). Thus, the Spirit knows no limits and reaches out to people of all faiths as well as those without any religious commitment – a growing number in this time of secularization. The church is called to discern the signs of the Spirit in the world and witness to Christ in the power of the Spirit (Acts 1:8) as well as be engaged in all forms of liberation and reconciliation (2 Cor. 5:18-19).

25. In the sufferings of the present time, the Spirit shares our "groans" and the childbirth pains of the whole of creation subjected to "bondage under decay" (Rom. 8:26, 21-22). Therefore, we are looking forward to the redemption of our bodies (Rom. 8:23) with hope and joy. The same Spirit of God that "swept over the face of the waters" (Gen. 1:2) in creation now indwells the church and works in the world often in mysterious and unknown ways. The Spirit will participate in the ushering in of the new creation when God finally will be all in all.

---

[6] *Ibid.*, § 13.

26. Since the time of the New Testament, two understandings of pneumatology can be discerned. One emphasizes the Holy Spirit as fully dependant on Christ, as being the agent of Christ to fulfil the task of mission, and has led to a missiology focussing on *sending* and *going forth*. The other understands the Holy Spirit as the source of Christ, and the church as the eschatological *synaxis* (coming together) of the people of God in God's kingdom. In that second perspective, mission as *going forth* is the outcome, not the origin of the church. Mission is the liturgy *after* the Liturgy. Because reconciliation is a prerequisite of the eucharist (the act that actually constitutes the church) it becomes a primary of mission in that perspective.

Liturgical Perspectives on Reconciliation

27. The church's mission, in the power of the Spirit, derives from the teaching, life and work of our Lord Jesus Christ. This is to be understood in reference to the expectations of Judaism. The core of this was the idea of the coming of a Messiah, who in the "last days" of history would establish his kingdom (Joel 3:1; Isa. 2:2, 59:21; Ezek. 36:24, etc.) by calling all the dispersed and afflicted people of God *into one place*, reconciled to God and becoming one body united around him (Mic. 4:1-4; Isa. 2:2-4; Psa. 147:2-3). In the Gospel of John it is clearly stated that the high priest "prophesied that Jesus should die...not for the nation only, but to *gather into one* the children of God who are scattered abroad" (John 11:51-52).

28. This reconciliation was experienced in the liturgical, more precisely "eucharistic" (in the wider sense), life of the early church. The early Christian community suffered from factions and divisions but, reconciled through the grace of our Lord to God, felt obliged to extend horizontally this reconciliation to one another by being incorporated into the one people of God through the eucharist, a significant act of identity, which was celebrated as a manifestation (more precisely a foretaste) of the coming kingdom. It is not accidental that the condition for participating in the Lord's table was, and still often is, an act of reconciliation with one's sisters and brothers which bears profound symbolic value and is remindful of the core of the gospel (Matt. 5:23-24). By sharing the "kiss of love", church members give each other a sign of reconciliation and commit themselves to the healing of relationships in the community. In a related manner, Paul challenges the Corinthians to take seriously the fact that their failure to share could jeopardize the very celebration of the Lord's supper (1 Cor. 11:20-21).

29. This eucharistic act is not the only liturgical rite of reconciliation in the healing process. Baptism, which presupposes an act of repentance, is a common sign of incorporation through the Spirit into the one body (1 Cor. 12:13; Eph. 4:4-5). The act of confession, which has sacramental significance for some churches, was originally meant as the necessary reconciling process with the community – a sacrament of reconciliation. There is also the act – or sacrament – of anointment for healing. For many churches the Lord's supper itself also has therapeutic meaning. These examples draw our attention to the importance of reconciliation and healing in the life and mission of the church.

30. These manifestations of the kingdom in the community were the starting point of Christian mission, the springboard of the church's witnessing *exodus* to the world. The missiological imperatives of the church stem exactly from this awareness of the church as a dynamic and corporate body of reconciled believers commissioned to witness to the coming kingdom of God. In striving to manifest the ministry of reconciliation (2 Cor. 5:18 ff) to the world, we become a reconciling community. This ministry to be "ambassadors for Christ" includes a commitment to the proclamation of the gospel: "We entreat you on behalf of Christ, be reconciled to God. For our sake he made him to be sin who knew no sin, so that in him we might become the righteousness of God." (2 Cor. 5:20 - 21)

In ecumenical perspective such evangelism "aims to build up a reconciling and reconciled community (cf. 2 Cor. 5:19) that will point to the fullness of God's reign, which is 'righteousness and peace and joy in the Holy Spirit' (Rom. 14:17)". This affirmation of the preparatory document for Salvador finds an echo in the recent WCC mission statement: "To speak of evangelism means to emphasize the proclamation of God's offer of freedom and reconciliation, together with the invitation to join those who follow Christ and work for the reign of God."[7]

3) Reconciliation as an Imperative for Mission

31. The powerful convergence of a new interest in reconciliation and healing within the churches, and a parallel new quest for healing and reconciliation in many societies around the world, have prompted us to rethink what God is calling us to in mission today. Remembering that the reconciliation we have received in Jesus Christ is to be shared in the world, we have come to see reconciliation as part of mission.

32. Mission as ministry of reconciliation involves the obligation to share the gospel of Jesus Christ in all its fullness, the good news of him who through his incarnation, death and resurrection has once for all provided the basis for reconciliation with God, forgiveness of sins and new life in the power of the Holy Spirit. This ministry invites people to accept God's offer of reconciliation in Christ, and to become his disciples in the communion of his church. It promises the hope of fullness of life in God, both in this age and in God's future, eternal kingdom.

33. The ministry of reconciliation also involves the work for reconciliation among persons and societies. In order to understand what this participation in God's mission of reconciliation may mean, we will focus upon the goals and processes of reconciliation and healing. This involves both some general thoughts and reflections upon the dynamics of how reconciliation and healing come about.

34. Reconciliation is and results from a process leading to peace with justice. The vision is to establish community, where brokenness and sectarianism are overcome and people live together with mutual respect and tolerance. Reconciliation results

---

[7] WCC Unit II, Churches in Mission: Education, Health, Witness: *Preparatory Papers for Section Work, Conference on World Mission and Evangelism,* Salvador da Bahía. Geneva, WCC, 1996, p. 19. *Mission and Evangelism in Unity Today, op.cit.,* § 62

in communication with one another without fear. It implies tolerance of others, inclusion and consideration of them. Reconciled community is where differences can be resolved through dialogue and without resort to violence.

35. Reconciliation is sought between *individuals*, in order to overcome divisions, enmity and conflicts from the past. Here the internal dynamics for both parties, for victims and wrongdoers must be explored. Reconciliation also needs to occur between *groups or communities*. In these instances social and structural relations will need special attention. And reconciliation sometimes needs to happen within and among *nations*, in which the whole structures of societies will need examination. In the first instance, between individuals, reconciliation is often about restoring dignity and a sense of humanity. In the second instance, reconciliation focuses upon how to live together, both as human beings and in the whole of creation. In the third instance, on national levels, the institutions of society itself will need attention for reconstruction to be possible.

36. Reconciliation is both a *goal* and a *process*. As individuals and societies we need a vision to keep us moving toward a future state of peace and well-being. But without understanding the process we can lose heart and sense of direction in our work. In actual practice, we will find ourselves moving back and forth between goal and process, since we need both in reconciliation and healing.

Dynamics of Reconciliation Processes

37. Attention needs to be given both to initiating the process of reconciliation and to sustaining it. The participants in this process are often divided into *victims* and *wrongdoers*. Sometimes the two parties are easily distinguished and identified, as for example in many cases of victims of rape and those who perpetrate the act. But in extended conflicts, victims may, at a later date, become wrongdoers, and wrongdoers become victims. This makes clear-cut categories less helpful. While Christian practice has special regard for the plight of victims, reconciliation and healing require restoration and healing both of the victim *and* repentance and transformation of the wrongdoer. These things do not always happen in a clear sequence, but becoming a "new creation" (2 Cor. 5:17) requires change in both.

38. Six aspects of the reconciliation and healing process need special attention. They are: **truth, memory, repentance, justice, forgiveness and love**.

Establishing the **truth** about the past is often difficult because abuses and atrocities have been shrouded in silence. Healing requires that the silence be broken and the truth be allowed to come to light. It allows for *recognition* of what has been hidden.

39. At other times, under a repressive regime for instance, there has been a systematic distortion of the truth. Lies prevail where truth should dwell. In such cases, the truth needs to be asserted. This is especially true when the language of reconciliation itself is misused. There have been instances where wrongdoers have called for "reconciliation" when they really mean that victims should ignore the wrongdoing done, and life should continue as though nothing happened. In

such cases, the meaning of the word "reconciliation" has been so poisoned that it cannot even be used. In other cases, wrongdoers urge hasty "reconciliation" so that the claims of the victims will not even be considered. They may do this by making Christians feel guilty for not being able to forgive quickly. Such false uses of the idea of reconciliation must be resisted.

40. At a national level, after prolonged conflict and struggle, Truth and Reconciliation Commissions have been established to seek out the truth about the past. The Commission in South Africa is perhaps the most well-known. The need for such commissions underscores how difficult it is to establish the truth, and how important it is for reconciliation and healing.

41. The Christian understanding of truth can help in such situations. The Spirit of God is the Spirit of truth (John 14:17), and Jesus "who is the way, and the truth, and the life" (John 14: 6), prayed that his disciples be sanctified by the Spirit of truth (John 17:17). Establishing the truth, especially after situations of conflict, can be difficult. Respect for the truth comes from knowing God wants the truth to be told (cf. the prophetic tradition).

42. **Memory** is closely linked to truth. How will the past be remembered, how shall we speak of it? Authentic memory should yield the truth about the past. Traumatic memories of acts of wrongdoing or atrocity often will need healing if they are to be the building blocks of a different kind of future. To heal memories means that they lose their toxic quality. When that happens, memories do not hold us hostage to the past, but empower us to create a future where the wrongdoing of the past cannot happen again.

43. Memories are not just about the past. They are the basis for identity. *How* we remember the past is both the basis for how we will live and relate to one another in the present, and how we will envision the future. For that reason, memory is central to the process of reconciliation and healing.

44. Memories that do not heal can inhibit reconciliation. Sometimes the healing takes more than a generation. In some instances victims are so submerged in their memories that they need help in coming free of them. This may imply to provide a space for the victims to express their anger. In a few instances, victims do not want to be healed, and use their memories to keep any progress from happening. Accompanying victims so that they can come free from traumatic memories is an important task of those who work for reconciliation.

45. Projects of recovering memory that has been suppressed or distorted are often important for building a different future together Publishing the results of Truth and Reconciliation Commissions,[8] or collecting recollections of what happened[9] are examples of this. Recovering memory can also be a threat to the wrongdoers who still hold power.[10]

---

[8] as in South Africa
[9] as in Guatemala
[10] the murder of Bishop Gerardi in Guatemala after he announced the results of such a report is a chilling reminder of this.

46. Recovering memory and allowing it to help us live in the present, as well as imagine the future, is central to Christian practice and witness. We celebrate the eucharist to remember what happened to Jesus: his betrayal, suffering and death, and how he was raised from the dead. It is the memory of what God has done in the story of Jesus that gives us hope and the Spirit of Christ who empowers us in our work of reconciliation.

47. In many cases of conflict there is a need for **repentance** (*metanoia*) before reconciliation can take place. Because there may be a situation of wrongdoing and guilt, personal or collective, that has caused the enmity or estrangement, true reconciliation cannot take place until the guilty part has repented of sin and wrongdoing. Jesus' proclamation of the kingdom of God was accompanied by a call for repentance and faith in the gospel (Mark 1:15). It is noteworthy that Jesus' call for repentance is motivated by the new time of salvation that is inaugurated by his coming. True repentance cannot be the result of threats and fear, but has to come from a realization of guilt and a wish and hope for a new reconciled relationship based on forgiveness (cf. Acts 2:38).

48. **Justice** is essential to the work of reconciliation. Three kinds of justice are needed. First, there is **retributive justice**, where wrongdoers are held accountable for their actions. This is important both for acknowledging that wrong has been done, and as a statement that such wrongdoing will not be tolerated in the future. Retributive justice should be the task of the legally constituted state. Punishment outside that forum can be renegade action or sheer revenge, and should be avoided. If the state itself is implicated in the corruption, it may be possible to achieve retributive justice by means of non-violent protest.[11] This will require great personal sacrifice.

49. Second, there is **restorative** justice, in which what has been taken wrongfully from victims is restored, either directly or in some symbolic way. This may be by reparation or compensation. In Luke's gospel, the story of Zacchaeus's encounter with Jesus (19: 1-10) shows how an authentic repentance resulting from meeting Christ can lead to a radical form of restitution. In other cases, for example when the perpetrator or victim has died, some other statement of reconciliation may need to be found – such as a public memorial.

50. And finally, there is **structural justice**, whereby the institutions of society are reformed to prevent instances of injustice from happening in the future. Dimensions of restorative and structural justice often need special attention. For example, to achieve economic justice, reform of global trade laws and the mechanisms of trade will be necessary. Gender justice will require attending to the special contributions of women to overcoming injustice and retaining right relations. To overcome sexism and racism structural reform will be necessary. In recent years, the need for ecological justice has come to the fore as well.

51. The Holy Spirit spoke through the prophets of old against injustice and anointed Jesus Christ to bring freedom to the oppressed (Luke 4:18-19). The Spirit

---

[11] as for example the "mothers of the disappeared" in Argentina

gives gifts of prophecy and boldness today as Christians struggle especially to aid in the process of restorative justice, and work toward the reforms that structural justice require. Biblical images of covenant – care for all, and right relations between God and humanity – support efforts for these reforms of society. These are illustrated by the collection from the churches taken up by the Apostle Paul to Jerusalem so that there might be "equality" between the churches in the mutual meeting of one another's needs (2 Cor. 8:14).

52. **Forgiveness** is often considered a specifically religious dimension of reconciling and healing. It is important to realize that forgiveness does not mean condoning past wrongdoing, or even foregoing punishment. Forgiveness acknowledges what has happened in the past, but seeks a different relationship both to the wrongdoer and to the deed. Without forgiveness, we remain locked in our relationships to the past and cannot have a different kind of future.

53. Along with having a Christian vision of the whole, seeking reconciliation for the human community today requires interaction with the different communities of faith. For us as Christians, this will call for some knowledge of how the other great religious traditions envision healing and wholeness, since many situations will require our acting together. In those situations also, we as Christians must be able to communicate our own contribution to the common task. Many cultures have their own spiritual and ritual resources for bringing about reconciliation and healing. Whenever possible, these need to be incorporated into our work toward reconciliation.

54. Forgiveness has special import for Christians. We believe that it is God who forgives sin (Mark 2:7-12). Jesus came among us preaching the forgiveness of sins (Luke 24:47), pointing to the graciousness of God and the possibility of overcoming the past for the sake of a different kind of future. Personal experience of acceptance and grace can be life-changing, inspiring individuals to reach out in love to others and transform society, as the story of Zacchaeus illustrates. After his resurrection, when he breathed the Holy Spirit into his disciples, Jesus sent them out with a ministry of forgiveness (John 20:21-23).

55. Forgiveness by God is bound up with our willingness to forgive others (see Matt. 6:12, 14-15). Because of this, Christians often say that we should "forgive and forget." We can never forget wrongdoing, as though it never happened. To ask victims to do this would be to demean them once again. We can never forget, but we can remember in a different way – a way that allows for a different relationship to the past and to the wrongdoer. That is what we are called to as Christians.

56. **Love** (*agape*) is the most characteristic feature of Christianity. The triune God, the Three-in -One expresses the perfect union of distinct persons, the supreme love, which encompasses everything. God reveals and manifests Godself as love, because God is love (John 3: 16; 1 John 4:7-21). Being created according to God's image and recreated through baptism, God's love "has been poured into our hearts through the Holy Spirit which has been given to us" (Rom. 5:5; cf. Gal. 5: 22). That is why the commandment to love our enemies (Matt. 5: 44) is not a commandment

that is impossible to fulfil. God never asks from us what God did not give already. To love enemies is simultaneously God's gift and the human personal contribution, "the more excellent way" (1 Cor. 12:31; 13: 1-8) which brings us to a holy life, to conformity with Christ, our model (Gal. 4:19), to his way of being and thinking: "We have the mind of Christ" (1 Cor. 2:16). Love encompasses the whole process of reconciliation as the very sign of its authenticity.

57. Truth, memory, repentance, justice, forgiveness and love are important and essential elements for holistic complete and true reconciliation. Experience has however shown that reconciliation is **not always complete**. Most of the stories told in the Bible are not stories of full reconciliation. The well-known stories of Sarah and Hagar, Jacob and Esau, Rachel and Leah, leave us wondering whether the characters were truly reconciled. Even the parable of the prodigal son makes no mention of the reconciliation between the two brothers. Most situations of intense conflict result in some reservations on either side that hinder complete acceptance and reconciliation. This is not to suggest that true reconciliation cannot take place, but rather to acknowledge that the reconciliatory process can take long, perhaps even a life time or longer for the eradication of hurt, suspicion and anger.

58. Another dimension of this is that the perpetrator of conflict may never repent, or seek forgiveness even after the period of conflict. Stories from South Africa and several other parts of the world attest to this fact. In such instances, victims may have to find ways to cope with the situation by moving away from the site of oppression, a form of resistance. The victim then often realizes that forgiveness may have to be given even when repentance is not forthcoming nor forgiveness sought by the perpetrator. The victim however must become able to live on and cope with the situation. Carrying around feelings of anger, hurt and bitterness is detrimental to the self and growth of the individual or community. There are other situations where the perpetrator is really seeking forgiveness, but does not receive it. In such cases, the perpetrator is the one who must find other ways to resolve his or her guilt. In can also happen that the victim needs to forgive him- or herself for having allowed something to happen and for having shown complicity in systems of oppression. It is important that such dimensions of the perpetrator's or victim's experience be duly considered in the dynamics of reconciliation.

59. Whether at the social, community or personal level reconciliation and healing are *goals* we seek within the ambivalence and brokenness of human existence. These goals are inspired by the biblical vision of the eschatological restoration of the original *shalom, the promised final realization of the kingdom of God*, when all will have been healed, made whole again and united in God. In contemporary human history, we may hope to reach levels of reconciliation or healing, or justice, peace, and the integrity of creation. Whereas the vision of full reconciliation and healing embraces the totality of God's creation, our contribution is limited as is our vision. But we are called to give corporate signs of God's reconciliation, for in so doing we renew hope. Indeed, seeking reconciliation and healing in our world requires a constant moving back and forth between imagining reconciliation within human life, society and creation as a goal and as the process of reaching that goal. This may be a long and difficult struggle and it cannot be carried through unless it is in a spirit of love that "bears all things, believes all

things, hopes all things, endures all things" (1 Cor. 13:7). In the process we do not lose hope and, at the same time, we focus our participation in the reconciling and healing work of the Holy Spirit in the whole creation.

4) The Reconciling Mission of the Church

60. The Holy Spirit transforms the church and empowers it to be missional: "The Holy Spirit transforms Christians into living, courageous and bold witnesses (cf. Acts 1:8)".[12] Therefore, for the church, mission is not an option but an imperative: "Mission is central to Christian faith and theology. It is not an option but is rather an existential calling and vocation. Mission is constitutive of and conditions the very being of the church and of all Christians". The church is by nature called to participate in God's mission: "Through Christ in the Holy Spirit ... participating in God's mission ... should be natural for all Christians and all churches"[13] (cf. the reference to the priestly ministry of the community in I Peter 2:2-12).

61. The church's mission in the power of the Spirit is to work for reconciliation and healing in the context of brokenness. Reconciliation constitutes an important focus and characteristic of the mission of God which bears consequences for the church's mission: "The church is sent into the world to reconcile humanity and renew creation by calling people and nations to repentance, announcing forgiveness of sin and a new beginning in relations with God and with neighbours through Jesus Christ"[14]. We expect full reconciliation as the establishment of *shalom* by God at the end of time that is the creation – or re-creation – of harmonious and just relationships. It is a holistic process, initiated by God and extended to the whole creation, both human and non-human. As we and all creation struggle for freedom from our bondage to decay, "the Spirit helps us in our weakness ... [and] intercedes for us with sighs too deep for words" (Rom. 8:22-26). In a context of broken relationships in the world today, the specific challenge for the church is to grasp more deeply the gift of God's reconciliation in its life and ministry on behalf of the whole created order.

Reconciliation in the Context of Brokenness

62. The primary broken relationship is between *God* and humanity. The gospel of reconciliation is a call to turn to God, to be converted to God and to renew our faith in the One who constantly invites us to be in communion with Godself, with one another and with the whole creation. We rejoice that through our Saviour Jesus Christ, this reconciliation has been made possible: "Through our Lord Jesus Christ we have now received our reconciliation" (Rom. 5:11). We are called to extend this reconciliation to the rest of the world in mission and to join our energies with that of the Spirit of God in creation.

63. At the heart of the brokenness today is the distortion and destruction of the integral bond that existed in the divine order, between humanity and the rest

---

[12] *Mission and Evangelism in Unity Today, op.cit.* § 13
[13] *Ibid.*, §§ 9 and 13
[14] *Ibid.*, §14

of *creation*. The human-centred separation of human and non-human creation has led to a tendency of some parts of humanity to conquer and destroy nature. Much of the ecological crisis we face today may be attributed to a lack of respect for life and the integrity of creation. An ecological healing – or "ecociliation" – is what Christians envisage: the reconciliation of "all things, whether on earth or in heaven" (Col. 1:20). In the Nicene-Constantinopolitan Creed we confess the Holy Spirit as the lord and the giver of life. Mission in the Spirit warrants a new perspective – a life-centred approach that will cause the earth to flourish and sustain human communities. This model of cosmic reconciliation and healing provides a powerful basis for reconciliation among humanity.

64. Brokenness is also felt in the area of *human relationships*. The image of God is distorted in estrangement and enmity, which is often related to power structures. These are manifested concretely in manifold forms of discrimination in the world at large on the bases of caste, race, gender, religion, sexual orientation, and socio-economic status. Mission in terms of reconciliation and healing in this context is about going beyond and transcending such frontiers and thereby restoring the consciousness of the image of God in humanity. In real terms, the mission of the churches is to strive to work in common for the dismantling of divisive walls – those within the church as well as outside. This means taking part in ecumenical attempts at reconciliation within and among churches and in people's struggles for reconstruction of society on the basis of justice and human rights, as well as providing a space for dialogue and debate where society or the churches remain profoundly divided. The body of Christ is endowed with various spiritual gifts (1 Cor. 12:8-10; see also Rom. 12:6-8). Exercised in the spirit of love (1 Cor. 13:1-3; Rom. 12:9-10), these build up the community and express its reconciled unity in diversity.

65. In a context where there are victims and perpetrators of injustice and exploitation, the church has a particular missionary role to play, namely that of a *bridge-builder*, between the poor and the rich, women and men, black and white, and so on. The Holy Spirit has been described as "the Go-Between God"[15] because of the Spirit's role in creating and sustaining communion (Eph. 2:18, 4:3). The "go-between" or "in-between" position is not be construed as a value-neutral position but acknowledged as a rather risky and costly position to be in. While taking the sides of the victims, the church also has the mission of reaching out to the victimizers with the challenges of the gospel. Mission at the point of "in betweenness" is simultaneously a mission of empowering the powerless by accompanying them and also of challenging the perpetrators of hurt to repent. In this way it becomes a mission of mutual life-giving.

66. Brokenness is also sadly a mark of today's *church*. The divisions among churches, both doctrinal and non-theological, are a challenge to the mission of reconciliation and healing. A divided church is an aberration of the body of Christ (1 Cor. 1:13) and grieves the Holy Spirit (Eph. 4:25-32). If churches are not able to reconcile one with the other, they are failing the gospel call and will lack credibility

---

[15] reference to John V.Taylor *The Go-Between God: the Holy Spirit and Christian Mission*. London, SCM, 1972

in witness. "Sent to a world in need of unity and greater interdependence amidst the competition and fragmentation of the human community, the Church is called to be sign and instrument of God's reconciling love... Divisions among Christians are a counter-witness to Christ and contradict their witness to reconciliation in Christ."[16] There has been a particular tendency of churches and Christian movements to split in and over mission work during the last century. Competition and conflict in mission, in development or inter-church aid, as well as proselytism, have proved to be a serious counter-witness to Christ's reconciling work. Christians and churches are called to undertake or strengthen reconciliation processes among themselves. There are signs of some theological convergence between opposed mission movements in recent years. And churches themselves have made significant progress towards shared baptism, eucharist and ministry and also toward common witness. We hope that these will lead to renewed relationships. The gospel of reconciliation is shared with integrity if the church is a reconciled and healing community.

67. If the goal and process of mission is to be reconciliation, it is imperative that the church revisit its past and engages in some introspection and self-examination about its *mission* in the world. Any credible mission by the church has to begin with the confession that not all of her mission has been a reflection of the mission which God has intended and which Godself carries out (*missio Dei*). If we have declared the love of God while hating our brother or sister, we are liars (1 John 4:20). Where Christian missionary enterprise was – and still is – complicit in an imperialistic project involving violence, causing destruction of indigenous cultures, fragmentation of communities and even division among Christians, it calls for repentance (*metanoia*). Repentance requires the confession of the sin of violent colonization in the name of the gospel. This is important for the "healing of memories", which is an integral part of the mission of reconciliation and healing. The church must take care to dress the wounds of the past (cf. Jer. 6:14 f).

68. While we confess these sins, we also acknowledge the fact that there has been, and is, much genuine Christian mission in the spirit of peace and reconciliation. Such mission results in peace with God, healed lives, restored communities and the socio-economic liberation of marginalized peoples.

Spirituality of Reconciliation

69. Mission in terms of reconciliation and healing calls for a corresponding spirituality: one that is healing, transforming, liberating, and builds relationships of mutual respect. A genuine spirituality for reconciliation and healing reflects the interaction of faith and praxis that constitutes witness (*martyria*). Witness presupposes a spirituality of self-examination and confession of sins (*metanoia*), leading to proclamation (*kerygma*) of the gospel of reconciliation, service (*diakonia*) in love, worship (*leiturgia*) in truth and the teaching of justice. The exercise of these spiritual gifts builds up reconciled communities (*koinonia*).[17]

---

[16] „The Challenge of Proselytism and the Calling to Common Witness", Appendix C of the *7th Report of the Joint Working Group between the Roman Catholic Church and the World Council of Churches*, Geneva-Rome 1998, p. 45, §§ 8 and 9

[17] *Mission and Evangelism in Unity Today, op.cit*, §7

70. The spirituality of reconciliation is one of humility and self-emptying (kenosis; Phil. 2:7), and at the same time an experience of the Holy Spirit's sanctifying and transforming power. In his struggle to reconcile Jews and Gentiles and other factions, the Apostle Paul declared that God's power is made perfect in weakness (2 Cor. 12:9; 1 Cor. 2:3-5). The spirituality of reconciliation is the spirituality of passion, resurrection as well as of Pentecost. In the global context of the return of imperialism – especially in the form of the hegemonic power of globalization – this self-emptying spirituality is a challenge both to the victims and perpetrators of systemic violence and injustice. The treasure we have is "in earthen vessels, to show that the transcendent power belongs to God and not to us" (2 Cor. 4:7). The church's mission in this context is once again to be in the "in betweenness" – between the wielders of power and the powerless – to empower the powerless and also challenge the powerful to empty themselves of their power and privileges for the sake of the dis-empowered. The spirituality of reconciliation challenges the power structures of local communities, including the churches, in particular where traditional majority or folk churches act in a hegemonious way.

71. A self-emptying spirituality is also a spirituality of cross-bearing. The church is called to bear the cross of Jesus Christ, by being with the suffering.[18] A spirituality of non-violent resistance is an integral aspect of reconciliation and healing in an age of continuing exploitation of the poor and the marginalized. In situations of oppression, discrimination and hurt, the cross of Christ is the power of God for salvation (1 Cor. 1:18).

72. The sacraments and liturgical life of the church should express the mission of reconciliation and healing. Baptism is an act of sharing in the death and resurrection of Jesus Christ. It is symbolic of the spirituality of cross-bearing, which is both a dying to self (Mark 8:34 and parallels) and a raising up to life (John 3:14, etc.). The eucharist is a sacramental act of healing, an act of remembrance, and a re-enactment of the breaking of the body of Christ for the sake of cosmic reconciliation. The bread of God, which comes down from heaven, gives life to the world (John 6:33). The sharing out of the bread and the wine among all calls for redistribution of wealth and the equality of the kingdom that Jesus Christ proclaimed. In prayer, the church intercedes with God for the world, standing in the "in-betweenness" in faith that God will bring reconciliation and healing. In preaching the word, the church brings comfort to the downtrodden, proclaims truth and justice, and calls all to repentance and forgiveness. The church's worship is itself a witness to the world of reconciliation in Christ, and in the power of the Spirit the church lives out this eucharistic witness in daily life.

73. Spiritual resources for reconciliation and healing are not confined to Christian faith traditions. This challenges us to take the inter faith dimensions of mission seriously, for reconciliation and healing in the holistic sense cannot be achieved without reconciliation amongst various faiths and cultures. One way of doing this is to appreciate and learn from the spiritual resources available in other faiths and

---

[18] For example, the "Ecumenical Accompaniment Programme in Palestine and Israel" aims to be with Palestinians and Israelis in their non-violent actions and concerted advocacy efforts to end the occupation.

cultures. Other traditions and experiences of healing and reconciliation, including those of indigenous communities, are of great value.

74. The recent ecumenical statement on dialogue reminds us that "interreligious dialogue is not an instrument to resolve problems instantly in emergency situations".[19] However, in times of conflict the relationships built up by patient dialogue during peacetime may prevent religion from being used as a weapon and, in many cases, pave the way for mediation and reconciliation initiatives. Dialogue presupposes mutual recognition, it signifies a willingness to reconcile and desire to live together. A process of dialogue can build up trust and allow for mutual witness, in this way it may be a means of healing. However, while dialogue is important, issues of truth, memory, repentance, justice, forgiveness and love may need to be addressed before dialogue is possible. The "in-betweenness" of the missionary praxis means that in some situations what is called for is the prophetic power of the gospel to critique religious practices and beliefs that promote injustice and to bring about repentance.

75. The ministry of the Holy Spirit – in which the church is privileged to share – is to heal and reconcile a broken world. In order to exercise this mission with integrity, the church must be a community that is experiencing healing and reconciliation in Christ. The spirituality of reconciliation is self-emptying and cross-bearing in order that the saving power of God may be demonstrated. The Holy Spirit endows the church with gifts and resources for this ministry and, in the spirit of dialogue, Christians are open to appreciate the resources that people of other faiths bring to it. The mission of the church involves going between the parties that are estranged or in conflict. This means accompanying them in their struggles and at the same time challenging the powers of injustice and violence to bring about reconciliation. The goal is to build up reconciled and healing communities which are again missional in commitment and practical ministry.

5) Equipping for Reconciliation: Pedagogy, Pastoralia and Vision

76. In the mission of reconciliation we are inspired by the gospel vision of peace on earth (Luke 2:14). In his preaching of the kingdom of God in both word and deed, our lord Jesus Christ showed us what the kingdom of God is like. It is the kingdom of truth and justice, repentance and forgiveness, in which the first are last and the leaders are servants of all. In the epistles, the apostles taught the churches how to be communities of reconciliation. These bring forth the fruit of the Spirit: love, joy, peace, patience, kindness, goodness, faithfulness, gentleness and self-control (Gal. 5:22-23). Members are called to love one another, live at peace with one another, and bless those who persecute them, leaving vengeance to God (Rom. 12:9-21).

77. However, many have proclaimed peace where there is no peace and only superficially treated the deep wounds caused by broken relationships and injustice (Jer. 6:14). Any pedagogical and pastoral approach to mission has to acknowledge

---

[19] *Ecumenical considerations for dialogue and relations with people of other religions. Taking stock of 30 years of dialogue and revisiting the 1979 guidelines*, Geneva, WCC, 2003, §28

the fact that the ministry of healing and reconciliation is a profound and often lengthy process that therefore requires long-term strategies (Rom. 8:25). Once the church believes that mission belongs to God, and that it is not a frenzied activity initiated by the church, then the church's mission will be oriented towards the long-term goal of creating communities of reconciliation and healing. The realization of our hope requires patience, pastoral sensitivity and an appropriate educational method.

78. Our sense of being human is key to this educational process. Human beings are essentially relational beings, linked together and active in the web of life. For our survival, we depend on one another and therefore we need to live in just relationships of trust and build communities of reconciliation and healing. From a Christian anthropological perspective, human beings are also forgiven beings, forgiven by God. Forgiveness as a theological category has ethical ramifications. The ministry of reconciliation and healing through forgiveness involves truth telling and justice. In other words, the pedagogy of justice is what makes forgiveness a radical concept. Forgiveness that undermines justice is not Christian forgiveness. Costly discipleship, which is integral to the ministry of healing and reconciliation, has to be justice-oriented.

79. Compassion for the broken and concern for life in all its fullness are the pastoral modes of Christian mission. One of the most important sources for learning about this ministry is the immense wealth of people's day-to-day life experience, especially that of the poor and the vulnerable. The church's involvement in people's life experiences, in their struggles to affirm life wherever it is denied, is perhaps the best learning process. Through this pedagogy of shared memories, the church will be enabled to carry out its mission effectively.

80. Whereas the emphasis is being put in this document on social reconciliation processes, insights can be drawn for renewing and strengthening the pastoral approach to conflicts between individual persons in family, work place and church. Reconciliation between persons also needs to address questions of truth, healing of memories, repentance, justice, forgiveness and love. Pastors, priests as well as lay members of the community have the most important and difficult task to find ways to journey with persons who suffer from deep wounds left by the hardship of life or inter-personal conflicts, to offer them a safe space for expressing their vulnerability, anger, helplessness, suffering and yearning. At personal level, too, to follow Christ's call to reconciliation may entail a long journey or process, needing time and the capacity to cope with success and failures, moments of hope and of despair, putting faith to the test. Not all churches have kept the tradition of the sacrament of confession and reconciliation, but all are encouraged to find a way to envisage their pastoral ministry in terms of the understanding of mission described in this document.

81. This pastoral healing ministry must be embedded in a community life where people find a home and a safe space in which joys and pains can be shared openly, where those feeling vulnerable find enough security to express what burdens them, a community in which love overcomes fear and judgment. Such

communities, nourished by the celebration of the eucharist, become then as such missionary entities, because the gospel which is preached is also lived and experienced. That such communities also have a role to play in society and be welcoming even to those who are not regular members was forcefully described by Paul in Romans 12. That passage also reminds us that a reconciling and healing mission may lead to suffer persecution. Since Christ, many missionary persons and communities have also been victims of violence and discrimination. But even in such cases, the commandment to love is to be the overarching characteristic of Christian witness to God's reconciliation.

82. Equipping for mission in a paradigm of reconciliation has significant implications for existing models of theological and mission education and training. Imbuing the church with a pedagogy of justice and a compassionate pastoral theology brings challenges for both the content and the mode of instruction. As Christians engaging in a ministry of reconciliation we will continue to require the knowledge of language, culture and religious traditions that will help us enter into the experience of others and serve them. However, equally importantly, we will need a theology and spirituality of reconciliation. We should together develop a theological understanding of how God effects reconciliation in the world and Christians' part in it. The church needs to learn and teach the dynamics and processes of reconciliation and the importance of the different dimensions of reconciliation ministry: establishing the truth, healing the memory, doing justice, receiving forgiveness and forgiving others. In order to overcome the contemporary culture of violence and counter the myth of redemptive violence, the church must demonstrate in its life and witness that justice and redemption is achieved through a non-violent resistance. This requires a spirituality of reconciliation that is self-emptying and cross-bearing for the sake of justice. We also have a responsibility to use and develop the spiritual gifts that, used in the spirit of love, build up community and overcome disunity and enmity (1 Cor. 12:8-10, 13:1-3; see also Rom. 12:6-10).

83. The main theme of the 2005 Conference on World Mission and Evangelism, "Come, Holy Spirit, heal and reconcile" calls our attention to the mission of the Spirit. According to St John's Gospel, the Holy Spirit who proceeds from the Father, is the *parakletos*, who accompanies us in our brokenness. The Spirit, the intercessor, is in the "in betweenness", going between the Father, the Son and all creation. The *parakletos* is the Spirit of truth who leads us into all truth and interprets to us the teaching of Jesus. The Holy Spirit unites us to God the Father and the Son and makes us part of the *missio Dei* to bring life to the world. The Spirit teaches us to abide in Christ and to love one another, thus witnessing to the love of Christ. In a situation of enmity, the Spirit comforts us and gives us courage to speak and declare the word of God. The *parakletos* consoles the suffering and convinces the world of sin and righteousness and God's judgement. The Spirit, who is our counsellor, is the Spirit of peace in a violent world (John 14:15-16:15).

84. The *parakletos* provides a model and the medium for the church's ministry of reconciliation. The Holy Spirit heals and reconciles by coming alongside to inspire, enlighten and empower. In the Spirit, we are enabled to affirm what is true

and at the same time to discern what is false and evil. The Spirit binds us together and in the Spirit we enjoy true communion and fellowship (2 Cor. 13:13). Though for a little while we, and all creation, groan like a woman in childbirth, the Spirit is our midwife and when the mission is accomplished we believe that our sorrow will turn to joy at the new life of reconciliation (John 16:20-22; Rom. 8:18-25).

The Final Vision

85. At the very end of the Bible, in the Book of Revelation, St John set down the vision given to him of the new heaven and new earth, the new creation that is the result of God's reconciling work in Christ (Rev. 21:1,5; cf. 2 Cor. 5:17-18). The New Jerusalem is the reconciled city where God dwells with God's people. In this city there is no longer any mourning or crying or pain because justice has been done; nor is there any darkness because everything is in the light of the glory of God. Through the centre of the city runs the river of life for the healing of the nations (Rev. 21:1-22:5). In the field of world mission we can, therefore, speak of the "oikoumene which is to come" (Heb. 2:5 cf. 13:14ff.), as an open society, where an honest dialogue between the existing living cultures can take place. The world today can and must become a *household*, where everyone is open to the "other" (as they are open to the Ultimate Other, i.e. God), and where all can share a common life, despite the plurality and difference of their identity. Reconciliation as a new mission paradigm results in a new understanding of the term *oikoumene* and its derivatives (ecumenism etc.). These terms no longer exclusively refer to an abstract universality, such as the entire inhabited world, or the whole human race, or even a united universal church. In other words they no longer describe a given situation, but substantial – and at the same time threatened – relations between churches, between cultures, between people and human societies, and at the same time between humanity and the rest of God's creation.

6) Questions for Further Study and Discussion

86. This attempt toward a theology of mission as reconciliation raises a number of questions that will need further and more detailed attention. These include:

- What are the practical implications of the call for *economic* reconciliation?
- What are the processes that can bring *Muslim-Christian* reconciliation in the present context?
- What contributions does *Pentecostal and charismatic* thinking and experience make to mission theology of reconciliation?
- In what ways can the theology of the Holy Spirit *(pneumatology)* further aid the practice of and reflection on reconciliation?
- How does a renewed focus on pneumatology transform humankind's relation with *creation*?
- What changes does mission as reconciliation suggest to existing paradigms of mission? In particular, what does it mean for the understanding of *conversion*?
- How can the importance of the spirit of reconciliation in mission

be effectively communicated to those using aggressive missionary methods?

- How can we resource and develop appropriate ways to *equip* local churches to become reconciling and healing communities?
- How can the churches *support* those specially called and gifted in the ministry of reconciliation?

Preparatory Paper No 11

The Healing Mission of the Church

INTRODUCTORY REMARKS

1. The present document has been prepared by a multicultural and interdenominational group of missiologists, medical doctors and health professionals. It builds upon the tradition of the WCC's Christian Medical Commission (CMC) and its most fruitful contribution to an understanding of the healing ministry of the church. This document does not repeat what remains well formulated in earlier texts of the World Council of Churches, such as the document "Healing and Wholeness. The Churches' Role in Health", adopted in 1990 by the Central Committee. That text situates the healing ministry within the struggle for justice, peace and the integrity of creation, and remains an essential contribution, the urgency of which has even grown in a now globalized world. The present study document concentrates mainly on some medical and theological-spiritual aspects of the healing ministry and their link with a recent ecumenical understanding of mission. It is offered as a background document to the 2005 Athens Conference on World Mission and Evangelism (CWME) and an important contribution to a dialogue on the relevance of its theme "Come Holy Spirit, heal and reconcile – Called in Christ to be reconciling and healing communities". It is to be read together with the study document recommended by the CWME Commission on "mission as ministry of reconciliation".[1] The present document does not pretend to make any final statement on healing or mission, but hopes to enrich the debate and enable Christians and churches to better respond to their calling.

1 THE CONTEXT

The Global Context of Health and Disease at the Beginning of the 21st Century

2. Global statistics on the incidence and prevalence of diseases, on the burden of diseases for communities and societies and on mortality rates, are based on a scientific concept of disease and epidemiological methods for measuring disease and its impact.[2] In medical science, disease refers to identifiable dysfunction of human physiology .We have to acknowledge that this approach is inherently different from a more holistic interpretation of health and diseases used in WCC circles,[3] and that is not quantifiable with current methods and therefore not easily suitable for statistical analyses.

3. It may anyhow be misleading to describe a global context because the situation is extremely complex and varies enormously between continents and societies, and increasingly also within societies and even within local communities depending on economic resources which influence living conditions, lifestyle behaviour and

---

[1] CWME Conference Preparatory Paper No. 10 on: www.mission2005.org
[2] Cf. Christina de Vries: "The Global Health Situation: Priorities for the Churches' Health Ministry beyond AD 2000". International Review of Mission (IRM) Vol XC, Nos. 356/357, p. 149ff.
[3] For the WCC definition, see § 31 below.

access to health care. Any overview will be grossly misleading if taken as an accurate description of local or regional situations.

4. Nevertheless some trends may be discerned. One can speak of a worldwide improvement in health if measured in terms of premature mortality and disability adjusted life years, except for those regions heavily affected by HIV/AIDS. *Infant mortality* which is a sensitive indicator for general living conditions and access to basic health care has reached very low levels in Europe and North America and is going down particularly in East and Southeast Asia as well as Latin America and the Caribbean. It is still very high or even increasing in a number of countries in Sub-Saharan Africa.

5. Other major trends include the *global increase in chronic disease*, particularly mental diseases and diseases affecting the elderly. Even in low-income countries there is an increasing number of adults suffering e.g. from coronary heart disease, cancer or diabetes which are the most common causes of morbidity and mortality in industrialized countries.[4] What is most disturbing is the general trend for a long-term increase in the number of people suffering from psychiatric diseases, particularly depression, both in countries of the North and the South. Accelerated and aggravated experiences of crisis and threat following rapid globalization processes seem to put excessive pressure on the human psychic system.

6. Currently the international community is engaged in a major review of the global health status as part of the process to assess progress toward the achievement of the Millennium Development Goals (MDG). Three of the eight MDGs are directly referring to health.[5]

7. The impact of *human-made climate* change and deterioration of the natural environment on the global health situation cannot yet be sufficiently mapped and measured, but raises serious concerns as to its potential devastating effects, not only locally but worldwide. Deforestation, for exampte, contributes to building up the greenhouse gases in the atmosphere which results in the depletion of the stratospheric ozone and increases ultraviolet radiation. This induces the suppression of immune systems and permit the emergence of cancers and certain infectious diseases that depend on cell mediated immune responses. Global warming leading to a rise of the surface water levels of oceans occasions the flooding of human dwelling places thereby increasing the incident of waterborne diseases. Global warming also leads to the resurgence of malaria and other infectious diseases in temperate countries and increases the danger of cardiovascular illnesses.

8. Despite the advanced technology, *the state of health of the world* is still preoccupying as shown in the 2004 World Health Organization report.[6]

---

[4] World Health Organization (WHO): *The World Health Report – Changing History* , Geneva, 2004
[5] United Nations: Report on Millennium Development Goals. Cf. www.un.org/millenniumgoals/ Reference is made here to #4: reduce by two-thirds the mortality rate among children under five; #5: reduce by three-quarters the maternal mortality ratio; # 6: Halt and begin to reverse the spread of HIV/AIDS. Halt and begin to reverse the incidence of malaria and other major diseases.
[6] WHO, op.cit.

It has therefore be pointed out that health and healing are not just medical issues. They embrace political, social, economical, cultural and spiritual dimensions. As it is stated in the WCC document "Healing and Wholeness, the Churches' role in Health": *"...although the 'health industry' is producing and using progressively sophisticated and expensive technology, the increasingly obvious fact is that most of the world's health problems cannot be best addressed in this way...It is an acknowledged fact that the number one cause of disease in the world is poverty, which is ultimately the result of oppression, exploitation and war. Providing immunizations, medicines, and even health education by standard methods cannot significantly ameliorate illness due to poverty...".*[7]

Unequal Access to Health Services – Health and Justice as Ethical Challenges

9. The fact remains that in large parts of the world people have no access to essential health services. The question of affordable *access to health care provisions* and the commercialization of health constitute yet other very complex and sensitive issues. On the one hand scientifically based health care becomes ever more expensive with increased levels of diagnostic and therapeutic sophistication widening the gap between those who can afford it and those who can't. This gets most pronounced in low-income countries but becomes increasingly visible also in high-income countries with reduced public expenditure on health. Christians have to be constantly reminded that access to health care is an essential human right and not a commodity that should be available only for those with sufficient financial resources.

10. On the other hand, there is an increased interest in addressing diseases of poverty, in particular the major infectious diseases HIV/AIDS, Tuberculosis and Malaria. The creation of "The Global Fund to Fight AIDS, Tuberculosis & Malaria" by the United Nations is a case in point. Christians have advocated strongly for increased attention to and financial resources for diseases of poverty to achieve greater equity in the distribution of resources. Several global campaigns or initiatives testify to this concern, such as the "Ecumenical Advocacy Alliance" and the "Ecumenical HIV/AIDS Initiative in Africa". On such global health questions, there are also increasing efforts at co-operation between various Faith-Based Communities.

11. Even if in some instances, good health care services help to alleviate poverty, health and healing cannot be disconnected from structural organization of our societies, the quality of relationship among people and the life style.

Increasingly widespread unhealthy life-style patterns[8] are a consequence of standards and interests of the food industry and of changing cultural behaviours promoted among others by media and the advertisement industry.

12. The present state could be summarized in terms such as:

---

[7] Cf. *Healing and Wholeness. The Churches' Role in Health. The report of a study by the Christian Medical Commission.* Geneva, WCC, 1990. Document received by the WCC Central Committee. Quote from page 1.
[8] Such as fast-food and other consumption trends leading to overweight of children and adults in affluent societies, addiction to drugs, over-consumption of TV and video, etc.

Today, in our globalized and highly commercial world, people are far from being all healthy, neither as individuals nor as communities, and this despite the many advances in preventive medicine and therapeutic skills.

♦ Many people don't have access to affordable medical care.
♦ While preventable diseases are still a major problem in many parts of the world, chronic illnesses often related to life style and behaviour are on the rise, causing much suffering all over the world.
♦ A growing number of people with mental illnesses are being recognized today.
♦ The costs of medical care have risen to prohibitive levels, making the technology unavailable to many and leading to medical systems becoming unsustainable.
♦ High technology has an inhuman face leading to people feeling isolated, and fragmented.
♦ Death in modern medicine is seen as failure and is aggressively fought to such an extent that people are not able to die with dignity.

13. People disenchanted with the established medical system are looking for more than treatment of a sick liver or heart. They want to be seen and treated as persons. Their diseases often lead them to ask spiritual questions and there is a growing search for the spiritual dimension of healing.

The importance of the role of the community in creating and maintaining health is being rediscovered in many of the affluent countries.

14. Scientific researchers have started to map what they call the "religious health assets" in order to provide basic data on potential material infrastructure and spiritual contributions by religious communities to national and international health policy.

A number of epidemiological studies carried out by medical professionals, mainly in the USA, highlighting the positive effect of religion and spirituality on health are enabling a new dialogue between the medical and theological disciplines.[9] Scientific medicine itself has become increasingly interested in the spiritual dimension of the human person.

Healing and Culture – Different Worldviews, Cultural Conditions and their Impact on Understanding Health and Healing

15. The way health and healing are defined, sickness and illness explained, depends largely on culture and conventions. In ecumenical mission circles, culture is usually understood in a wide sense, including not only literature, music and arts, but values, structures, worldview, ethics, as well as religion.[10]

---

[9] Cf. Harold G. Koeching, Michael E. Muccullogh, David B. Lason, eds, *Handbook of Religion and Health*, New York, Oxford University Press, 2001.
[10] The question of the relation between gospel and cultures was seriously addressed at the world mission conference in Salvador in 1996, cf. Christopher Duraisingh (ed.), *Called to One Hope. The gospel in diverse cultures*. Geneva, WCC, 1998.

16. It is in particular the combination of religion, worldview and values that impacts people's specific understanding of and approach to healing. Since culture varies from continent to continent and from country to country or even within countries and groups of people, there is no immediate universal common understanding of the main causes of sickness and illness or of any evil affecting humans.

17. There are cultures in which supernatural beings are seen as the real ultimate causative agents for ill health, particularly on mental disorders. In such worldviews, people go to traditional healers and religious specialists for exorcism and deliverance from evil spirits and demons. Only then can they have the guarantee that the ultimate cause of their suffering has been dealt with. This would not exclude parallel treatments of symptoms with herbs, traditional or industrially manufactured drugs.

18. Masses of people integrate popular religious beliefs and culture in their understanding of health and healing. We may call this popular religiosity and belief in health. This belief may involve veneration of saints, pilgrimages to shrines and use of religious symbols such as oil and amulets to protect people from evil spirits or evil intentions that harm people.

19. Others, in particular Asian cultures, also point to the importance of harmony within the human body as the necessary pre-condition for a person's health, well-being and healing. *Shibashi*, e.g., an ancient Chinese practice of nature-oriented movements attune the body to the rhythm of nature producing an energizing effect. The traditional belief is that healing and health are actual effects of balance in the flow of energy that are affected from within and outside the human body. The clogging of centres of energy (*chakras*) or obstruction in the flow of energy causes illness. Acupuncture or finger pressure are other modalities of balancing the flow of energy.

20. Out of different worldviews culture-specific medical sciences and systems developed in some of the major civilizations of the world. In particular since the Enlightenment, these were disregarded by the Western medical establishment, but are now again increasingly considered worthy alternatives for the treatment of specific illnesses.

21. As a result of advances in medical science and of intercultural exchanges, some people, in particular in Western contexts, develop new life-styles emphasizing walking, jogging, aerobic exercise, healthy diet, yoga and other forms of meditation, massage and going to sauna and spa as a way to achieve wellness, health and healing. These may well bring relief from stressful situation and some chronic illnesses like cardiovascular diseases and diabetes mellitus.

22. Certain forms of nature-centred religiosity and indigenous and emerging secular cultures also point to the relationship between cosmology or ecology and health and healing. There is a growing, however still insufficient awareness of the importance of linking ecology and health. The determinants of health are clean water and air and a safe space for all living creatures. Deforestation has

profoundly damaged the water supply, polluted the air, and destroyed the habitats of many living creatures turning them into "pests" and creating ill health among human beings and other elements of creation. Very close associations of animals and human beings are now the cause of new forms of epidemics such as the emergence of Avian Flu, a severe and potentially fatal viral infection that is transferred from ducks and chickens to human beings. The tsunami event and post-tsunami situation highlights the importance of taking care not only of human beings but of the whole of creation and of attuning oneself to the rhythm of nature.

2 HEALTH AND HEALING AND THE ECUMENICAL MOVEMENT

23. In ancient times, the art of healing belonged to priests. They were consulted in the case of disease and often were regarded as mediators of healing. The unity of body, mind and spirit was understood and accepted.

The Centrality of Healing in the Mission of the Early Church

24. It is worth recalling that the growth of the early church in the 2nd and 3rd century was – among other factors – also due to the fact that Christianity presented itself as a healing movement to the early Mediterranean societies. The importance of the different healing ministries within the church is reflected by the early accounts of mission in the New Testament. Many writings of the early church fathers also affirm the centrality of the church as a healing community and proclaim Christ as the healer of the world over against Hellenistic religiosity.

25. In affirming that God himself in the life of his Son has lived through experiences of weakness unto even experiencing death himself, Christianity revolutionized the understanding of God and profoundly transformed the basic attitudes of the faith community to the sick, the aged and the dying. It contributed decisively to break up the conventional strategies and mechanisms of exclusion, of discrimination and of religious stigmatization of the sick and the fragile. It put an end to the association of the divine with ideals of a perfect, sane, beautiful and un-passionate existence. The different attitude to the sick, to the widows and to the poor proved to be a vital source for the missionary success and vitality of the early church. The monasteries continued to be islands of hope - by caring for the sick.

Medical Science and Medical Missions

27. Over the centuries the development of science and technology, and especially since the Enlightenment, have led to a change in the understanding of the human being and of health. Instead of being regarded as an indivisible unity, the human being was fragmented into body, mind and soul. Medical professionals tend to view a disease as a malfunction of a wonderful and complicated machine to be repaired with the help of medical skills, neglecting the fact that human beings have a soul and a mind. The rise of the disciplines of psychology and psychiatry accentuated this divide taking over the care of the mind. As a result, there was loss of the understanding of the concept of wholeness, as well as of the role of the community and of spirituality in health.

28. Medical missions came about some time later, formally in the 19th century, leading to the setting up of church related health care systems in many parts of the world where missionaries were active. Health care was seen by some as an essential part of the mission of the sending church or missionary organization. Though these mission hospitals provided compassionate care of high quality at low cost, the western medical model of health care was often superimposed on indigenous local cultures with their own therapeutic and healing traditions. However, many medical missionaries engaged in training indigenous people in the art of healing and nursing from the very start of their medical mission.

A Holistic and Balanced Understanding of the Christian Ministry of Healing

29. A carefully designed, most comprehensive study process initiated by the World Council of Churches' Christian Medical Commission (CMC) in the seventies and eighties showed that many factors or influences are responsible for forms of illness and broken relationships; growing feelings of void and lack of spiritual orientation in people's lives; weaken the natural defences of the body to cope or defend oneself from infections or bio-chemical disturbances in bodily functions or other forms of physical, emotional, or mental disorders; cause imbalance in the flow of energy leading to obstruction and manifestation of dis-ease; provoke enslavement or addiction from evil desires or influences that hinder the person's response to God's saving grace.

30. According to an anthropology rooted in the biblical-theological tradition of the church, the human being is seen as "multidimensional unity".[11] Body, soul and mind are not separate entities, but inter-related and inter-dependant. Therefore, health has physical, psychological and spiritual dimensions. The individual being is also part of the community, health has also a social dimension. And because of the interaction between the natural environment (biosphere) and persons or communities, health has even an ecological dimension.

31. This has led the World Council of Churches to offer the following **definition of health**:

> Health is a dynamic state of well-being of the individual and society, of physical, mental, spiritual, economic, political and social well-being – of being in harmony with each other, with the material environment and with God.[12]

Such a holistic view underlines that health is not a static concept in which clear distinction lines are drawn between those who are healthy and those who are not. Every human being is constantly moving between different degrees of staying

---

[11] A conception developed in particular by Paul Tillich. Cf. Paul Tillich: "The meaning of health" (1961) in Id., *Writings in the Philosophy of Culture/ Kulturphilosophische Schriften (Main works/Hauptwerke* 2) ed. by M. Palmer, Berlin-New York, 1990, pp. 342-52. Paul Tillich, "The relation of religion and health. Historical considerations and theoretical questions" (1946), in: *Ibid.*, pp. 209-38. Id., *Systematic Theology III. Life and the Spirit, History and the Kingdom of God.* Chicago, 1963, pp. 275-82.
[12] CMC study on "Healing and Wholeness", op.cit. (note 6), p. 6

healthy and of struggling with infections and diseases. Such an understanding of health is close to the one emerging in the more recent debate and research on health promoting factors.[13]

Such a holistic view also has consequences on the understanding of the church's mission:
The Christian ministry of healing includes both the practice of medicine (addressing both physical and mental health) as well as caring and counselling disciplines and spiritual practices. Repentance, prayer and/or laying on of hands, divine healing, rituals involving touch and tenderness, forgiveness and the sharing of the eucharist can have important and at times even dramatic effects in the physical as well as social realm of human beings. All the different means are part of God's work in creation and presence in the church. Contemporary scientific medicine as well as other medical approaches make use of what is available in the world God has created. Healing through "medical means" is not to be thought of as inferior (or even unnecessary) to healing through other or by "spiritual" means.

32. There are churches and social contexts (particularly in western post-Enlightenment and modern societies) in which a one-sided emphasis and attention was given to the achievements of contemporary scientific medicine and the physical aspects of health and healing. Here a new openness and attention is needed for the spiritual dimensions in the Christian ministries of healing. There are other contexts and churches in which – due to a different world view and the non-availability of modern western medical systems – the importance of spiritual healing is highly valued. Here also a new dialogue between spiritual healing practices and approaches in modern medicine is essential.

Recent Attempts to Deepen the Understanding of the Healing Mission of the Church

33. One of the most thorough recent studies was conducted on behalf of the Church of England by a working party commissioned by the House of Bishops. It produced a remarkably encompassing report developing a definition of healing as a "process towards health and wholeness.... It embraces what God has achieved for human beings through the incarnation of Jesus Christ.... God's gifts of healing are occasionally experienced instantly or rapidly but in most cases healing is a gradual process taking time to bring deep restoration to health at more than one level." [14]

34. It is both significant that at the beginning of the 21st century several important ecumenical church meetings such as the Lutheran World Federation's (LWF) assembly in Winnipeg, Canada, the assembly of the Conference of European Churches (CEC) in Trondheim, Norway and the General Council of the World Alliance of Reformed Churches (WARC) in Accra, Ghana have focussed directly or

---

[13] One example are the discussions around the conception of "salutogenesis" developed by the medical sociologist Aaron Antonowsky, focusing on what helps maintaining health and well-being in body and soul, instead of focussing on factors producing illness.
[14] *A Time to Heal . A Report for the House of Bishops of the General Synod of the Church of England on the Healing Ministry.* London, Church House Publishing, 2000.

indirectly on the healing ministry of the church in a world torn by suffering and violence. The following extract from the most recent mission document of the LWF shall stand for many of those efforts:

> According to the scriptures, God is the source of all healing. In the Old Testament, healing and salvation are interrelated and in many instances mean the same thing: "Heal me, o Lord, and I shall be healed; save me, and I shall be saved" (Jeremiah 17:14). The New Testament, however, does not equate being cured from an ailment with being saved. The New Testament also makes a distinction between curing and healing. Some may be cured but not healed (Luke 17:15-19), while others are not cured but healed (2 Corinthians 12:7-9). "Cure" denotes restoring lost health and thus carries a protological view. Healing refers to the eschatological reality of abundant life that breaks in through the event of Jesus Christ, the wounded healer, who participates in all aspects of human suffering, dying, and living, and overcomes violation, suffering and death by his resurrection. In this sense, healing and salvation point to the same eschatological reality.[15]

Recent Dialogue of Worldviews re. the Reality of Spiritual Powers

35. In recent years, largely because of the rapid growth of Pentecostal-charismatic movements and their influence across the ecumenical spectrum, terms such as "power encounter", "demon[ology]" and "principalities and powers" have become topics of missiological interest and research today as has the question of divine healing in particular. Exorcism, casting out evil spirits and "witch demonology" are also terms more frequently used in certain Christian circles today.[16]

> Talk about demons and evil spirits is, of course, not a new phenomenon either in Christian theology or church life. The Christian church, throughout its history – especially during the first centuries and later, more often among enthusiastic, charismatic renewal movements – has either appointed specially gifted/graced persons to tackle evil forces (exorcists) or at least acknowledged the reality of spiritual powers.

36. The rapid proliferation of Christian churches among the cultures outside of the West, has also contributed to the rise to prominence of the theme of demonology. Christians in Africa, Asia, Latin America, and the Pacific tend to be much more open to the idea of the reality of these forces. In many of those cultures, there is a widespread involvement with spiritual powers even apart from Christian faith.

One of the main reasons why the Western churches – especially the mainline Protestant churches – eschewed the whole topic of spiritual powers for several centuries has to do with the specific nature of their worldview going back to the influence of the Enlightenment. Christian theology and the way clergy was trained

---

[15] *Mission in Context. Transformation – Reconciliation – Empowerment. An LWF contribution to the understanding and practice of mission.* Geneva, LWF, 2004, pages 39-40.
[16] cf. IRM Vol. 93, Nos 370/71 July/October 2004 on "Divine Healing, Pentecostalism and Mission".

did not only ignore the topic but often also helped "demythologize" even the biblical talk about demons and spiritual powers. Earlier documents of WCC on healing and health have not tackled the issue adequately either.[17] Currently, a paradigm shift is taking place in Western culture – often referred to as "postmodernity" – which is challenging a narrow rationalistic world-view and theology.

3 HEALTH AND HEALING IN BIBLICAL AND THEOLOGICAL PERSPECTIVE

God's Healing Mission

37. God the Father, Son and Spirit leads creation and humanity towards the full realization of God's kingdom, which the prophets announce and expect as reconciled and healed relationships between creation and God, humanity and God, humanity and creation, between humans as persons and as groups or societies (healing in the fullest sense as "shalom": Isaiah 65:17-25). This is what in missiology is referred to as *missio Dei*. In a trinitarian perspective, the creational, social-relational and spiritual-energetical dimensions of healing are interdependent, interwoven.

While affirming the dynamic reality of God's mission in world and creation, we also acknowledge its profound mystery which is beyond the grasp of human knowledge (Job 38 f). We rejoice whenever God's presence manifests itself in miraculous and liberating, healing, changes in human life and history, enabling life in dignity. We also cry out with the Psalmist and Job to challenge the Creator when evil and unexplainable suffering scandalize us and seem to indicate the absence of a merciful and just God: "Why, O God? Why me, Lord? How long?" It is in a profoundly ambivalent and paradoxical world that we affirm our belief and hope in a God who heals and cares.

38. As Christians, we acknowledge the perfect image of God as manifest in Jesus Christ, who came to witness through his life, deeds and words how God cares for humanity and creation. The incarnation of God in Christ affirms that God's healing power is not saving us from this world or above all material and bodily matters but is taking place in the midst of this world and all its pain, brokenness and fragmentation and that healing encompasses all of human existence.

Jesus Christ is the core and centre of God's mission, the personalization of God's kingdom. In the power of the Holy Spirit, Jesus of Nazareth was a healer, exorcist, teacher, prophet, guide and inspirator. He brought and offered freedom from sin, evil, suffering, illness, sickness, brokenness, hatred and disunity (Luke 4: 16ff, Matthew 11:2-6). Hallmarks of the healings of Jesus Christ were his sensitivity to needs of people, especially the vulnerable, the fact that he was "touched" and responded by healing (Luke 8: 42b- 48), his willingness to listen and openness to change (Mark 7: 24b- 30), his unwillingness to accept delay in alleviation of suffering (Luke 13: 10-13) and his authority over traditions and evil spirits. Jesus' healings always brought about a complete restoration of body and mind unlike what we normally experience in healings.

---

[17] Take as an example the CMC study of 1990, Healing and Wholeness, *op.cit.*

39. He inaugurated the new creation, the "end of time" (*eschaton*) through signs and wonders which do point to the fullness of life, the abolition of suffering and death, promised by God as announced by the prophets. But these miraculous actions were not more than signs or signposts. Christ healed those who came or were brought to him. He did not however heal all the sick of his time. The kingdom of God, already present, is still expected. "Healing is a journey into perfection of the final hope, but this perfection is not always fully realized in the present (Rom. 8:22)".[18]

40. Jesus' healing and exorcist activity points in particular to the accomplishment of his ministry at the cross: he came to offer salvation, the healing of relationship with God, what Paul later described as "reconciliation" (2 Cor. 5). This he did through service and sacrifice, fulfilling the ministry of the "wounded healer" prophesized by Isaiah (52:13 – 53:12). Christ's death on the cross is thus both protest against all suffering (Mark 15:34) and victory over sin and evil. By resurrecting Christ, God vindicated his ministry and gave it lasting significance. The cross and resurrection of Christ affirms that God's healing power is not staying apart and above the reality of pain, brokenness and dying but is reaching down to the very depth of human and creational suffering bringing light and hope in the uttermost depth of darkness and despair. The image of the resurrected Christ may be encountered among people who suffer (Matt. 25:31-46) as well as among vulnerable and wounded healers (Matt. 28: 20 and 10:16, 2 Cor. 12: 9, John 15:20).

41. In ecumenical missiology, the Holy Spirit, Lord and life-giving, is believed to be active in church and world. The ongoing work of the Holy Spirit in the whole of creation initiating signs and foretastes of the new creation (2 Cor. 5:17) affirms that the healing power of God transcends all limits of places and times and is at work inside as well as outside the Christian church transforming humanity and creation in the perspective of the world to come. God the Holy Spirit is the fountain of life for Christian individual and community life (John 7:37-39). The Spirit enables the church for mission and equips her with manifold charisms, including (e.g.) the one to heal (cure) by prayer and imposition of hands, the gift of consolation and pastoral care for those whose suffering seems without end, the charism of exorcism to cast out evil spirits, the authority of prophecy to denounce the structural sins responsible for injustice and death, and the charism of wisdom and knowledge essential to scientific research and the exercise of medical professions. But God the Holy Spirit also empowers the Christian community to forgive, share, heal wounds, overcome divisions and so journey towards full communion. The Spirit pursues thus, widens and universalizes Christ's healing and reconciling mission. Groaning in church and creation (Rom. 8), the Spirit also actualizes Christ's solidarity with the suffering and so witnesses to the power of God's grace that may also manifest itself paradoxically in weakness or illness (2 Cor. 12:9).

42. The Spirit fills the church with the transforming authority of the resurrected Lord who heals and liberates from evil, and with the compassion of the suffering

---

[18] Group report from a consultation with Pentecostals in Ghana in 2002, published in *IRM* July/October 2004, *op.cit.*, p. 371.

Servant who dies for the world's sin and consoles the downtrodden. A Spirit-led healing mission encompasses both bold witness and humble presence.

Health, Healing and the Concept of Spiritual Powers

43. One of the dominant traits in which the healing ministry of Jesus is presented in the NT is that of ultimate authority over all life deforming and life destroying powers including death (Luke 7:11-17; John 11:11; Mark 5:35-43). The biblical worldview takes for granted the reality of the unseen world and attributes power and authority to spirits and the spiritual world.

44. In Jesus Christ the kingdom of God was at hand (Matt.4:17, Luke 11:20) making demons "shudder" (James 2:19) because they realized that Christ had come to "destroy the works of the devil." (1 John 3:8; see Col. 2:15). Since numerous biblical healing narratives refer to demons and evil spirits as the cause of disease, exorcism becomes – consequently – one of the most common remedies (Mark 1: 23-28; 5:9; 7:32-35; Luke 4:33-37; Matt. 8:16; John 5:1-8) for diagnosis rules therapy. There is thus indeed a form of healing which in the Bible is presented as a power encounter between Christ and the evil forces, a specific form of the healing mission particularly highlighted in several churches today, especially those with Pentecostal and Charismatic background.

45. Through resurrection and ascension, Christ has overcome all evil powers. In the liturgy, the church celebrates this victory. Through its witness and mission, the church manifests that the powers – all the powers – have been defeated and so stripped of their binding influence on human lives. Those who follow Christ dare in his name to denounce and challenge all other powers, thus bringing good news: "Go, preach, saying, the kingdom of heaven is at hand! Heal the sick, cleanse the lepers, raise the dead, cast out demons!" (Matt.10:7, cf. Mark 16:9-20).

46. This implies that the churches' ministry of proclaiming the gospel has to consciously address and name the powers, taking up the struggle with evil in whatever way it presents itself. These powers are not to be tampered with but recognized, because their reality rests in the hold they have over people who relate to them as the vital coordinates in life.

This issue of relationship between demonology/powers and healing needs careful study. How to interpret the reality and influence of powers in contemporary contexts and cultures is one of the urgent ecumenical debates.[19]

Illness, Healing and Sin. The "Already and Not Yet" of the Kingdom

47. Whereas in Christ evil and sin have been overcome, there are still many disasters, illnesses, deficiencies and diseases (physical, moral, spiritual and social) that seem to deny the arrival of the kingdom of God. The Bible knows the tradition saying that disease or disaster can be divine answer to sin, individual or collective. The prophets have repeatedly challenged God's people to repent from its disobedience to God's word. The New Testament knows of the potential

---

[19] See below, chapter 5.

relation between sin and sickness (1 Cor. 11: 28-34). There is however a strong insistence by Jesus on denying any direct relationship between personal sin and sickness: "Who sinned? This man or his parents?... this is to manifest the power of God." (John 9:2). Similarly, in his answers to questions related to disasters, Jesus leaves open the question of their origin (Luke 13:1-5) and instead points to the urgency of turning back to God and follow the life he offers.

48. Suffering continues in the period between Easter and the end of history. The gospels do not explain this mystery. But the Spirit strengthens the church for its healing and reconciling mission and enables people to cope with continuing suffering and illness in the light of Christ's redemption. Because Christ has paid the price for all sin and brings salvation, no power has final damaging influence on those who put their confidence in God's love manifested in Christ (Rom. 8 : 31 - 39).

49. In the end, Christ will hand over the kingdom to his Father (1 Cor. 15: 24), free of illness, suffering and death. In this kingdom healing will be complete. There is found the common root of healing and salvation (salus). "He will wipe every tear from their eyes. Death will be no more: mourning and crying and pain will be no more" (Rev. 21: 4).

4 THE CHURCH AS A HEALING COMMUNITY

Church, Community and Mission

50. The nature and mission of the church proceeds from the Triune God's own identity and mission with its emphasis on community in which there is sharing in a dynamics of interdependence. It belongs to the very essence of the church – understood as the body of Christ created by the Holy Spirit– to live as a healing community, to recognize and nurture healing charisms and to maintain ministries of healing as visible signs of the presence of the kingdom of God.[20]

51. To be a reconciling and healing community is an essential expression of the mission of the church to create and renew relationships in the perspective of the kingdom of God. This means to proclaim Christ's grace and forgiveness, to heal bodies, minds, souls and to reconcile broken communities in the perspective of fullness of life (John 10:10).

52. It has to be reaffirmed what the document *Mission and Evangelism in Unity today*[21] stated, i.e. that "mission carries a holistic understanding: the proclamation and sharing of the good news of the gospel, by word (*kerygma*), deed (*diakonia*), prayer and worship (*leiturgia*) and the everyday witness of the Christian life (*martyria*); teaching as building up and strengthening people in their relationship with God and each other and healing as wholeness and reconciliation into *koinonia* – communion with God, communion with people and communion with creation as a whole."

---

[20] This refers to congregations, as well as church-related health care institutions and specialized diaconical services.
[21] CWME conference preparatory document No 1.

Healing the Wounds of Church and Mission History

53. When Christian churches speak of the healing ministry as an indispensable element of the body of Christ they must also face their own past and present, sharing a long and often conflictual history with each other. Church splits, rivalry in mission and evangelism, proselytism, exclusions of persons or whole churches for dogmatic reasons, condemnations of different church traditions anathematized as heretical movements, but also inappropriate collaboration between churches and political movements or economic and political powers, have left deep marks and wounds in many parts of the one body of Christ and continue to have a harmful impact on interdenominational relationships. Christians and churches are still in deep need of healing and reconciliation with each other. The agenda of church unity remains an essential part of the healing ministry. The ecumenical movement has indeed been and still is one of the most promising and hope giving instruments for the necessary processes of healing and reconciliation within Christianity. What such processes mean and imply has been described in the document "Mission and the ministry of reconciliation" recommended by the CWME commission in 2004.[22]

The Local Christian Community as a Primary Place for the Healing Ministry

54. The Tübingen consultations in 1964 and 1967[23] affirmed that the local congregation or Christian community is the primary agent for healing. With all the need and legitimacy of specialized Christian institutions like hospitals, primary health services and special healing homes it was emphasized that every Christian community as such - as the body of Christ - has a healing significance and relevance. The way people are received, welcomed and treated in a local community has a deep impact on its healing function. The way a network of mutual support, of listening and of mutual care is maintained and nurtured in a local congregation expresses the healing power of the church as a whole. All basic functions of the local church have a healing dimension also for the wider community: the proclamation of the word of God as a message of hope and comfort, the celebration of the Eucharist as a sign of reconciliation and restoration, the pastoral ministry of each believer, individual or community intercessory prayer for all members and the sick in particular.[24] Each individual member in a local congregation has a unique gift to contribute to the overall healing ministry of the church.

The Charismatic gifts of Healing

55. According to the biblical tradition the Christian community is entrusted by the Holy Spirit with a great variety of spiritual gifts (1 Cor. 12) in which charisms relevant to the healing ministry have a prominent role. All gifts of healing within a

---

[22] CWME conference preparatory document No 10, *op.cit.*

[23] Two consultations held at the German Institute for Medical Mission (Difäm) in Tübingen, Germany, who were at the origin of the creation of the Christian Medical Commission and the health work of the WCC. Cf. *The healing Church. The Tübingen consultation 1964*. Geneva, WCC, 1965, and James C. McGilvray, *The Quest for Health and Wholeness*. Tübingen, Difäm, 1981.

[24] Cf. the excellent chapter on healing community in the CMC document "Healing and Wholeness", *op.cit.* p. 31f.

given community need deliberate encouragement, spiritual nurture, education and enrichment but also a proper ministry of pastoral accompaniment and ecclesial oversight. Charisms are not restricted to the so-called „supernatural" gifts which are beyond common understanding and/or personal world view, but hold to a wider understanding in which both talents and approaches of modern medicine, alternative medical approaches as well as gifts of traditional healing and spiritual forms of healing have their own right. Among the most important means and approaches to healing within Christian tradition mention should be made of

- the gift of praying for the sick and the bereaved
- the gift of laying on of hands
- the gift of blessing
- the gift of anointing with oil
- the gift of confession and repentance
- the gift of consolation
- the gift of forgiveness
- the gift of healing wounded memories
- the gift of healing broken relationships and/or the family tree
- the gift of meditative prayer
- the gift of silent presence
- the gift of listening to each other
- the gift of opposing and casting out evil spirits (ministry of deliverance)
- the gift of prophecy (in the personal and socio-political realms)

The Eucharist as the Christian Healing Event Par Excellence

56. The celebration of the eucharist is considered by the majority of Christians as the most prominent healing gift and unique healing act in the church in all her dimensions. While the essential contribution of the eucharist for healing is not understood in the same manner by all denominational traditions, the sacramental aspect of Christian healing is more deeply appreciated and expressed in many churches today. In the eucharist Christians experience what it means to be brought together and to be made one, constituted again as the body of Christ across social, linguistic and cultural barriers, however not yet across denominational divides. The remaining division between churches, which prevent a common celebration at the Lord's table is the reason why many Christians have difficulties in grasping and experiencing the eucharist as the healing event par excellence.

57. The eucharistic liturgy provides however the setting and visible expression for God's healing presence in the midst of the church and through her in mission to this broken world. The healing dimension of the eucharist is underscored by the tradition reaching back to the early church requesting reconciliation with the brother or sister prior to sharing the sacrament. It is expressed also through the mutual sharing of the peace and forgiveness of sins between God and the believers in the liturgy of confession. Very early evidence is also there for the Christian practice to share the eucharist with the sick and to bring it to homes and hospitals. The body of Christ broken for the suffering world is received as the central gift of God's healing grace. Every eucharistic celebration restores both the community of the church and renews the healing gifts and charisms. According

to ancient sources the liturgical tradition of anointing the sick with oil is rooted in the eucharistic celebration. In both Roman Catholic and Orthodox traditions the oil used for anointing the sick[25] is sanctified by the local bishop in the liturgy of benediction of the oil during Holy Week (chrismation mass), thereby rooting the healing ministry of the church both in the eucharist and in the cross and resurrection of Christ.

The Healing Dimension of Worship in General and Special Healing Services

58. For all Christian denominations and church traditions it holds true that the worshipping community and the worship itself can have a deep healing dimension. Opening oneself in praise and lament to God, joining the others as a community of believers, being liberated from guilt and burdens of life, experiencing even unbelievable cures, being enflamed by the experience of singing and of praise are a tremendously healing experience. It must however also be acknowledged that this can never be taken for granted. Inappropriate forms of Christian worship including triumphalistic "healing services" in which the healer is glorified at the expense of God and where false expectations are raised, can deeply hurt and harm people. In many places, still, special monthly or weekly services are experienced as authentic witness to God's healing power and care. Indeed, in such worship, explicit recognition is given to the needs of those seeking healing from experiences of loss, of fragmentation, of despair or physical illness. In many church traditions worship events combine the eucharist with the ritual of personal prayer for the sick and the laying on of hands and are an appropriate response both to the mandate of the church and the longing for healing within the population. The contribution of Pentecostalism and the charismatic movement both within and outside the historical churches to the contemporary renewal of the understanding of the healing dimension of worship and of mission in general has to be acknowledged in this context.

Deepening a Common Understanding of a Christian Healing Spirituality

59. It is clear for all Christian traditions that Christian healing ministries cannot be seen as mere techniques and professional skills or certain rituals. All of them depend on a Christian spirituality and discipline which influences all spheres of personal as well as professional life. Such spirituality depends on faith in God, following Christ's footsteps, on how the body is treated, how the limitations of space and time are dealt with, how pain and sickness are coped with , how one eats and fasts, prays and meditates visits the sick, helps the needy and keeps silence in openness to God's Spirit. There is a need for discernment as to what constitutes authentic Christian spirituality. There exist theologies and forms of Christian practice that do not contribute to healing. Distorted forms of spirituality or piety can lead to unhealthy lives and questionable relationship with God and fellow human beings.

---

[25] It was only in the middle ages that they were narrowed down to a sacramental sign reserved to the dying as "extreme unction".

The Ordained and the Laity in the Healing Ministry

60. In many congregations it can be observed that only ordained people are allowed to extend signs of blessing and prayers of healing for people who are in need. Biblical evidence reminds us however that the Spirit and the Spirit's gifts have been promised to all members of the people of God (Acts 2:17, 1 Cor. 12:3 ff) and that every member of the church is called to participate in the healing ministry. Churches are encouraged to support the gifts and potentials particularly of lay people both in local congregations as well as in health care institutions. Empowering people to act as ambassadors of the healing ministry is an essential task of both the ordained ministers and deacons in the church as well as the Christian professionals working in various health related institutions.

61. How each church can best recognize the mandate of the local community, express the responsibility of the ordained ministry and of lay people in the healing ministry, depends on its own tradition and structure. For example, the Church of England has appointed in many places a healing advisor on the level of the diocese. This minister is responsible for encouragement, education and also spiritual and pastoral advice for emerging healing ministries in cooperation with the regional bishop. The healing ministry of the church thereby receives a visible recognition and support in the church as a whole instead of just being delegated to specialized institutions or restricted to the local situation.

The Need for Educating Christians for the Healing Ministry – integration *versus* Compartmentalization

62. There is a growing consensus that education for the different forms of Christian healing ministry is not as widespread and developed as it ought to be in the various sectors of church life. Explicit teaching on a Christian understanding of healing in many programmes of theological education is absent or still underdeveloped. However recently efforts have been made to include HIV/AIDS in the curricula of institutions of theological education in Africa. But many training and educational programmes are taking place only within the different fields of specialized competence. Nurses, doctors, diaconal workers are educated within their own professional fields. There is no interaction between different education programmes and fields of competencies, and there is a lack to introduce issues and basic themes of Christian healing within the mainline stream of ministerial and adult education in general.

The Healing Ministry of the Community and Healing Professions

63. The deliberations of the consultations at Tübingen in 1964 and 1967 and the setting up of the CMC in 1968, with the development of the concept of Primary Health Care (PHC) in the 1980s created a PHC movement that began with great hope for change, but has not been sustained. The divide created between high technology based medicine on the one hand and primary health care on the other has been detrimental to the struggle for a better and healthier world. While committed Christian professionals developed outstanding programmes in

primary health care, the congregational involvement in the PHC movement was patchy and minimal. Though the access and justice issues were addressed to some extent in that movement, the spiritual aspects were not addressed appropriately. Traditional systems of medicine in many countries have been unnecessarily condemned by the modern allopathic system of medicine and have developed in isolation and in competition to it, creating problems of relation between Christian communities and traditional health specialists.

64. Additional dramatic changes in society and health systems have brought increased tensions in recent years for many of those who are working within the established medical systems, in particular in industrialized countries and centres. Increasing pressures to rationalize health care, to reduce costs and medical personnel tend to prevent doctors, nurses and assistants to relate to a holistic approach in health and healing. At the same time, the need for addressing the whole person in health care has become more than obvious in many parts of the world. How medical personnel will be able to respond to these contradictory requests remains an open question. It is encouraging to discern signs and signals of a new quest and openness for cooperation with religious organizations, particularly Christian churches, in many secular institutions of the established health system.

65. Christian churches should be open and receptive to listen and learn from the situation of those facing the ever more growing contradictions and shortcomings within the established medical systems.

The health professionals on their part should recognize that health issues move beyond the individual to the community which is a social network with many resources and skills that can promote health. Health professionals are challenged to see themselves as part of a broader network of healing disciplines that include the medical, technical, social and psychological sciences, as well as religions and traditional approaches to healing. This wider view will help the professionals to integrate suffering into the concept of health and enable people with incurable physical problems to be healed persons. It will also encourage the health professionals to share information with and empower the patient to feel responsible and take decisions for their own health.

66. The primary health care approach in the community should be backed by adequate secondary and tertiary care facilities. The referral system should be reciprocal and mutually supportive.

Healing Ministry and Advocacy

67. While this document concentrates on the medical and spiritual aspects of the healing ministry, it acknowledges that there exists a wider definition of healing which includes efforts of persons, movements, societies and churches for fundamental transformation of structures which produce poverty, exploitation, harm and sickness or illness. The earlier CMC study of 1990[26] is still considered

---

[26] *Healing and Wholeness, op.cit.*

a valid guideline for that wider aspect of the healing ministry, which gained even more urgency with the HIV/AIDS pandemic. The 1990 document considers health to be a justice issue, an issue of peace, and an issue related to the integrity of creation. Consequently it requests a healing congregation to "take the healing ministry into the political, social and economic arenas:

- advocating the elimination of oppression, racism and injustice,
- supporting peoples' struggle for liberation
- joining others of goodwill in growing together in social awareness,
- creating public opinion in support of the struggle for justice in health". [27]

68. All Christians, especially those active in healing ministries and in medical professions, those gifted with the charisms of prophecy, are called to be advocates for such a holistic approach on national and international political scenes. Because of their specific competence and experience, they bear a special responsibility to speak with and on behalf of the marginalized and the underprivileged and contribute to strengthen advocacy networks and campaigns to put pressure on international organizations, governments, industries and research institutions, so that the present scandalous handling of resources be fundamentally challenged and modified.

Training

69. Because of all these aspects of the church's mission in terms of health and care, training for medical and health professionals will be a key area for appropriate action. Congregations and those who work in the pastoral areas too need training on the holistic approaches to health and the specific contributions they can make as alluded to in this document.

70. The challenge is for Christians to continue to engage communities- in such a way as to incorporate the pedagogy of healing in the church, so as to

- Motivate and mobilize communities to identify the core issues of ill health, to own the issues and to take effective action
- Identify with the holistic understanding of the healing ministry in the gospel
- Work with wider societies to bring about difference in peoples health and life

5 OPEN QUESTIONS AND NECESSARY DEBATES

71. This chapter contains items on which there is ongoing debate among Christians from different denominational traditions and/or cultural backgrounds. This does not mean that all affirmations below are contested. But the scope and consequences of some are subject of debate.

---

[26] *Healing and Wholeness, op.cit.*
[27] *Ibid.*, p. 32.

All Healing Comes from God
Christian Healing, Spirituality and non-Christian Healing Practices

72. That all healing comes from God is a conviction shared by most if not all Christian traditions[28]. There is however a debate as to the consequence of such an affirmation for the approach of people and traditions or healing practices of other religions.

73. Affirming the presence of God's healing energies at work in the whole of creation, thanks and praise should be given for all different means, approaches and traditions which contribute to the healing of human persons, communities as well as creation, by reinforcing their healing potentials.

74. In many contexts where a strong longing for healing is felt both within as well as outside the Christian churches the question of Christian openness towards and reliance on healing practices rooted in other religions (such as various traditional religious medicinal approaches, but also Yoga, Reiki, *Shiatsu*, Zen-Meditation etc.) is however much debated within churches and Christian health related institutions. To what extent is Christian healing spirituality compatible with healing practices from other religions? Are those reconcilable and in harmony with basic principles of Christian spirituality?

75. Christian spirituality should show openness to all means of healing offered as part of God's ongoing creation. At the same time there are healing practices which associate themselves with a religious worldview which can be in contrast to basic Christian principles, and some Christians are particularly attentive to such dangers. For other Christians still, caution is requested, because evil spiritual powers might disguise their destroying effect behind apparently beneficial healing practices.

76. No healing practice is just neutral. It needs critical theological assessment. This is not to say that any Yoga or Reiki practices, for example, have no place in Christian parish centres. They can be practised, many Christians in the West believe, in ways which do not lead to a dissolution or fundamental distortion of Christian faith and the Christian community. The church has always been aware that God can reveal aspects of how creation works and contributes to healing through peoples of other languages, cultures and even religious traditions and this also applies to the realm of medical treatment, alternative medicine and alternative healing practices.

77. But caution or even explicit rejection are recommended wherever
   - religious dependency is created on the healer or Guru,
   - absolute spiritual, social or economic obedience is demanded,
   - human beings are kept in a spirit of threat, anxiety or bondage due to healing practices,
   - the success of a healing is made dependant on fundamental changes in the religious worldview of Christians.

---

[28] cf. *IRM* July-October 2004, *op.cit.* (dialogue with Pentecostals); cf. also LWF mission statement, *op.cit.*, p. 39. The affirmation that all healing comes from God is already to be found in the documents resulting from the Tübingen consultation of 1964, cf. *The Healing Church*, *op.cit.* p. 36.

78. As the biblical tradition shows, Christians are invited and commissioned to test everything, hold on to the good and abstain from every kind of evil (1 Thessalonians 5: 21-22). When encountering practices of healing and energetic therapeutic work rooted in other religions, Christians should always first of all feel encouraged to rediscover the rich diversity and ancient spiritual traditions of healing within the Christian church itself.

Debate on the Concepts of Demonology and Power Encounter

79. Traditionally, the term "demonology" in Christian theology has been part of the doctrine of angels (angelology). Demons/demonic powers denote the "dark" side of the spiritual reality. The term "power[s]" in theological and ecumenical discourse is used in more than one way. Often and in particular in ecumenical circles it is used in relation to political violence and oppressive social structures.

80. Among Pentecostal-Charismatic Christians – but also beyond, among those who continue in the tradition of classical Christianity – the term "powers" usually mean spiritual powers, evil spirits, demons. Consequently "power encounter" is understood as an encounter between the (spiritual) power of God and other gods/ spiritual realities. These Christians believe that the true God will show off God's power over others. While it is important that such dialogue does not simplify the complex intricacies of spirit worlds thriving in – and alongside – the age of post-modernism it should at the same time resist any attempt to turn the Holy Spirit into a powerful means to an end as if the church had to vindicate God.[29] The church is to witness for the living God. The church's task is not to prove God right.

81. An ecumenical challenge to the churches is to acknowledge the various meanings assigned to the talk about powers and try to resist reductionism. While the traditional way of relating "powers" to spiritual forces seems to be the primary biblical connotation, the understanding of powers in terms of social and political realities is also present in the Bible (cf. e.g. the temptation story in Matt. 4:1-11 and Luke 4: 1-13) and may be seen as a legitimate interpretation of the Christian message.

82. The Pentecostal-Charismatic interest in power encounter poses serious challenges and can be subject to theological and pastoral concerns. The idea of "power encounter" as explained above may lead to a triumphalistic, aggressive presentation of the gospel. In some cases, "spirits" are attributed influence and power beyond what appear to be appropriate theologically, blurring the meaning of individual and collective responsibility.

83. This being the case demonology and exorcisms present cognitive and spiritual challenges to those churches whose frame of reference and theology is shaped by a post Enlightenment scientific rationality as is that world-view to the one explaining events through referring to spiritual beings. An appropriate intercultural and ecumenical dialogue for the sake of the churches' ministry of healing as a whole seems urgent.

---

[29] God vindicates the church instead: Mt. 10:19-20; Lk. 21:15; Mk. 13:11.

Sharing Resources and Insights in Christian Healing within the Ecumenical Fellowship

84. Many church traditions have their own rich insights and liturgical as well as theological treasures and can contribute to a holistic understanding and new appreciation of the Christian ministry of health and healing today. The Anglican, Orthodox and Roman Catholic traditions offer distinct and different healing liturgies. It is encouraged to make these known among other denominations and traditions and to share such formulas which exist within the ecumenical community of churches.

Study and Dialogue on Demonology

85. It would be a worthwhile task for the WCC mission desk to initiate a wide scale study process on the topic of demonology and powers since, as mentioned, it is a topic that Christians and Christian communities are tackling in their everyday life. One part of the study task would be to consider the issue of rehabilitating the office of exorcist as Christian ministry in those church traditions where it does not exist.

Ecumenical Initiative on Healing Spirituality

86. It could be well considered whether for the years to come an ecumenical initiative is needed to deepen the Christian healing spirituality and to encourage related formation courses for voluntary workers, professional health care workers and ordained ministers.

The need for round tables on the future of health, spirituality and healing

87. Established institutions of health care in many countries are in a process of transformation and institutional crisis, partly due to economic factors and financial instability, lack of proper management and leadership, rising costs of high technology medicine, changed patterns in the behaviour of patients, lack of compliance of the patients and the demographic imbalances in many Western societies. Historically speaking Christian mission had played a pioneering role in bringing about and shaping the health systems in many countries of the South. It also has a responsibility in contributing to overcoming the crisis of the established institutions of health care at the beginning of the 21st century. In accordance with the tradition of the Christian Medical Commission and recent proposals[30] it is recommended that the various Christian medical commissions and associations existent in the different regions of the world join hands and establish interdisciplinary dialogue forums on the future of health care and health systems both in the West as well as in the South. Ways of exchanging and strengthening the collaboration between the various regional Christian medical associations should be sought in order to give new profile to the Christian ministry of healing and make it more visible and effective before the eyes of the world.

---

[30] cf. results of the consultation held in Hamburg in 2000, published in *IRM*, Vol. XC, Nos 356/357, January/April 2001, on the theme "Health, Faith and Healing".

Preparatory paper No. 13

Religious Plurality and Christian Self-Understanding

Introduction

The present document is the result of a study process started in response to strong suggestions made during the 2002 meeting of the WCC Central Committee to the three staff teams on Faith & Order, Interreligious Relations, Mission & Evangelism and their respective commissions or advisory bodies. The question of the theological approach to religious plurality had been on the agenda of the WCC many times, reaching some consensus in 1989 and in 1990.[1] In recent years, it was felt that a new approach to this difficult and controversial issue was needed.

Some 20 scholars from different contexts and denominations, specialized in religious studies, missiology or systematic theology and linked to the three mentioned WCC networks met for a first brain-storming consultation in Bossey, Switzerland, in October 2003. On the basis of their discussions, a small editorial group established a first document in March 2004. Intensive further drafting work prepared the way for the final consultation in October 2004, again in Bossey, during which the theological paper was revised for wide distribution as a discussion paper.

The document is the fruit of a good cooperation between scholars participating in the work of Faith & Order, Interreligious Relations and Mission & Evangelism. Such a collaboration is quite unique in the recent history of the ecumenical movement.

It must be emphasized that the paper has so far not been submitted to any governing or advisory body of the WCC and does not represent a position adopted by the Faith and Order Commission, the Commission on World Mission and Evangelism or the Reference Group on Interreligious Relations and Dialogue. It is shared as a document for discussion and debate and does not pretend to contain a final or ecumenically agreed wisdom on the issue of Christian self-understanding in a religiously plural world.

The three programme staff persons who accompanied the process:

Jacques Matthey
Mission & Evangelism

Hans Ucko
Interreligious Relations
& Dialogue

Kersten Storch
Faith & Order

---

[1] For the world mission conference of 1989, cf. F.R.Wilson, ed., *The San Antonio Report*, Geneva, WCC, 1990, in particular pp. 31-33. For the 1990 consultation in Baar, Switzerland, see *Current Dialogue* No. 19, January 1991, pp. 47-51.

Religious Plurality and Christian Self-Understanding

Preamble

"The earth is the Lord's and all that is in it, the world and those who live in it."
(Ps. 24:1)

"For from the rising of the sun to its setting my name is great among the nations, and in every place incense is offered to my name, and a pure offering; for my name is great among the nations, says the Lord of hosts." (Mal. 1:11)

"Then Peter began to speak to them: I truly understand that God shows no partiality, but in every nation anyone who fears him and does what is right is acceptable to him." (Acts 10:34-35)

1. What do the experiences of the psalmist, the prophet, and Peter mean for us today? What does it mean to affirm our faith in Jesus Christ joyfully, and yet seek to discern God's presence and activity in the world? How do we understand such affirmations in a religiously plural world?

I. The Challenge of Plurality

2. Today Christians in almost all parts of the world live in religiously plural societies. Persistent plurality and its impact on their daily lives are forcing them to seek new and adequate ways of understanding and relating to peoples of other religious traditions. The rise of religious extremism and militancy in many situations has accentuated the importance of interreligious relations. Religious identities, loyalties, and sentiments have become important components in so many international and inter-ethnic conflicts that some say that the "politics of ideology," which played a crucial role in the twentieth century, has been replaced in our day by the "politics of identity".

3. All religious communities are being reshaped by new encounters and relationships. Globalization of political, economic and even religious life brings new pressures on communities that have been in geographical or social isolation. There is greater awareness of the interdependence of human life, and of the need to collaborate across religious barriers in dealing with the pressing problems of the world. All religious traditions, therefore, are challenged to contribute to the emergence of a global community that would live in mutual respect and peace. At stake is the credibility of religious traditions as forces that can bring justice, peace and healing to a broken world.

4. Most religious traditions, however, have their own history of compromise with political power and privilege and of complicity in violence that has marred human history. Christianity, for instance, has been, on the one hand, a force that brought the message of God's unconditional love for and acceptance of all people. On the other hand, its history, sadly, is also marked by persecutions, crusades, insensitivity

to indigenous cultures and complicity with imperial and colonial designs. In fact, such ambiguity and compromise with power and privilege is part of the history of all religious traditions, cautioning us against a romantic attitude towards them. Further, most religious traditions exhibit enormous internal diversity attended by painful divisions and disputes.

5. Today these internal disputes have to be seen in the light of the need to promote mutual understanding and peace among the religions. Given the context of increased polarization of communities, the prevalent climate of fear and the culture of violence that has gripped our world, the mission of bringing healing and wholeness to the fractured human community is the greatest challenge that faces the religious traditions in our day.

The Changing Context of the Christian Faith

6. The global religious situation is also in flux. In some parts of the Western world, the institutional expressions of Christianity are in decline. New forms of religious commitment emerge as people increasingly separate personal faith from institutional belonging. The search for authentic spirituality in the context of a secular way of life presents new challenges to the churches. Further, peoples of other traditions, like Hindus, Muslims, Buddhists, Sikhs etc., who have increasingly moved into these areas, as minorities, often experience the need to be in dialogue with the majority community. This challenges Christians to be able to articulate their faith in ways that are meaningful both to them and their neighbours; dialogue presupposes both faith commitment and the capacity to articulate it in word and deed.

7. At the same time, Christianity, especially in its evangelical and Pentecostal manifestations, is growing rapidly in some regions of the world. In some of the other regions, Christianity is undergoing radical changes as Christians embrace new and vibrant forms of church life and enter into new relationships with indigenous cultures. While Christianity appears to be on the decline in some parts of the world, it has become a dynamic force in others.

8. These changes require us to be more attentive than before to our relationship with other religious communities. They challenge us to acknowledge "others" in their differences, to welcome strangers even if their "strangeness" sometimes threatens us, and to seek reconciliation even with those who have declared themselves our enemies. In other words, we are being challenged to develop a spiritual climate and a theological approach that contributes to creative and positive relationships among the religious traditions of the world.

9. The cultural and doctrinal differences among religious traditions, however, have always made interreligious dialogue difficult. This is now aggravated by the tensions and animosities generated by global conflicts and mutual suspicions and fears. Further, the impression that Christians have turned to dialogue as a new tool for their mission, and the controversies over "conversion" and "religious freedom" have not abated. Therefore dialogue, reconciliation and peace-building across the religious divides have become urgent, yet they are never achieved

through isolated events or programmes. They involve a long and difficult process sustained by faith, courage and hope.

The Pastoral and Faith Dimensions of the Question

10. There is a pastoral need to equip Christians to live in a religiously plural world. Many Christians seek ways to be committed to their own faith and yet to be open to the others. Some use spiritual disciplines from other religious traditions to deepen their Christian faith and prayer life. Still others find in other religious traditions an additional spiritual home and speak of the possibility of "double belonging". Many Christians ask for guidance to deal with interfaith marriages, the call to pray with others, and the need to deal with militancy and extremism. Others seek for guidance as they work together with neighbours of other religious traditions on issues of justice and peace. Religious plurality and its implications now affect our day-to-day lives.

11. As Christians we seek to build a new relationship with other religious traditions because we believe it to be intrinsic to the gospel message and inherent to our mission as co-workers with God in healing the world. Therefore the mystery of God's relationship to all God's people, and the many ways in which peoples have responded to this mystery, invite us to explore more fully the reality of other religious traditions and our own identity as Christians in a religiously plural world.

II. Religious Traditions as Spiritual Journeys

The Christian Journey

12. It is common to speak of religious traditions being "spiritual journeys." Christianity's spiritual journey has enriched and shaped its development into a religious tradition. It emerged initially in a predominantly Jewish-Hellenistic culture. Christians have had the experience of being "strangers", and of being persecuted minorities struggling to define themselves in the midst of dominant religious and cultural forces. And as Christianity grew into a world religion, it has become internally diversified, transformed by the many cultures with which it came into contact.

13. In the East, the Orthodox churches have throughout their history been involved in a complex process of cultural engagement and discernment, maintaining and transmitting the Orthodox faith through integration of select cultural aspects over the centuries. On the other hand, the Orthodox churches have also struggled to resist the temptation towards syncretism. In the West, having become the religious tradition of a powerful empire, Christianity has at times been a persecuting majority. It also became the "host" culture, shaping European civilization in many positive ways. At the same time it has had a troubled history in its relationship with Judaism, Islam and indigenous traditions.

14. The Reformation transformed the face of Western Christianity, introducing Protestantism with its proliferation of confessions and denominations, while the Enlightenment brought about a cultural revolution with the emergence of modernity, secularization, individualism, and the separation of church and state. Missionary expansions into Asia, Africa, Latin America and other parts of the world raised questions about the indigenization and inculturation of the gospel. The encounter between the rich spiritual heritage of the Asian religions and the African Traditional Religions resulted in the emergence of theological traditions based on the cultural and religious heritages of these regions. The rise of charismatic and Pentecostal churches in all parts of the world has added yet a new dimension to Christianity.

15. In short, the "spiritual journey" of Christianity has made it a very complex worldwide religious tradition. As Christianity seeks to live among cultures, religions and philosophic traditions and attempts to respond to the present and future challenges, it will continue to be transformed. It is in this context, of a Christianity that has been and is changing, that we need a theological response to plurality.

Religions, Identities and Cultures

16. Other religious traditions have also lived through similar challenges in their development. There is no one expression of Judaism, Islam, Hinduism, Buddhism etc. As these religions journeyed out of their lands of origin, they too have been shaped by the encounters with the cultures they moved into, transforming and being transformed by them. Most of the major religious traditions today have had the experience of being cultural "hosts" to other religious traditions, and of being "hosted" by cultures shaped by religious traditions other than their own. This means that the identities of religious communities and of individuals within them are never static, but fluid and dynamic. No religion is totally unaffected by its interaction with other religious traditions. Increasingly it has become rather misleading even to talk of "religions" as such, and of "Judaism", "Christianity", "Islam", "Hinduism", "Buddhism" etc., as if they were static, undifferentiated wholes.

17. These realities raise several spiritual and theological issues. What is the relationship between "religion" and "culture"? What is the nature of the influence they have on one another? What theological sense can we make of religious plurality? What resources within our own tradition can help us deal with these questions? We have the rich heritage of the modern ecumenical movement's struggle with these questions to help us in our exploration.

III. Continuing an Ongoing Exploration

The Ecumenical Journey

18. From the very beginnings of the church, Christians have believed that the message of God's love witnessed to in Christ needs to be shared with others. It is

in the course of sharing this message, especially in Asia and Africa that the modern ecumenical movement had to face the question of God's presence among people of other traditions. Is God's revelation present in other religions and cultures? Is the Christian revelation in "continuity" with the religious life of others, or is it "discontinuous", bringing in a whole new dimension of knowledge of God? These were difficult questions and Christians remain divided over the issue.

19. The **dialogue programme** of the World Council of Churches (WCC) has emphasized the importance of respecting the reality of other religious traditions and affirming their distinctiveness and identity. It has also brought into focus the need to collaborate with others in the search for a just and peaceful world. There is also greater awareness of how our ways of speaking about our and other religious traditions can lead to confrontations and conflicts. On the one hand, religious traditions make universal truth claims. On the other hand, these claims by implication may be in conflict with the truth claims of others. These realizations, and actual experiences of relationships between peoples of different traditions in local situations, opened the way for Christians to speak of our relationship with others in terms of "dialogue". Yet there are many questions awaiting further exploration. What does it mean to be in dialogue when the communities concerned are in conflict? How does one deal with the perceived conflict between conversion and religious freedom? How do we deal with the deep differences among faith communities over the relationship of religious traditions to ethnicity, cultural practices, and the state?

20. Within the discussions in the **Commission on World Mission and Evangelism** (CWME) of the WCC the exploration of the nature of the missionary mandate and its implications in a world of diverse religions, cultures, and ideologies have drawn on the concept of *missio Dei*, God's own salvific mission in the world, even preceding human witness, in which we are in Christ called to participate. Several issues of CWME's agenda interact with the present study on religious plurality: What is the relation between cooperation with people of other religious traditions (for justice and peace), involvement in interreligious dialogue, and the evangelistic mandate of the church? What are the consequences of the intrinsic relation between cultures and religions for the inculturation approach in mission? What are the implications for interfaith relations if mission focuses, as the 2005 Conference on World Mission and Evangelism suggests, on building healing and reconciling communities?

21. The WCC's **Plenary Commission on Faith and Order**, meeting for the first time in a Muslim-majority country (in Kuala Lumpur, Malaysia, 2004) spoke of the "journey of faith" as one inspired by the vision of "receiving one another". The Commission asked: How do the churches pursue the goal of visible Christian unity within today's increasingly multi-religious context? How can the search for visible unity among the churches be an effective sign for reconciliation in society as a whole? To what extent are questions of ethnic and national identity affected by religious identities, and vice versa? The Commission also explored broader questions arising in multi-religious contexts: what are the challenges which Christians face in seeking an authentic Christian theology that is "hospitable" to

others? What are the limits to diversity? Are there valid signs of salvation beyond the church? How do insights from other traditions contribute to our understanding of what it means to be human?

22. It is significant that all three programmatic streams of the WCC converge in dealing with questions that are relevant for a theology of religions. In fact, attempts have been made in recent conferences to deal with, and formulate, positions that take the discussions forward.

Recent Developments

23. In its search for consensus among Christians about God's saving presence in the religious life of our neighbours, the world mission conference in San Antonio (1989) summed up the position that the WCC has been able to affirm: "We cannot point to any other way of salvation than Jesus Christ; at the same time we cannot set limits to the saving power of God." Recognizing the tension between such a statement and the affirmation of God's presence and work in the life of peoples of other faith traditions, the San Antonio report said that, "we appreciate this tension, and do not attempt to resolve it." The question following the conference was whether the ecumenical movement should remain with these modest words as an expression of theological humility, or whether it should deal with that tension in finding new and creative formulations in a theology of religions.

24. In an attempt to go beyond San Antonio, a WCC consultation on theology of religions in Baar, Switzerland (1990) produced an important statement, drawing out the implications of the Christian belief that God is active as creator and sustainer in the religious life of all peoples: "This conviction that God as creator of all is present and active in the plurality of religions makes it inconceivable to us that God's saving activity could be confined to any one continent, cultural type, or group of people. A refusal to take seriously the many and diverse religious testimonies to be found among the nations and peoples of the whole world amounts to disowning the biblical testimony to God as creator of all things and Father of humankind."

25. Hence, developments in Mission and Evangelism, Faith and Order, and the Dialogue streams of the WCC encourage us to reopen the question of the theology of religions today. Such an inquiry has become an urgent theological and pastoral necessity. The theme of the 9th WCC assembly, "God in your grace, transform the world", also calls for such an exploration.

IV. Towards a Theology of Religions

26. What would a theology of religions look like today? Many theologies of religions have been proposed. The many streams of thinking within the scriptures make our task challenging. While recognizing the diversity of the scriptural witness, we choose the theme of "hospitality" as a hermeneutical key and an entry point for our discussion.

Celebrating the Hospitality of a Gracious God

27. Our theological understanding of religious plurality begins with our faith in the one God who created all things, the living God present and active in all creation from the beginning. The Bible testifies to God as God of all nations and peoples, whose love and compassion includes all humankind. We see in the covenant with Noah a covenant with all creation that has never been broken. We see God's wisdom and justice extending to the ends of the earth, as God guides the nations through their traditions of wisdom and understanding. God's glory penetrates the whole of creation. The Hebrew Bible witnesses to the universal saving presence of God throughout human history through the Word or Wisdom and the Spirit.

28. In the New Testament, the incarnation of the Word of God is spoken of by St. Paul in terms of hospitality and of a life turned toward the 'other.' Paul proclaims, in doxological language, that "though he (Christ) was in the form of God he did not regard equality with God as something to be exploited, but emptied himself, taking the form of a slave, being born in human likeness. And being found in human form he humbled himself and became obedient to the point of death – even death on a cross" (Phil. 2:6-8). The self-emptying of Christ, and his readiness to assume our humanity, is at the heart of the confession of our faith. The mystery of the incarnation is God's deepest identification with our human condition, showing the unconditional grace of God that accepted humankind in its otherness and estrangement. Paul's hymn moves on to celebrate the risen Christ: "Therefore God has highly exalted him, and given him the name that is above every name" (Phil. 2: 9). This has led Christians to confess Jesus Christ as the one in whom the entire human family has been united to God in an irrevocable bond and covenant.

29. This grace of God shown in Jesus Christ calls us to an attitude of hospitality in our relationship to others. Paul prefaces the hymn by saying, "Let the same mind be in you that was in Christ Jesus" (Phil. 2: 5). Our hospitality involves self-emptying, and in receiving others in unconditional love we participate in the pattern of God's redeeming love. Indeed our hospitality is not limited to those in our own community; the gospel commands us to love even our enemies and to call for blessings upon them (Matt.5: 43-48; Rom.12: 14). As Christians, therefore, we need to search for the right balance between our identity in Christ and our openness to others in kenotic love that comes out of that very identity.

30. In his public ministry, Jesus not only healed people who were part of his own tradition but also responded to the great faith of the Canaanite woman and the Roman centurion (Matt. 15: 21-28; 8: 5-11). Jesus chose a "stranger", the Samaritan, to demonstrate the fulfilling of the commandment to love one's neighbour through compassion and hospitality. Since the gospels present Jesus' encounter with those of other faiths as incidental, and not as part of his main ministry, these stories do not provide us with the necessary information to draw clear conclusions regarding any theology of religions. But they do present Jesus as one whose hospitality extended to all who were in need of love and acceptance. Matthew's narrative of Jesus' parable of the last judgment goes further to identify openness to the victims of society, hospitality to strangers and acceptance of the

other as unexpected ways of being in communion with the risen Christ (25: 31-46).

31. It is significant that while Jesus extended hospitality to those at the margins of society he himself had to face rejection and was often in need of hospitality. Jesus' acceptance of the peoples at the margins, as well as his own experience of rejection has provided the inspiration for those who show solidarity in our day with the poor, the despised and the rejected. Thus the biblical understanding of hospitality goes well beyond the popular notion of extending help and showing generosity toward others. The Bible speaks of hospitality primarily as a radical openness to others based on the affirmation of the dignity of all. We draw our inspiration both from Jesus' example and his command that we love our neighbours.

32. The Holy Spirit helps us to live out Christ's openness to others. The person of the Holy Spirit moved and still moves over the face of the earth to create, nurture and sustain, to challenge, renew and transform. We confess that the activity of the Spirit passes beyond our definitions, descriptions, and limitations in the manner of the wind that "blows where it wills" (John 3:8). Our hope and expectancy are rooted in our belief that the "economy" of the Spirit relates to the whole creation. We discern the Spirit of God moving in ways that we cannot predict. We see the nurturing power of the Holy Spirit working within, inspiring human beings in their universal longing for, and seeking after, truth, peace and justice (Rom. 8:18-27). "Love, joy, peace, patience, kindness, goodness, faithfulness, gentleness, self-control", wherever they are found, are the fruit of the Spirit (Gal. 5:22-23, cf. Rom. 14:17).

33. We believe that this encompassing work of the Holy Spirit is also present in the life and traditions of peoples of living faith. People have at all times and in all places responded to the presence and activity of God among them, and have given their witness to their encounters with the living God. In this testimony they speak both of seeking and of having found wholeness, or enlightenment, or divine guidance, or rest, or liberation. This is the context in which we as Christians testify to the salvation we have experienced through Christ. This ministry of witness among our neighbours of other faiths must presuppose an "affirmation of what God has done and is doing among them" (CWME San Antonio 1989).

34. We see the plurality of religious traditions as both the result of the manifold ways in which God has related to peoples and nations as well as a manifestation of the richness and diversity of human response to God's gracious gifts. It is our Christian faith in God, which challenges us to take seriously the whole realm of religious plurality, always using the gift of discernment. Seeking to develop new and greater understandings of "the wisdom, love and power which God has given to men (and women) of other faiths" (New Delhi Report, 1961), we must affirm our "openness to the possibility that the God we know in Jesus Christ may encounter us also in the lives of our neighbours of other faiths" (CWME San Antonio 1989). We also believe that the Holy Spirit, the Spirit of Truth, will lead us to understand anew the deposit of the faith already given to us, and into fresh and unforeseen insight into the divine mystery, as we learn more from our neighbours of other faiths.

35.   Thus, it is our faith in the Trinitarian God, God who is diversity in unity, God who creates, brings wholeness and nurtures and nourishes all life, which helps us in our hospitality of openness to all. We have been the recipients of God's generous hospitality of love. We cannot do otherwise.

V. The Call to Hospitality

36. How should Christians respond in light of the generosity and graciousness of God? "Do not neglect to show hospitality to strangers, for by doing that some have entertained angels without knowing it" (Heb. 13: 2). In today's context the "stranger" includes not only the people unknown to us, the poor and the exploited, but also those who are ethnically, culturally and religiously "others" to us. The word "stranger" in the scriptures does not intend to objectify the "other" but recognizes that there are people who are indeed "strangers" to us in their culture, religion, race and other kinds of diversities that are part of the human community. Our willingness to accept others in their "otherness" is the hallmark of true hospitality. Through our openness to the "other" we may encounter God in new ways. Hospitality, thus, is both the fulfilment of the commandment to "love our neighbours as ourselves" and an opportunity to discover God anew.

37. Hospitality also pertains to how we treat each other within the Christian family; sometimes we are as much strangers to each other as we are to those outside our community. Because of the changing world context, especially increased mobility and population movements, sometimes we are the "hosts" to others, and at other times we become the "guests" receiving the hospitality of others; sometimes we receive "strangers" and at other times we become the "strangers" in the midst of others. Indeed we may need to move to an understanding of hospitality as "mutual openness" that transcends the distinctions of "hosts" and "guests".

38. Hospitality is not just an easy or simple way of relating to others. It is often not only an opportunity but also a risk. In situations of political or religious tension acts of hospitality may require great courage, especially when extended to those who deeply disagree with us or even consider us as their enemy. Further, dialogue is very difficult when there are inequalities between parties, distorted power relations or hidden agendas. One may also at times feel obliged to question the deeply held beliefs of the very people whom one has offered hospitality to or received hospitality from, and to have one's own beliefs be challenged in return.

The Power of Mutual Transformation

39. Christians have not only learned to co-exist with people of other religious traditions, but have also been transformed by their encounters. We have discovered unknown aspects of God's presence in the world, and uncovered neglected elements of our own Christian traditions. We have also become more conscious of the many passages in the Bible that call us to be more responsive to others.

40. Practical hospitality and a welcoming attitude to strangers create the space for mutual transformation and even reconciliation. Such reciprocity is exemplified in

the story of the meeting between Abraham, the father of faith, and Melchizedek, the non-Israelite king of Salem (Gen. 14). Abraham received the blessing of Melchizedek, who is described as a priest of "God Most High". The story suggests that through this encounter Abraham's understanding of the nature of the deity who had led him and his family from Ur and Harran was renewed and expanded.

41. Mutual transformation is also seen in Luke's narrative of the encounter between Peter and Cornelius in the Acts of the Apostles. The Holy Spirit accomplished a transformation in Peter's self-understanding through his vision and subsequent interaction with Cornelius. This led him to confess that, "God shows no partiality, but in every nation anyone who fears him and does what is right is acceptable to him" (10: 34-35). In this case, Cornelius the "stranger" becomes an instrument of Peter's transformation, even as Peter becomes an instrument of transformation of Cornelius and his household. While this story is not primarily about interfaith relations, it sheds light on how God can lead us beyond the confines of our self-understanding in encounter with others.

42. So one can draw consequences from these examples, and from such rich experiences in daily life, for a vision of mutual hospitality among peoples of different religious traditions. From the Christian perspective, this has much to do with our ministry of reconciliation. It presupposes both our witness to the "other" about God in Christ   and our openness to allow God to speak to us through the "other". Mission when understood in this light, has no room for triumphalism; it contributes to removing the causes for religious animosity and the violence that often goes with it. Hospitality requires Christians to accept others as created in the image of God, knowing that God may talk to us through others to teach and transform us, even as God may use us to transform others.

43. The biblical narrative and experiences in the ecumenical ministry show that such mutual transformation is at the heart of authentic Christian witness. Openness to the "other" can change the "other", even as it can change us. It may give others new perspectives on Christianity and on the gospel; it may also enable them to understand their own faith from new perspectives. Such openness, and the transformation that comes from it, can in turn enrich our lives in surprising ways.

VI. Salvation Belongs to God

44. The religious traditions of humankind, in their great diversity, are "journeys" or "pilgrimages" towards human fulfilment in search for the truth about our existence. Even though we may be "strangers" to each other, there are moments in which our paths intersect that call for "religious hospitality". Both our personal experiences today and historical moments in the past witness to the fact that such hospitality is possible and does take place in small ways.

45. Extending such hospitality is dependant on a theology that is hospitable to the "other". Our reflections on the nature of the biblical witness to God, what we believe God to have done in Christ, and the work of the Spirit shows that at the

heart of the Christian faith lies an attitude of hospitality that embraces the "other" in their otherness. It is this spirit that needs to inspire the theology of religions in a world that needs healing and reconciliation. And it is this spirit that may also bring about our solidarity with all who, irrespective of their religious beliefs, have been pushed to the margins of society.

46. We need to acknowledge that human limitations and limitations of language make it impossible for any community to have exhausted the mystery of the salvation God offers to humankind. All our theological reflections in the last analysis are limited by our own experience and cannot hope to deal with the scope of God's work of mending the world.

47. It is this humility that enables us to say that salvation belongs to God, God only. We do not possess salvation; we participate in it. We do not offer salvation; we witness to it. We do not decide who would be saved; we leave it to the providence of God. For our own salvation is an everlasting "hospitality" that God has extended to us. It is God who is the "host" of salvation. And yet, in the eschatological vision of the new heaven and the new earth, we also have the powerful symbol of God becoming both a "host" and a "guest" among us: "See, the home of God is among mortals. He will dwell with them as their God; they will be his peoples ..." (Rev. 21: 3).

March 2005

THE CONFERENCE

Descriptive Introduction to the Programme of the Athens Conference

Aims and Style

The aim and objectives adopted by the CWME Commission and confirmed by the WCC Central Committee suggested that the Athens Conference would have a **different style** to that of its predecessors. The commission decided in particular to move away from planning conference sections, in which delegates would struggle in groups, sub-sections and section plenaries to formulate and adopt theological or strategic reports intended to be received or adopted by the conference plenary. That scheme had been used by most if not all the preceding conferences, with more or less success. In Athens, the main emphasis was put on creating safe spaces for sharing in an almost "liturgical" setting for confidence to be built among participants. The conference method and mode should reflect and express the theme of healing and reconciliation with a pneumatological emphasis. The Athens conference was also shorter than most of the earlier mission conferences.

The **venue** of the conference, the Aghios Andreas centre, is a holiday resort owned by the Greek army and used by its officers and their families. It had been used as a media village during the International Olympic Games in 2004. Situated directly on the seashore, it is made up of dozens of small bungalows with ample outside space for meeting, as well as some central buildings for offices and the restaurant. Tents had been installed for the plenaries, the worship and most of the synaxeis. The venue was ideal for a conference of this type.

Daily Schedule

Principles
The daily schedule indicated that the main emphasis was to be put on creating spaces for sharing, dialogue, debate, listening, presenting experiences and case studies or theological reflections.

Each day began with Bible meditation in home groups, followed by commonly held morning prayer in the worship tent, and one plenary session on a different aspect of the conference theme every day. In the afternoons participants could choose among a number of parallel running *synaxeis* (workshop offerings) before coming again all together for evening prayers. The day ended as it had begun with open space for intimate sharing in the home groups.

The programme aimed at offering several possibilities for participants to approach and perhaps experience healing and reconciliation at different levels: personal, inter-personal in sharing groups, in study groups and in common reflection in plenaries and prayers in the worship tent.

Some details

For the first time in such a mission conference, an opportunity was provided to offer pastoral counselling to everyone who requested it. Throughout the week of the conference, a group of counsellors and pastors, representing different denominations, regions and sensitivities, both women and men, were available on call or by appointment for **person-to-person counselling**.

A major role was assigned to the **"Home Groups"** consisting of approximately 10 -12 persons. These were a place for biblical meditation, silence, prayer and mutual pastoral support, based on personal sharing, story telling and reflection. These groups met every morning for *Lectio Divina*, a form of Bible meditation. It was a new experience to use this method in a major WCC event, which proved to be inspiring, not least as a discipline to listen. The same home groups met again for a debriefing session in the evening, allowing people to share experiences of the day, questions, frustrations, and to prepare for the following day.

Plenaries were limited to one session a day. Each plenary had a specific approach to the overall conference theme. It should provide introductions or reflections on the theme from a variety of points of view. This meant that the plenaries gave the floor to a variety of persons for relatively short inputs, in forms of speeches, interviews, round tables, personal stories or short case studies, with some visual presentation. Plenary debates had been planned for the last days of the conference, when confidence had been built among participants, but time did not allow it as expected.

The afternoons were left for two consecutive sessions of **"Synaxeis"** (workshops, gatherings, and offerings of different kinds). Participants were free to choose the synaxis in which they would participate. Up to ten synaxeis were running parallel to one another. That meant there were twenty different offerings each afternoon. A wide range of methodologies were used, allowing participants to contribute to the debate from knowledge and experience, to question, discuss and share in a big-group setting.

The conference aimed at having a rich **spiritual** life and a certain liturgical flow, with elements of liturgy finding a place in the day-to-day activities of the meetings, as well as offering a framework to the overall flow of the conference during the week. All morning and evening prayers were open to all participants and took place in a worship tent. Morning prayers were held following the tradition of specific denominations. An existing beautiful outdoor chapel provided space for individual prayers, liturgical services by denominations and healing services. A wall of prayer was provided for written, spoken or silent prayers, individually or accompanied.

On Sunday, May 15 participants were invited to visit local churches in Athens. On that same evening (Pentecost in the Western calendar) all participants gathered for an open sending service at the Areopagos, in the centre of the classical town of Athens, near the Acropolis, in the place where the apostle Paul had first preached the gospel to the Athenians.

Programme of the Plenaries

May 10: Opening Plenary: "Come, Holy Spirit, Heal and Reconcile!"
The Opening plenary served two purposes. As well as being the opening and welcoming plenary, it was an introductory plenary on the conference theme.
Participants were welcomed by the CWME moderator, Ruth Bottoms, before theological introductions and welcomes were given by Archbishop Christodoulos of Athens and all Greece and the WCC general secretary.
The second part of the plenary focused on the thematic prayer; "Come, Holy Spirit...", through two pneumatological inputs:
Kirsteen Kim, honourary lecturer at the University of Birmingham and chair of the British and Irish Association for Mission Studies spoke on "How do we know when the Spirit comes? The question of discernment"; and
Wonsuk Ma, a Korean Pentecostal missionary and theologian spoke on "'When the poor are fired up': The role of pneumatology in Pentecostal-Charismatic mission".

May 11: "Called in Christ to be Reconciling and healing communities"
The second plenary dealt with the other part of the conference theme, focusing on the role and quality of the community/church in mission and its contribution to healing and reconciliation.
First, a woman from Latin America, a delegate from a Pentecostal church, brought a personal testimony, witnessing to the healing powers of her church community and of the Holy Spirit in situations of brokenness. Two theological introductions followed:
Sam Kabue of Kenya, co-ordinator of the Ecumenical Disability Advocates Network (EDAN), presented a speech on "Addressing disability in a healing and reconciling community"; and
Athanasios N. Papathanasiou, Greek Orthodox missiologist, who teaches at the Higher Ecclesiastical School in Athens, spoke on: "Reconciliation: the major conflict in post-modernity. An Orthodox contribution to a missiological dialogue".

May 12: Mission and Violence – building a culture of peace
A Decade to Overcome Violence Mid-term event
The ambiguous relationship between Christian life, witness, mission and violence were the focus of the third plenary, co-organized by CWME and the coordinator and reference group of the Decade to Overcome Violence (DOV).
The plenary was opened with a liturgical procession of symbols of violence in the form of placards brought to the front stage by young people from various regions. After an audio-visual presentation of the DOV, Fernando Enns, a Mennonite theology professor and ecumenical DOV leader from Germany, introduced the second part of the plenary. Personal testimonies were then brought by Janet Plenert, a Mennonite from Canada, Alix Lozano, a Mennonite from Colombia and Viola Raheb, a Lutheran and Christian educator from Palestine, all witnessing to the ambivalent relationship between mission and violence. A round table led by Fernando Enns then provided the opportunity for further reflections on the link between mission and violence, with the additional participation of Tinyiko Maluleke, African missiologist teaching at the University of South Africa, who offered challenging concluding thoughts. The plenary closed with prayer.

May 13: Healing

Under the overall theme of "Healing", two major foci were addressed, through panel interviews. In the first, "Healing in a post-modern context", Fr Bernard Ugeux, a Roman Catholic anthropologist and theologian from France, and Erika Schuchardt, a German counselling expert, focused on different aspects of the healing ministry seen from a context of secular societies witnessing strong yearning for individual and personal healing. Dr. Tito Paredes, an Evangelical social anthropologist from Peru, facilitated the panel.

The second panel, "HIV/AIDS and healing" focused on people living with HIV/ AIDS and the question of healing in this context. The floor was mainly given to persons living with HIV or having long experience of the significance of healing communities as response to the pandemic. Speakers were Gracia Violeta Ross Quiroga, a young Evangelical woman who has become the spokesperson of those living with HIV/AIDS in Bolivia, Anthony Allen, a psychiatrist living in Kingston, Jamaica, and Japé Heath, an Anglican priest in South Africa, himself HIV-positive. Sara Bhattacharji, a medical doctor from India, facilitated the panel.

Due to the particular style and method chosen for this plenary, no texts of prepared speeches can be reproduced. A short press release provides some insight on the importance of the matters addressed by the panel participants.

May 14: Reconciliation

The last thematic plenary focused on reconciliation. Two case studies were given, highlighting present and future reconciliation problems:

Pepine Iosua, church minister and fisherman from Kiribati addressed the urgent plight of his people: "Rescuing victims in their home islands"; and

Lunga Lungile Magqwagqwa ka Siboto, bishop of the Ethiopian Episcopal Church, from South Africa, reflected on his experience as ecumenical accompanier in Israel and Palestine: "A cloud of witnesses".

Robert Schreiter, C.PP.S., concluded the plenary with a systematic presentation of "Reconciliation as a new paradigm for mission".

May 14: Final plenary

The final plenary heard significant oral summaries of their findings by members of the reflectors' group, and received a challenging message by the young delegates and stewards. Then it moved to the discussion on a draft "Letter from Athens". A message committee had been working throughout the week to draft such a letter. In the middle of the week, the draft had been shared with all participants for comments and discussion in home groups. More than 120 individual comments, additions and corrections had then been received by the committee, who prepared a revised draft, which was presented to the final plenary. It decided, in a first general indication of opinion, that the text did provide the basis for a conference letter. During the detailed discussion the plenary realized that it would not have time to go through the whole text, so as to adopt it; thus, the work in progress was sent to the commission meeting immediately following the conference for reworking and adoption on the basis of the plenary discussions and of remarks which could be shared with the commission. The final version of the letter is included in this book.

Text based on a report prepared by Beate Fagerli, conference organizer, revised and augmented by Jacques Matthey, CWME Commission secretary.

SPIRITUAL LIFE

Introduction

(From the Conference worship book)

The theme of the World Mission Conference is both a prayer and an affirmation: Mission is the work of the Triune God whose will is that all may share in God's life – a life of fullness and wholeness; and calls us to participate in that mission. In the spirit of that prayer and affirmation the Conference on World Mission and Evangelism, in Athens, will embark on a spiritual journey on the road to that wholeness. It will attempt to be an experience of healing and reconciliation. It is thus a different conference in style and orientation from the preceding ones.

The main emphasis will be put on creating spaces for prayer and celebration, and for theological reflections, sharing, dialogue, debate, listening, presenting experiences and case studies.

A major role has been assigned to what the CWME Commission calls the "home groups" consisting of approximately 10-12 persons. Each official participant will belong to one of these homes. They will be places for biblical meditation (in the style of *lectio divina*), prayer and mutual pastoral support, based on personal sharing, story telling and reflection. These groups will meet at least once each day.

Such liturgical elements need not follow any rigid pattern, but could happen simultaneously in different places, and as the Spirit leads. There are planned elements that will be for the whole conference including common celebrations, confession, affirmation of faith, etc., but the smaller groups too may also experience the elements of such a liturgical flow as they go through the day.

Liturgical spaces include the worship tent, the outdoor chapel decorated with flowers and healing plants, the wall of prayer and the beach. A number of daily liturgical symbols, such as hands, oil, light, stones, water, have been identified in line with the whole thematic flow of the Conference. Throughout the meeting it will be important to maintain the sacredness of the spaces that are provided for sharing and dialogue. A "pastoral team" of facilitators, of people with communication and counseling skills will be available to conference participants.

The Conference spiritual life committee has prepared morning prayers according to the Orthodox, United Protestant, Pentecostal and Roman Catholic traditions. The opening, closing and sending worships are inter-confessional. Evening prayers follow the same structure each day and have both common and changing elements.

In addition to the corporate prayer times, there will be healing services offered by different traditions, as part of the many "synaxeis" on offer in the programme.

The Gift of a Cross: Symbolism is Rich at Opening Prayer service

By Theodore Gill*

The wood of olive trees uprooted near Bethlehem during the ongoing Israeli-Palestinian crisis is transformed into an emblem of hope and reconciliation.

Receiving the cross

On the shore of the Aegean Sea, a small craft delivered a cross of olive wood from Bethlehem at morning prayer on the first day of the Conference on World Mission and Evangelism (CWME) near Athens. It came as a gift from the Christian churches of Jerusalem, a reminder of the birthplace of Christianity and the contemporary struggles of the people there. An ecumenical delegation from Jerusalem also presented cross-shaped pendants for each participant. The crosses, large and small, had been fashioned from olive trees uprooted in and around the city of Bethlehem, from Palestinian land that was confiscated as barriers were constructed.

As the cross was lifted ashore, a throng of worshippers greeted the delegation from Jerusalem with liturgical chants and litanies, and then processed behind the cross from the seashore to the worship tent, singing a song based on the CWME theme, "Come Holy Spirit, heal and reconcile!"

The Right Rev. Riah Abu Al-Assal, Anglican bishop of Jerusalem and the Holy Land, brought greetings from the Christians of the Holy Land as well as "from all who are working to make peace in the Middle East".

Bishop Al-Assal presented the cross as "the symbol of our salvation, our redemption. Even among the many different traditions of Christianity, I can find no Christian controversy about it. We agree that through the cross, through pain, through suffering and death, God in Jesus Christ reconciled the world to himself. And God has entrusted us with a wonderful ministry of reconciliation. Our mission and evangelism will never be realized until we achieve reconciliation, with God and among ourselves."

He warned against a naïve peacemaking that fails to recognize the importance of struggling against evil and seeking justice. But "in struggling against the powers of evil," the bishop concluded, "we need always to resort to the weapons of God, never to the weapons of the evil-doers. Otherwise, we will be defeated."

---

* Theodore Gill is senior editor of WCC Publications in Geneva, Switzerland, and an ordained minister of the Presbyterian Church (USA).

As olive oil was used to illuminate a traditional lamp in the tent, worship leader Ruth Bottoms, an ordained Baptist minister from the United Kingdom and moderator of the conference, recalled the olive branch borne to Noah by a dove, and the oil of anointing that served as a biblical sign of God's power in healing and reconciliation.

The symbolism of the olive tree is rich in Jewish and Christian tradition, yet it is also significant in the pre-Christian culture of Athens. Classical mythology holds that Athena became the patron goddess of the city through the gift of an olive tree, which remains the emblem of Athens to this day. The history of Christian mission preserves many such examples of the transformation of religious imagery.

As the CWME gathers in prayer this week at the foot of the Bethlehem cross, they bear witness to the potential for transformation symbolized in a cross of olive wood: from brutal uprooting to the healing of communities, from suffering to hope, from violent conflict to the possibility of reconciliation.

(from WCC Media - Conference features)

The Patriarchs and Heads of Churches in Jerusalem

A Message for the Mission and Evangelism Conference Athens – May 2005

We bring you greetings from all the Heads of Churches in Jerusalem and their various communities as you gather to consider the next stage in the work of Mission and Evangelism of the Christian Churches.

This Cross is a token of our love and prayers that God will richly bless all of you and guide your deliberations. It was made by Christian craftsmen in Bethlehem, whose very livelihoods are in danger because of the on-going situation in the Holy Land. The wood used come from olive trees uprooted to make way for the advancement of the so-called "security fence". The Cross has been ingeniously constructed by putting olive wood tiles together – a clear reminder to all of us that our witness is more positive and effective the more our various Churches are seen working and witnessing together.

Jesus said, "I, when I am lifted up from the earth, will draw all people to myself." (John 12:32). So we believe the stronger our witness together the greater the power of the Cross to draw men and women to Christ, who offers healing and reconciliation to the world.
The Cross comes also with representatives of our various families of Churches to remind all of you that we seek to be a vital, living witness in the Holy Land to our Risen Lord. However, the efficacy of our witness calls for the prayers and support of the whole of Christendom across the world. Though each of us is called by God to witness to the love demonstrated by the Cross in our various homelands nevertheless we would ask you to help and encourage all Christians of the Holy Land to be "Living Stones".

We wish you all the Peace of the Risen Christ.

Lectio Divina Bible Meditations

The Scripture passages are printed in a format that allows you to underline or highlight words or phrases, or make any other note as a help for your meditation. Time and sequence are directed by the "home group" leader. Each phase of Scripture meditation lasts about 15 minutes. It is preferable to allow the time for each member to complete a phase rather than rushing to the end of all phases. If there is time pressure just stop where you are but then always go to phase IV to finish the session.

The home group starts with a few moments of silence and/or prayer/hymn asking for the Spirit's presence. The use of the Conference hymn "Come Holy Spirit, Heal and reconcile" is recommended.

I – LISTENING TO THE WORD

A member of the group will be asked by the home group leader to read the Scripture slowly.

As I listen, I notice any word or phrase that seems important to me today. During silent meditation, it may be helpful to use a pencil to underline significant words or phrases at this point.

The home group leader asks the members to read aloud a word or phrase that struck them. No explanation is necessary. Comments are not advisable.

II – LISTENING TO ONE ANOTHER

Another member of the group will then be asked to read the Scripture again, slowly.

Another time of silent meditation follows this reading. In this silence I ask myself **What does the text say to me personally today?"**

The home group leader then invites each person to share with the group his/her reflection.

This is a time for listening, not for discussion or debate.

III – RESPONSE AND PRAYER

A third reader reads the same Scripture once more, even more slowly.

A third time of silent meditation follows, while I ask myself: **"How do I respond in prayers and in action?"**

The home group leader invites the members to share a prayer, or reflection.

This time, individuals may want to give thanks, express repentance, petition or intercession – these personal prayers of response may be shared. The group may respond by confirming the prayer with "Amen".

IV – CLOSING

The group may then bring this time of meditation to an end by saying together the Lord's Prayer and/or the blessings.

Note: It is important not to start a debate on what people share. In this kind of approach, one leaves side by side the shared insights of each participant. People may well repeat something already said if it matches their own reflections.

Bible texts used in the home groups:

Ezekiel 37:1-14
Ephesians 2: 11 – 22
John 18:15-27 and 21: 15-19
Luke 8: 40- 52
Isaiah 52:13 – 53:12

Come, Holy Spirit, Conference Hymn

Sister Celine Monteiro   Sister Celine Monteiro

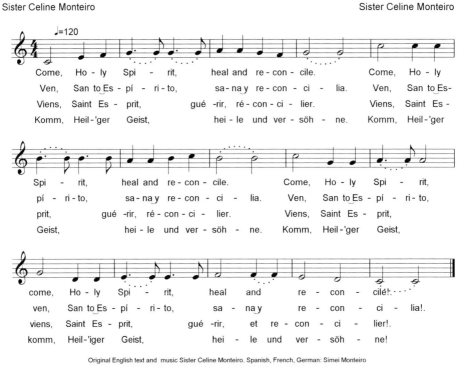

Original English text and music Sister Celine Monteiro. Spanish, French, German: Simei Monteiro
© WCC-COE. 150, Route de Ferney, CH-1211, Geneva 2, Switzerland

"Sending Service" on the Areopagus Embraces Unity amid Diversity

Following in the footsteps of Saint Paul, WCC general secretary Samuel Kobia proclaimed Christian unity in "a fellowship that exceeds our capacity to define it".

Common prayer and reflection within a historic setting in downtown Athens provided a climax to the spiritual life of the 13th Conference on World Mission and Evangelism. On Sunday evening, May 15, participants joined members of local churches on the Areopagus (sometimes translated as "Mars Hill") where the apostle Paul proclaimed the gospel of Jesus and his resurrection to first-century Athenian philosophers (Acts 17:18-34).

Participants processed up the lower slopes of the Acropolis as Greek actors re-enacted Paul's journey to the same spot. As they arrived at the Areopagus, gathering music was provided by the children's choir of St. Joseph school, the youth choir and mandolins of St Panteleimon church and the modern chamber orchestra of Athens playing with invited soloists. Prayers and biblical readings were offered in five languages by Christians from all points of the compass.

In his sermon, WCC general secretary Samuel Kobia recalled that "Paul was right here at the Areopagus, to confront the clever and the wise with the truth of the gospel of Christ. The Epicurean and Stoic philosophers held Paul in contempt, wondering what 'this babbler' was trying to say. But empowered by the Holy Spirit this babbler not only outdebated them, his message lived on to transform the lives of millions."

For many Christians it was the day of Pentecost, so Kobia also discussed the account of that event in Acts 2: "Among other things, the Holy Spirit represents the gift of understanding. At Pentecost diversity was overcome by a power that transcends it, the power to understand, to hear in one's own language." Kobia found this revelation essential to Christian mission. "The gospel is not our gospel that is to be translated from our language and experience to others for their benefit; rather, the gospel is that good news of Jesus Christ that all are privileged to hear, and the unity of what we hear overcomes the diversity of who we are. As Christians, we are members of a fellowship that exceeds our capacity to define it."

Kobia elaborated on how the universality of the gospel is given expression in particular contexts. Today, he said, those who hear and believe are called to take up such challenges as the false idols of wealth and power, war and violence, oppression of women and minorities, inequities of economic globalization and the stigma against those who live with HIV/AIDS.

Sending forth this congregation from Athens, Kobia exhorted them: "Like the apostle Paul and the disciples of Christ, who heard the good news as they were, where they were, and they were never the same again, let us allow the same Holy Spirit to come upon us, to convict us and transform us in such a way that we shall never be the same again."

(from WCC Media - Conference features)

THE GIFT OF UNDERSTANDING

*By the Rev. Dr Samuel Kobia**

> *"The Holy Spirit, whom the Father will send in my name,*
> *will teach you everything, and remind you of all that I have said to you."*
> *(John 14:26)*

In the fourteenth chapter of John we find Jesus expounding on ideas and concepts that the disciples find difficult to comprehend. Jesus was teaching them about the way, the truth, the life – and love.

The philosophical depth of these concepts was proving difficult for the disciples to follow. They already must have been sufficiently confused when Jesus went on to tell them that:

> I am in the Father, and the Father is in me, and since I
> am also in you and you in me, then the Father will be in
> you ... and because I live, you also will live (v. 19) ... and
> if you love me, my Father will love you, and I and the
> Father will come and make our home with you. (v. 24)

At least three of the disciples were honest enough to admit that they were finding it rather difficult to follow the thread of thought. Thomas was very frank and told Jesus that they had no idea where Jesus was going, much less the way that would take him there (v. 5). Philip told Jesus that they would be satisfied if Jesus showed them the Father (v. 8). And Judas (not Iscariot) demanded to know why Jesus would reveal himself to them, but not to the world (v. 22).

This particular discourse was so difficult for the disciples to comprehend that Jesus finally told them that, if they couldn't conceptualize what he was talking about, "then believe me because of the works themselves" (v. 11).

It is against this backdrop that we should understand the text for our message this evening. I wish to base my reflections on the 26th verse of John 14, "... the Holy Spirit, whom the Father will send in my name, will teach you everything, and remind you of all that I have said to you." The advocate, the Holy Spirit promised by Jesus to the disciples, did indeed come. In our message today I would like to reflect on what happens when the Holy Spirit comes. The very theme of the Conference that is now coming to an end begins, "Come Holy Spirit ..." What actually happens when the Holy Spirit comes?

As we learn from Pentecost, many things happen when the Holy Spirit comes. Among other things, the coming of the Holy Spirit represents **the gift of understanding**, and this is the theme of our meditation this evening.

---

* The Rev. Dr Samuel Kobia, a pastor of the Methodist Church in Kenya, is the general secretary of the World Council of Churches.

At Pentecost the gift of understanding overcame the curse of confusion that occurred at Babel. The project in the Plain of Shinar was motivated by human ambition and selfishness: people agreed to build a proud tower unto heaven and "make a name for ourselves". As a result, the unity of the human beings was destroyed in the very attempt to frustrate the divine purpose and will, and henceforth people were made the parochial captives of our own languages, divided by our inability to hear or to be heard, to understand or to be understood. Because human beings sought to compete with, or even to play, God... because of human pride at great achievements... because of human disregard for God's design – the diversity of language at Babel was reduced to a curse, and differences in language have served too often in this world to erect walls of ethnocentrism behind which we hide and from which we protect ourselves against others.

Pentecost is the New Testament sequel to the Babel narrative, when the Holy Spirit intervenes to correct the failings and divisions of humanity. Among other things, the Holy Spirit represents the gift of understanding. At Pentecost diversity was overcome by a power that transcends it, the power to understand, to hear in one's own language, one's own accent or regional dialect, the wonderful works of God.

The gift of understanding did not diminish the diversity of that great crowd at Pentecost; the people did not cease to be who they were, Medes, Persians, Elamites. They were not reduced to some vague generality without past or place. No, they did not become less than they were, they became more than they had been, for they became at one with all those who heard and understood that God was alive and active in this world and eager that they, all of them, should participate in God's purposes. It is the reality of the particular that makes the universal so powerful and appealing.

And that has been our experience at this mission conference. Each day when we gathered for worship we prayed the Lord's Prayer, each in our diverse languages; we have shared our experiences from the diverse contexts in more than 105 countries represented by over 600 participants; we have told each other stories and testimonies about God's great deeds in our lives. In that way we have enriched each other's spirituality, and deepened our understanding of our unity in diversity. The realities of our particularities made the universal much more powerful and meaningful.

The unity of Christ's holy, catholic, and apostolic Church is a unity that is based upon an understanding of who and what God is and has done, is doing and will do in our lives, in our churches, in our countries. The understanding that unites the faithful is an understanding of the mighty works of God, but there is another understanding at work as well, and that is our understanding that others hear of the same mighty works of God in their own tongues. The gospel is not our gospel that is to be translated from our language and experience to others for their benefit; the gospel, rather, is the good news of Jesus Christ that all are privileged to hear, and the unity of what we hear overcomes the diversity of who we are. As Christians, we are members of a fellowship that exceeds our capacity to define it. The gift of understanding that we receive from the Holy Spirit transcends logic and diversity and is a gift of the spirit of unity: unity of the Church of Jesus Christ and unity of humankind within the one household of God.

During our time together here in Athens we have prayed and sung on numerous occasions, "Come Holy Spirit ..." And we shall continue to say and sing this prayer long after we have gone back to our respective places and countries. This is because the coming of the Holy Spirit defines the mission of the Church in a wider context that is inclusive, celebratory and filled with a renewed invigoration of faith.

We have already noted that the building of the tower of Babel was a selfish human endeavour driven by a rebellious spirit whose logic was driven by idolatry and lust for power. In our world today, we detect a similar logic that is driving the prevailing tendency to create and sustain a global system that concentrates economic power in fewer hands and controls most of the world's resources, condemning millions of poor people to a wretched life and to death.

When the Holy Spirit blesses us with the gift of understanding, we are enabled to discern a world that is broken, fractured, divided and violent – a world that is in need of healing and reconciliation.

When the Holy Spirit blesses us with the gift of understanding, we are enabled to discern a humanity that is fast losing the capacity to relate as human beings; human beings are treated increasingly as commodities, and the worth of individuals is measured against their ability to consume.

When the Holy Spirit blesses us with the gift of understanding, we are enabled to discern the danger in which we have put the rest of the creation. That creation, to use a Pauline image, groans for liberation – as do all human beings who suffer oppression.

When the Holy Spirit blesses us with the gift of understanding we are enabled to speak God's good news with conviction despite the apparent odds against us. Paul was right here at the Areopagus, to confront the clever and the wise with the truth of the gospel of Christ. The Epicurean and Stoic philosophers held Paul in contempt, wondering what "this babbler" was trying to say. But, empowered by the Holy Spirit, this babbler not only outdebated them, his message lived to transform the lives of millions. And 2000 years later, our presence here, having come from all corners of the earth, is a powerful testimony to the success of the gospel that St. Paul proclaimed to the Athenians for the first time.

At the time of Paul's visit to this very place, standing in front of the Areopagus he saw how extremely religious the Athenians were – and yet that which they worshipped too often left them lacking in understanding. Just so, in our world today, we seek the empowerment of the Spirit to see modern idols for what they are: the mammon of our time. At a time of economic globalization, money has been elevated to the level of an idol – without it you are nothing, and for it even human beings are trafficked and sold. And this happens in many capitals of countries in the North, East, West and South. Those most affected by the processes of globalization are young people.

Let us pray for the Holy Spirit to bless our young people with understanding and enable them to see visions and dream dreams that will make it possible for another world to emerge: another possible world that is more just, more caring, more participatory, more peaceful. Let us pray that the young people at this conference and in our congregations and parishes will bring fresh thinking and energy into the ecumenical movement and into our churches, and that our young people will find a more meaningful and fulfilling life, and carry that as their mission to inspire other young people whose lives are empty and meaningless.

And, today being the Sunday that in the Orthodox tradition is dedicated to women in honour of Mary Magdalene, Mary the mother of James, and Salome – who were the first to witness the empty tomb, let us praise God for the spiritual courage of these women who were also the very first to hear the good news from the risen Lord himself, and literally ran with the breaking news to tell the disciples. We praise God for the ministry of women who have since continued to be the strength of our congregations and parishes. Let us pray that the Holy Spirit will increase the capacity of women in the churches and in society at a time when humanity is in need of courage and hope for a more humane society, as well as respect for life.

Let us pray that the Holy Spirit will bless all of us here, and our brothers and sisters in Christ everywhere else, to emulate the apostle Paul and boldly proclaim the good news even when it means confronting the powers and principalities of our time, even when it means speaking truth to power, even when it means taking risks in overcoming violence and all other forms of oppression and discrimination in our communities.

Sisters and brothers in Christ, our world today is in serious need of a moral compass. Therefore part of our mission and calling today is to engage in spiritual discernment, so we may be able to distinguish the authenticity of the competing claims that offer supposed solutions to humanity's maladies.

As we leave this place, this very special place, the hallowed place in which Saint Paul stood and from which he proclaimed the good news of the risen Christ, the saviour of the world, Lord of the whole inhabited earth, let us embrace with graciousness the generosity of Jesus who pours out his spirit to this world in need of a saviour.

Let us go from this place with renewed energy from the risen Christ, and may the prayer "Come Holy Spirit..." help us to overcome our differences and unite our diversity through the gift of understanding. Like the apostle Paul and the disciples of Christ, who heard the good news as they were, where they were, and they were never the same again, let us allow the same Holy Spirit to come upon us, to convict us and transform us in such a way that we shall never be the same again.

Pentecost is the festival of the Holy Spirit whose gift is that of understanding, of knowing who and whose we are. As we go forth, let us celebrate once again that gift to the apostles and to us, as we pray that what transformed them may transform us, and, as we pray "Come Holy Spirit", may transformation come to the world God so loved that he sent his only Son... to teach us how to live and relate to God and one another... to die for us and for our salvation... to defeat death by rising again from the dead to the glory of the triune God... so that today we may say together:

Christ is risen! He is risen indeed.

Go forth, and proclaim the good news. Amen.

PLENARY PAPERS

"Come Holy Spirit, Heal and Reconcile" Welcoming Address

H.B. Archbishop Christodoulos of Athens and of All Greece

On behalf of the Orthodox Church of Greece, and at the same time on behalf of all the people of Athens and of all Greece, it is with great joy and fraternal love that I welcome here in Athens all the participants of the XIIIth Conference on World Mission and Evangelism of the WCC. In this Paschal period, almost ten days after the celebration of the Holy Easter and the Resurrection of Christ allow me to greet you all with the ancient and existential greeting which constitutes the core of our identity and witness as Christians: XPICTOC ANECTH, Christ is Risen!

Our joy is even greater because this event has gathered in the same place sisters and brothers from all over the world and from a Christian constituency much wider than the WCC. This place is Athens, the capital of Greece, a country especially privileged by God's love. Our country was indeed privileged by the grace of our Lord to receive the gospel in our mother tongue. In fact, the entire New Testament, the very heart of our Bible, was originally written in Greek. We are grateful and quite honoured that Athens was selected to host this important and timely conference. Our Church, which historically is a result of Apostolic mission, is to this very day deeply committed to witness and evangelism, focusing on the same aspect underlined by the Apostle St Paul in his historic speech to the Athenians at Areopagus (Acts 17:23-31), namely on the Resurrection. Our mission, the mission of the Orthodox Church, the mission of spreading the gospel all over the world, in the spirit of the forthcoming Pentecost, starts from our Divine Liturgy, the eucharistic synaxis of the people of God, in which the Resurrection of our Lord, the ontological and existential foundation of our hope that is in us (I Pe 3:15), is Sunday after Sunday and on any other occasion, doxologically re-enacted, thus becoming in our tradition the springboard for mission to the end of the inhabited world *(oikoumene)*.

The Church of Greece has responded from the first moment, more than a year ago, both to the invitation and to the challenge extended to her by the WCC to be the hosting Church for this conference on the general theme "Come, Holy Spirit, Heal and Reconcile". The decision of the Holy Synod to host such a major ecumenical event, the first ever in an Orthodox setting, despite our past bitter experience from aggressive missionary activities and hostile actions against our people (Crusades, uniatism, and more recently activist proselytism), was based on three reasons:

a) on our determination to join our forces with other Christians in dialogue and common witness, especially nowadays when, from one end of the world to the other, the human person is tortured at the social and political level, because of urbanization and globalization which annul any difference between personalities and make invalid the unique character of each individual person;

b) on the positive developments within the WCC, evidenced in the recommendations of the Special Commission; and

c) on the holistic understanding of mission, being developed in recent years within WCC. Especially, we considered this conference important and providential among other world mission conferences of this kind, because of its new shift in mission paradigm, which makes it resonate with the theology, spirituality and contextual realities of our Orthodox Churches. We Orthodox do not only benefit from the ecumenical encounter and dialogue but also bring challenges coming from our history of long mission experience and our mission theology with echoes from the time of the early Christian communities.

Especially with regard to the Orthodox Church of Greece, I would like to stress that our Church, without foresaking her traditional achievements, is characterized by a visibly extrovert tendency to make new "openings" to the world, in the spirit of Pentecost, within the frame of mutual understanding and cooperation with every constructive agent to man's profit, and by the need for direct contacts and relations among people. This tendency results from the fact that our Church acknowledges the vital importance of the values of friendship, respect, freedom and love for the person itself, independently of religious, cultural and social differences. Within this context of the Pentecost, in which the Holy Spirit plays a specific role, the Church of Greece welcomes members of the WCC from different countries of the globe, emphasizing the significance she gives to the world fellowship of Churches "which confess the Lord Jesus Christ as God and Saviour according to the scriptures... to the glory of the one God, Father, Son and Holy Spirit". After the successful organization here in Athens of the Olympic Games, almost a year ago, the Church of Greece is willing to offer the possibility to the member Churches of WCC for a fruitful exchange of missionary experiences.

You are all well aware of the constant complaints, concerns, and even objections of the Orthodox concerning a number of issues (from the decision-making procedures, and the forms of common prayer, to ecclesiology); you may have even experienced, or heard of, the vocal reactions of a segment of our Orthodox community against our decision to host this event. For the last forty years or so there were reasons, some justified and some unjustified, that made the Church of Greece, though one of the founding members of the WCC, to limit her participation to it to the least necessary point. The recent developments with the "Special Commission on the Orthodox Participation in the WCC" have convinced us that a new era in WCC-Orthodox relations is about to be inaugurated. We are grateful to the organizers of this conference that for the first time the agenda of a World Mission Conference was set with Orthodox sensitivities in mind.

All these, as well as our determination to witness our Orthodox faith to the world in a visible manner, will hopefully result in the awareness that Orthodoxy has an important role to play within the wider Christian community, faced with a growing hostility against our faith. Our church has never denied dialogue; on the contrary, she seeks dialogue along the line of St Markos Evgenikos of Ephesus, the bastion of our faith, who stated that "when some differ from others and do not enter into dialogue, the difference between them seems to be greater. But when they enter into dialogue and each part listens carefully to what the other is saying, their difference is found to be much smaller".

Allow me to reflect from our Orthodox theological perspective on some very important aspects of your conference. First of all I rejoice on the liturgical dimension, quite evident in the title or theme of the conference which is shaped in a prayerful manner, i.e. as an invocation of the Holy Spirit to heal and reconcile. In post-modernity the importance of liturgy, and of the experience in general, are significant elements for our Christian witness, equally significant as the proclamation of the gospel. Almost all Christian missionaries recognize today that the exclusive emphasis on the verbal proclamation of the gospel and the rational comprehension of truth dangerously diminishes the effective reception of the gospel. Many people nowadays remind us that we have to open our mind towards knowledge--science, development, finance, profit.

However, the same people forget that these are not enough for hope to be reborn. Hope is only asserted when we empathize with Resurrection. The Resurrection of the Lord is the crack through which we gain a deeper look into our eschatological horizon. We might feel pain for last century's historical calamities, where some Christians by name were the protagonists, but we are not imprisoned in historical time, we do not render it absolute, we do not worship the idolized aspects of ourselves, those of knowledge or technology. And we do not seek to solve every problem completely "here and now", we do not live under the illusion that everything depends on us. Within the light of the Resurrection neither the world nor the individual is condemned to a hopeless freedom, which in the last century was praised as the breakthrough of liberating humanism. In our Orthodox tradition what constitutes the essence of the Church is not her mission in the conventional sense, but the Eucharist, the Divine Liturgy; the mission is the meta-liturgy, the *Liturgy after the Liturgy*.

That is why mission is understood not only as "going out", as proclaiming the Gospel, but also as a silent witness. Despite all the hardships and difficulties in oppressive and/or minority contexts our Church preserved her faith and transmitted it not as an ideology but as a way of life defined by the values of the gospel. And the contribution of our liturgy and our monastics in this respect was tremendous.

It is for the first time, as I could recall, that a mission conference adopts a more humble ethos and language, renouncing the over-optimistic tones and messianic programmatic missionary agendas of the earlier years; its theme is not an activist and programmatic statement, but a prayer, a prayer to God to heal, reconcile, strengthen and make all God's people living witnesses to the Risen Lord, and powerful examples of reconciling and healing communities. By this, it is acknowledged that mission is inherent to the church, to all the people of God, not only to some specialized ministries; it is also recognized that the missionary responsibility of all Christians consists in being living witnesses in word and deed; and above all it is underlined that the conversion of the people does not stay within the responsibility or the power of the missionary but rather of God *(missio Dei)*. From the very beginning it was God who added new people to the number of the early Christian communities and not the Apostles themselves (Acts 2:47). We as co-workers of God *(synergia)* pray, witness and act with humility; but God, through Christ in the Holy Spirit is doing the conversion.

My second comment is also taken from the slogan of the conference. The very fact that the Holy Spirit takes the initiative in mission is a very sound theological foundation of any acceptable missionary activity. The emphasis of course on pneumatology, at least as it is evidenced in Orthodox theology, does not by any means de-centre Christ, who is "the way, the truth, and the life" (Jn 14:6), and the sole Saviour of humanity (Acts 4:12). To put it in a slightly different way: an authentic Christian missiology must not attempt to replace a Christocentric universalism, despite all its shortcomings, with a Spirit-centred universalism. Rather, a pneumatology that is conditioned by Christology (and vice versa) provides a balanced missionary activity, since it relocates both Christology and pneumatology within the traditional Trinitarian framework. This is quite evident in the full title of your conference, since the pneumatological nuance of the above-mentioned slogan is perfectly supported by the Christological emphasis of the title proper: "Called in Christ to be reconciling and healing communities".

This takes me to my third point: the mission as a "ministry of reconciliation" (II Cor 5:18). We rejoice that the central focus of the conference is healing and reconciliation. In our ages long Orthodox theology the concept of sin was always perceived as breaking and alteration of relationship and estrangement of the human race from God, from one another and with the whole of creation; never, or rather very seldom, as a legalistic guilt. It was on these grounds that salvation is understood as a process of healing and reconciliation of humanity with God, with one another and with the whole of creation. Healing and reconciliation is a fact which has been achieved in Christ, the Incarnated, Crucified and Risen Son of God and which is to be appropriated by all of us in the Church, through the power and work of the Holy Spirit.

Salvation, as ontological healing and restoration of the fallen humanity and creation, brings about transformation, transfiguration, renewed relationships with God, the source of life and existence, with one another, and with the cosmos around us. Christ has died for us, has raised our fallen humanity and has ascended it to heaven and seated it at the right hand of the Father. However, what Christ has done for us once and for all *(ephapax)* has to be appropriated by each of us in a personal (but by no means individualistic) way in the Church. Each of us is also called to die to the "old man" in order to rise again into a new being in Christ. God in Christ and in the power of the Holy Spirit has the initiative, but each of us has to respond to God's call and to engage synergistically in working out his or her salvation and in bringing about the Kingdom of God "on earth as it is in heaven" (Mt 6:10).

It was for this reason that our Orthodox Church has given healing and reconciliation a sacramental dimension. The Holy Unction is a communal liturgical service, a *Sacramentum* that bestows the gifts of divine grace and renews in each person the eschatological reality of wholeness, glorification, love and immortality in Christ. As such it heals human and spiritual pain and rehabilitates the communion and communication of the faithful with God. Healing and reconciliation actually permeate all the worship services of our Church. However, the sacraments are not magic rituals. Sickness and death, the inescapable indignities that plague and limit human life, are not forms of divine retribution but rather a result of the world's alienation from, and broken relations with, God. Christ, who took on our infirmities and bore our diseases, has liberated life from its brokenness through his resurrection. By overcoming the world, Christ has given humanity peace, joy and access to imperishable life in the Kingdom of Heaven.

And now I will come to the practical consequences of the above sketchy theological reflection. Your conference is an important and timely one, because of the many and difficult challenges which confront all Christians today. The world we live in today, in many cases, is no longer the same with the world our Church lived in the past and developed her mission theology and praxis. The growing effect of globalization, (as a cultural and not as a financial phenomenon any more), the opening of the national frontiers and the increased movement of populations from one place to another put our Christian witness in a totally different situation than that of the past. Traditionally and historically mono-religious societies are becoming multi-religious, and faithful Christians live together with people of other faiths, other races, traditions, languages, share the joys and the pains of the same society, engage in mixed marriages or other social or family events. We have to try hard to preserve our traditional Christian values, our spiritual identity, our faith, our individuality, despite the fact that no contemporary society could claim to be Christian *per se*. More and more people of other faiths live together with Christians and struggle with the same challenges of atheism, agnosticism and anti-religious secularism. In such situations, there is a need for a new articulation of both our Christian identity and our mission, without of course compromising our faith. In such new contexts we are called to be signs of healing and reconciliation. The historical wounds between churches, nations, smaller communities, even families, have to be treated in a spirit of humility and in an attempt of healing them and reconciling people, as we look to the future. This is even more urgent now, in the post-11 September situation, than in earlier times.

The consequences which globalization, terrorism and the war on terror bring about require that Church rediscover her prophetic voice. When peoples are more and more impoverished while the rich are becoming richer and the modern economists and politicians motivate their decisions and actions (both on war and on economy) as "historically unavoidable", the Church has to raise her voice and to be on the side of peace, the poor, the marginalized, and the powerless. It has to be a powerful witness to the values of the gospel, to reaffirm that our Lord is the "prince of peace", and the earth and all of it belongs to God. As the Fathers of our Church so eloquently declared in their time, all the resources of the earth have to be shared by all. Peace without justice is a chimerical pursuit.

In a time, when the secular states, disturbed by the values of the Gospel, try to push the faith and its social and moral values into the private sphere, the church is called to witness to the values of the Kingdom and not to conform herself to what pleases the politicians and the businessmen of this world. The Church does not exist in order to follow powers that oppose God's will, but in order to give witness of faith, strength and truth. The Christians, who are also citizens of modern societies, should not give up witnessing to the values of the gospel and should not remain silent in front of the contemporary tendencies of some modern secularized states that try to impose on their people standards and values which are foreign to them. In such cases, while looking for healing and reconciliation, the Church should position herself in a counter-culture attitude and dare to tell "the rulers" the will of God, as the prophets did in the past and the Fathers of the Church in their time.

Last but not least, our missionary attitude should be always supported and nourished by love. Christ has won the world, has destroyed the gates of hell by perfect love, that love which led him to die on the cross. Love is the secret weapon which brings about remorse for the sins of the past, leads to healing of memories and reconciliation among estranged people. "Who will separate us from the love of Christ?" asks rhetorically St Paul the Apostle. "Will hardship, or distress, or persecution, or famine, or nakedness, or peril, or sword? No, in all these things we are more than conquerors through him who loved us. For I am convinced that neither death, nor life, nor angels, nor rulers, nor things present, nor things to come, nor powers, nor height, nor depth, nor anything else in all creation, will be able to separate us from the love of God in Christ Jesus our Lord" (Rom 8:35-39). The key and the way to healing and reconciliation are humility and love towards God and towards one another.

In the cradle of democracy, in the main entrance to Europe, that St Paul the Apostle preached, in the country that creatively assessed the human centric culture and respect of the ancient Greeks, and received the Gospel in the mother tongue of its inhabitants, our Church of Greece is extremely happy and honoured to welcome you all and host the World Conference on Mission and Evangelism of the WCC.

May the grace of our Lord Jesus Christ, and the love of God the Father, and the «healing and reconciling» communion of the Holy Spirit be with us all and empower us on our common journey to witness to the gospel in an authentic holistic way. I wholeheartedly wish you success to your work.

Opening Remarks

Rev. Dr Samuel Kobia is the General Secretary of the World Council of Churches

Introduction

First, I wish to extend my profound thanks – and those of the World Council of Churches – to the Church of Greece, as well as the churches of Greece, for their invitation to hold the first mission conference of the new millennium in Athens where the apostle Paul proclaimed the gospel boldly, while still showing respect for the culture of Athens and the traditions held precious by the Greeks.

I am also pleased to welcome all of you who have followed in the footsteps of Paul, coming to participate in this event. You come from many places and represent the rich diversity celebrated at Pentecost. Quite a number of you are well acquainted with World Council of Churches conferences and assemblies. I am delighted to see you here again amid the beautiful surroundings of Agios Andreas. On the other hand, this may be the first opportunity for others of you to join brothers and sisters from such a wide variety of backgrounds in a WCC event. I particularly want to welcome you! Your presence enriches our fellowship, and I am keen to learn how God is at work in your lives and communities.

On his second missionary voyage, the apostle Paul came to Athens from Thessalonica by way of Beroea, passing along the Aegean coastline where we gather today. The sails of the ship that bore him were filled with breezes like those we now feel, blowing over this same sea. May that knowledge inspire us as we continue the Christian journey, and may the ecumenical ship be propelled by winds of the Spirit.

Healing and Reconciliation in the Contemporary Context

Mission and evangelism have to do with calling and conversion. In our global context, I would like to suggest that we are being summoned to a threefold conversion in our thinking and attitudes.

First, we are being called to rethink our assumptions concerning the geography of mission. It is well known that the demographic centre of Christianity has been steadily shifting from the North to the South. In the middle of the first century, this centre was in or near Jerusalem; in the following centuries it shifted to Europe, where it long remained. But statisticians now locate Christianity's centre of gravity near Timbuktu in the Sahara desert, and it continues to migrate southward. Africa has moved from the periphery of the church's consciousness to its centre. Our vision must undergo a corresponding conversion, if we are to attend to what God is doing in the world today.

Second, we are called to recognize that this change in global dynamics is not merely geographical, but carries with it implications that are spiritual, moral, theological, missiological. Forms of expressing our faith that grew out of European culture are no longer normative; for example, Pentecostal and charismatic spirituality is now flourishing in both South and North. The life of Christian communities in the South is not necessarily defined by concepts that are the heritage of Europe's 11th-century Great Schism, nor of the 16th-century Reformation. Are we open to mission from directions we have not anticipated, borne by brothers and sisters who have received gifts of the Spirit that were never monopolized by European or North American intermediaries? We are all too aware that ministries from unexpected sources, though often providing healing, joy and comfort, may also create tensions and disunity among churches. It is my hope that this conference will encourage broad dialogue on Christian witness, joined by participants from diverse traditions.

Third, as we seek to overcome tensions between North and South, we must also be converted to a new sense of unity joining the East and West. Athens is one of the most honoured cities of eastern Christianity, and our conference has received the gift of a cross from the churches of Jerusalem as a sign of fellowship and solidarity. As we become aware of new manifestations of the Spirit in unaccustomed regions of the world, we must not allow ourselves to become detached from the truth, tradition and theology of historic communities that have faithfully served God for 2,000 years. The World Council of Churches has begun to deepen its fellowship through a dialogue concerning the meaning of Orthodox participation in the WCC, and we hope to continue this process of healing and reconciliation as we examine questions of mission in light of the renewal of our ecclesial relationships.

Healing, Reconciliation and Peace

The call to mission requires us to look beyond our own communities for the sake of the whole world. In the week ahead, we have the opportunity to ponder what healing and reconciliation mean within the context of the world surrounding us.

The secular world, like the church, is no stranger to division. Some world leaders seem adept at manipulating religious identities for narrow nationalistic and economic ends. I think of religiously fuelled racism, culture wars and the clash of civilizations. Politicians are not solely to blame – there are too many exponents of particular religions who intentionally discount people of different beliefs and encourage aggressive behaviour towards them. Such "identity politics" prepare the ground for sowing seeds of conflict, civil unrest and war.

We are meeting at the mid-point of the WCC's Decade to Overcome Violence, an initiative by the churches and their ecumenical partners to teach the ways that make for peace. I encourage this mission conference, focusing on a theme of healing and reconciliation, to highlight peace and non-violence as gospel imperatives. In Christ, God is revealed as a healer who offers reconciliation and forgiveness as gifts of pure grace. We are called to discipleship in Christ's way: "Love your neighbour as you love yourself." Unfortunately this remains a counter-cultural message, no matter where we find ourselves. Communities that are true to Christ are called to make clear that their identity provides ground for cooperation, dialogue and respect, for Jesus assured us that it is the peacemakers who are blessed. If humanity is to live more peacefully in a more just world, Christianity as well as other religions must announce their refusal to be used as pawns on a political chessboard.

So perhaps the time has come for confession, and repentance. This is a mission conference. "Mission" carries heavy historical baggage, having played a part in fostering division and conflict – between peoples, and even between families of churches. Let us acknowledge that there is often a risk of being disrespectful of others and their traditions when one is highly motivated to promote and defend a significant cause and message. There have been times when we Christians have been insensitive to others, and worse, both outside the churches and within them. For this we are truly sorry.

But even when Christians are performing at our best, the prophetic dimension of the gospel is likely to cause offence. We are called to be ambassadors of Christ, as Paul said, and sometimes an ambassador is required to convey an essential message despite its unpopularity. While this is true, it must never be forgotten that the message we bear is ultimately a message of love, not of condemnation.

Mission as Reconciliation and Healing

The theme of our conference is longer than most: "'Come Holy Spirit, Heal and Reconcile!' Called in Christ to be healing and reconciling communities." Some observers have seen it as two distinct themes, but once again the ecumenical movement discerns an underlying unity in diversity.

"Come Holy Spirit, Heal and Reconcile!" This is a prayer, representative of a spirituality founded on experience of God as healer and source of unity. In this prayer, we express our faith and urge the Holy Spirit to manifest the presence of the Triune God within the life of our conference, and in all our actions and interactions.

"Called in Christ to be healing and reconciling communities" is a modest exercise in ecclesiology. It invites us to begin defining the sort of church that our world needs: a church that bears witness to the gospel in word and deed; a church that is alive in worship and learning; a church that opens its doors to outsiders; a church engaged with those who suffer, and with those who struggle for justice and peace; a church that provides services to all who are in need; a church that is faithful.

In the World Council of Churches, we are also contemplating another theme, another prayer. Next February, the WCC's Ninth Assembly will gather in Porto Alegre, Brazil to explore the theme, "God, in Your Grace, Transform the World!" This is an intercession that lies at the heart of our missiology. In one form or another, this has always been the theme, the prayer, of Christ's church in mission: "God, in your grace, transform the world!" We know that it is possible for us to become what we are called to be – the one, holy, catholic and apostolic Church – only through the grace of the Triune God. We trust that, through the power of

God's Word and Spirit, the Creation may be redeemed and made new. In healing us as persons created in God's image, in reconciling us as communities, the Holy Spirit builds us up in love, transforming us into the body of Christ, in order that we may play the part that God has assigned us in the healing, the reconciliation, the transformation of all people, and of the whole Creation.

We have come to Athens, as did the apostle Paul, confident of the presence and guidance of the Spirit. And so we are bold to pray: "Come Holy Spirit, heal and reconcile! ... God, in your grace, transform the world!"

And may Almighty God, the Father, Son and Holy Spirit, remain with us, now and always. Amen.

"Come, Holy Spirit": Who? Why? How? So What?

Kirsteen Kim *

When the apostle Paul stood in front of the Areopagus, he began by connecting with the spirituality of the ancient Athenians. He affirmed their search for God and the spiritual awareness of their poets, who proclaimed that God is Spirit "in whom we live and move and have our being" and that, as God's "offspring", we are spiritual beings. Paul attempted to use the Athenians' spiritual language to tell about the Creator God and the Christian gospel. At the same time he discerned a spirit of idolatry that distracted them and prevented them from repentance and practical obedience to the Holy Spirit of God, as manifested in Jesus and his resurrection (Acts 17:16-34). It was difficult for Paul to bridge the spiritualities of the Jewish and Greek world in this way – there was a lot of misunderstanding and he had limited immediate success in terms of new Christians – but from our standpoint 2,000 years later, we can see this is a Christian city and we know how the use of Greek thought and language contributed to the formation of Christian theology, particularly to our understanding of God the Holy Spirit. So I consider it doubly appropriate that here in Athens we pray, "Come, Holy Spirit!" However, in order to appreciate what we are praying, I consider it important to ask four questions: Who? Why? How? So what? Who is the Spirit? Why does the Spirit come? How does the Spirit come? So what do we do?

(1) Who/What is (the) Spirit? The Spiritual Context of Mission

Gathered here we represent a variety of spiritualities and we are in mission in different spiritual contexts. Will we engage positively with one another's spirituality as Paul did? To do this, we need to discover what we and our neighbours mean

* Dr Kirsteen Kim is tutor and mission programme coordinator at the United College of the Ascension, Selly Oak, honourary lecturer of the University of Birmingham, and currently chair of the British and Irish Association for Mission Studies. Dr Kim's research on mission pneumatology draws on various contexts: Britain, where she grew up; South Korea, her husband's home country; USA, where she did part of her studies; and India, where she taught missiology as a missionary of the Presbyterian Church of Korea. Her first monograph, *Mission in the Spirit* was published by ISPCK, Delhi in 2003. This is a revised and slightly expanded version of the speech she delivered at Athens (ed.).

by "spirit" and by Holy Spirit. My research into the Holy Spirit and mission arises from my personal experience of different spiritual contexts. Growing up in the British churches in the first stirrings of the charismatic movement in the 1960s and 70s, there was much talk of the Holy Spirit. However, in that materialistic context, the concept of "spirit" did not seem to connect with anything outside the church. It made little sense to me or many of those around me, who seemed to have given up belief in anything "spiritual". However small the place assigned to the Holy Spirit, each denomination seemed to have a different notion of what was referred to. In my Reformed Church tradition, the Holy Spirit was invoked chiefly to illumine the Word. The Quakers knew the Spirit as the "inner light" for which they waited in silent meetings; whereas in the house church, the Spirit caused loud singing, dancing, and brought about miraculous healing. At the Christian Union, we emphasized the mighty spirit that gave the first Christians courage for evangelism; whereas at the Anglo-Catholic church it was a very mysterious spirit that seemed to waft through the incense. Then there was the Keswick tradition of the sanctifying spirit that would protect from immorality, and Celtic spirituality, which connected the Holy Spirit with life, nature and creativity.

When we lived in my husband's home country of South Korea, all these ideas about the Spirit were there too but there was also a wider awareness of ancestor spirits, and spirits of popular Buddhism and traditional shamanistic belief. The Protestant churches I knew would have nothing to do with these spirits but looked back to their origins in the outpouring of the Holy Spirit in the 1907 Korean revival. Korean Christians seemed to have unlimited confidence in the availability of spiritual power to achieve goals in any sphere of life, together with an inner yearning – expressed in agonized prayer – to have more power to achieve victory. At seminary in the United States, there seemed to be more of a climate of fear of the spiritual world. It was the "Third Wave" of the charismatic movement and there was talk of "spiritual warfare". There was also rising interest in the Holy Spirit, and the theology of the Trinity.

My students in India were very interested in the Holy Spirit, at least partly because of the Pentecostal movements offering healing that were attracting many new members. At the same time the spiritual power of Hinduism was very evident, not just in the temples but also in the streets and in politics. To talk about the Spirit and spirituality seemed natural to Indians as these are very meaningful concepts in their society, yet the Western textbooks said little that was relevant and I felt ill-equipped to answer their questions. However, some Indian theologians – many of them Roman Catholic – were reflecting on God as Spirit in a way that was positive toward Indian thought and movements.

Back in Britain after ten years away, I was struck by a new openness toward spiritual experience of all kinds and interest in New Age spirituality and pagan spirits. It seems to me that if we can connect the spirit-language of the Bible with contemporary spiritual experience, we may be able to communicate the good news of Jesus Christ in a way that is more meaningful in a post-modern age. In each country – and even in different Christian denominations – the spiritual milieu and the cultural meaning of the word "spirit" are different, and this gives a different nuance to the meaning of the biblical testimony to the Holy Spirit.

Our gospel will only be meaningful if we express it in a way that is recognizably spiritual in our mission context.

(2) Why Does the Spirit Come? The Mission of the Spirit

The next question to ask in a mission conference such as this is: Why does the Spirit come? Or, to put it another way: What is the mission of the Spirit? The Bible tells stories of occasions when the Spirit came and reveals the Spirit's mission. I find it helpful to think of the Spirit's coming in three ways: at Pentecost, in and of Jesus Christ, and in creation.

At Pentecost, Jesus' followers – the Twelve, the women and all those gathered in that upper room in Jerusalem – were transformed by the Spirit's coming. Their lives were never to be the same again. The day the Spirit came was the birth day of the church (Acts 2:41-42); and, simultaneously, Pentecost was the start of the Christian mission that spread into all Judea and Samaria and to the ends of the earth (Acts 1:8). The followers of Jesus – Jew and Gentile alike – were caught up in a movement of the Spirit that was to lead them to deny themselves, sell their possessions, and share their lives with strangers. Some of them were persecuted, forced to leave their homes and abused for the witness they bore. On the other hand they had the excitement of seeing signs and wonders, and of experiencing healing and deliverance. They became reconciled to one another and to God, and were empowered by the Spirit to live courageous lives and to help and serve others. Throughout the Acts of the Apostles, the Holy Spirit is seen to initiate, guide and empower the Christian mission (Bosch 1991: 114). As Samuel Rayan has written, the Holy Spirit "is no tranquilizer" to give us peace that puts us to sleep, the Spirit comes to enable us to recreate our earth (1998: 7).

For the first Christians, as for us, the Spirit comes to us as a second birth. In our fallen state, we do not know what it is to live life in its fullness until the Spirit comes in baptism and we are reborn (John 3:5-6). But when the Spirit came in Jesus Christ, it was different; at his very conception in the womb of Mary, Jesus was constituted by the Spirit (Luke 1:35), like the Church of which he is the Head. From babyhood and through childhood, many who saw him recognized the Spirit of wisdom and power that was in him, until one day by the Jordan River that special status was confirmed to Jesus and to John when the Holy Spirit descended on Jesus in the form of a dove and a voice came from heaven saying, "this is my beloved Son" (Mark 1:10-11 and parallels). The implications of Jesus' anointedness by the Spirit, his Messiah-ship are worked out in the gospel stories of his ministry and passion – in times of testing, in saving acts, in concern for the poor, in prayer-life, in challenging preaching, in wise teaching, in love for friends and for enemies, in suffering and sacrificial death – showing us how to live in the Spirit, and in his resurrection to new life (Rom. 8:11). The Spirit in Jesus is the light that shone in the darkness, the new wine that everyone shared at the wedding in Cana in Galilee (John 2:1-11), it is the water of life that Jesus offered to the abused woman at the well (4:7-26), the wind that blew Jesus across the lake to his disciples in the boat (6:16-21), the saliva that healed the eyes of the blind man (9:1-12), the voice that called, "Lazarus come out!" (11:17-44), the purifying water with which the Teacher washed his disciples' feet (13:1-20), the life-blood that poured out of Jesus' side on the Cross (19:31-37); and it is the flaming glory with which Jesus was glorified (17:24), and the breath that Jesus breathed into his disciples saying, "Receive the Holy Spirit" (20:19-23).[1]

In the earthly ministry of Jesus Christ, the economy of the Spirit and the economy of the Word coincided. Jesus Christ is both the receiver and the giver of the Holy Spirit. The Spirit of God animated Jesus Christ and shone forth from him (2 Cor. 4:6), and so from that time, Christians have found it appropriate to refer to the Holy Spirit as the Spirit of Jesus or the Spirit of Christ. This is the Spirit whose mission is to glorify God and give life in its fullness, and who is the distinguishing mark of all Christians. Rayan comments,

> Perhaps the finest name given to Jesus is "He who baptizes with the Holy Spirit", the one who presents us with the basis and core of Christian identity and Christian distinctiveness.... That seems to be the meaning of John: "There was, of course, no Spirit as yet, because Jesus had not yet been glorified" (John 7:39)" (1998: 37).

Nevertheless, the Spirit was also known before the coming of Jesus Christ. The leaders of Israel were empowered by the Spirit. The Spirit of the Lord stirred the judges and took possession of them: Gideon's victories (Judg. 6:34) and Samson's might (15:14) were due to the Spirit that was with them. The creative spirit of those who made and furnished the tent of meeting was divine (Ex. 31:1-5). Moses' authority (Num. 11:17), David's courage (1 Sam. 16:13) and Solomon's wisdom (2 Chr. 9:23) were gifts of the Spirit. The Spirit spoke through the prophets (Neh. 9:30) and they looked forward to the coming of a servant of the Lord, who would fulfil not only the letter but also the Spirit of the law (Isa. 11:2). They also foresaw a time when the Spirit would be poured out on all flesh – young and old, male and female, high and low (Joel 2:28-29). The effect of the Spirit would be to raise the dead, to bring dry bones together into living beings (Ezek. 37:13,10), to soften hard hearts so that God's law would be naturally expressed in their lives (Ezek. 11:19-20), to cause dreams, visions and prophesy of the truth (Joel 2:28-29). The outpouring of the Spirit would be a sign of the end to which the whole world is moving (Isa. 32:14-20).

The people of Israel also looked back to the beginning of time when, at the creation, the Spirit hovered over the waters (Gen. 1:2). They were aware that God's involvement in the world was by the Spirit as well as the Word, and that, by the Spirit, God's presence was infused throughout the whole creation (Ps. 139:7). They sometimes felt the force of this in the elements of wind, water and fire, and in the earth itself (Ps. 148:7-8). They saw the evidence of the Spirit's sustaining role in all life (Ps. 104:30). They also knew that humanity was created in a special way when God breathed the Spirit into the first human being (Gen. 2:7; cf. 6:17), and that human beings at their best show spiritual awareness: a sense of justice,

---

[1] I am indebted particularly to the work of Vandana (1989) for drawing my attention to the symbols of the Spirit in John's gospel, especially water.

kindness toward their neighbours, and a desire to know God (Mic. 6:8). They experienced God's presence and activity in the world – sometimes in surprising and unforeseen ways (Hab. 1:5).

These three ways in which the Spirit came (and comes) are inter-related. The Apostle Paul explains that the new community begun at Pentecost is significant for the future of the whole creation (Rom. 8:19-23) because, due to the resurrection of Jesus Christ from the dead, the church has the Spirit as a foretaste, a guarantee or a down-payment of the liberation and new life which God desires for all (2 Cor. 1:22; 5.5; Eph. 1:13-14; Rom 8:23). And, conversely, the church's identity is bound up in the Spirit of God, known to us in Jesus Christ, with whom we bear witness in all times and places (Rom. 8:14-17; cf. Rayan 1998: 10). Reflecting on Pentecost, Rayan points out the centrality of the Holy Spirit to Christian identity: "our life and our world stand bathed in the Holy Spirit, the Spirit of God and of Jesus Christ.... [This] is the heart of the Gospel and of Christian hope" (1998: 10).

(3) How Does the Spirit Come? Discerning the Spirit(s) in Mission

The Father sends the Spirit into the world and, as followers of Christ, we are privileged to participate in that mission (Rom. 8:14-17). If this is so, then the first act of mission is discernment to discover the way in which the Spirit is moving that we may join in (Dunn 1998: 72). To join with the Spirit in mission, we not only need to pray "Come, Holy Spirit!" but we also need to ask how the Spirit comes and how we will recognize the Spirit. This ability to discern is the fruit of wisdom. When God gave Solomon wisdom, what he asked for and what he received was "an understanding mind ... able to discern between good and evil" (1 Kings 3:9,12). Discernment is not an easy task, it is a complex process and an inexact science. The Spirit "blows where it chooses" (John 3:8) and cannot be pinned down and captured in a box. As for electrons, there is an uncertainty principle for the Spirit: the presence of the Spirit cannot be pinpointed precisely, though the indications are there. In this world our knowledge is partial but we can begin to know.

"Discernment of spirits" is listed as a gift of the Holy Spirit (1 Cor. 12:10). Justin Ukpong argues that it means, "To identify God's action in the universe and in human affairs today" (Ukpong 1990: 81). Two important points arise from this verse: First, we need the Spirit to discern the spirits, since discernment is a gift of the Spirit. Secondly, in its use of the plural "spirits" it raises a dilemma: Are we seeking to discern one Spirit or to distinguish between many different spirits? In large measure my research suggests that this depends on world view or cosmology. Whether we talk about spirit (singular) or spirits (plural) may indicate the difference between a philosophical approach and popular religion. Furthermore, the language of "spirits" may be used by different people with widely differing reference. For example, some regard spirits as highly personal beings that possess individuals or places; for others the discourse of spirits (plural) is a helpful way of imagining political, social and economic struggles; still others find such talk confuses what they regard as the real issues. If we do consider other spirits, there are a number of different attitudes to them. For some all spirits are equated with demons or evil spirits to be cast out. Yet others recognize good spirits – angels, for example (Heb. 1:14) – that bring protection and good fortune. There may be other spirits that are more ambiguous but can be cooperative if approached in the right way (Kim 2004).

People have different ways of discerning the spirits according to their spiritual context. Muslims, Hindus, Buddhists and those of other faiths will use their own criteria to recognize where God is at work, or what is holy or spiritual. Those of a secular persuasion may apply still other criteria to discern what is true and right. However, for the Christian, discerning the Spirit is essentially seeing Jesus Christ. It cannot be otherwise because it is the Christian testimony that Jesus Christ is the focus of the Spirit's activity, the one in whom all the fullness of the Father is manifest (e.g., Col 2:9; see Bevans 1998). But seeing the likeness of Christ and his ministry in different situations must not amount to making the whole world Christian, either explicitly or implicitly. And the question of whose spiritual vision is most closely in touch with God or Ultimate Reality or the universe will only be answered at the end. In the meantime, discussion among people of different world views about what we value will help us live together in our common home, the earth. However, the Christian contribution to this debate will always be Christ-centred.

Before we can begin to discern, we also need to decide where to look. I have noticed that we search for the Spirit in different places. We may look up to see the Spirit descending from heaven, bestowing authority and sanctifying. We may experience in nature the Spirit below, the ground of our being. We may expect the raw power of the Spirit rushing in from outside to purify and transform. We may look deep within to encounter the spirit in the depths of our being. Or we may look primarily for the Spirit in those around us, in the fellowship of the Christian community and in our neighbours. We cannot look everywhere at once but let us keep an open mind on this issue. The ministry of the Holy Spirit is as broad as the work of God the Father and expressive of the life of God the Son. What distinguishes the Spirit from the other persons of the Trinity is not differences of concerns or goals but his/her being as spirit, which allows him/her to come and go freely, to be among us, alongside us, and within us.

What are the signs of the Spirit coming? I find four biblical criteria for discernment, though none leads to conclusive identification of the Spirit. The first is ecclesial: the confession of Jesus as Lord (1 Cor. 12:3; 1 John 4:2). We hope and expect to find the Spirit in the Christian community, where Jesus Christ is known and worshipped. However it is well to remember that the Spirit defines the church not the other way round. Calling "Lord, Lord" is not necessarily a guarantee of the right spirit (Matt 7:21-22). The second criterion is ethical: the evidence of the fruit of the Spirit: love, joy, peace, patience, kindness, generosity, faithfulness, gentleness, and self-control (Gal. 5:22). The Spirit changes our lives, producing Christ-likeness. At the same time, good works alone are not always a sign of the life of the Spirit – they may be the result of unregenerate legalism (Rom. 7:6) – it is the heart and character that matters.[2] The third criterion is charismatic:

---

[2] The first two criteria were recognized in the reports of the Canberra Assembly in 1991 (see Kinnamon: 256).

the practice of the gifts of the Spirit (1 Cor. 12:4-11; Rom. 12:6-8).[3] Where there is empowerment to prophesy, ministry, teaching, exhortation, giving, leading, compassion, and so on, we have good reason to believe God is at work (by the Spirit). However exercise of a spiritual gift is not a sign of the Spirit's presence if it lacks love (1 Cor. 13:1-3). The fourth criterion is liberational being on the side of the poor.[4] The effect of the Spirit's anointing on Jesus Christ was that he preached good news to the poor (Luke 4:18) and this must be a touchstone for all claims to be filled with the Spirit. When discerning the Spirit in any Christian activity, we need to ask whose interests are being served; who is benefiting from this?

Stanley Samartha once wrote that the claim that the Spirit is with us is not ours to make; it is for our neighbours to recognize (1981: 670). Paul urged the Corinthians to prophesy in love because this would disclose or discern the secrets of the unbeliever's heart and "that person will bow down before God and worship him, declaring, 'God is really among you'" (1 Cor. 14:20-25). Discernment is matter for ecumenical debate as well as individual conscience. It requires wide horizons – in view of the breadth of the Spirit's mission, openness – in view of the unpredictability of the Spirit's movements, and humility since the Spirit is the Spirit of Almighty God. Many questions about discernment are not around criteria but about power. Who has the power to discern the Spirit for others? We are not obliged to accept someone else's identification of what is spiritual, however strong their tradition, however weighty their theology, or however much power they wield, if their exercise of that authority is incompatible with the Spirit of Christ. At the Eighth WCC Assembly in Canberra (1991), the Orthodox participants warned "against a tendency *to substitute a 'private' spirit, the spirit of the world or other spirits for the Holy Spirit*" (italics original; in Kinnamon 1991: 281). We should all remember that if we mistake the Holy Spirit for an unclean spirit, we may blaspheme against the Holy Spirit, a sin which cannot be forgiven (Mark 3:29; Matt. 12:31-32).

(4) So What Do We Do? Mission in the Spirit

In the light of what we have discussed of the nature of "spirit", the mission of the Spirit and the need for discernment, how shall we then live and what should we do in mission? Since Jesus Christ has set us free from the law of sin and death, we are called to live "in the Spirit" (Rom. 8:1-11). As we do so, we are naturally caught up in the excitement and struggles of God's mission (Boer 1961). We have often focussed on mission as a task to be achieved, a goal to be reached, when it is actually a gift, a promise of the Spirit (Acts 1:8). Mission is a spiritual practice of Christians and churches, a spirituality. As such it involves our values, motives and life-style as well as our specific mission practice and action. If mission takes place "in the Spirit" (Kim 2003), then it will be carried out in a way that is Christ-like. The process of mission will be as important as the results. The means of mission will be in accord with its end.

In the course of mission, we encounter many diverse spirits and powers in the world, whether we regard these as supernatural entities or natural forces, or simply

3 This suggestion from the Pentecostal-Charismatic movement has been made by Amos Yong (2000).
4 This has been suggested by liberation theologian Samuel Rayan (1998: 132).

use this language as a metaphor for socio-economic powers. We need wisdom to distinguish good from evil, and to know who/what to work with and whom/what to fight against. We need courage to stand up to the harmful spirits that are not on the Lord's side and spell injustice and death. Enlightenment and encouragement are ours in the Holy Spirit, who comes to help and equip us as we wage a spiritual struggle against rulers, authorities, cosmic powers and spiritual forces (Eph. 6:12). This may involve rebuking demons and casting out evil spirits in the name of our Lord and Saviour Jesus Christ and after his example. We can have confidence that, however powerful and threatening, all "thrones", "dominions", "rulers" and "powers" are only creatures of God and, at the end, will be reconciled in Christ (Col. 1:15-20). In other cases, it may be that those who are not against us are for us (Mark 9:40). At the very least, we may need to give them the benefit of the doubt, and perhaps even cooperate with them for specific purposes. In showing hospitality to strangers, we may be entertaining angels without knowing it (Heb. 1:14; 13:2). There are good as well as bad forces at work. A mission theology of the Holy Spirit should allow us to appreciate creativity and love wherever it is found and affirm whatever is true, honourable, just, pure, pleasing and commendable (Phil. 4:8).

In this conference we are focussing our attention on the Spirit's role as healer and reconciler. Both these ministries encourage a comprehensive appreciation of the Holy Spirit. Only if we have a vision of the full personhood of the Spirit, will we have a mature understanding of what it means to heal and reconcile. For many, the Spirit implies "spiritual" and this has to do with meditation, contemplation and other religious or mystical practices and techniques. For others, the Spirit debunks much of this and primarily drives action for social transformation and development. In spiritual healing, we learn to hold both these aspects of the Spirit – presence and activity – together. Moreover, the Spirit is the Spirit of truth (John 16:12-13), and may appear sharp and severe as s/he convicts the world of sin, righteousness and judgement (John 16:8). Yet the Spirit is also the Spirit of love (Rom. 5:5) who inspires sympathy and encourages dialogue. In our vision of the Spirit's reconciling role, we realize the need to balance truth-telling with listening, justice with peace. The presence and activity of the Holy Spirit is boundless and bridges both creation and redemption (Taylor 1972: 25-41). As Christians, we see the Spirit is at work to heal and reconcile in our hearts and in the church, and we also affirm that God, by the Spirit, is healing and reconciling the world, both through human development and by sustaining the eco-system, to bring well-being and joy (Acts 14:17). Wherever and however the Spirit is present and active, the Spirit leads to Jesus Christ, who reveals the Father.

So, together in the Spirit and discerning the spirits, we look out for the coming of the Spirit revealed to us in Jesus Christ that we may catch onto – and be caught by – the Spirit's movement in the world, which is God's mission. Come, Holy Spirit!

References Cited

Bevans, Stephen B.
    1998   "God Inside Out: Toward a Missionary Theology of the Holy Spirit",
           IBMR 22/3 (Jul), pp 102-105; "Jesus, Face of the Spirit: Reply to Dale
           Bruner", *IBMR* 22/3 (Jul), 108-109.

Boer, Harry R.
1961   Pentecost and Missions (Grand Rapids, MI: Wm B. Eerdmans Pub. Co.).

Bosch, David J.
1991   *Transforming Mission: Paradigm Shifts in Theology of Mission* (Maryknoll, NY: Orbis Books).

Dunn, James D.G.
1998   *The Christ and the Spirit: Collected Essays. Vol. 2: Pneumatology* (Edinburgh: T & T Clark).

Kim, Kirsteen
2003   *Mission in the Spirit: The Holy Spirit in Indian Christian Theologies* (Delhi: ISPCK)

Kim, Kirsteen
2004   "Spirit and 'spirits' at the Canberra Assembly of the World Council of Churche, 1991, *Missiology: An International Review* XXXII/3 (July), pp 349-365

Kinnamon, Michael (ed.)
1991   *Signs of the Spirit.* Official Report of the Seventh Assembly of the WCC, Canberra, 1991 (Geneva: WCC).

Rayan, Samuel
1998   *Come, Holy Spirit* (Delhi: Media House; originally published 1978)

Samartha, S.J.
1981   "Milk and Honey – Without the Lord?", *NCCR* 101/12 (Dec), pp 662-671

Taylor, John V.
1972   *The Go-Between God: The Holy Spirit and the Christian Mission* (London: SCM Press)

Ukpong, Justin S.
1991   "Pluralism and the Problem of the Discernment of Spirits" in Emilio Castro (comp.), *To the Wind of God's Spirit: Reflections on the Canberra Theme* (Geneva: WCC), pp 77-86.

Vandana (Sister)
1989 [1981] *Waters of Fire* 3rd edn (Bangalore: ATC; New York: Amity House, 1988; first published, Madras: Christian Literature Society, 1981).

Yong, Amos
2000   *Discerning the Spirit(s): A Pentecostal-Charismatic Contribution to Christian Theology of Religions.* JPT Supplement Series 20 (Sheffield: Sheffield Academic Press).

"When the Poor Are Fired Up": The Role of Pneumatology in Pentecostal-Charismatic Mission[1]

*Wonsuk Ma**

1. As We Begin...

During the 100 years of the modern Pentecostal-Charismatic movement, it has made many impacts on Christianity, yet its role in mission is extremely significant. The explosive growth of churches, particularly in non-western continents, is but one example. As discussed below, there are several important roles of the Holy Sprit that are evident in the mission practices of Pentecostal-Charismatic believers.

However, before we take this journey of discovery, it will be helpful to clarify several issues. The first is the complexity of Pentecostal-Charismatic Christianity today. Many have argued that the "fountainhead" of the movement is found in North America at the turn of the 20th century, especially at the Azusa Street Mission (1906-1909) under the leadership of the African-American preacher William J. Seymour. However, more evidence has been presented to contest this theory, with India and Korea being examples. Also, the stunning "discoveries" of the so-called "indigenous Pentecostals" from Africa and Asia appear to support the theory of "multiple fountainheads" for the origin of Pentecostal-Charismatic Christianity.[2] In fact, we may be arriving at the notion that "the church is charismatic" after all, from its inception.

As I try to represent this fastest-growing segment of Christendom, I do so with evident limitations. First, Pentecostal-Charismatic Christianity is not homogenous. It encompasses classical (or denominational) Pentecostals, Charismatic (or Neo-) Pentecostals and indigenous (or Neo-Charismatic) Pentecostals. The last category is particularly problematic because of its diversity and also because some groups in this classification advocate questionable doctrines with which orthodox Christians are not comfortable. This gives rise to the possibility of having groups that may be "more Pentecostal, but less Christian." Second, the pneumatology of groups broadly classified as Pentecostal or Charismatic is not "standardized." For example, while classical Pentecostals feature a unique experience called "baptism in the Holy Spirit", many other groups may not necessarily subscribe to such a doctrinal statement but are, nonetheless, open to the supernatural work of the Holy Spirit. The rapid growth and vast diversity of this movement also poses a challenge in defining the parameters of the movement; but, as I attempt to

---

* The Rev. Dr Wonsuk Ma is a Korean Pentecostal missionary to the Philippines involved in tribal evangelism and church planting. He also serves as Vice President for Academic Affairs while lecturing Old Testament and Pentecostal Studies at Asia Pacific Theological Seminary, Baguio, Philippines. (Since 2007, Dr Ma is the Executive Director of the Oxford Centre for Mission Studies, OCMS, Oxford, UK.)
[1] A similar, revised version of the original paper presented at the Conference on World Mission and Evangelism, May 2005 in Athens, Greece, was published in *Transformation* 1 (24), January 2007, pp 28-34.
[2] For a good review, see Hwa Yung, "Endued with Power: The Pentecostal-Charismatic Renewal and the Asian Church in the Twenty-first Century," *Asian Journal of Pentecostal Studies* (2003), pp. 63-82.

represent this loosely identified group of Christians all over the world, here is a minimal working definition for our discussion:

Segments of Christianity which believe and experience the dynamic work of the Holy Spirit, including supernatural demonstrations of God's power and spiritual gifts, with consequent dynamic and participatory worship and zeal for evangelism.[3]

My reflection comes with two main points: Pentecostal-Charismatics represent the "poor," for whom poverty and sickness are a part of their lives, and the core of Pentecostal-charismatic pneumatology is "empowerment" for witness.

2. The Spirit and the "Poor"

- "Religion *of* the Poor"

Early Pentecostals at the turn of the 20th century were "poor" in many ways. Most participants of the Azusa Street revival came from the lower socio-economic bracket of society. Urban African-Americans and ethnic immigrants, with "sprinkles of whites", made up this controversial epicentre of one of the most significant revivals in modern church history[4] Practically marginalized by society, and sometimes by established churches, they understood themselves to be the eager recipients of the Messiah's message of hope, who came "to preach good news to the poor" under the anointing of the Holy Spirit (Luke 4:18).[5] These socially "dislocated" found such strong solidarity among themselves, courageously going against commonly accepted social norms such as racial segregation, that they forged a social and spiritual culture where the hopeless found a space to experience God's grace and power. This "haven for the disinherited" created a powerful drawing force to make Pentecostal Christianity a "religion of the poor".[6] The context of "poor", as the socio-spiritual context of Pentecostal-Charismatic Christianity, has left several unique contributions.

This characterization is important in that Pentecostalism is a religion *of* the poor, not *for* the poor. Marginalized by existing churches, this group of people coming from the lower socio-economic strata found themselves to be the main players in the church. Their "primal spirituality" is expressed in the participatory and expressive worship as well as testimony times. The very fact that the Holy Spirit chose to visit them through powerful experiences such as healings, baptism in the Spirit, prophecy and miracles, as well as drastic conversion experiences, was in itself a social upliftment.

---

[3] Wonsuk Ma, "Asian Pentecostalism: A Religion Whose Only Limit Is the Sky," *Journal of Beliefs and Values* 25:2 (Aug 2004), pp. 191-204 (192).

[4] E.g., William W. Menzies and Robert P. Menzies, *Spirit and Power: Foundation of Pentecostal Experience: A Call to Evangelical Dialogue* (Grand Rapids, MI: Zondervan, 2000), p. 22 argues: "The uniqueness of the modern Pentecostal revival lies in its very survival—surviving long enough to gain a hearing in the larger church world and to emerge as a significant component of the Christian world."

[5] Scripture quotations are from New International Version.

[6] David Martin, *Pentecostalism: The World Their Parish* (Oxford: Blackwell, 2002), p. 4. Also Robert M. Anderson, *Vision of the Disinherited: The Making of American Pentecostalism* (Peabody, MA: Hendrickson 1992).

The cross is received from the churches in Jerusalem

Opening prayers, gathering on Aghios Andreas' beach

Aghios Andreas, seafront

Registration desk

Procession to the worship tent

The first Conference newspaper is out !

Rev. Ruth Bottoms, Conference moderator, with
Rev. Dr Sam Kobia, WCC general secretary, and the late
Archbishop Christodoulos of Athens and all Greece

One of the many tents for synaxeis

Synaxis on multicultural ministry

Lectio Divina in home groups

Home group

Rev. Ruth Bottoms, Conference moderator, with Bishop Ioannis of Thermopylae, moderator of the Athens Local Arrangements Committee

Opening prayer for forgiveness, healing and peace

On the way from prayer to plenary

Conference bookshop

Beate Fagerli and Dimitrios Passakos, the organizers

Coffee break – discussion with and among Pentecostals

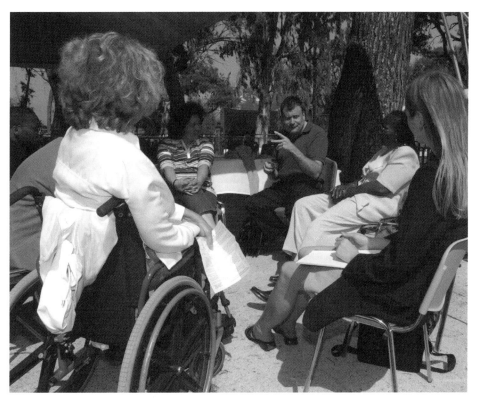

People living with disabilities made a significant contribution

Language groups during plenary on community

Plenary on community – theatre performance

Greek cultural evening

Stewards' group

Worship tent

Plenary on mission and violence – theatre performance by young participants

Plenary on DOV – Tinyiko Maluleke, Viola Raheb, Janet Plenert, Fernando Enns

Aghios Andreas' outdoor chapel

Rev. Anna Ljung and Fr Alkiviadis Calivas, co-moderators, Spiritual Life Committee

Synaxis on Christian identity and religious plurality

Morning prayer

Intercessions

Plenary

Common prayer

Coffee break

Stewards, plenary tent

Final plenary. Intervention of reflectors' group

Members of the Athens Local Arrangements Committee

Procession with world mission conferences' banners

United in common prayer

Preparing for the final celebration at entrance of Dionysios Areopagitis

Procession "in the footsteps of St Paul" on Dionysios Areopagitis

Areopagos – (from left to right)
Rev. Dr George Mathew Nalunnakkal, vice-moderator of the conference,
Rev. Ruth Bottoms, moderator of the conference, and
Rev. Dr Sam Kobia, WCC general secretary

Areopagos – gathered for the final celebration

Areopagos – musical introduction

In the footsteps of St Paul – 2000 years later

As observed in many non-western continents such as Latin America and Asia, Pentecostal believers have achieved upward social mobility, and this has been viewed as God's special blessing. This is also the reason why Pentecostal mission has been traditionally focused on evangelism (the spiritually lost) and care for the poor and marginalized. In many cultures where women are considered not appropriate for ministry, the Pentecostal faith has brought "liberation" for them. One such example is the cell system of David Yonggi Cho of Korea. In this highly male-dominant society, Cho organized, trained and empowered lay women to exercise their ministry gifts over a vast number of cell groups of the Yoido Full Gospel Church.

- Immanence of God

The "outpouring" of the Holy Spirit in the early 20th century brought several powerful paradigm shifts for the poor. First, their self-understanding changed drastically: from the marginalized to the conspicuously "called" for God's ministry. Second, it was also seen as a strong eschatological sign for the immediate return of the Lord, and this brought urgency to their divine call to minister. Third, this "apostolic" movement had a strong restorational expectation in the early church. Having inherited the holiness spiritual traditions, supernatural interventions of God, such as healings and miracles, were regularly expected. Even if "classical Pentecostalism" did begin in North America, their beliefs exhibited a strikingly holistic worldview where the supernatural world intersects with the natural world on a daily basis.[7] Fourth, their unique experience of baptism in the Holy Spirit and other supernatural manifestations made this a religion of experience.

This emphasis on God's immanence (closeness) and the unique religious worldview strongly suggests its potential for explosive growth in the non-western world and that is exactly what we have had in the past 100 years. Testimonies of healings, exorcisms, miracles and the like are heard daily. Unlike many other Christian traditions, Pentecostal-charismatic spirituality includes the real level of daily human existence, including particularly physical and material aspects, as well as spiritual dimensions. This is a "religion with flesh and bones",[8] and compares well with many church traditions where the Holy Spirit and his work is moved to ethical, moral and spiritual levels, quickly bypassing the physical and material dimensions.

3. When They Are "Fired Up" for Service

There are several important studies enumerating distinct characteristics of Pentecostal mission. One of them, for example, is by Allan Anderson, a South African Pentecostal missiologist. His list includes: 1) pneumatocentric mission; 2) dynamic mission praxis; 3) evangelism, central missiological thrust; 4)

---

[7] Among others, this may come under the category of the "Black Root" of Pentecostalism. Walter J. Hollenweger, *Pentecostalism: Origins and Developments Worldwide* (Peabody, MA: Hendrickson, 1997), pp. 18-24 for the Azusa Street Mission.
[8] Wonsuk Ma, "Jesus Christ in Asia: Our Journey with Him as Pentecostal Believers" (A paper presented at the Asian Consultation, Global Christian Forum, May 2004, Hong Kong) to be published in *International Review of Mission*, Vol. 94, No 375, October 2005, pp. 493-506.

contextualization of leadership; 5) mobilization in mission; and 6) a contextual missiology.[9] In order to highlight several important characteristics of the work of the Holy Spirit in Pentecostal mission, I have selected several models, including two individuals and several organizations. Not all may overtly identify themselves as "Pentecostal", but either their link with Pentecostal Christianity or their unique practices reflect its influence. As any real case is a complex matter, duplication of certain elements is unavoidable.

- The Holy Spirit as the Initiator of Mission: "One-way Ticket Missionaries"

The distinct missionary nature of Pentecostal experiences, particularly baptism in the Spirit, is well attested in the stream of missionaries who went out of, and were influenced by, the Azusa Street Mission. Gary McGee argues that within five years of the Pentecostal revival in Los Angeles, at least 200 Pentecostal missionaries from North America served in various parts of the world. [10] Reinforced by eschatological urgency, many Pentecostal believers, often not properly trained, clergy as well as laity, men as well as women, young as well as old, devoted their lives for evangelism. Vinson Synan termed them "missionaries of the one-way ticket" with several useful examples.[11] According to him, they were "evangelists and missionaries who went out with little or no institutional or financial support".[12] However, in my opinion, the most crucial genius of this new breed of missionaries lies in their expectation not to return home in their lifetime, but work "to the end of their lives" in mission fields. There is no doubt that their shared eschatological urgency must have contributed to this determination, but equally powerful is their passion for the lost.

Synan has several powerful examples, many of whom indeed never returned home, but planted a seed which now blossoms powerfully: Ivan Efimovich Veronaev who introduced the Pentecostal message to his homeland Russia, Willis Collins Hoover, the father of Chilean Pentecostalism, and Daniel Berg and Gunnar Vingren who began the Brazilian Pentecostal movement. Lillian Trasher (1888-1961), a Spirit-filled 23-year old believer, broke her engagement and sailed to Egypt. There she founded the very first orphanage in the country and once cared for 1,200 orphans, widows, single mothers and blind women.[13] Although she received a heroic welcome in her brief 1955 visit to the States after 25 years of ministry without furlough, she was no doubt a missionary with a one-way ticket. She and many early Pentecostal missionaries and evangelists exhibited a lifestyle of commitment to mission that is uniquely Pentecostal.

---

[9] Allan Anderson, "Towards a Pentecostal Missiology for the Majority World," *Asian Journal of Pentecostal Studies* 8:1 (2005), pp. 29-47.
[10] Gary B. McGee, "Mission, Overseas (N. American Pentecostal)," *The New International Dictionary of Pentecostal and Charismatic Movements*, revised and expanded edition, eds. Stanley M. Burgess and Eduard M. van der Maas (Grand Rapids: Zondervan, 2002), pp. 885-901 (888).
[11] Vinson Synan, *The Spirit Said "Grow": The Astounding Worldwide Expansion of Pentecostal and Charismatic Churches* (Monrovia, CA: MARC, 1992), pp. 39-48.
[12] Synan, *The Spirit Said "Grow,"* p. 39.
[13] The entire issue of *Assemblies of God Heritage* 4:4 (Winter 1984-85) is on Trasher's life and ministry. This volume is electronically available at http://www.agheritage.org/pdf2/Heritage/Winter-1984-1985. pdf#Page7 (checked: July 26, 2005).

- "Prophethood of All Believers": Youth With A Mission (YWAM)

Established by a Pentecostal minister in 1960, this powerful mission group has mobilized Christian youth for mission all over the globe. Loren Cunningham, the founder, once saw "waves on a map" which "turned into young people, going to every continent, sharing the good news about Jesus."[14] YWAM's ministry is focused on evangelism, training and mercy ministry with 900 bases (or centres) in over 140 countries, with a staff of over 11,000.[15]

The most significant "Pentecostal" tradition observed in YWAM is the "liberation" of ministry from elite clergy to the hands of every believer. For Pentecostals, one of the most important passages is Acts 1:8, "But you will receive power when the Holy Spirit comes on you; and you will be my witnesses in Jerusalem, and in all Judea and Samaria, and to the ends of the earth." The coming of the Holy Spirit (or "baptism in the Spirit" as they call it) is for empowerment, and empowerment is for witnessing. Cunningham had difficulty in convincing his own Pentecostal denominational leadership to envision mobilizing youth for mission. Its training programme practically aims to turn the "ministered" to the "ministering" believers. The life-changing testimonies of participants are heard almost daily. In order to be a "missionary" in this organization, what is required is one's willingness to give time and talent in mission, be it a week or a year. Now, this tradition of "democratization of ministry" is being expressed in various creative ways in many parts of the world. In the academic realm, a new expression has been suggested: "prophethood of all believers", such possibly becoming an active move from the traditional notion of "priesthood of all believers".[16]

- "God of Healing and Miracle": David Yonggi Cho

Perhaps best known as the pastor of the largest single congregation in the world, Yoido Full Gospel Church, Cho has changed millions of lives throughout his 45-years of ministry. He was born in 1936 and grew up in Korea under an oppressive colonial rule, went through the difficulties of war, and spent a hopeless youth, with a terminal case of tuberculosis.[17] His encounter with Christianity, particularly a Pentecostal-type, is described as follows:

> On what was thought to be his deathbed he was visited by a Christian girl who was a friend of his sister. His Buddhist parents had forbidden her to visit their home, but she persisted and gave Cho a Bible, preaching the gospel to him. Soon Cho became a Christian and his health began to improve dramatically.[18]

[14] "History of YWAM" (http://www.ywam.org/contents/abo_his_introhistory.htm, 2004), accessed: April 27, 2005.
[15] "Introducing YWAM" (http://www.ywam.org/contents/abo_introduction.htm, 2004), accessed: April 27, 2005.
[16] Earlier used in James Luther Adams, ed., *The Prophethood of All Believers* (Boston: Beacon, 1986), the expression is recently appropriated to Pentecostal beliefs by Roger Stronstad, *The Prophethood of All Believers: A Study in Luke's Charismatic Theology* (Sheffield: Sheffield Academic Press, 1999).
[17] Among many biographies of Cho, see Nell L. Kennedy, *Dream Your Way to Success: The Story of Dr. Yonggi Cho and Korea* (Plainfield, NJ: Logos International, 1980).
[18] Young-hoon Lee, "The Life and Ministry of David Yonggi Cho and the Yoido Full Gospel Church," *Asian Journal of Pentecostal Studies* 7:1 (2004), pp. 3-20 (4).

His radical experience of God's love and power through healing made him an evangelist of a "good God" who heals and blesses those who seek him. Coming from a Buddhist religious tradition and extremely poor social conditions, his message has been consistently about a God who loves and cares for the daily needs of his people. Stories of God's miraculous healing, blessing and restoration (of families, relationships and the like) filled the pages of the *Shinang-gye* (World of Faith), once the most popular monthly magazine (both religious and secular) in the country. It impacted not only Christians, but also the entire society as the magazine was read in schools, military camps, prisons etc.[19] Now he terms this as a "ministry of hope".

His ministry and theology demonstrates a holistic worldview, including the physical and material aspects of human life, as much as the spiritual level. A bowl of rice and healing of terminal diseases in a poverty-stricken society are as important as the matter of sin and salvation. In the "majority world", if the most powerful and loving God cannot heal a person, he is not as useful as the ancestor spirits many have been relying on for such needs. God is expected to be the saviour, not only after this life, but also during this earthly existence. This is where the work of the Holy Spirit comes in with "signs and wonders." Often the demonstration of God's power through the Holy Spirit triggers a "people's movement" or conversion by groups. This partly explains the phenomenal growth of the Pentecostal-charismatic churches all over the world.

- Priority of Inner Change and Evangelism: Teen Challenge

Established by an American Pentecostal minister, David Wilkerson, in 1958,[20] this drug rehabilitation programme has become the "oldest, largest and most successful programme of its kind in the world," with over 170 centres in the United States and 250 worldwide.[21] The "National Institute on Drug Abuse Report" found at the same website argues that the drug rehabilitation programmes of Teen Challenge records a 70 percent success rate, while most secular programmes reach a 1-15 percent success rate.[22] The programmes include residential rehabilitation facilities, seminars among youth for education and prevention and others. The residential programme involves a strong spiritual component which underlines the theological assumption that any transformation of a society begins with individuals, and a change in a person begins with his or her inner (in this case, spiritual) being. This inner change involves not only a conversion experience, but also an encounter with God's reality, often through baptism in the Holy Spirit. For instance, the first entry in the testimony section reads, "John Melendez was spiritually lost and confused on the streets of New York, as a teen and young man."[23] As human suffering begins with a spiritual loss, the restoration should also begin with the spiritual component of a human being.

---

[19] Myung Soo Park, "Korean Pentecostal Spirituality as Manifested in the Testimonies of Members of Yoido Full Gospel Church," *Asian Journal of Pentecostal Studies* 7:1 (2004), pp. 35-56.
[20] David Wilkerson, *Cross and the Switchblade* (New York: B. Geis Associates, 1963) details the story of Teen Challenge.
[21] "About Us" (http://www.teenchallenge.com/index.cfm?infoID=1&centerID=1194, 2005), accessed: April 27, 2005.
[22] "National Institute on Drug Abuse Report" (http://www.teenchallenge.com/index.cfm?studiesID=3), accessed: April 27, 2005.
[23] "Can a Drug Addict Really Change?" (http://www.teenchallenge.com/index.cfm?testimonyID=1, 2005), accessed: April 27, 2005.

The practice of Teen Challenge epitomizes two Pentecostal values. The first is the primacy of evangelism as a Pentecostal mission focus. Driven partly by the eschatological conviction that the Holy Spirit was poured upon them for the last-minute harvest before the return of the Lord, many committed their lives to "reaching the lost". They were church planters and evangelists. Everything they did, be it mercy ministry or training, was to achieve the ultimate goal of evangelism and church planting.

The second is the Pentecostal pattern of social ministry. Many of the social ministries were to care for the "poor," such as girl's and boy's homes in India, orphanages in Egypt and many other countries, educational programmes in Latin America, feeding and educational programmes in India, vocational training schools in Korea, etc. This value is aptly expressed in a well-known statement: when asked by a fellow Christian in Latin America if there are any social programmes among Pentecostals, the answer was, "We are social programmes!" Although this "care for victims" is not good enough to remove structural evil in this world, Pentecostals have modelled the ministry of Jesus as their paradigm found in Luke 4:18-19.

▪ Empowered for Witness: Brother Badol's Story[24]

Brother Badol was a young man who lived in Papasok, a village of the Kankana-ey tribe, deep in the mountains of the northern Philippines. Reachable only by foot, this totally isolated community had served ancestor spirits and many gods for generations. About twenty grass-roofed houses welcome rare visitors, who are usually exhausted from the long mountain hike.

Badol and his wife lost their two young children on the same day. A simple fever took both lives. As advised by village elders, he offered animal sacrifices to appease the angry ancestor spirit who took them. During this time, a Christian worker visited his community once in a while and introduced a God who made pine trees, pigs and humans. He told them that this God loved everyone dearly, and that he also hears prayers, even if there is no animal offering.

Badol and his wife soon had two new children, but they also died young, following another epidemic which took many lives in the village. He decided to try this new God who seemed to be quite different from the spirits he had served. Of course, this was never easy, as the entire village expected him to be punished by the spirits, but they still began their strange new worship in their house. Very soon, a neighbour quietly asked him if this new God could heal his dying child. Badol laid his hand upon the motionless baby and prayed in the name of Jesus who had given life to her. The next Sunday, the entire family, with the now recovered baby, joined the "church". Badol believed that the Holy Spirit came not only to save him from darkness, but also to empower him so that he could share the gospel with effectiveness. In fact, the villagers regularly asked him to pray for the sick, and most of them were healed miraculously.

---

[24] The full text available in Julie C. Ma, *Mission Possible: The Biblical Strategy for Reaching the Lost* (Oxford: Regnum International; Baguio, Philippines: APTS Press, 2005), pp. 18-22.

About fifteen years later, everyone in Papasok serves this new God who can heal the sick. Badol and his wife had ten more children and none died. He visited nearby villages and shared this good and powerful God with them. Because of this missionary work, seven villages have their churches.

This story from our place of ministry in the Philippines epitomizes millions of Pentecostal-Charismatic believers all over the world who are never properly recognized as "ministers" or "missionaries", and yet, are faithfully and powerfully carrying out God's call for mission. The coming of the Holy Spirit as promised in Acts 1:8 has been understood as "Pentecostal missiology": The Spirit calls, empowers and sends his people to the ends of the earth to be his witnesses. The Holy Spirit, whom they experienced through healings, miracles and empowerment, is also expected to perform miracles and healings. Even the promise of the Lord for supernatural power as recorded in Mark 16:15-18 is understood in the context of mission:

He said to them, "Go into all the world and preach the good news to all creation. Whoever believes and is baptized will be saved, but whoever does not believe will be condemned. And these signs will accompany those who believe: In my name they will drive out demons; they will speak in new tongues; they will pick up snakes with their hands; and when they drink deadly poison, it will not hurt them at all; they will place their hands on sick people, and they will get well."

- "The Spirit Who Makes Us One": Azusa Street Mission

Among the many challenging traditions observed in this renewal movement, the work of the Holy Spirit to remove human barriers is distinct. This incredible anti-cultural phenomenon against the social norm of that day appeared in two fronts. The first was the multi-racial composition of the mission. Under the leadership of an African-American holiness preacher, twelve leaders were an equal mixture of black and white. An observer, who happened to be Seymour's teacher, reported the eruption of this spiritual movement in a distasteful flavour:

Men and women, whites and blacks, knelt together or fell across one another; frequently a white woman, perhaps of wealth and culture, could be seen thrown back in the arms of a big "buck nigger", and held tightly thus as she shivered and shook in freak imitation of Pentecost. Horrible, awful shame! Many of the missions on the Pacific coast are permeated with this foolishness, and in fact, it follows the Azuza [sic.] work everywhere.[25]

However, this congregation where "the 'colour' line is washed by the blood"[26] is a powerful demonstration of what the Holy Spirit can do in a complex and troubled world. The other was the ecumenical nature of the mission. The participants of the Azusa Street revival came from a variety of Christian traditions. Stories abound about how a visitor, theologically suspicious, was overwhelmed by the presence

---

[25] Charles F. Parham, "Free-Love," *The Apostolic Faith* [Baxter Springs, KS] 1:10 (December 1912), pp. 4-5.
[26] Frank Bartleman, *Azusa Street*, foreword by Vinson Synan (Plainfield, NJ: Logos International, 1980), p. 54.

of the Holy Spirit and ecclesial differences suddenly disappeared. This ecumenical potential was again presented during the Charismatic renewal when "Spirit-filled" members of various churches (often from mainline churches, including the Roman Catholic) were able to celebrate common faith with genuine Christian love and appreciation.

This unique demonstration of the Spirit's work was short-lived, at least in the Azusa Street revival. Soon, various Pentecostal denominations were organized, often along racial lines. Also, the ever-increasing number of Pentecostal-Charismatic congregations from splits remains as a testimony against its spiritual tradition. However, the recent spread of the "Pentecostal" practices (or culture) in singing and worship has reminded us of its potential to bring a divided humanity (including the church) together through the Holy Spirit.

4. As Concluding...

This presentation is purposefully brief and incorporates narratives (to be truthful to the Pentecostal testimonies). The role of Pentecostal-Charismatic churches and believers in fulfilling God's mission will become increasingly important in the coming years. Particularly significant will be the role of the non-western churches, which I represent, with their explosive growth and increasing challenges. This will require the active exchange of experiences with the members of the world church.

The highlighted strengths are shared, not to argue that the Pentecostals have at last found the secret formula for world evangelization, but to humbly present to the church community at large that the Lord has brought this movement with its unique set of gifts to the body of Christ, particularly in fulfilling God's missions mandate. The 100-year history of the Pentecostal-charismatic movement is an unfortunate combination of the Spirit's empowerment and human shortcomings, and we Pentecostals know this all too well.

As a "new kid on the block", Pentecostals have much to learn from the historic churches with their rich histories and traditions. At the same time, the rise of a new movement (particularly the renewal type) such as this in itself serves as God's reminder to his people of his missionary mandate to the world. If the Pentecostal-Charismatic movement can serve this purpose by strengthening and renewing the body of Christ through its healing and restorational potential, its primary historical calling is fulfilled. May this be the case by the help of the Spirit. Thus, come Holy Spirit and empower us for your mission!

"Called in Christ to Be Reconciling and Healing Communities"

A personal testimony

I was born into a Christian home, the daughter and granddaughter of Pentecostal pastors. I was brought up and educated with love and devotion, being the youngest child with two older brothers.

From childhood I was given instruction on the Christian way and learned to love Jesus. When I came to an understanding of the plan of salvation, I was baptized and received the gift of the Holy Spirit with speaking in tongues.

From my youngest days, I took part in church work. I was a teacher, and later the superintendent, in the Sunday School, youth leader and a teacher in Bible study courses. I studied in preparation for Christian service and have worked, and still do, in all sorts of useful activities.

I have two daughters who are twenty and eighteen years old, both of them faithful to God and active in the church.

I have been separated for fifteen years and divorced for twelve.

God has been faithful to me and never disappointed me. With his help I have been able to move forward, run my household, and support it financially, emotionally and spiritually. Christ has freed me, not only from sin, but also from all emotional hang-ups that could hold me back.

Since we are considering the theme "Come, Holy Spirit, Heal and Reconcile", it seems to me that it could be helpful to give my testimony on this...

When I was 31 years old, I married a man of the same age after being engaged for one year and two months. I had noticed that he had some personality problems, but I thought that with my love, understanding and ability to solve problems they could be dealt with. I excused his attitude because of his family background and convinced myself that it would all be different when we got married, because he was basically a good decent person and he loved me very much.

Soon after we were married I realized that it was not going to be easy to live together, but I was emotionally stable and I believed that it was a situation that I could cope with.

But, as it turned out, the more time passed, the more difficult things became. We were almost always arguing.

His sudden mood changes confused me: at one moment I was utter rubbish, and at other times he wept, begging my forgiveness and saying that I was the best woman in the world!

He swung so easily from being aggressive to being tender and loving, that my mind and my feelings could not cope.

He blamed me for everything that went wrong in the home, with my daughters, with him. If I was not able to solve a problem for him, it was my fault, and he often gave up working, because, he said, the problems got on his nerves.

I became the head of the household, financially, emotionally and spiritually, but it was leaving me physically and emotionally drained.

To begin with, I tried to hide the situation, but later I came to see that we needed help, and so I approached my church for assistance. The pastor and the leaders attempted to help us by giving us advice and supporting us in order to save our marriage. As it was a difficult situation, the pastor recommended us to go to a specialist marriage guidance counsellor. To begin with, my husband refused to go, because he believed that no one from outside could solve our internal problems. So, at the suggestion of the counsellor, I began attending alone, until, because of my persistence, he did agree to come with me. We did receive counselling for a time, but then the counsellor decided that what was needed was psychological treatment, due to my husband's emotional instability, which he flatly refused. So, with him promising to change his ways and asking for forgiveness, we continued a little longer, but we went back to the same situation and I did not manage to change it.

I became so exhausted that I lost all motivation and felt that my life was meaningless. I was in tears for more times than I could imagine, I was becoming a zombie, and came to understand why it was that there were people who took their own lives. I blamed God for what was happening to me, thinking that it was not fair, because I had lived a good life, serving God, but the Holy Spirit reminded me of past situations, and I seemed to hear inwardly his sweet voice saying to me, "My daughter, I kept on telling you again and again, but you made the decision."

When I accepted that I had made the wrong decision, I asked God for forgiveness and received strength from where I had none and decided to do something to put my own life in order. I began by talking with my pastor in order to receive advice according to the Word of God. I remember that I said to him, "I am not getting any younger and I am making no progress in finding a solution to my problem. I should like to separate from my husband, but I do know that God disapproves of my decision and so I grit my teeth and keep going with the relationship, even though it is destroying me, because I do not want to do anything displeasing to God." I can still hear in my mind my pastor's words, which made sense to me, when he said:

"This is not the God we preach. We believe in a forgiving and merciful God. Merciful means that he is giving you another chance. God wants your good and your personal fulfilment, and so he would not compel you to keep up a relationship that is destroying you. If you want to be a martyr and continue, that is your decision and not God's, but you will have to accept the logical consequences of being separated."

It did not prove possible to change the other person. I did not succeed in saving my marriage, but it was possible to rebuild my own life, and so I decided on a separation. My daughters were two and four years old, and I was physically and emotionally ill and spiritually depressed.

The doctors dealt with my low physical condition. With the support of family, friends and the church community I recovered emotionally, and they helped me to grow stronger spiritually so that I could be useful to God, to my family, to society and to the church.

At that time I offered to resign from my church activities, because, as I was separated from my husband, I did not wish to be a cause of conflict in the congregation, but the leaders and the community did not accept my resignation: "It's as if you had been knocked down by a truck – you are injured, but you are still alive – and our job is not to bury you but to find the necessary means by which you can be healed and restored."

My husband stopped attending our church, because he thought that in practice they should have made me persevere with our marriage, and he accused me of adultery because of my decision to separate. He was advised by our pastor to receive pastoral care from another pastor in a different church in order to recover. A pastor friend of his took him on and devoted much time and energy to him, but, every time that he seemed to be recovering, he again relapsed, fell out with the leaders and stopped attending the church, or moved to another one.

The days following were not easy. My young daughters lived with me in my parents' home and spent the weekends with their father. I had to provide for my daughters, because their father has never, to this very day, contributed to maintaining them, and, to top it all, he tried to turn them against the church, my father – whom the girls adored – and me by saying that we were in the wrong, and this gave rise to constant arguments.

A further heavy blow was when I discovered that he was drinking heavily. Not knowing the situation, I was leaving the girls in his care for part of each weekend, but one day he got drunk in their presence, and that further damaged relationships, both with me and with my daughters, who were frightened and bewildered. Despite everything, we did not reject him, but tried to make him understand that he should seek help in order to regain his self-respect, but that the decision was his.

For my part, I used all the resources provided by the church (pastoral counselling, healing groups, workshops and retreats) to recover and experience healing, not only of my own wounds but also those of my daughters.

On the other hand, I had recovered physically, but I was still carrying a heavy emotional burden, because I had counselled many young people and I was feeling that, having failed in my marriage, I was not being a good example. And then, in a meeting which we called "With open hearts", where we could express our feelings and receive positive ideas from other group members that would help us to surmount our problems, I was given healing words, especially from two young people. One young man said to me "on the day when you forgive yourself, we shall all be more happy". And a girl said to me, "I have known you for as long as I can remember, and I can remember every book that you have given me and every piece of advice that you have given me. I have always admired you and that has not changed. I want to be like you." Then some mothers asked me to continue advising their daughters. I believe that on that day God used those individuals in our community to enable me to recover and to tell me that I still had a lot to give.

Later, with the support of members of the congregation I was able to take out a loan to buy an apartment, where I am at present living with my two daughters.

Today I can say that my inner wounds have been bound up and healed by a community that has known how to work with me and be alongside me, and they have been healed by the power of the Holy Spirit. So I am able to give my testimony without feeling pain as I do so, and with the intention that it will serve to help others experiencing conflict. I have been reconciled with myself, and in my dealings with my ex-husband. I do not feel bitter towards him and I wish him well and that he will recover.

My daughters have been taught to respect and help their father, even though they do not share his ideas or his lifestyle. And today, as young women who have grown up in a healing community, they try to ignore many problems with their father, so as to avoid a breakdown in their relationship with him and to see if it is possible for him to rebuild his life. They are both working, and studying at the university. They love God with all their heart and share actively in the life of the church.

At the present time, I am the executive secretary of my church, and of ministries such as "Crusade to Every Home" and "International Bible Society". I work full time in the service of the church. I work closely with the pastor and am a member of his team, and that enables me to put my point of view as a woman in the service of the church.

Today I realize how important it is to be a healing community, but I also realize that it is a personal decision. There is nothing magical about it. It is a process that begins when we want it to, and decide to walk each day obeying and being faithful to God, to our leaders and to the community that gives us a sense of security.

I am convinced and I want to say that we must ourselves take responsibility for changing what is negative into something positive with the authority and strength given us by the Spirit of God. It is my desire that many can say with me:

"Thank you, Holy Spirit, for healing me and reconciling me to myself, to the society around me and especially to those who at some time or another have caused me pain."

Addressing Disability in a Healing and Reconciling Community

*Samuel Kabue**

This presentation is made within the overall theme of CWME, which is "Called in Christ to be reconciling and healing communities". The emphasis of the plenary is on "community". And the way community life may or may not have healing and reconciling quality and effect. I have attempted to explore this in the light of persons with disabilities in the contemporary church and society.

The terms "healing" and "reconciling" are all so common to us, especially in the ecumenical fraternity, that it is assumed they mean the same and evoke the same positive feelings in all of us. This is certainly not the case. To the people of South Africa to whom apartheid is still fresh in their memory, and to the peoples of Sudan who are just emerging out of many years of conflicts that have brought about a lot of suffering, the terms will have an understanding of bringing hope and a sense of creating harmony with neighbours that were once enemies. In societies that are still hopelessly torn apart by armed conflicts and dominated by the experience of death and suffering, the terms will have no meaning and their use will be considered as consistent reminder of the suffering. Even among persons with disabilities in the church and society, the terms will have very different meanings and experience depending on the circumstances of various individuals.

As the WCC Interim Statement "A Church of All and for all" rightly points out, "No social group is ever the same, and disabled people are no exception to the rule. We come from a variety of cultures, and are thus culturally conditioned in the same manner as every person. We have experienced different kinds and levels of medical care and differing social attitudes. We have come to an acceptance of our disabilities by diverse routes. Some of us have been disabled since birth, either by congenital conditions or by the trauma of birth itself, while others have been victims of accidents or have had disabilities develop later in life."[1] This makes the two terms have very different meaning to different individuals contrary to the common view of the society as observed in the statement that "In the case of disability, it is often assumed that healing is either to eradicate the problem as if it were a contagious virus, or that it promotes virtuous suffering or a means to induce greater faith in God."

If your disability is as a result of sickness or accident, the term healing comes with the yearning and hope for recovery as long as you have not accepted the disability as a new condition in your life. To those who have been disabled since birth and have gone through the necessary processes of adjustment, the term healing has little to do with their disabilities until others remind them of this understanding. To them, disability and sickness are two very different things and healing applies to sickness and not to disability.

* Samuel Kabue is executive director of the Ecumenical Disability Advocates Network (EDAN), a programme of the World Council of Churches based in Nairobi.
[1] The references and quotes are from "A Church of All and for All", taken from Arne Fritzon and Samuel Kabue, eds, *Interpreting Disability. A Church of all and for all*, Geneva, WCC, 2004, pp.64-88.

Let me make it clear at this point that there is no doubt in my mind and to many persons with disabilities whom I know that divine healing is biblical and applicable in the Christian faith. However, its understanding as it relates to persons with disabilities is made complex by differing teachings, doctrines and theology. Some of these have made the word healing anathema in the ears of persons with disabilities. This is especially the case where disabled people become vulnerable to easy commercial fixes and religious groups, which offer miraculous healing in the setting of superficial acceptance and friendship. A few scenarios illustrate this:

Take the case of a well-known evangelist from abroad who jets with his whole team of assistants to a city in Africa. Prior to his arrival, the city is alight with posters and media announcements about his powers to heal and inviting all those vexed with all manner of infirmities for healing. An entire school for the physically disabled turns up at the stadium where the evangelical crusade is taking place with all the hope for cure. An altar call for those with needs is made after the sermon and the enthusiastic ushers push forward all the children on their wheelchairs and crutches to the front. A moving prayer is made and everyone is called upon to receive healing by jumping out of the wheelchairs and throwing off their crutches. The ushers assist the children by pulling them off the wheelchairs and taking away crutches. Although in the confusion some get badly hurt, no cure takes place and the crowd scatters, some carrying with them the crutches as evidence of some imagined cure and in the process inflicting more suffering on those poor children left in the field, unable to move.

Another example is that of a mature Christian with a disability who turns up to such an evangelical gathering with the simple objective of listening to the word of God from the reputed evangelist and thereby receives spiritual blessings. An altar call is made for those who would like to accept the Lord and those who have needs requiring prayers. The enthusiastic ushers believing, rightly or wrongly that the disabled Christian must have come to seek healing pushes him in the front without any consultation or even consent. No healing takes place and as the crowd scatters away the "poor" disabled is left alone, still with his disability, the reason given being that he had no faith. Hypothetical as this may seem, these are live experiences in the part of the world where I come from and I have personally been a victim of such circumstances. As can therefore be seen, whereas healing can bring joy and relief, it can also bring pain, frustration and raises serious theological questions.

One might want to ask, are the healing stories today a matter of faith, reality or imagination? Are some, if not most of the evangelists who claim divine healing especially where it refers to cure or fixing up of impairments that cause disabilities, true to their proclamations or are they seeking self-glory impervious to the humiliation, embarrassment and frustration on the part of those who are the subjects of their attempted healing missions? Most important, in this modern age of information, communication and technology, with all the assistive devices to enable persons with disabilities to function in the society and to take part in nearly all aspects of societal life, is miraculous cure or fixing of impairments in the body the central reason for presenting those who bear these impairments to

God? Were this the case, then the soul which is the ultimate subject of the gospel mission is less important than the physical body. People, irrespective of their bodily condition need to hear and to be reached with the gospel. They need to partake in getting the gospel to others. Their impairments can neither be a cause for their remission of sin nor an excuse for their failure to play their part in the extension of the kingdom. This is best illustrated by the example of St Paul who, having a bodily condition he calls a thorn in the flesh that troubled him, prayed three times to have it taken away. Instead of a cure, God assured him that divine grace was sufficient to uphold him. In the process, Paul gets the revelation that God's strength is perfected in weakness (2 Cor. 12: 7-8). Is that same grace not sufficient to persons with disabilities to march on as crusaders of the gospels and partakers of the kingdom?

I have mentioned differing teachings, doctrine and theology. These have at times led to serious and unhelpful paternalistic and patronizing attitudes in the church. The interpretation and belief among some churches that there is a relationship between disability, sickness and sin has made them develop an attitude of pity and sympathy to those people who are disabled or sick. To them, the presence of people with disabilities in the church is a sign that the church is unable to combat the devil that is the source of these infirmities. The response to this is endless prayers for those in this condition and when these prayers do not yield the expected result, the victim is blamed for having no faith. The consequent relation is that the person in question will opt to stay away, not only from that particular church but also from the Christian faith. This explains why more often than not, persons with disabilities feel alienated, marginalized, embarrassed and, in some cases, offended by the treatment meted out to them by the church.

While we cannot blame a church for the interpretation of the Bible that they may adopt, it is necessary in this age that a more inclusive and empowering theology and, therefore, interpretation of the Bible be adopted. Although Jesus in his language in some of the gospel healing stories seems to have associated healing with forgiveness of sins, he is at the same time the one who led the way in departing from this line of thoughts. Referring to the man born blind (John 9: 1-3), contrary to the belief expressed by his disciples that the man must have been blind because of either his own sins or those of his parents, Jesus made it clear that his blindness had nothing to do with sins. He was blind so that God's work may be made manifest in him. The interpretation to the gospel healing stories needs to take this line of thought.

The healing stories in the New Testament and especially those in the gospel had a hidden dimension that modern society should consider as it deals with disability in the current concept of healing and reconciliation. In the first place, Jesus made precedence in including the sick and the disabled as a focus of concern in his ministry. He chose to use healing to unite them with the rest of the society. Prior to his time, they were excluded, ignored and considered unclean. His reconciling mission meant good news for the poor, release for oppressed, recovery of sight to the blind and freedom for the oppressed (Luke 4: 18).

Healing as a means of reconciliation in respect of ministry to persons with disabilities had two complementary dimensions: cure and restoration. Restoration has been seen in this context as what could be defined as healing to distinguish it from cure. Jesus' mission had to take into consideration the aspect that the society of the day best understood. That was the cure though it was only a means to the end and not necessarily the end. What was, and still is, most important in our reconciliation message is the acceptance, inclusion and restoration into the mainstream of the society. In order to understand this aspect of the mission, let us take a few further examples.

When the blind Bartimaeus (Mark 10: 46-52) received his sight, we are told that he joined with the rest of the crowd that followed Jesus. He became one of them and was no longer isolated, excluded and ignored. He was no longer the blind beggar on the roadside. Not only was he cured from his blindness, he was restored and reconciled with the rest of the society which previously had rebuked him, screamed at him, spoke at him instead of speaking to him, considered him different, inferior and imperfect.

In the story of the physically disabled man at the Beautiful Gate (Acts 3: 1-10), it is clear that on gaining strength in his legs, he entered the temple and joined with the rest in worship and praise to God. Prior to that, he was a stranger who, though always in the sight of the temple, had no business with what went on there. His cure was the means of his reconciliation not only with the people but also with God. He became a worshipper like the rest of the community. He was no longer different as he had been reconciled with his people.

In the John 5: 1-18 story of the man who had been at the pool of Bethsaida for 38 years, we are told that he met with Jesus later after his cure in the temple. This might probably be the first time that he had ever been to a temple because his disability, according to the Jewish culture and religion, made him unclean and therefore unworthy of being in a holy place. Like the other two, he had been restored, set free, made human and therefore reconciled with the rest of the Jewish people.

There are approximately 26 different scripture references about people with such infirmities as paralysis, blindness, deafness or physical disabilities in the gospels. There are, in accordance to the Judeo-Christian culture and practice of the day, some main distinct characteristics in all of them. They have no names, they are poor, unemployed, beggars or servants. They are patronized, treated with contempt, publicly rebuked and humiliated. It is from this state of affairs that Jesus declares that he came to set the captives free and to give release to the oppressed. His healing mission, though at times within the language of forgiveness of sin as this is what the Jews understood, was precisely to set free those who had lived in the bondage of oppression, ridicule and humiliation. He invited them to his banquet table contrary to the expectations of the prevailing norm and practice.

As already mentioned in the WCC interim statement, at the beginning of the 21st century, as was the case before the Christian era, sectors of the population who are unable to compete or to perform at the levels that society demands are vitiated, despised or, in more contemporary terms, discarded. Among them, we find a high proportion of people with sensorial, motor and mental disabilities. We will find them living in any of the great cities of the world: men and women of all ages, ethnic backgrounds, colours, cultures and religions who, because they have a disability, live in abject poverty, hunger, dependence, preventable disease and maltreatment by those who are "able".

It is the role of the church in this new century to face the reality of humanity in the image of a disabled Jesus on the cross; the reality of people with disabilities who are rejected and abandoned. It is painful that the churches throughout the world have not addressed more vigorously the sufferings of marginalized, poor, blind, deaf, and physically and mentally limited people. We do not need pity, or mercy, but compassionate understanding and opportunities to develop our vocations, possibilities and abilities.

In their efforts to attain peace, preserve the environment, ensure the equality of women and the rights of the child, care for the aged, churches and Christians should also include the struggle for the full realization of disabled persons in their agendas.

Suffices to mention that over the past twenty years, positive attitudes towards disability and disabled persons have increased in our churches and Christian institutions. While far from being universal, this is a welcome development. But it is important to be aware that, in some parts of the world and in some churches, there has recently been a return towards over-protection and even disregard of disabled persons. In some places, evangelical groups have manipulated us. Even worse than being ignored, manipulating disabled people could become the church's newest sin.

In light of this, it is necessary for the church to consider defining healing in dealing with persons with disabilities in the widest possible meaning to ensure that all aspects of their lives are sensitively and realistically covered. One helpful option is to define dealing with disabilities in a way that makes a clear distinction between healing and cure. Healing is understood to be the removal of oppressive systems, whereas curing has to do with physiological reconstruction of the physical body. In this kind of theology, disability is a social contract and healing is the removal of social barriers. From this perspective, the healing stories in the gospels are primarily concerned with the restoration of the person to their communities, although for the purpose of making it illustrative for the Jews, the gospels described cure of physiological conditions.

The prevailing emphasis on physical healing of the body found in the charismatic theology is not the only problem persons with disability encounter in the church. The more liberal theology of the traditional organized churches too has its share of keeping persons with disabilities outside. In the first place, the charity approach to disability has been the most negative aspect in their address to disability concern. They are largely responsible for the growth and maintenance of a "helping" profession, which relegates persons with disabilities to a receiving role. Helping becomes an excuse for exclusion and this is characterized by separate schools, rehabilitation centres and other caring institutions. Very few churches have developed procedures for initiation of persons with disabilities, and especially the intellectually disabled, into sacraments prerequisite to full church membership.

In the process of caring, persons with disabilities are not considered to have anything to offer in the church. Even those well exposed and willing to serve find it very difficult to be incorporated into the life of the church. Being educated in these church-run institutions does not seem to make any difference. They are assumed to be disabled and therefore needing to be served rather than to serve. Their place is seen to be in special institutions set aside and not in the central operation of the church. No wonder that, although many persons with disabilities are educated in these church-run institutions, the church is unable to account for their whereabouts after their school life. They do not feel welcome and as such they do not associate with the church. The few bold ones who persist find their presence largely ignored. It will be an open fact, for example, that most of such churches represented in this conference or in any international or regional ecumenical fora, there will already be established mechanism to ensure that representation of women, youth and clergy is ensured. We had difficulties to get any persons with disabilities to Athens because no church wanted to consider them in their delegations since they do not fall in the classifications they are familiar with of women, youth and clergy. The situation is no different in the WCC members, regional and national ecumenical organizations. Thus, persons with disabilities are not considered to belong and are therefore largely not included in the life of the church.

In summing up the fundamental theological principle that guides the WCC interim statement, it is made clear that the integration of disabled people within the church gives testimony to God's love as expressed by all his sons and daughters. It is a continuation of Christ's healing mission. It can also be an example and an inspiration in those societies in which disabled people suffer from humiliating marginalization.

Whether the church is involved in provision of care, rehabilitation, chaplaincy or ministry to or with disabled people, it must recognize the central assumptions of equality and dignity within the Christian message and promote it at the fore of all its work.

The church is by definition a place and a process of communion, open to and inviting all people without discrimination. It is a place of hospitality and a place of welcome, in the manner that Abraham and Sarah received God's messengers in the Old Testament (Gen. 18). It is an earthly reflection of a divine unity that is at the same time worshipped as Trinity. It is a community of people with different yet complementary gifts. St Paul reminds us: "For as in one body we have many members, and not all members have the same function, so we, though we are many, are one body in Christ, and individually we are members one of another..."
It is a vision of wholeness as well as of healing, of caring and of sharing at once. Just as the body is one and has many members so it is with Christ (1 Cor.12:12).

We all accept and proclaim that this is what the church is and stands for. It is the basis of our unity as Christians. Then why is it that, all too often, certain people among us and around us (usually those whom we consider as being unfamiliar or as strangers, as different or perhaps disabled) are marginalized and even excluded? Wherever this happens, even by passive omission, the church is not being what it is called to become. The church is denying its own reality. In the church, we are called to act differently. As St Paul says, the parts of the body which seem to be weaker (we should notice that he does not say "actually are weaker") are indispensable (1 Cor. 2:22).

As the Interim Statement concludes, in our attitudes and actions towards one another, at all times, the guiding principle must be the conviction that we are incomplete, we are less than whole, without the gifts and talents of all people. We are not a full community without one another. Responding to and fully including people with disabilities is not an option for the churches of Christ. It is the church's defining characteristic.

Reconciliation: The Major Conflict in Post-Modernity

An Orthodox Contribution to a Missiological Dialogue

*Athanasios N. Papathanasiou**

Diseases such as AIDS today, or leprosy in earlier times, push those suffering from them to the margins of society - or keep them within society, provided there is some guarantee that everyone else will be safe. These diseases are of such nightmarish proportions that this social logic seems well-founded. So of course it sounds like sheer absurdity when we hear the witness of the monasticism of the Egyptian desert (ca. 5th century). Abba Agathon, we are told, was aflame with such love that he wanted to find a leper and exchange his own body for that of the leper![1]

What sort of perspective, we may ask, can give rise to an attitude such as this? What understanding does it indicate of "oneself" and the "other", of "disruption" and "co-existence"?

We are living in the midst of a state of world-wide flux described by the ambiguous term "post-modernity".[2] On the international stage, it seems that we have the intersection of two antithetical tendencies. On the one hand, certain specific forces

* Dr Athanasios N. Papathanasiou has graduated in law and in theology and holds a doctorate in theology. He teaches at the Higher Ecclesiastical School, Athens, and is the editor-in-chief of the theological quarterly *Synaxe*, published in Athens. Here he wishes to thank Dr Elizabeth Theokritoff for her linguistic help with this paper.

[1] "Sayings of the Desert Fathers", Agathon, 26, *Patrologia Graeca* 65, 116C; *The Sayings of the Desert Fathers: The alphabetical collection* (Benedicta Ward, tr.), Mowbrays, London 1975, p. 20.
[2] It is disputed whether the term "post-modernity" indicates a truly new period in history following the demise of modernity and the Enlightenment, or simply the most recent stage of modernity. See Charles Van Engen, "Mission Theology in the Light of Post-Modern Critique", *International Review of Mission* 343 (1997), pp. 437-461 and Petros Vassiliadis, "The Universal Claims of Orthodoxy and the Particularity of Witness in a Pluralist World", in: *The Orthodox Churches in a Pluralistic World. An Ecumenical Conversation* (Emmanuel Clapsis, ed.), WCC Publications / Holy Cross Orthodox Press, Geneva / Brookline 2004, p. 195.

of globalization (such as technology and economics) reinforce monoculture and tend towards turning the world into a homogeneous "global village".[3] On the other hand, however, we see the rise of the conviction that in reality, not only is there not *one* world, but every single local human context forms a water-tight and self-contained world, with its own "truth" which is valid for itself alone;[4] holistic interpretations of the cosmos (the so-called grand narratives) are rejected as being without foundation.[5]

There are of course a variety of views on these questions; we have mentioned these two extreme views by way of example so as to be able to paint in bold strokes the spectrum within which the Christian faith is called to bear witness. Post-modernity brings to the fore a fundamental truth that has been ridden roughshod over by aggressive missionizing and cultural expansionism. This is the truth that human life is not ahistorical and abstract, but concrete and many-sided. But post-modernity also presents a challenge to Christian theology: to the degree that the various contexts are understood as entirely self-contained, the belief is that their meaning comes from within themselves, from their own constituent elements.

If, however, genuine reality actually does consist of enclosed, self-sufficient clusters, how then is modern man to evaluate realities such as conflict and reconciliation? Is it justified, for example, to accept reconciliation as a *holistic* vision, and correspondingly to condemn hatred as a holistic nightmare; or are we obliged to accept both as equally legitimate, as elements of particular clusters which cannot be subject to a *holistic* critique? To put it another way: can there be a perspective that will not sacrifice the unity of humanity, but will not stifle its discrete particularities in imperialistic fashion either? To be still more concrete: is it possible to give a firm answer to the question of what constitutes "disruption" and "reconciliation", what is a "wound" and what is "healing", if that answer is not based on a firm doctrine of the world and the human being? As Anastasios, archbishop of Tirana and all Albania, put it in the plenary address to the San Antonio Conference on World Mission and Evangelism (1989), "the simplistic anthropology that encourages a naive morality by passing our existential tragedy by does not help at all".[6]

EXISTENCE AS A CALL TO RECONCILIATION

In contrast with the beliefs that the world derives meaning from itself or from some divine element that forms a constituent part of it, the Christian faith introduces a radically new perspective, a perspective based on the logic of relationship between

---

[3] Cf. Marshall McLuhan – Bruce P. Powers, *The Global Village. Transformations in World Life and Media in the 21st Century*, Oxford University Press 1992. On the "compression of time and space" see David Harvey, *The Condition of Postmodernity*, Blackwell, Oxford 1989, p. 240 and Anthony Giddens, *The Consequences of Modernity*, Polity Press, Cambridge 1990, p. 14.
[4] A presentation of the gradations of the post-modern position and a theological dialogue with them is attempted by Sue Patterson, *Realist Christian Theology in a Postmodern Age*, Cambridge University Press, Cambridge 1999, pp. 7-11.
[5] See, for example, Zygmunt Bauman, *Intimations of Postmodernity*, Routledge, London 1992 and Sheila Greeve Davaney, "Theology and the Turn to Cultural Analysis", in: *Converging on Culture. Theologians in Dialogue with Cultural Analysis and Criticism* (Delwin Brown et al., eds.), Oxford University Press, Oxford 2001, p. 5.
[6] Anastasios of Androussa, "Thy Will be Done; Mission in Christ's Way", *New Directions in Mission and Evangelization* (James A. Scherer - Stephen B. Bevans, eds.), Orbis Books, vol. 2, Maryknoll, New York 1994, p. 33.

genuinely *distinctive* subjects. The world, by its very nature, is subject to decay and death. If by any chance it does exist spontaneously, then it will never get beyond that fate. If, however, God is indeed wholly Other, and if he is indeed as Trinitarian theology claims (in other words, if he really is endless life and unbroken communion), then the world has the monumental possibility of coming to participate in God's life – in a new mode of existence, a mode of existence that cannot be provided by any of its own constituent parts. The possibility for such opening-up is a structural datum in human nature.[7] Participation in God's life is not something *additional* to being complete as human beings. On the contrary, it is the very *attainment* of our completeness as human beings. The same applies to creation as a whole. The unification of the parts of the world and its reconciliation with God is ministered by man acting as "microcosm" and "mediator"[8] – certainly not as the proprietor or rapist of the world. This dynamic (which, *inter alia*, offers Christian theology the possibility of a meaningful attitude towards the ecological question and the task of reconciliation between man and the world) must be conceived of as a historical action which finds its proper place in the perspective of the eschatological renewal of the cosmos; but we will refer to this perspective later on.

This means that sin consists in man affirming his autonomy, enclosing himself in his own essence and, ultimately, in death. Thus death is interwoven with individualism, while life is paired with relationship. The hope of the entire cosmos is based on the *otherness* of God vis-à-vis the world, and salvation is understood as *communion*.

This brings us to a point on which the Eastern Fathers insist, and which has always seemed a paradox to Western thought, at least until modern times.[9] I am referring to the theology that approaches the mystery of the Holy Trinity by giving priority to the persons rather than the essence. To speak of "priority" here does not, of course, mean that the one is temporally prior to the other. It means that the hypostasis is not defined individually, on the basis of the properties of its essence; it is defined on the basis of the fact that it exists in communion with the other hypostases. In this perspective, I have authentic existence when otherness is not something parallel or opposite to my own identity, but *an element of* my identity. Truth and communion coincide.[10] This coincidence has a significant impact on the human being's religious identity. The meeting point with Christ is not an ideology, but the person of our fellow-man. It is impossible to come to know the truth of Christ outside the mystery of communion with the other (Mat. 7:21-23, 25:34-45, John 17:20-23). At the same time, precisely because the Church's doctrine is an expression of this understanding and an invitation to this experience, is of vital importance to seek out this doctrine and remain faithful to

---

[7] See Panayiotis Nellas, *Deification in Christ; Orthodox Perspectives on the Nature of the Human Person*, St Vladimir's Seminary Press, Crestwood, 1987.

[8] Cf. Lars Thunberg, *Microcosm and Mediator; The Theological Anthropology of Maximus the Confessor*, Open Court, Chicago / La Salle, Illinois 19952. See also Elizabeth Theokritoff, "Embodied Word and New Creation: Some Modern Orthodox Insights Concerning the Material World", in: *Abba: The Tradition of Orthodoxy in the West* (John Behr, Andrew Louth and Dimitri Conomos, eds.), St Vladimir's Seminary Press, Crestwood 1985, pp. 221-238.

[9] Cf. Willie J. Jennings, "Person (Person and Individualism)", in: *Dictionary of the Ecumenical Movement* (Nicholas Lossky et al., eds), WCC Publications, Geneva 20022, pp. 907-908; John Zizioulas, Metropolitan of Pergamon, "Communion and Otherness", *St Vladimir's Theological Quarterly* 38.4 (1994), pp. 347-361.

[10] See John Zizioulas, *Being as Communion*, St Vladimir's Seminary Press, Crestwood, 1985, pp. 101-105, 134.

it. Given this, whenever we set *truth* and *love* in opposition to each other in one way or another, we end up in a state of schizophrenia.

Here, then, is the meaning of conversion to the trinitarian mode of existence as revealed by the Trinitarian God. Both this conversion and the invitation to it are something totally different from proselytism or from any "colonization of mind".[11] Nor is it a decision that gives one the illusion of having assured salvation. Rather, it is a journey which constantly needs to be reaffirmed, and which never achieves finality within history. We might rather speak of an *asceticism of conversion*. Why asceticism? Because, given that the God of Christianity is acknowledged as a personal being - that is, as a being which desires, plans, acts, responds (and, consequently, not as something impersonal and inert) - humans are invited to embark on a sort of 'athletic training': they are invited to accept the invitation of this God, to become his disciples and friends, to engage in a personal relationship to him. Personal relationships have a grandeur about them; nevertheless, they also carry a risk. They may thrive, but they may also break down. Personal relationship involves the uncertainty that accompanies freedom; it lacks the assurances provided by mechanical procedures or magic. Thus, those among us who are convinced unreservedly that we have secured the Holy Spirit in our life and actions should at least acknowledge God's right to disagree with the choices we have made. If I am to be truly Christian, I must be ready to confess that I do not have God in my pocket!

Our desire to denounce proselytism with all its negative features (aggressive recruitment, narrowly individualistic piety, cultural alienation etc.[12]) is altogether legitimate; but if in the process we also denounce conversion, we will be doing an injustice to the Gospel message and impoverishing man. What makes us human is our capacity to question whatever appears as given and self-evident and, consequently, to judge what is meaningful to life, what promotes life and what distorts it. If man is not open to striving after this quest, he degenerates into a mere product of biological, cultural and ethnic randomness. Unless it is accepted as part of our anthropology that the orientation of the human being in all its dimensions (personal, cultural, political etc.) *can* change, repentance and reconciliation make no sense.

Division between human beings is a wound, a trauma. But we can contribute to the healing of division only by experiencing it truly *as* a trauma, not by closing our eyes to it. It is obvious that *imperialism* is contemptuous of otherness, since its aim is to impose its own "truth" on others. There is also, however, another attitude that is in reality contemptuous of otherness - one that is supposedly the absolute antithesis of imperialism. This is the belief that all truth claims, all faiths, all traditions and all cultures are basically saying the same thing, or that all convictions must be unquestionably accepted as valid.

---

[11] The phrase is taken from Brian Stanley's interesting article "Conversion to Christianity: The Colonization of Mind?", *International Review of Mission* 366 (2003), pp. 315-331.
[12] On this question, see for example Petros Vassiliadis, "Mission and proselytism. An Orthodox Understanding", *International Review of Mission* 337 (1996), pp. 257-275; issue on: "Religious Freedom and Proselytism", *The Ecumenical Review* 50 (1998); issue on: "Christian Conversion and mission", *International Bulletin of Missionary Research* 28 (2004).

This tendency is not imperialistic; it is however *paternalistic*, and it is likewise a problem because although it does not attack "othernesses" directly, in reality it bypasses them because it does not acknowledge that they have real content. It does not recognize any true difference; difference is illusory. For this reason, it does not dare to attempt the sort of encounter with others that might be critical, but would provide genuine opportunities for the enrichment of those who partake in it together. The Holy Spirit is connected with communion (2 Cor. 13:13). Do we not fall into a contradiction, however, if we appeal to this truth in theological perspectives that in reality wrench the Holy Spirit out of communion? This can happen whenever Pneumatology, Christology, Ecclesiology and Trinitarian doctrine are divorced from one another,[13] and the Spirit is presented as all-embracing, presumably encompassing even views that deify individualism or legitimize the sovereignty of death! Thus one of the most generous gestures towards reconciliation may be the humble willingness to engage in dialogue and take upon ourselves the pains of brotherly debate.

CONVERSION TO THE KINGDOM

On the basis of what we said earlier, reconciliation has existential and cosmic dimensions. It is not first and foremost a matter of going *back* (as the prefix re- might suggest) but of going forward. In other words, it is not a matter of human beings returning to some lost paradise, but rather of the entire universe attaining to that future for which it was created, but which has yet to become a reality. Here I am referring, of course, to the eschatological kingdom of God, where decay, evil and death will be abolished. Whereas in general the future is regarded as an effect of the past, for the church the cause of the past (and of the present) is precisely the future. The incarnation of the Son did not take place as a result of the (past) fall of our forefathers, but for the sake of the (future) transformation of creation into the kingdom.

The character of the kingdom is of crucial significance, since it is well attested that different types of eschatology have their own profound impact on missionary theory and methods.[14] Thus, it is of especial importance that the kingdom should be understood as something meta-historical - as a reality that is not to be identified with a stage in history. What I am talking about is neither a withdrawal to an individualistic model of mission, nor an esoteric eschatology, nor indeed a flight from the vision of justice and peace on earth. I am talking about what that pioneer of the ecumenical movement, the late Fr Georges Florovsky, called "inaugurated eschatology".[15] The Kingdom has already been inaugurated, but not yet fulfilled. Its

---

[13] Cf. Zizioulas' comments on heresy and schism as choices which have practical, existential consequences, and cause *otherness* to degenerate into *disarray*, "Communion and Otherness", *op.cit.*, p. 356. We certainly cannot deal with these issues in detail here. Let us simply note, however, that Pneumatology is not subsequent to the Incarnation of the Son; the Incarnation is itself Pneumatologically conditioned. Besides, the Orthodox belief that God's energies in the cosmos are uncreated affirms that the Holy Trinity (while being ontologically / essentially the ultimate Other) has always been truly and immediately present and active in the world and in history.

[14] See Jürgen Moltman, *The Coming of God. Christian Eschatology*, SCM Press, London 1996, pp. 12-22; David Bosch, *Transforming Mission. Paradigm Shifts in Theology of Mission*, Orbis Books, New York 1992, pp. 498-510.

[15] Georges Florovsky, *Bible, Church, Tradition* (The Collected Works, 1), Büchervertriebsanstalt, Vaduz/Belmont 1987, pp. 35-36 and idem, *The Metaphysical Premises of Utopianism* (The Collected Works, 12), op. cit., 1989, pp. 75-93. See also Athanasios N. Papathanasiou, *Religion, Ideology and Science*, Alexander Press, Montreal 2004, pp. 10-19.

fulfillment is conceived as a future, post-historical event that inspires and demands historical action and struggle on the side of the victims and the oppressed, but, at the same time, it leaves the history open to the future, to human freedom and to God's unpredictable initiatives. If a certain phase in history is declared in advance to be final, inevitable and irrevocable - that is, to be the point after which history can supposedly go no further - then this opens the way to oppression or theocracy. The experience of the church and the torments of humankind can well testify to that. Remember the way in which the empires (Eastern and Western alike) saw themselves, or how the identification of the Millennium with certain social models led in many cases to the imperialistic imposition of western values, capitalism and technology.[16] For the same reasons, reconciliation needs to be understood as a continuous and open-ended process of self-criticism and repentance on every level (personal, theological, social, economic etc.).

TRANSFIGURATION INTO THE CHURCH

The Orthodox Divine Liturgy begins with an invocation of both the Holy Trinity and the kingdom at the same time: "Blessed is the Kingdom of the Father and of the Son and of the Holy Spirit". History is illumined by the light of the Last Times, the *eschata*. Thus the *eschata* are imprinted upon the present in such a way as to reveal the relational mode of existence of the Trinity and the communal character of the kingdom: that is to say, they are imprinted on the present as church. The church is neither an association of individuals nor a secular organization. Being the body of Christ "she is [...] neither confining the Spirit of God to her institutional organization seen as a sociological unit, nor imprisoning the individual by human authority [...]. There are no limitations to the grace of God, but, within this limitless grace, the Church represents the new action of God in Christ, through the Spirit, as an act of redeeming and of gathering all people into One fellowship".[17] It is indicative that the Greek equivalent to "to forgive" is *syn-chorein*, which means to "come together", to "meet the others".[18] Forgiveness is not a juridical decision, but the restoration of the communion which has been damaged by sin.

The church is the first fruits of creation's new mode of existence, the anticipation of the kingdom and the servant of the *missio Dei*.[19] This means that mission is not something that has to do only with what the church does, but first and foremost with what the church *is*.[20] It is indicative that the eucharist, the sacrament that

---

[16] Brian Stanley, *The Bible and the Flag. Protestant Missions and British Imperialism in the Nineteenth and Twentieth Centuries*, Apollos, Leicester 1992, p. 59; David J. Bosch, op.cit., pp. 319-327; Timothy Yates, *Christian Mission in the Twentieth Century*, Cambridge University Press 1994, pp. 75-76, 179; *Das Recht des Menschen auf Eigentum* (Johannes Schwartländer - Dietmar Willoweit, eds.), Kehl am Rhein, Strassburg 1986, p. 2.

[17] N. A. Nissiotis, "An Orthodox View of Modern Trends in Evangelism", in: *The Ecumenical World of Orthodox Civilization (Russia and Orthodoxy, v. II), Essays in honor of Georges Florovsky* (Andrew Blane, ed.), Mouton, The Hague – Paris 1973, pp. 189-190.

[18] H. Liddell – R. Scott, *Greek-English Lexicon*, Clarendon Press, Oxford 1996 rev., p. 1669.

[19] On the introduction and use of this term, as well as questions connecting it with the church, see Jacques Matthey, "God's Mission Today: Summary and Conclusions", *International Review of Mission* 367 (2003), p. 582.

[20] See Athanasios N. Papathanasiou, *Future, the Background of History; Essays on Church Mission in an Age of Globalization*, Alexander Press, Montreal 2005, p. 13. In his "Editorial" [*International Review of Mission* 372(2005), p. 6], Jacques Matthey pertinently notes how in the 1960s, ecumenical interest moved from overemphasizing the missionary role of the Church to downgrading it, to focus today once again on the relationship between Church and mission.

makes the church, is at the same time a missionary event: whenever the church community celebrates the eucharist, it is witnessing to the kingdom which we await; as Saint Paul says, it proclaims the Lord's death until he comes (1 Cor. 11:26), and thus interprets the *interim* (the time between the first and second comings of Christ) as the time for mission. Here the problem of Christian division arises. This problem cannot be discussed at length here; let us however present it in broad outline. The disarray in the Christian world can neither be passed by as if it did not even exist, nor can it be legitimized as if it were not even a problem. The inability of the Christians today to subscribe to the same apostolic faith, which would enable them to partake in the same holy eucharist, constitutes a major obstacle to the realization of common mission and evangelism[21] (apart, of course, from initiatives for witness, reconciliation and cooperation which are feasible in several areas). There is likewise a problem when apostolic faith is conceived as a fleshless ideology; that is, when it is indeed proclaimed, but in reality is not allowed to permeate the way the church body is constructed and to transform its everyday life. So Christian communities still have a long way to go, as regards both relations with each other and their own interior life. And to make headway here requires four inseparable preconditions (which we have already mentioned several times above):
- experience of disunity as pain;
- willingness for encounter with the other;
- reluctance to minimize the importance of theology; and
- readiness for repentance.

Ecclesial existence implies what we underlined earlier - conversion to the Trinitarian mode of existence, and an orientation towards God's kingdom. As a result, the church members betray her authentic self when they lapse into confessionalism or power games, or when they slip into the arrogant conviction that they are the proprietors of grace. It is characteristic that Orthodox worship has a profound epicletic character. We see this, for example, in the celebration of the eucharist, the event in which the vision for cosmic reconciliation is made manifest: here the church community beseeches the Holy Spirit to transform the bread and wine into the body and blood of Christ here and now. It is the new action of the Spirit that makes the church to be church, not simply the recollection of its action in the

---

[21] It was in the early 1970s that Fr. John Meyendorff (criticizing the merger of the International Missionary Council and the World Council of Churches in 1961, at the Fourth Assembly of the WCC in New Delhi) wrote that "mission in its ultimate theological meaning [...] cannot grow out of a divided Christendom, but only from the One Church, and leads to conversion to this One Church". See John Meyendorff, "The Orthodox Church and Mission: Past and Present Perspectives", *St Vladimir's Theological Quarterly* 16 (1972), p. 63. For the various approaches to this issue see Yates, *op.cit.*, pp. 129-132. See, for example, Ion Bria, "Witness (Common Witness)", *Dictionary of the Ecumenical Movement*, op.cit., p. 1208, who takes the moderate position that: "Common Christian witness cannot replace the theological debate searching for the unity on a common faith, but it can help Christians to realize, through their unity in evangelism and mission, the visibility of their incomplete universality". One should take into account that on the part of the WCC ("Mission and Evangelism in Unity Today", *"You are the Light of the World": Statements on Mission by the World Council of Churches 1980-2005*, WCC Publications, Geneva 2005, p. 64) it is stated that "the search for ways of witnessing together in unity and cooperation [...] avoiding any form of confessional rivalry or competition [...] does not imply an unrealistic super-church ecclesiology; neither does it deny the intrinsic relationship between mission and ecclesiology".

past.[22] And so, being animated by the Spirit in this way, the church bears witness to the Resurrection in the face of death in all its forms, without falling into a dichotomy which divides spiritual life from the material side of life. Characteristic is a testimony from the work of St Gregory Palamas (14th. c.), an ascetic bishop and teacher of "deification" (which is often misunderstood as mysticism and a retreat from history). In order to explain the true meaning of fasting, he quotes the prophet Isaiah (58:5-10), who places especial emphasis on healing as solidarity: the kind of fasting I have chosen, says the Lord, is "to loose the chains of injustice, [...] to set the oppressed free and break every yoke [...]. Then [...] your healing will quickly appear".[23]

Abba Agathon's wish, to which we referred at the beginning, is nothing other than an indication of the kenotic, ecclesial mode of existence. It is a way of affirming in practice the outpouring of the Trinitarian life and the Incarnation of the Son, who took upon Himself the pain of the world with a love offered without any preconditions (religious, cultural, ideological, ethnic).

Avoiding the simplistic interpretations which see globalization and post-modernity only as a melting-pot, or, to the contrary, only as an inevitable clash of civilizations, we are called to see the present state of affairs as an occasion for *critical creativity*. By the term *creativity* I mean that the church is not allowed to understand herself as a remnant of a sacred era belonging to the past. The cultural data of the present can never be for her merely something that surrounds her. They must be seen as the material through which God will appear to the people of today. These data make up the actual life of real, tangible people, that life which must be offered to the Holy Spirit and be grafted into the flesh of Christ. This does not mean simply imitating a glorious past. It demands a new creative work which must however be undertaken with caution, not with a naiveté which would threaten to drive the church into secularization. The qualifier *critical* (implying discretion, investigation and judgment) is intended to shed light on this point. The mission of the church is not only to embrace the realities of the world, but also to judge them. The Holy Spirit is constantly at work in the world, but not everything that is happening in the world is necessarily the work of the Spirit. As is well known, Christ's incarnation did not legitimize the human datum called slavery, nor did his resurrection herald reconciliation with the datum called death. It is precisely because the notions of encounter, koinonia and partnership are of fundamental significance, that the criteria for their realization are of crucial importance. It is therefore of great interest to look into many other issues through this prism. Take, for example, the optimistic modern sociological theories about "cultural hybridization",[24] which more or less

---

[22] Similarly, the Church experiences Christ's resurrection as the culmination of his action in history and as the sign of the final resurrection, the first fruits of the coming transformation and liberation of the universe from decay (1 Cor. 15, Col. 1:18, Acts 26:23). Thus, the eucharistic gathering does not derive its content solely from remembrance, but also from the anticipation of the final resurrection, as implied by Paul (1 Cor. 11:26) and as explicitly proclaimed in Eastern liturgical anaphoras. See Anton Hänggi – Irmgard Pahl, *Prex Eucharistica. Textus a variis liturgiis antiquioribus selecti*, Editions Universitaires, Fribourg 1968, p. 248 (cf. pp. 112, 120).

[23] Gregory Palamas, "Sermon 13", Patrologia Graeca 151, 161C-165B. (Scripture taken from the *Holy Bible, New International Version*, International Bible Society 19843).

[24] Cf. Emmanuel Clapsis, "The Challenge of a Global World", in: *The Orthodox Churches in a Pluralistic World*, *op.cit.*, p. 54-59.

claim that the present global situation cannot be read only as an anguished struggle for the survival of existing cultural entities, but as an opportunity for new cultural syntheses to appear. We should think how far views such as these converge in a fruitful way with those elements of the Christian experience that are able to build cultures of coexistence and social justice, avoiding equally both fragmentation and totalitarianism.

The challenge here is how to become faithful listeners to the Spirit who blows wherever it pleases; how to learn to be co-workers with a transcendent God who, because he is incarnate in particular human contexts without being confined within those contexts, brings reconciliation to a shattered world and the healing of every form of leprosy.

PLENARY MAY 12

Mission and Violence - Building a Culture of Peace

A Decade to Overcome Violence – Mid-term event

In the beginning of the plenary on Wednesday morning May 12, 2005, youth delegates and stewards took to the stage of the main tent. Without resorting to spoken words, nine young performers enacted the shattering of a community circle and desecration of the cross through acts of racism, colonialism, exclusion, ecological destruction and prejudice against the poor, women and persons with HIV/AIDS. These victims were portrayed by women, but the remaining man was labelled as a victim of his own ignorance.

As the audience sang the conference theme "Come, Holy Spirit, heal and reconcile", dozens of stewards and youth delegates proceeded to the stage where they liberated those who had been bound, raised the fallen and began to restore the broken community.

Following the projection of a video introducing the DOV, Rev. Dr **Fernando Enns**[1] took over as moderator of the plenary:

"Sisters and Brothers,
We are gathering in the presence of a truly violent world."
Therefore we pray: "Come, Holy Spirit, heal and reconcile"

To a great extent, the theme of this important Conference on World Mission and Evangelism was inspired by and chosen because of the Ecumenical Decade to Overcome Violence – Churches seeking reconciliation and peace 2001-2010.

At the 8th Assembly of the WCC in Harare, Zimbabwe we, the churches from around the world, have committed ourselves to this Decade:
- because we do not believe that violence is the final word;
- because we do not agree that there are moments in times of crisis and conflict when the people of God have to step back and agree to the use of violence;
- because we do not believe any longer that we will overcome evil by evil, but by doing good.

We have committed ourselves to this Decade:

- because we truly believe that the Apostle Paul is referring to us, the ecumenical family, when he says in his letter to the Corinthians, that we are a "new creation", "from God who reconciled us to himself through Christ and gave us the ministry of reconciliation " (2 Cor 5);

---

[1] Dr Fernando Enns, from the Mennonite Church in Germany, spoke as a faculty member in systematic theology and ecumenical studies at Heidelberg University in Germany. He is a member of the WCC Central Committee and of the reference group for the Decade to Overcome Violence.

- because we are beginning to understand that the church not only has a mission, but as a true *koinonia* of the Triune God is a mission itself – to witness the love of Jesus Christ, a love that is active, non-violent, emphatic and compassionate – reaching out far beyond our own community;

- because we listen and we hear that in Christ we are called to be healing communities – for the healing of all. All nations, ethnic groups, different traditions and denominations, men and women, persons living with disabilities, young and old, rich and poor, and yes all of creation. In order to become what we are in the messianic perspective: a healing *koinonia* – because we are healed in Christ.

When we launched the DOV internationally at Berlin in 2001, at the very symbolic site of the Brandenburg Gate, that had been a separating site for so many years and was finally an open gate again – the delegates of the churches agreed to these goals:
- to address holistically the wide varieties of violence, direct and structural, in homes, communities and in international arenas;
- to overcome the spirit, logic and practice of violence;
- to relinquish any theological justification of violence;
- to affirm anew the spirituality of reconciliation and active non-violence;
- to create a new understanding of security in terms of cooperation and community instead of domination and competition;
- to learn from the spirituality and resources for peace-building of other faiths; and
- to reflect on the misuse of religious and ethnic identities in pluralistic societies.

Today we celebrate the mid-term of this wonderful ecumenical journey called DOV in which so many churches around the world are taking part. The celebration will continue until next year's WCC Assembly in Porto Alegre, Brazil. We deliberately do this here, at the Conference on World Mission and Evangelism 2005, because we need to listen anew to this calling of the churches: to become healing and reconciling communities, to become a faithful church.

But: this mid-term is also a time of honest confession:
- we have not always listened carefully to this very calling;
- at times our churches have been tempted to justify injustice and violence theologically, in order to maintain and to perform power; and
- we have been misled at times in our respective traditions, when the mission of the church has contributed to the violence in the world.

Today we honestly admit, that there is at least an ambivalent relation of violence and mission. The gospel has not always been experienced as the liberating, reconciling and healing word of God.

The eagerness of some in our churches has violated cultures and communities, it has at times supported racism and oppression, even torture, and this has added to the violent conflicts in the world.
And in situations of violence, the churches have not always been the confessing

church, not always fulfilling its ministry of reconciliation, but instead have become one-sided or simply closing their eyes, turning away from conflict.

This failure needs to be confessed, this ambivalence needs to be analyzed, – which hopefully will lead us into a better and deeper understanding of our confession and calling in Christ.

As our general secretary, Sam Kobia, has put it in the opening plenary when he said: "I encourage this mission conference, focusing on a theme of healing and reconciliation, to highlight peace and non-violence as gospel imperatives. In Christ, God is revealed as a healer who offers reconciliation and forgiveness as gifts of pure grace. We are called to discipleship in Christ's way."

Enns then introduced the three persons who would intervene in different ways in the plenary:

Rev. Janet Plenert, from the Mennonite Church in Canada – one of the Historic Peace Churches – also representing the Mennonite World Conference.

Viola Raheb, a Lutheran from Palestine, member of the DOV reference group. For many years Viola has served as head of schools in Palestine. She now lives in Austria.

Prof. Tinyiko Maluleke, Presbyterian Church in South Africa. He is also a member of the international DOV-reference group and teaches theology and missiology at the University in Pretoria.

They intervened by plenary presentations followed by a panel discussion. Finally, Prof. Maluleke summarized the reflections shared and the significance of the plenary on mission and violence.

Janet Plenert[1]

It is a double pleasure for me to be here this morning. Double, because I have the privilege to speak not just for me, but for my sister in Christ who should also be here with us today. Due to systemic violence and injustice, she, as a Colombian woman, could not come. I, as a North American of privilege, could come. So I will share my time between my story and hers so that her voice may also be heard. First, my story.

I met Laurina and was immediately drawn to her gentle and loving spirit. I asked her if she was a Christian. "No, not yet," she said, "but my whole family is Christian." Over the next months as I got to know her, she began to tell stories of her family – her Christian family. The father had locked his drunk wife out of the house one night. The cousin had threatened to beat her sister. The grandparents

---

[1] At the time, Janet Plenert was executive director for International Ministries of Mennonite Church Canada. Currently she is the executive secretary of Mennonite Church Canada Witness. She lives in Winnipeg, Canada.

hadn't talked to each other for days. Her uncle had refused food to his sister, her mom. "What kind of Christians were these?" When I questioned her about this, certain that I had misunderstood her when she said they were Christians, she assured me they were. "But it doesn't change the way they behave," she said, "but they go to church most evenings, then come back and keep on with the same way of relating to each other".

This is a critical issue in the perpetuation of inter-personal violence. The kind of Christianity my friend's family understood, was a Christianity that limited the redemptive, life-giving good news of the gospel to be a message of salvation alone, rather than the transformative, powerful message of salvation, healing and hope that changes communities and is a sign of the kingdom among us. Becoming a Christian is about *belief* in Christ, is about salvation, it is also about *belonging* to a faith community that holds us accountable for our actions and transformation, and it is about the necessary change in our *behaviour* to reflect as full a gospel teaching as possible. When we fail to hold these three B's (belief, belonging and behaviour) together and in balance, we fail to experience the redemptive blessing that Jesus Christ our Lord intended when he came to us.

I am from a historic peace church that has taught the importance of these three aspects. Sometimes, European and North American Mennonites have over-emphasized the need to belong to our community, to the point where we became exclusionary and isolated. We have marginalized others or not opened the door widely enough for others to enter. Some time we have marginalized women within our community. This marginalization of others is a sin and a form of violence. Mennonites are known as hard working, dedicated people with a strong work ethic and an ethic of serving others. Sometimes we have called ourselves "The Quiet in the Land" to refer to our peaceful existence. But we have sinned, I believe, in what we have failed to do. We have been too quiet about our conviction of peace and non-violence as gospel imperatives, to use Rev. Sam Kobia's words.[2] We have sometimes refused to participate in the perpetuation of violence, while allowing others to continue in their violent ways. We must become, as Mennonites, the "Quiet in the Land" no more. We must take our message of behaviour, belief and belonging, of non-violence and peace as gospel imperatives and we must pronounce that to all those around us. And, as a Canadian, I must confess my culture's obsession with materialism that drives the global systemic violence of over-consumption for the privileged few in the world. *Forgive us Lord, for we know not what we do.*

I will now share the story of my friend and sister from Colombia.

"I am Alix Lozano, a woman, a mother, pastor and theologian. I have been on my faith journey with the Mennonite Church for 23 years. I am currently the director of the Mennonite Biblical Seminary of Colombia.

"Colombia is located in the extreme north-west of South America. It borders Ecuador, Peru, Brazil, Panama and Venezuela and has two ocean borders, the

---

2 Cf. Opening remarks by the WCC General Secretary, pp 147-50.

Atlantic and the Pacific. It is a country of great cultural, environmental and agricultural diversity. We produce coffee (some of the most delicious in the world), bananas, potatoes and rice. We have mineral richness – precious stones, gold, emeralds. We also have oil and fresh water for all. Our population is about 45 million and is multi-ethnic with Indigenous and African roots. We are a country of wonderful people who are pro-active, hard-working, caring, welcoming, who love to laugh and who are happy in spite of the adversities in our lives. We love life.

"But we also have a history that must be considered, especially in the past 500 years. We have survived genocides and homicides through the invasion of the Spanish and in the name of the conquest. They destroyed our ancestors and took our riches. Our ancestors were fooled into giving up our gold. The Spanish arrived, raped our women and permanently influenced our culture with weapons and threats. They abused our land, violated our ancestral rights and our human rights, all in the name of the conquest and evangelism, all through the cross and the sword.

"How ironic! It is precisely the land of our conquerors from Europe that today has prohibited me from participating in this important Conference on World Mission and Evangelism because of its absurd and expensive visa requirements. Except that this time they are not asking for gold, but rather Euros, but in such exaggerated quantities that it is an excuse to continue having a hegemony and discrimination against those they have exploited and where they have left behind an abominable legacy.

"I was invited to share a testimony about how we understand mission in a context of violence. For us in Colombia this is just a change of words, because violence (the sword) has been a constant companion to mission (the cross). *Evangelization by means of the Cross and the Sword* was the motto of the *Conquistadores* (Conquestors).

"A bit about our reality of violence. Colombia is in the midst of one of the most critical and painful moments in our history. Although it hasn't always been so violent a country, violence has often been present in our history. Internally, we have had a chronic series of wars: fourteen years of war of independence against Spanish domination, eight civil wars, fourteen local wars, two world wars, two coups, political confrontations, internal uprisings and the longest internal armed conflict on the continent.

"For more than 50 years, we have lived with a socio-political and economic war. My parents lived in a context of violence, I and my children were born into this same violent context. I sincerely hope and pray that my grandchildren and all future generations will be generations for whom war will be something of the past. For this to happen will take a long time. Today it is no longer Spain who wishes to conquer us, but we have the United States and their economic interests to contend with. In the name of fighting terrorism and narcotics trafficking, they appeal to the international community for solidarity and a multilateral intervention in our country. But this is already happening. In addition to the famous Plan Colombia of the US, we now also have our own programme called *Plan Patriota*, (Patriotic Plan) which was made public in Colombia just last week. This is one of the most ambitious military plans in the history of Colombia, and until now one of the best kept governmental secrets. Never before has a military force of 18,000 men been assigned to one single military operation. Never before has the United States gotten so directly involved in our war.

"We understand that we have a mission, and this is the mission of God. It is not our mission, it is God's mission. So the work of the church is to discover the mission of God, no matter where it is. Then we must align ourselves with the activities of God in the world. How can we move ahead in participating in God's mission in this context of violence?

"One of the consequences of this absurd war is the phenomenon of internally displaced persons in Colombia. Millions of rural people have had to abandon their land, or face death, because of internal conflict. They arrive in the cities disoriented, without belongings, with only their lives in their hands. Some of them arrive at the doors of the Mennonite church. There they share their pain, their tragedy, their fears, their anguish and receive help for their immediate needs as well as pastoral care. The church is thus converted into a place of refuge, of shelter. Some begin to participate in the church and slowly begin to rebuild their lives. Others continue to be persecuted. Some are received by the church in Canada as refugees. In this way the church becomes a place of peace, free of the presence of armed groups.

"This is one of the concrete examples of how we understand that the mission of God can be lived out in a context of violence. Aligning ourselves with the intention of God who always takes the side of the poor, the needy, the persecuted, the marginalized.

"I hope that this conference provides inspiration and challenge for each of you. May the Holy Spirit move among you, through every people, nation, race and language so that we may continue celebrating life in the midst of despair. I could not be present with you, but *you have heard my voice*. This is a miracle and a step towards overcoming one kind of violence. Denial of a visa could not silence me.

"Shalom from Alix Lozano".

Viola Raheb

I come from the land from which mission started more than 2000 years ago. Yet it is a land that has become the target of mission in the last decades with many free churches, specially from the US context, coming to establish a presence in the Holy Land, without relationship to the local churches. Therefore, I would like to share with you some aspects of the ambivalent relation between mission and violence in the context of Palestine.

In 1987, the first *intifada* started. It was the first resistance movement in the last decades, initiated mainly by young people, aiming at ending the illegal occupation of Palestine by Israel. At that time, we had a guest preacher from the US in our Christmas Lutheran Church in Bethlehem. His preaching text was loving one's enemy. Thinking of the North American context our guest forgot that the Palestinian context differs enormously. In his elaborations loving one's enemy was a call to be friendly to the enemy, to love ones enemy, without consideration of the concrete political situation and its implications.

While he was preaching a young man left the church. After the service the young man said if loving one's enemy and being a Christian means being passive in regard to the political situation, then he would rather not be a Christian. For the young man, who grew up in a context in which the enemy is a real entity, a real challenge, the idea of a sentimental approach to the issue of loving one's enemy seemed to be a passive approach to the life-threatening reality.

On the eve of Christmas 1987 someone wrote graffiti on the walls of our Christmas Lutheran Church in Bethlehem: "Dear Jesus Christ, we apologize for not being able to celebrate your birthday, but our land and our people are bleeding."

But if not in the midst of sorrow and pain, when else can we celebrate Christmas? If not in the midst of suffering, when else can we celebrate the wonder of God becoming human, taking us and our situation seriously? These two questions, the one of the young man in the church and the one of the anonymous person on the wall of our church, were but only two of the many questions and challenges young people brought to the church and to the theologians in Palestine regarding what it means to be a Christian here and now in Palestine in a very concrete context of occupation. This movement of young people questioning the relation of their faith to the daily challenges in Palestine, helped the church and the theologians reflect on what became to be known as Palestinian contextual theology. A long journey of theological reflection started. Many conferences, books, articles were the outcome. So, when the second *intifada* started in 2000 the local church in Palestine was no longer waiting for the questions to be raised but rather it had developed by then a pro-active role in responding to the challenges raised by the brutal reality of life in Palestine day by day.

In the introductory film on the DOV, which we had just seen, Bishop Munib Younan, the Bishop of the Evangelical Lutheran Church in Jordan and the Holy Land, made a clear statement in this regard: "The church needs to address the roots of violence." The journey between 1987 and 2000 made it evident that the church is challenged to address the questions, sorrows and realities of its followers in its theological and diaconical work. But the film also gave us a glimpse of another role of the churches that is beyond reflection. The sentence, which the bishop defined as a mission of the church did not remain a theoretical approach. If you have carefully followed the images from Palestine in the film, then you would have been able to recognize clergy from the different churches in Palestine standing at one of the many checkpoints, holding a vigil stating their mission.

During the theological journey of the last decades, the church came to realize that it is not enough to raise questions or develop answers, but that a concrete involvement is needed. The church cannot be a spectator in such a context, it needs to be a pro-active agent in transforming the reality.

We do not need churches that preach the importance of overcoming violence. We need churches that are pro-active in developing non-violent approaches and methodologies in overcoming violence.

In 2000, Bethlehem was under continuous attack and bombardment. The people were afraid to leave their homes after five pm. The city became more and more a ghost town, with empty streets and a fearful atmosphere. In this time, the International Centre of Bethlehem wanted to set an example of a non-violent approach. Therefore, we called upon the people and the students in our Lutheran schools to join us on a candle-light march through the empty streets of Bethlehem. Our message was that we will not allow violence to take over our lives. Our goal was to take back our streets and our life.

During the march one parent of a student in our schools asked us, "Why are you asking the children to do this, this is dangerous?" We explained that we did not force any one to come, it was an offer, an invitation to be pro-active. The man responded saying that his son told him that if he (the father) will not join then he does not have enough courage to change the situation. The reaction of the students was an outcome of a discussion we had at our schools in preparation for the march. One of the debates we had was: What needs more courage to stand in front of a caterpillar, or to march through the dark and fearful streets of Bethlehem after five pm? The answer for this young student was clear, as it was for us who had organized it.

In the last years the church in Palestine is more and more involved in developing creative alternatives in facing the harsh realities of the occupation, that are becoming day by day more suppressive. The accompaniment programme of the WCC, is such an alternative. It was the idea and the request of the local churches to the WCC and its members to come and join in developing such an alternative approach. The church in Palestine is doing its best to help transform this violent conflict. The EAPPI (the Ecumenical Accompaniment Programme in Palestine and Israel) programme is a chance and a challenge to our sisters and brothers around the world to also be active in journeying together.

I would like to end with a quote from the German theologian Dietrich Bonnhoeffer, who wrote that "if tomorrow would be the day of justice, then we would give up our work for a just world, but if not, then we would continue to work for another world that is possible."

The DOV and the Challenges before Us: Ten Concluding Reflections

Tinyiko S. Maluleke[1]

Introductory Remarks

As an African, it is significant for me that the idea of a Decade to Overcome Violence (DOV) emerged in Africa at Harare, in 1998. Even before that, it was at a special WCC Central Committee meeting in South Africa, where Bishop Stanley Mogoba of the Methodist Church of Southern Africa had declared: "Apartheid is dead, but violence is still with us." His words inspired an ecumenical initiative for peacemaking and non-violence in several cities of the world. All of these were the first stirrings which culminated in the ecumenical project now known as the Ecumenical Decade to Overcome Violence.

Indeed, the cold war may have ended, but many parts of the world are engulfed in violence. Twenty-seven years later, Nelson Mandela may be out of prison, but in his country, women are still being raped and children are still being violated.[2] The African Union (AU) and the New Partnership for Africa's Development (NEPAD) are crucial, new and progressive initiatives for Africa, but much of the continent remains in turmoil and conflict. We often hear encouraging noises regarding the new phenomenon called the African Renaissance from Lagos and Johannesburg, but the Sudan, DRC and Somalia are still not in peace. Since the advent of the so-called new world order, following the collapse of the former Soviet Union, we have not seen any decrease in war and violence; rather we have seen an alarming increase.

The DOV: What It Is and What It Should Be

First, I wish to underline that the DOV is an invitation for churches and their members to vigilantly analyze our situations so that we are able to recognize the new mutations and practices of violence in our world and in our society today. Violence was once hidden in communism and fascism; it was integral to colonialism and embedded in apartheid. Just because these "isms" appear to have disappeared from the face of the earth, it does not mean that the violence they bred and the violence on which they are based is also gone. In order for the DOV to become effective and meaningful, we will have to be vigilant and skilled in our ability to unmask the spaces, practices and beliefs in which violent conduct and behaviour are rooted. As Mercy Oduyoye (1995:171) points out with regard to overcoming violence against women, legislation alone will never succeed in combating violence: Legislation by modern governments will go the way of missionary

---

[1] Tinyiko Sam Maluleke – a member of the DOV Reference Group - is executive director for research at the University of South Africa, Pretoria, South Africa. He currently also serves as the president of the South African Council of Churches. This text is a revised version of his concluding reflection at the end of the DOV plenary at the mission conference in Athens 2005.

[2] Sarojini Nadar (2006:79) points out a study cited in *The Cape Times*, 24 October 1991 conducted by Lloyd Vogelman of the University of the Witwatersrand from the Centre for the Study of Violence and Reconciliation which said: "South Africa has the highest rape statistics in the world for a country that is not at war. It is estimated that 1 in 2 women will be raped in her lifetime in South Africa."

pronouncements until the fundamental religious beliefs are demythologized and the masks of "patri-kyriarchy" exposed. The most effective interventions against violence are those that happen before violence actually breaks out. In order to be able to do this, we shall have to devise ways of perceiving systems, relations, structures, beliefs and practices which produce violence and be able to intervene before it manifests itself.[3]

Second, the DOV is at once a choice and a commitment of the churches. In other words, the DOV is the business of all the member churches and the business of all their members. This is a message that comes through strongly when we consider the genesis of the idea as well as its unfolding over the past years. So, the answer to the question "Who is going to do this work in Geneva?" is, "The DOV is not a Geneva job. It is the business of all of us." The Decade is the business of all the churches and all the members of these churches.

To this end the DOV reference group, of which I am a member, is seriously thinking of strategies that will locate the DOV at the centre of the lives of the churches, where the churches are. In this way we hope to lay to rest the mistaken idea that the DOV is something located in, and driven from, WCC headquarters in Geneva. A specific way in which we hope to do this is to have an annual regional focus, a focus which will be used to stimulate DOV activities in all regions.[4]

Third, serious engagement with the work of the DOV, forces us to grapple with our own identity, nature and calling as members of the ecumenical family and as members of the Christian community. Essentially, being Christian should be and is antithetical to violence. Yet many times, our claims to be Christian do not seem to have led to peaceable and non-violent solutions. Our very notions of community and membership appear to be the basis of violence. Therefore, we need to continue to be sensitive to, and grapple with what it means to belong, so that we can deal with all forms of potential and built-in violence in the way in which we define membership and belonging. Many of the definitions and markers of belonging in many Christian communities have immense potential for violence – insiders vs. outsiders, top dogs vs. underdogs, men vs. women, saved vs lost, born-agains vs "churched" etc. Indeed, the very notion of community itself can be perverted so that being a member of a community can become oppressive as weaker members of communities are often required to make extreme sacrifices in order to be considered worthy of membership.

Fourth, in engaging seriously with the DOV agenda, we are all forced back to the question of our understanding and practice of Christian mission. Although we have learned that the church is missionary by its very nature; that the church cannot be but in mission; although we have learned all about the Christian mission being the

---

[3] Karen Buckenham has pointed out with regard to rape that: "To prevent rape, we need to challenge societal beliefs and cultural values that promote and condone sexual violence. The silence surrounding rape by society at large, including the church, denotes its acceptance, and allows it to continue." (Buckenham n.d.: 29; See also, Maluleke and Nadar 2002: 5-17)

[4] Notwithstanding the efforts made by these campaigns, these "decades" have not always been successful in involving those churches on the margins. For example Nadar (2005:61) points out that "the ecumenical decade in solidarity with women ended in 1998, yet some churches [Pentecostal and Evangelical in particular] were not even aware that such a decade existed."

missio Dei; in some ways, mission continues to be one of the most misunderstood dimensions of the church and of Christian life. How else can we explain the fact that "going into mission" has often had violent repercussions?[5] One is thinking here of several forms of violence – violence against culture, against peoples, against women, against children. These forms of violence have at times been promoted if not unleashed in the course of "Christian mission". Crucial mission texts have often been interpreted in violent ways: The commandment to multiply and have dominion over the earth (Genesis 1:28) has been used as justification for uncurbed plunder. Similarly Jesus' commandment for his disciples to "go into the world" (Matthew 28: 18-20) has sometimes been appropriated as license to go into different parts of the world in cultural and religious arrogance and intolerance. Some utterances of Paul about church life and ministry have been selectively read in ways that promote violence against women both inside and outside the church (1 Corinthians 14:33-35; Colossians 3:18, I Peter 3:1); it is time, perhaps, for us to go back in search of alternative, neglected, more peaceable forms of, and rationales for, mission. As Marilyn Legge (2004:119) has argued, mission needs to be "rethought as the relation between a particular understanding of church (as shaped by context and location) and a particular understanding of the world (where both are governed by justice/right relations)."

Fifth, the challenges outlined in the preceding point above do not merely – or only – relate to texts we have interpreted and "lived" in violent ways. It also relates to those "texts" in the Bible and in our national canons which appear to promote violence and/or appear to promote acquiescence to it. At issue here are not merely the texts we pervert and bend towards violence, but those that appear to promote and legitimize violence themselves. Such texts include the many in the Old Testament which have been dubbed "texts of terror" (Trible 1984). These are texts describing acts of terror and violence, often without censure and sometimes appearing to recommend, if not justify, such acts.

The Old Testament is particularly replete with such texts where several acts of violence are either described in neutral terms or grafted into one divine "purpose" or the other. Such acts include rape, murder, betrayal as well as blanket extermination of peoples and their properties. Notably, several such texts portray women and children as (intended) victims. One of the challenges we must put before ourselves as part and parcel of the DOV project is to take yet another look at these "texts of terror" and to do battle with them. Sadly, in many churches, these texts are avoided like the plague. How often do we hear sermons on the rape of Tamar (2 Samuel 13:1-22) or the murder of the nameless girl who was the only child of Jephthah (Judges 11)?[6] How often do we hear Bible studies about the nameless concubine (Judges 19) who was offered to be gang-raped and left for dead?

Unless we are brave enough to confront these texts, let them speak to us and allow ourselves to speak back at them, we shall not have begun to deal with the

---

[5] The church's direct involvement in violent history such as the crusades, slavery and apartheid are just some cases in point.

[6] Gerald West (2000: 38) comments that these texts are "seldom read and never on a Sunday".

culture of violence in both biblical and our own times.

Sixth, during our times, it has become clear that profit, materialism and consumption have become some of the main drivers of violence.[7] In pursuit of profit, multinational corporations have little regard for the safety and welfare of people and the environment. Similarly, materialism and the unbridled accumulation of products and goods often lead to violent relationships between people and between people and the environment. This is anthropocentrism in its most selfish and inward-looking form. Unless we can influence the values which drive humanity at both communal and individual levels in counter-hegemonic ways, we are unlikely to make a serious dent against violence. Unless we can confront the very human values which produce violent relations, we will not be able to stem the growing tide of violence in the world. It is relevant to the DOV initiative that we search together for motifs other than profit, materialism and consumption which can act as glue in the creation of a new society of human beings.

Seventh, we have to constantly ask ourselves who and where God is in our violent world. Often our notions of God connive with the forces of violent and coercive power rather than subvert them. In many ways, we often succumb to notions of God (and of church) as "prosperous", "wealthy", "conquering", "multi-national", "powerful". Therefore, the very symbols of violence we (should) detest also appear to be most potent signs of who God is.[8]

In our theologies and ecclesiastical practices, we often reflect these violent ambitions and leanings. Any wonder that as Christians and as churches we often appear to lose our nerve at the very point when we must confront the worldly powers which perpetuate violence? Could it be that deep down we actually see nothing wrong with violent forms of power as long as they claim to be for our own good and as long as they claim to be for "law and order"? Could it be that as religious people, we have already bought into the dominant forms of power, law and order, and are happy to ascribe these to God so that we see God in them and them in God? In this regard, it may help us to remember that God manifests not in the powerful and wealthy but in the weak, despised and the poor.

God is, therefore, located in the spaces occupied by those at the receiving end of violence. The poor are the face of God and not the powerful, the wealthy and the conquering. Until we shift our gaze from the powerful and wealthy to the poor and marginalized, from those who perpetuate violence (however noble their intentions) to those who are victimized by violence we shall not be able to contribute to peace and non-violence. Above all we have to disabuse the powers that be and any other power group of the idea that we are beneficiaries of their violence. Those governments which claim to engage in violence 'in order to protect our lifestyles' must be told that we do not need their protection. Those extremist groups which claim to be engaging in violence in order to protect us – some of

---

[7] In depth theological reflection has been done on the effects of globalization in recent times. Theologians such as Russell Botman (2004) and Steve de Gruchy (2002 and 2003) have explored economic globalization as a threat to human dignity and the "oikos" of God.

[8] Feminist theologians have been at pains to point out the destructive nature of our symbols and metaphors of God as king, warrior and husband.

them demanding that we become thankful to them, must be told that we do not need their protection! We must look all such governments and power-groups in the eye and tell them that we are not interested in being protected by them and that they must stop using us as justification for carrying acts of violence. We must say to them: "Your army is there, not for us, you are doing this not for us, we are not benefiting from this, this is your project for your own benefit and not for ours."

Eighth, we need to face up to our complicity in the violent systems of the world as Christians and as churches. We must come to a realization now that violence is not something out there in the world and it is not something perpetuated by others who are unlike us. It is time that we faced up to the fact that violence is not only being manufactured in our theologies and ecclesial structures and practices, it is alive and kicking in the very midst of the church of God.9 It is therefore important that we muster enough courage not only to admit to this, not merely to confess it, but to describe its presence with a view to designing ways through which we can root violence out of church life. Therefore, in the graffiti of our church walls and in our letters to Jesus, as it has been suggested, in the presentation of Viola Raheb, our letters must do more than summarily confess our complicity. We must describe our complicity in violence and we must propose initiatives and activities in which we shall engage in order to orient ourselves away from violent ways.[10]

Ninth, we have to go beyond naming violence, beyond sheer description and even beyond sheer analysis. It is indeed possible to reinforce violence by being obsessed with its terrorizing descriptions, its mind-boggling statistics, and by engaging cold analysis of the phenomenon. There is a sense in which the better we describe and analyze violence the more intractable it seems and in some ways the more attractive it looks. There is virtue in naming it and it is necessary for us to describe violence, but these must not become ends in and of themselves. As the DOV declares in its name, violence is something to be overcome and not merely something to be named, confessed and analyzed.

Tenth, as hinted in the previous reflection, we must confront the idea that violence is "sexy", "inevitable", "effective", a "necessary evil" or "our only salvation". This is a massive task given the globalized industry that encompasses the military, security industry, mass media, Internet and film industries. In these industries there is a growing glamourization of violence, not only as something effective but as something hip and sexy. In this way the young are brought up to think of

---

[9] See Maluleke and Nadar (2002:5-17), where they argue that the silence of the church on issues of violence does not render the church innocent but in fact renders the church even more guilty of being complicit in violence. In fact they go as far to argue that the churches are "co-conspirators" in covenants of death. Isabel Phiri (2000 -85-110) also showed how in her study of 25 women from Christian homes, 84 percent of them said that they had experienced violence at the hands of their husbands. They were also all wives of leaders in the church. Her study concluded that it was biblical beliefs, such as those on submission, which made these women stay in abusive relationships.

[10] Again perhaps we need help here from our feminist sisters, especially our African sisters, who argue that it is impossible to merely theorize about violence. Our theories must result in a transformation of our societies through concrete action for change. See for example, Oduyoye 1992, 1995a,1995b, Gnanadason 1993, Rakoczy 2000.

violence as fun and games even as violence is re-enforced as something inevitable. In extreme cases, children are taught to think of violence as the 'final solution' to any and all problems of life. Here, the churches must dig deepest into their non-violent spiritualities, practices and roots. It is my contention that all Christian churches have resources for the fight against violence if they would dare to be true to their histories, their calling and their deepest traditions. The South African churches have not, in my opinion even begun to tap on the rich resources and lessons of their non-violent struggle against apartheid. Nor have the churches of North America adequately exploited the legacy of Martin Luther King, Jr. In the same way the South African churches have not even begun to tap into the legacy of Archbishop Desmond Tutu. Similarly, I am not sure if we have made maximum benefit from the lessons of the German Confessing Church tradition up to and during World War II.

Finally, I would like to urge all of us and all churches to conduct ourselves and our business in ways that refuse to accept violence as a way of life. We do not have to accept violence as a way of life, even from those who claim to be doing it for our comfort and convenience. We should reject such comfort and such convenience premised and built on violent foundations.

Bibliography

Botman, R. 2004. "Globalization's threat to human dignity and sustainability", *Reformed World* Volume 54, 127

Buckenham, K, "Rape" in *Violence Against Women Resource Pack. PACSA Manual for Churches*, Pietermaritzburg, 29

De Gruchy, S. 2002. "Life, Livelihoods and God: Why Genetically Modified Organisms oppose Caring for Life" in *The Ecumenical Review*, July 2002. (Geneva: World Council of Churches)

De Gruchy, S. 2003. "Of agency, assets and appreciation: Seeking some commonalities between theology and development" in *Journal of Theology for Southern Africa*, Vol 117, (November 2003). pp 20 – 39

Gnanadason A. 1993. *No longer a secret – the church and violence against women*, Geneva: World Council of Churches Publications.

Legge, M. J. 2004. "Negotiating Mission: A Canadian Stance". *International Review of Mission*, 93, 368: 119-130

Maluleke T.S and Nadar S. 2002. "Breaking the covenant of violence against women" in *Journal of Theology for Southern Africa*, 114, 5-17

Mananzan, Mary John, et al., eds. 1996. *Women Resisting Violence: Spirituality for Life*. Maryknoll: Orbis

Nadar S. 2006. "Texts of Terror—The Conspiracy of Rape in the Bible, Church and Society: The Case of Esther 2:1-18," in *African Women, Religion and Health: Essays in Honor of Mercy Amba Ewudziwa Oduyoye*, (Eds.) Phiri, I A and S. Nadar. Maryknoll, New York: Orbis Books, 77-95

Nadar. S. 2005."On Being the Pentecostal Church: Pentecostal Women's Voices and Visions" in *On Being Church: African Women's Voices and Visions*, (eds.) Phiri, I A and S. Nadar. Geneva: World Council of Churches, 60-79

Oduyoye, Mercy Amba, ed. 1992. *The Will to Arise: Women, Tradition, and the Church in Africa*. Maryknoll: Orbis

Oduyoye, Mercy Amba. 1995a. *Daughters of Anowa: African Women and Patriarchy*. Maryknoll: Orbis

Oduyoye M. A. 1995b. "Violence against women: window on Africa". *Voices from the Third World – EATWOT women theologians on violence against women*, Vol. XVIII No. 1

Rakoczy S (Ed) 2000. *Silent No Longer: the Church Responds to Sexual Violence*, Pietermaritzburg: The Natal Witness Printing and Publishing Company

Schüssler Fiorenza E. 1995. "Ties that bind: domestic violence against women" in *Voices from the Third World – EATWOT women theologians on violence against women*

Thistletwaite S. 1989. "Every two minutes: battered women and feminist interpretation" in J Plaskow and CP Christ (Eds) *Weaving the Visions: New patterns in feminist spirituality*, San Francisco: Harper and Row, 302-313

Trible, P. 1984. *Texts of Terror: Literary Feminist Readings of Biblical Narratives*. Philadelphia: Fortress Press

West, G.O. 2000. "Tamar's Story: A Text of Terror", In Rakoczy Susan (Ed).*Silent No Longer: The Church Responds to Sexual Violence*. Pietermaritzburg: Southern African Catholic Bishop's Conference

Closing Prayers at Plenary on DOV

Leader: Ruth Bottoms.

Young people bring candles on to the stage, later they move to the placards which they had placed on it during the introductory theatre play.

The assembly sings "Come, Holy Spirit, heal and reconcile"

Silence

O God,
may your people break the silence that has too often surrounded issues of violence.

May the resources of the world be shared, that all may have access to clean, sparkling water and good food.

Stay the life-denying forces of globalization, may there come new, just systems of trade among the nations.

Light, O God, the touch-paper of peace-making that will lead to disarmament and demilitarization.

Teach us to care for the earth, radiating love instead of contamination.

Be present in the darkness of those in despair with no sense of self-worth, and light a way back to wholeness.

For those who have been abused, the woman who has been raped, the wife who has been battered, grant healing in their inner beings, the light of hope in their eyes.

And for the oppressor, the bully, the torturer, the ignorant, and for us – a prayer for transformation, by your power.

Silence for personal prayers (remembering also the stories shared during this plenary).

God of life and love and light,
hear our prayers that violence may be overcome;

so may the gospel be shared bringing peace and wholeness, life and light and hope, in the name of Christ, we pray.

AMEN

The Lord's Prayer *(each prays in his or her own language)*

PRESS RELEASE ON HEALING PLENARY*

"God healed me completely, although I am still living with HIV"

Gracia Violeta Ross only understood the meaning of her first name (grace) after discovering she was HIV-positive.

At that point in her life, she thought she was going to die soon, and asked God for forgiveness for a lifestyle that she felt had separated her from God's will. "God healed me completely then, although I am still living with HIV," she told participants at the Conference on World Mission and Evangelism in Athens.

Ross, a 28-year old Bolivian who grew up in an evangelical family, spoke at the conference plenary session on Friday, 13 May. Her moving testimony strongly made the point that healing and cure don't necessarily come together. "Actually my life became better after becoming HIV-positive."

Ross shared the floor with Johannes Petrus Heath, an Anglican priest from Namibia living with HIV, Erika Schuchardt, a professor at the University of Hanover, Anthony Allen, a psychiatrist from Jamaica, and Bernard Ugeux, a Roman Catholic theologian from France.

All five agreed that in both highly modernized societies and those ravaged by poverty and lack of basic health care, people yearning for healing of body and soul knock at the door of churches that are not always open. While healing doesn't necessarily mean physical cure, churches are called to be inclusive communities where people feel accepted and experience God's love and compassion.

"We need a theology of healing that includes the person, the community and the society," Allen affirmed. Such a theology has to "help Christians to deal with the stigma and discrimination that condemn people living with HIV/AIDS," Japé said. For that to happen, the theology must state clearly that "sickness, and particularly HIV/AIDS, are never a punishment for sin," Ugeux added.

Equipped with such a theology, Christian communities are able to provide the "welcoming space of acceptance and non-discrimination that allows people to face the crisis that illness poses to their lives," Schuchardt said.

(World Council of Churches - News Release)

---

* See remark in introduction on page 128

RECONCILIATION
RESCUING VICTIMS IN THEIR HOME ISLANDS
Pepine Iosua[1]

Introductory Remarks

I praise God and thank the WCC for the privilege of sharing a narrative study case from the Republic of Kiribati in reference to the South Pacific in general.

The presentation focuses on how our people understand and struggle with the impacts of climate change, especially "sea rise", in the Pacific understanding of the creation, and what the reconciling and healing mission of God is to these people and to the world at large.

Creation Perspective

The purpose of creation is for the praise of God. Creation was, and is, not done out of indispensability, but rather, owing to his grace and preference, therefore the creation work elucidates glimpses of God's love, wisdom and power.

This creation work is exceedingly superior, as witnessed by God himself who, after his creating work, rested and saw it to be good. The "resting" of God on the seventh day does not refer to his withdrawal from creation, but referring to his contentment with the goodness of his work.

The creation story narrated in Genesis seems to describe an ideal partnership pattern with God and creation. This partnership envisages and authenticates the unavoidable interdependency known these days as the ecosystem.

Jesus is the visible underlying cause of creation, and when the world was corrupted by sin, Jesus, with the love of God, was sent to rescue the 'world' from perishing. The word "world" is used here as inclusive of all the material world and not just humankind.

People's Responsibilities to God and Creation

The created world was entrusted to human beings to care for with love and to enjoy its benefits, but also as a sign of the relationship with the Creator.

As caretakers, humans are liable and answerable to the Creator and his affinity to creation. Humanity is not to exploit God's blessings selfishly, but wisely, globally, in a sustainable and responsible manner. In doing this, humanity is not to bring about an incessant destructive exhaustion of natural resources, because this world is fragile and limited. Humanity should give nature a chance to restore its

---

[1] The Rev. Dr Pepine Iosua is a pastor, theologian and fisherman from Kiribati.

reproductive potential, and only then will we be able to harvest plentifully when the time comes. For the Israelites, the land was given a one-year rest after every seven years of use.

This world is our global home, it is our life, we exist in it as an interdependent whole. Humanity, therefore, is to work hard towards the reconciliation and healing of our damaged world for the full glorification of God by his own creation, as he expected from the very beginning.

If we live up to our duties, God will use nature as a blessing to us, but if we do not conform to our duties as caretakers, nature will become a curse to us.

The Pacific Islands

The smallest, most fragile and most vulnerable islands on the planet are in the Pacific where the mean temperature varies between 27-34 degrees C elsius. The islands are low coral atolls, no more than five metres above sea level. Although small and insignificant, these small islands are not of secondary importance in God's creation; they are equally precious to and loved by God like the big countries.

Understanding a Reconciling Mission Together

The reality of climate change can be seen and experienced in the Pacific. Scientifically, a research done from the University of Hawaii in 1972 -1974 confirmed the rise of sea level to be between 3-4 mm annually. The United Nations Framework Convention and its Kyoto Protocol 1999, more recently confirmed the already increasing sea level from the past and claimed that it will rise drastically by 2100 by 50 centimetres. The two latest studies by our local social experts also reinforce a common understanding of the pragmatic consequences of climate change as experienced in the Pacific. In particular, the increase of heat ruins the lives of trees and peoples, the rise of sea level incites brackish and salty water, which will sooner or later cover the islands; erosion vanishes historical areas, disfigures and shrinks parts of the land, forcing people to move from coastal areas to the inland; extreme changes of tides, currents, weather, temperature and seasons cause confusion, more frequent and unpredictable storms, droughts, floods, diseases, diminishing marine and land resources, and more and more frequent drifting of fishermen.

The Pacific governments and churches are striving for survival, and sending out an SOS (Save Our Souls) rescue call for the world for help. The Kyoto Protocol is one of the most effective and applicable global solutions to the calamitous impacts of climate change. The superpower wealthy countries of the North that we trust for their global concerns, such as restraining "terrorism", are more concerned with attacks than the rise of sea levels, which will not only extinguish a few, but an entire human race and the islands themselves.

The problem is that we are sinners who have failed to be responsible caretakers in upholding the affluence of creation by selfishly and destructively exploiting it for our own luxury. We become the enemy of creation by causing its suffering to God who is in and beyond nature. The world has been wounded and is now groaning and crying for healing.

We commit the sin of irresponsibility to God, to the creation and to fellow human beings. Therefore we should confess to God the Creator, change genuinely by dying as our old selves and being re-born in a new life in Christ who rescued the world. We are to reaffirm the loving stewardship commitments, in words and in our healing and reconciling mission together globally. We will certainly be forgiven and reconciled with God, with is creation and with one another, and consequently receive the blessings of God and his creation abundantly.

In line with the above, the Pacific Church leaders cry out for global commitment:

1. We affirm our responsibility to care for the earth as our response to God's love for creation;

2. we declare forcefully the urgency of the threat of human-induced climate change to the lives, livelihoods, societies, cultures and eco-systems of the Pacific Islands;

3. we dedicate ourselves to engaging our churches in education and action on climate change;

4. we commit ourselves to ecumenical collaboration among our churches and with other religious and secular bodies in the Pacific that will increase the effectiveness of our national and regional efforts;

5. we call our sisters and brothers in Christ throughout the world to act in solidarity with us to reduce the causes of human-induced climate change. We issue this call particularly to churches in the industrialized nations, whose societies are historically responsible for the majority of polluting emissions;

6. we express our appreciation to the World Council of Churches for its support to the Pacific churches on the issue of climate change and request that the voices of the Pacific become increasingly reflected in the WCC Climate Change Programme;

7. we pressure all countries to ratify and implement the Kyoto Protocol, especially industrialized nations such as the United States of America and Australia which have not ratified the protocol.

8. we encourage companies that are major producers or consumers of fossil fuels to support a transition toward less carbon-intensive economies, reduced energy usage and the development of cleaner, renewable energy sources;

The Dignity of Humankind

People are more important than money, for they were created in the image of God, not created for money. Humankind was borne into a particular world which became a home so dear. The trees, birds, animals and other living and non-living things around us became part of the individual person's life.

The fear of the rise of sea levels forces some to reluctantly migrate to the big countries. These people lost their home islands, their identity, freedom, and political independence, as they migrated or were obliged to go to another foreign country, culture, and government which is another form of re-colonization.

Invitation

This is our SOS cry and an invitation to all people to listen objectively and lovingly. May this cry be the "chorus" of your heart, your mind, your prayers, your words and your doings. It will be much better if you come to see, experience and rescue the dying victims in their home islands, heal the groaning, wounded and crying creation, and be reconciled with the suffering and crying God in the Pacific.

These people are your brothers and sisters, created by the same God and living on the same planet. But they are dying victims in and with their home-islands. They are crying for justice and the dignity that they have been deprived of. A complete disappearance of this race and the islands is at hand, please come before it is too late. Come with compassion, sympathy and consolation, and may we see your love and commitment covering the whole earth and sea below and rising up even through the ozone layer as high as possible, so that the groaning creation be healed and the suffering Creator be pleased.

The time is running out, and people of the islands of hope firmly put their trust in "you", the members of the global family, and in God our Father, our Almighty Creator and Sustainer of the Universe.

"A Cloud of Witnesses"
Lunga Lungile Magqwagqwa ka Siboto[1]

Introduction

I have been asked to share in this Conference, on the eve of Pentecost 2005, some experiences and reflections of a participant in the Ecumenical Accompaniment Programme in Palestine and Israel (EAPPI) of the World Council of Churches.

I will do this with regards to:

1. Whether and how our current discourse on and quest for reconciliation in many societies around the world can be related to the situation in Palestine-Israel. As well as an interpretation of the ministry of the EAPPI in the light of concerns for reconciliation.

2. A search for a definition or formulation of a ministry and role of the church in situations where one party in a conflict may be seen as a victim.

The Accompaniment Programme

The programme comes in the context of the WCC's "Decade to Overcome Violence". It specifically came into being as a response to a request from church leaders in Jerusalem. The WCC was invited to send a physical presence of the church from the rest of the world. The church was urged to go beyond just issuing resolutions, and back its words with practical action. We now have a veritable "cloud of witnesses".

The focal point of EAPPI is ending the occupation of Palestinian Territories by Israel. I was a member of the second group of four South Africans that came to Palestine and Israel from September to December, 2004. South African participation was, and still continues to be, possible by the financial support from Sweden through the Swedish International Development Co-operation Agency (SIDA). Our group of South Africans was, in turn, part of the ninth group of 28 accompaniers, from seven countries. Teams consisting of two to four persons were placed in eight different centres.

To date, 198 Ecumenical Accompaniers have come to Jerusalem from more than 30 churches and ecumenical partners in 12 countries: Canada, Denmark, France, Germany, Ireland, Aotearoa-New Zealand, Norway, South Africa, Sweden, Switzerland, the United Kingdom and the United States of America.

The first official group arrived in August 2002 after a pilot project sent by Denmark's Danchurchaid and Icelandic Church Aid.

South Africa came on to the scene only in 2004. I, together with a Danish Baptist

---

[1] The Rt Revd Lunga Lungile Magqwagqwa (Xaba) ka Siboto is bishop of the Southern Diocese of the Ethiopian Episcopal Church in South Africa. The bishop lives in Port Elizabeth, South Africa.

minister and a Lutheran pastor from Berlin, were based in Bethlehem.

Activities

1. Joining in worship services and witnessing to hope in a just peace with believers. Besides worshipping regularly with identified congregations, in Bethlehem we joined religious sisters in reciting the rosary along the Separation Wall on Friday evenings.

2. Meeting various groups and people, Palestinian and Israeli, Christian and Muslim, who believe in peace and are peace activists involved in programmes towards a just and peaceful resolution to conflict.

3. Making public presentations on the ministry of the EAPPI, and sharing comparative insights and perspectives from our own national and regional contexts, where appropriate. The story of the Berlin Wall and its eventual demise as well the South African experience during and after institutionalized apartheid and racial discrimination found some resonance among the majority, if not all, of the Palestinians we met.

4. Being physically present and mediating peace in situations where there is a potential for violence. These included monitoring Israeli army and police checkpoints, assisting in the harvesting of olives where farmers and landowners are fearful of the intimidation of Israeli settler communities.

5. Recording of incidents of violations of human rights.

6. Exploring with believers, lay and clerical, possible theological responses to the situation of conflict.

7. Learning from, and working in collaboration with, local leadership of communities living in stressful conditions.

Observations

1. Demographics

Christians are a small minority in the Occupied Territories, whereas Islam commands considerable following. There is a high degree of resentment among Christian Palestinians with what is perceived as a lack of interest, on the part of Christians in other parts of the world, in the plight of Christians in Palestine. Those who can afford the cost, usually choose to emigrate because of lack of hope that the occupation will end anytime in the near future. A significant feature in the conflict is the debate around entitlement to land which is often related to the ratio of numerical strength between Palestinian and Israeli communities. Continued presence and positive influence of internationals, including accompaniers, is valued as a practical demonstration of care.

2. The Israeli State Machinery

This reminds me so much of the Apartheid regime which boasted what, at the time, was reputed to be the second most powerful military force in Africa after that of Egypt. The pervading presence of the Israeli security system gives the impression that it is intended to be, and is in fact, the major legitimizing factor for continued Israel's existence: checkpoints, both land–based and "flying"; the intermittent drone of military aircraft over the skies; and the "Separation Wall" that limits movement from and into the Palestinian territories, thus severely undermining the ability of Palestinians to find employment opportunities within the state of Israel. Palestinians are forced to carry identity documents for inspection at checkpoints and random searches inside Israel.

What also baffles the observers is that too much lends credence to allegations of expansionist tendencies by the State of Israel. There is fear among Palestinians that when, if ever, a final settlement is achieved prospects of a viable statehood for them will have diminished to insignificant levels. Any authority that is dependent on fear is burdensome to itself spiritually and financially and is, arguably, not sustainable in the long term.

It is also, in my view, in the interest of both the Israelis and Palestinians that a solution be found that can be owned and respected by all parties.

3. The International Community

In spite of numerous resolutions of the U N, and a legal opinion of the International Court of Justice, there seems to be little enthusiasm on the part of UN member states to take practical steps to "persuade" Israel to conform to international law. One of the undertakings made by accompaniers was to take the issues of the occupation to their own peoples and governments. South African accompaniers held a number of meetings with diplomats at our Embassy to Israel in Tel Aviv and our representative to the Palestinian Authority in Ramallah. Meetings have also been held with the National Council of Churches, and plans and strategies are being devised towards engaging the governments in a concerted and well thought out manner.

Personal Reflections

1. Two Identities of One Entity

Aboard the El Al flight from Johannesburg to Tel Aviv, I was struck by the absence of Palestine in the in-flight magazine of the airline. It reminded me of the road signs in apartheid South Africa directing people to residential areas of native people which was minimal. People, coming from outside the country, who showed interest in the oppressed majority were warned of the danger posed by visiting in these areas which hid the reality of the existence of these communities, both from the white population and the rest of the world. It is also the case for visitors to the Holy Land who are warned by Israelis that it is not safe to visit Palestinian areas.

When our group visited Nablus (Shechem) for Sunday worship a soldier at the checkpoint asked our coordinator from Jerusalem whether we needed protection. As I thought about this I realized that I felt much safer any time of the day or night in Bethlehem, a Palestinian area, than I did at an Israeli checkpoint or in Israeli-controlled West Jerusalem.

Maps of the area produced from the Palestinian side give different place names from those of the Israelis. This struck me as a significant aspect of the nature of the conflict. There exists, in my opinion, in many aspects of life in Palestine and Israel, two perceptions, realities and truths about the same entity.

2. A South African Perspective

It is in this context that, I propose issues around reconciliation may well be explored. Since just before, and well after, the inception of the new political non-racial dispensation in South Africa, the combined notion of truth and reconciliation featured heavily in public discourse. Two understandings of the concept "reconciliation" exist in my country.

For one small but vocal and influential section which are those citizens of European extraction, reconciliation was achieved with the inauguration of democracy in 1994. These persons strongly oppose government policies that seek to redress the imbalances that are the legacy of both the colonial and apartheid regimes. On the other hand, the majority of the non-European population ascribes to the ideal that, reconciliation should be understood as a process that identifies the cause of "disease" of apartheid and resolves them for the well-being of all parties.

I would argue that for the Palestinians and Israelis there is a need first of all to consider reconciliation with regard to their respective perceptions of reality.

The Church and Reconciliation

The church has a biblical mandate to be involved in this ministry.

Consequently, from now on we regard no one according to the flesh; ... And all this is from God, who has reconciled us to himself through Christ and given us the ministry of reconciliation, namely God was reconciling the world to himself in Christ, ... and entrusting to us the message of reconciliation. So we are ambassadors for Christ, as if God was appealing through us. (2 Cor. 16:18-20)

In a majority of Pauline writings, the issue of reconciliation is between humanity and God. We do, however, also have references where reconciliation is to take place between human beings. The Ecumenical Accompaniment Programme is on course in attempting to achieve reconciliation between Palestinians and Israelis. We may draw inspiration from St Paul's words to the Ephesians:

But now in Christ Jesus you who once were far off have become near by the blood of Christ. ... he is our peace, he who made both (Gentiles & community of Israel) one and broke down the wall of enmity, through his flesh, ..., that he might create in himself one new person in place of the two, thus establishing peace, and might reconcile both with God, in one body, through the cross, putting that enmity to death by it. He came and preached peace to you who were far off and peace to those who were near. (Eph. 2:13-17)

If reconciliation can be achieved for communities in the Middle East, I believe a new and redeeming paradigm can be gained for the world. Jerusalem, the city of peace, is a religious site of great significance for three of the world's major faiths -- Christianity, Islam and the Judaism The point of departure for Christians in this venture is not to seek subjugation of one by the other. It should not seek political interest for itself. Again, St Paul warns us not to be tempted and swept into the politics of hate and vilification that dominates the news today. Our motivation derives from acting on God's mandate. The God, who made us all, in his own image, reminds us through the words of Paul's letter to the Ephesians not to conform to the dominant ideologies of vilification, but to transform them:

For our struggle is not with flesh and blood but with the principalities, with the powers, with the rulers of this present darkness, with the evil spirits in the heavens. So stand fast with your loins girded in truth, clothed with righteousness as a breastplate, and your feet shod in readiness for the gospel of peace. (Eph. 6:12, 14-15)

In presentations to both Palestinians and Israelis EAPPI accompaniers constantly made the point and argued for the pursuit of a non-violent but active struggle to end the occupation. This requires courage and commitment as we know from experience that those opposed to a just peace may not be restrained from visiting violence on those engaged in non-violent struggles.

We, in South Africa, bear testimony to the impact of those people who do not just stop at making pronouncements on matters of conscience where communities in stressful situations are concerned. We draw inspiration from those who act out their social concerns. If the world had not stood up, often in the face of opposition and pressure from powerful political and economic forces, we would still be on "ground zero", if not worse, in South Africa. International alliances, often of ordinary people, created a powerful and irresistible surge of pressure on the Nationalist Party government of South Africa in the 1980's. The Christian community's involvement in our struggle is still cherished in our land. Upon returning from Palestine and Israel, I was interviewed by *Challenge* magazine, a Christian publication in my country.

In beginning the interview, *Challenge* noted that: "EAPPI is modelled on the Ecumenical Monitoring Programme in South Africa (EMPSA), which was active between 1990 and 1994 and was responsible for bringing over 400 volunteers to the anti-apartheid movement.".

If Christians of the world had just gone on to mind their own business, Nelson Mandela, Desmond Tutu and other peace loving luminaries from South Africa would only remain possibilities in the minds of those who knew them. The African

National Congress, now the government in South Africa, and other liberation formations had been banished and officially designated as terrorist organizations. It was criminal to associate with them and to advance any of their aims.

I have seen a similar marginalization of the communities in the West Bank. The amount of goodwill towards Israelis, in spite of the prevailing conditions of Palestinians, is so reminiscent of our own desire to embrace our compatriots of European descent, while their own governments made every effort to cut all ties of communication between us.

What is needed by communities living in stress is, as has been demonstrated before, a cloud of witnesses to the hope in, and of, Jesus which needs to be made evident to be believed. The ministry of reconciliation falls in the category of deeds which St Peter describes as good and about which he has this to say in his first epistle:

Now who is going to harm you if you are enthusiastic for what is good? But even if you should suffer because of righteousness, blessed are you. Do not be afraid or terrified with fear of them, but sanctify Christ as Lord in your hearts. Always be ready to give an explanation to anyone who asks you for a reason for your hope, but do it with gentleness and reverence, keeping your conscience clear, so that when you are maligned, those who defame your good conduct in Christ may themselves be put to shame and perhaps repentance. For it is better to suffer for doing good, if that be the will of God, than for doing evil. (1 Pet. 3:13-17)

Reconciliation as a New Paradigm of Mission
Robert Schreiter[1]

The Emergence of Reconciliation in the Discussion of Mission

There have been references and echoes of the theme of reconciliation in the theological discussion of mission throughout the previous century, but it is only in the last decade and a half that it has emerged as an important way of talking about Christian mission. David Bosch's 1992 magisterial work, *Transforming Mission*, makes no mention of it. Stephen Bevans and Roger Schroeder's recent book, *Constants in Context* published in 2004, on the other hand, has multiple references to reconciliation. What has happened?

It has been the experience of trying to come to terms with a violent past, the need to end hostility, and the long work of reconstructing broken societies that have pushed reconciliation forward into the attention of many people, especially those concerned with the work of the Church. The fact that many recent conferences on mission have been taking up this theme, and that it figures into the title and preparatory documents of this Conference, indicates how far we have come.

[1] The Rev. Dr Robert J. Schreiter, C.PP.S., is Vatican II Professor of Theology at Catholic Theological Union in Chicago, USA, and professor of theology and culture at the University of Nijmegen, The Netherlands. He is the author of many books and articles on reconciliation.

In this presentation, I would like to explore how reconciliation might be seen as a paradigm or model of mission. I begin with looking at how the idea of reconciliation might be seen as revealing to us the heart of the Gospel. Then I will look at the understanding of reconciliation today, both as a *process* for engaging in mission and as the *goal* of mission.

Reconciliation: The Heart of the Gospel

Although the word "reconciliation" does not occur as such in the Hebrew Scriptures, and only fourteen times in the New Testament, the Bible is replete with stories of reconciliation, from the stories of Esau and Jacob, and Joseph and his brothers, to Jesus' parables, especially that of the Prodigal Son. These stories lay out for us the struggle that goes on in trying to achieve reconciliation. Many of them end before reconciliation is actually reached—something that mirrors much of our own experience.

It is the Apostle Paul, especially, that sets out for us the Christian understanding of reconciliation. For Paul, God is the author of reconciliation. About this he has no doubt. We but participate in what God is bringing about in our world. One can discern three processes of reconciliation in which God is engaged. The first is God's reconciling a sinful humanity to God's own self. This is set forth especially in Paul's Letter to the Romans (5:1-11), where Paul describes the peace we now have with God, who has poured out love in our hearts through the Holy Spirit who has been given to us. We have been reconciled to God through the death of the Son, Jesus Christ. It is through Christ that we have now received reconciliation. This act of God reconciling us, rescuing us from our sin, is sometimes called *vertical reconciliation.* As such, it is the basis for all other forms of Christian reconciliation. It is also central to Paul's own experience of Christ, having been converted from the persecution of the church to being made, "out of due time", an apostle of Jesus Christ.

The second kind of reconciliation of which Paul speaks is brought about between individual human beings and groups in society. The paramount example of this reconciliation is between Jews and Gentiles. Here the description of how this reconciliation is effected through the blood of Christ is presented in Ephesians (2:12-20), the Gentiles, without hope or promise, are made alive together in Christ, who has broken down the wall of hostility that divided them, and made them fellow citizens in the household of God. This second kind of reconciliation is sometimes called *horizontal reconciliation.*

The third kind of reconciliation situates God's work through Christ in the context of the whole of creation. In the hymns beginning the letters to the Ephesians and Colossians, God is seen as reconciling all things and all persons—whether in heaven or on earth—in Christ (Eph. 1:10), making peace to reign throughout all creation through the blood of Christ's cross (Col. 1:20). This kind of reconciliation is sometimes called cosmic reconciliation and represents the fullness of God's plan for creation, to be realized at the end of time.

Paul sees the church participating in the reconciling work of God through a ministry of reconciliation, captured succinctly in Paul's presentation of this in 2 Corinthians (5:17-20):

> So if anyone is in Christ, there is a new creation: everything old has passed away; see, everything has become new! All of this is from God, who reconciled us to himself through Christ, and has given us the ministry of reconciliation; that is, in Christ God was reconciling the world to himself, not counting their trespasses against them, and entrusting the message of reconciliation to us. So we are ambassadors for Christ, since God is making his appeal through us; we entreat you on behalf of Christ, be reconciled to God. (NRSV)

It is the vertical reconciliation that makes the horizontal and cosmic dimensions possible. It is within this framework of vertical, horizontal, and cosmic reconciliation that we are to see Christian mission. That mission is rooted in the missio Dei, the going forth of the Holy Trinity in the acts of creation, incarnation, redemption, and consummation. Through the Son, God has brought reconciliation to the world, overcoming sin, disobedience and alienation that we have wrought. Christ reunites us with God through his saving death, which God confirms in the resurrection and the revelation of transfigured life. The Holy Spirit empowers the church to participate in this ministry of the Son and the Spirit in reconciling the world. The church itself is in need of constant reconciliation, but becomes the vehicle for God's saving grace to come to a broken and disheartened world.

One might summarize this biblical understanding of reconciliation under five brief headings:

1. God is the author of all genuine reconciliation. We but participate in God's reconciling work. We are, in Paul's words, "ambassadors of Christ" (2 Cor. 5:20).
2. God's first concern in the reconciliation process is about the healing of the victims. This grows out of two experiences: the God of the great prophets of the Hebrew Scriptures and the God of Jesus Christ cares especially about the poor and the oppressed. Second, so often the wrongdoers do not repent, and the healing of the victim cannot be held hostage by unrepentant wrongdoers.
3. In reconciliation, God makes of both victim and wrongdoer a "new creation" (2 Cor. 5:17). This means two things. First of all, in profound wrongdoing it is impossible to go back to where we were before the wrongdoing took place; to do such would be to trivialize the gravity of what has been done. We can only go forward to a new place. Second, God wants both the healing of the victim and the repentance of the wrongdoer. Neither should be annihilated; both should be brought to a new place, a new creation.
4. Christians find a way through their suffering by placing it in the suffering, death and resurrection of Christ. It is this pattern of our suffering in that of Christ that helps us escape its destructive power. It also engenders in us hope.

5. Reconciliation will only be complete when all things are brought together in Christ (Eph. 1:10). Until that time we experience only partial reconciliation, but live in hope.

The Ministry of Reconciliation as Process

How does the church participate in this reconciliation? What concrete forms does it take? Because of the wider interest in reconciliation in the world today—it is far from being only a Christian concern—the language of reconciliation is often unclear. At times it has been manipulated and distorted to serve other ends. As Christians we need to be as clear as we can about what we mean by reconciliation and how we go about the ministry of reconciliation.

Let me begin by saying that reconciliation is both a process and a goal. It is both an ongoing work in which we participate and a final point at which we hope to arrive. Let us first look at it as a process. I will focus here on the horizontal or social dimension of reconciliation. The church participates in the vertical dimension through its sacraments and in the cosmic dimension as well, both in its liturgy and its concern for all of creation. These too constitute part of reconciliation as a model of mission. But, because the thinking on the horizontal dimension is more recent and new to many, I will devote more time to it here.

Participation in the horizontal dimension of reconciliation is about participating in God's healing societies that have been wounded deeply and broken by oppression, injustice, discrimination, war and wanton destruction. This healing begins with truth-telling, the breaking of the codes of silence that hide wrongdoing against the poor and vulnerable members of society. Truth-telling also means overcoming and correcting the lies and distortions that bring unearned shame on the innocent and isolate people from one another so as to exercise hegemony over society. *Truth-telling* has to be a constant effort to tell the whole truth, both for victims and about wrongdoers. Truth-telling as a practice in this sense must encompass four things: a truth that resonates with my experience of events, in language I can understand, conforming to my understanding of truthfulness, and from someone I can trust.

For a Christian, truth-telling is more than relating facts in a credible manner. It involves also God, who is the author of all truth. Truth in its Hebrew sense *('emet)* is part of the nature of God: it is reliable, it is enduring, it is steadfast, and it is faithful. It is truth-telling at this deep, theological level that is the basis for healing a broken society. What that means on a practical level is that the church must endeavour to create safe, hospitable spaces where truth can be spoken and heard, where the silence can be broken, where pernicious lies can be undone and overcome.

With truth comes the pursuit of *justice.* To seek justice without efforts to establish truth runs the risk of engaging in vengeance instead of true justice. The struggle for justice (and it is a struggle, wrongdoing does not give up easily) is many faceted. It involves *punitive justice* that punishes wrongdoers in a lawful way to mark that a renewed society acknowledges the wrongdoing that has been done and will not tolerate it in the future. Second, it involves *restorative justice* which restores the dignity and the rights of the victim. Third, it requires *distributive justice*, since the unjust wresting away of the goods of the victim makes healing and the creation of a just society nearly impossible. Finally, it requires *structural justice*, that is, the restructuring of the institutions and processes of society so that just action becomes part of the rebuilt society. Reallocating resources, equity in human rights, guaranteed access to health, shelter, food, education and employment are all parts of creating a just society.

A third aspect of reconciliation as a process is the *rebuilding of relationships.* Without relations of equity and trust, a society quickly slides back into violence. Work on these relationships has to happen at many levels. For victims, it involves the *healing of memories* so that one does not remain beholden or hostage to the past. It is an overcoming of the toxin that memories of violence, oppression, and marginalization contain. It means *repentance and conversion* on the part of those who have done wrong, acknowledging the wrongdoing and taking the steps to approach the victim in order to apologize and make reparation. It means making the difficult journey toward forgiveness. Here the process of rebuilding relationships is often short-circuited. Amnesty is given or impunity is bestowed to wrongdoers even before the victims are allowed to speak. A shroud of forgetfulness and oblivion is drawn over the past. Forgiveness is not about forgetting, but coming to remember in a different way—a way that removes the toxin from the experience for the victim and creates the space for repentance and apology by the wrongdoer. Forgiveness means remembering the past, but remembering it in a way that makes a different kind of future possible for both victim and the wrongdoer.

Reconciliation as Goal

Truth-telling, struggling for justice, working toward forgiveness: these are the three central dimensions of the social process of reconciliation. In all situations I know, they are never undertaken on a level playing field; the consequences of oppression, violence, and war are not predisposed to honesty, justice, and even good intentions in all parties. Nor are the processes, for the most part, orderly. And they never seem to be complete. In fact, we usually experience them as truncated, prematurely foreclosed, hijacked by the powerful. What are we to do?

This brings me to the other understanding of reconciliation; namely, reconciliation as goal. Talk of reconciliation often skips too easily from the end of overt violence to an imagined peace. It circumvents the messy and protracted process of truth-telling, seeking justice, working toward forgiveness. We expect that peace will blossom and flourish after long periods of war. We expect democracy to rise up, phoenix-like, from the ashes of dictatorship and authoritarian rule. But such is not the case. We can find ourselves acquiescing in half-measures, half-truths, compromised solutions.

It is important not to confuse reconciliation as process with reconciliation as goal.

In order to stay in the process, we must fix our eyes on the goal. For Christians, it is God who is working reconciliation; we are but agents in the process, participating in what God is doing. God is our strength; God is our hope. It is God who is bringing this about. Here we experience the difference between optimism and hope. Optimism is what grows out of the confidence in our own resources and capacities. It comes out of us. The enormity of wrong and sin that we face in protracted war and oppression far exceeds what we are able to accomplish. Hope, on the other hand, comes from God. It is God drawing us forward, like he did Abraham and Sarah. We live in faith, the assurance of things hoped for (cf. Heb. 11:1). With our eyes fixed on God and God's promises, we can maintain the strength of heart, of mind, and of will to continue our participation in what God is doing for the world.

The Church: A Community of Memory and of Hope

So where does this place the church? Its participation in the *missio Dei*, understood here as God's reconciling the world to God's own self, is marked especially by three things. The ministry of reconciliation makes of the church, first of all, a community of memory and, second, a community of hope. Its mission, in word and deed, of the message of reconciliation makes possible what is perhaps for many the most intense experience of God possible in our troubled, broken world.

The church is first of all a community of memory. It does not engage in the forgetfulness urged by the powerful upon the vulnerable and poor—to forget their sufferings, to erase their memories of what has been done to them, to act as though wrongdoing never happened. The church as a community of memory creates those safe spaces where memories can be spoken of out loud, and begin the difficult and long process of overcoming the rightful anger that, if left unacknowledged, can poison any possibilities for the future. In safe spaces, the trust that has been sundered, the dignity that has been denied and wrested away, has the chance of being reborn. A community of memory is concerned too about truthful memory, not the distorting lies that serve the interests of the wrongdoer at the cost of the victim. A community of memory keeps the focus of memory as it pursues justice in all its dimensions—punitive, restorative, distributive, structural. Not to pursue and struggle for justice makes the truth-telling sound false and the safe spaces created barren. A community of memory is concerned too with the future of memory, that is, the prospects of forgiveness and what lies beyond. The difficult ministry of memory, if it may be called that, is possible because it is grounded in the memory of the passion, death, and resurrection of Jesus Christ: the One who was without sin and was made sin for us, so that we might become the justice of God (cf. 2 Cor. 5:21).

Living in the memory of what Christ has gone through—suffering and death, yet not forgotten and indeed raised up by God—is the source of our hope. Hope allows us to keep the vision of a reconciled world alive, not in some facile utopian fashion, but grounded in the memory of what God has done in Jesus Christ. Paul captures this well in another passage in 2 Corinthians:

But we hold this treasure in clay vessels, so that it may be made clear that this extraordinary power belongs to God and not to us. We are afflicted in every way, but not crushed; perplexed, but not driven to despair; persecuted, but not forsaken; struck down, but not destroyed; always carrying in the body the death of Jesus, so that the life of Jesus may also be made visible in our bodies (2 Cor. 4:7-10).

Reconciliation belongs to God, not to us. Despite all we go through, we do not lose heart, since we carry the death of Jesus in our bodies, so that through us his life might be made visible. This is the vocation of the church, its calling to the ministry of reconciliation, its proclamation of the death and resurrection of Christ in the church's own body. If we so preach with our bodies, God's reconciling work can be made known to a broken world. Mission, as our Orthodox brothers and sisters have so helpfully reminded us, is the liturgy after the liturgy. Our action is not just political action or action for justice (although it is also all of these). It is participation in something much larger than ourselves: the work of the Triune God in bringing about the healing of the world.

MESSAGE FROM THE YOUNG PEOPLE TO THE CONFERENCE

Honoured gathering, dear friends:

As the representatives of the youth of the Christian community all around the world, we now deliver you a message and urge you to listen.

How old was Jesus when he first delivered his message? According to the WCC standards he would have been considered a youth. He would have been placed into a special category, offered a pre-conference and have a lovely misspelled T-Shirt.

Surely we youth delegates and stewards appreciate the opportunity we have been given to participate, and we have done our best in order to let the voice of young people sound loud and clear.

In our minds there is a conference after this conference that takes place in our homes and in our communities where we are expected to carry on the message received here. We appeal to you to overcome barriers of communication between the different church traditions and to continue praying for the other churches and our common witness to the world. We also appeal to you to continue to stand up, to take position and action against the various forms of violence in the world. It is our task to confront challenges like the HIV-pandemic, domestic violence and ecological violence with one interconfessional voice; and to repent wherever our churches do not resist violence.

Therefore we urge all participants who experienced these blessed days in Athens to take care of the seeds planted in our hearts during this conference, to share what we have seen and heard and to carry out the message of healing and reconciliation to our world.

We remind you of the WCC goal of 25% youth participation in every major event, but clearly we have failed to reach this goal here in Athens, for only 5% of this conference's participants are youth, and they have not played an active role.

In eight months' time we have a great opportunity to change this trend – for the focus of the General Assembly in Porto Alegre is on youth! We challenge you to listen to the young people of your communities and give them the chance to contribute to the ecumenical mission.

Young people are important participants in their home communities, and therefore young delegates are crucial in delivering fresh messages all around the world and acting as a bridge between discussion and action.

SYNAXEIS

INTRODUCTION TO SYNAXEIS

Sample of Materials Used During Synaxeis

The Greek word "*synaxis*" refers to a "gathering of people" around a theme. The word is also a liturgical term. In the context of the CWME conference, it was used as the collective term for the variety of offerings given, such as workshops, study groups, panel discussions, introductions, video presentations etc.

Synaxeis were offered by participants and resource persons, and were intended to reflect the variety of concrete mission work and/or theoretical missiological reflection specifically relating to the theme of the Conference, and aiming at using participatory methods. Thus, the *synaxeis* offered a wide range of issues and methodologies from which participants could choose. The *synaxeis* covered many more important mission issues and reflections on healing and reconciliation than could possibly be addressed in the plenaries. Whereas they offered plenty of space for engaged discussions, debate and sharing of case studies, each of them brought together only a sample of all conference participants, and generally those who had chosen that subject rather than the full range of opinions and experiences.

It is impossible in a book documenting the Athens conference to give even an approximate idea of the richness of the experiences and reflections shared during the afternoons. All those preparing *synaxeis* had been asked to provide documents for the book, both in paper and electronic form. The style and quality of the documents collected during the conference was somewhat uneven, and electronic versions could be obtained only in certain cases. Needless to say, the use of power-point presentations gives headaches to any editor, since such documents are not in a form which is easily transformed into a readable text.

For these reasons, the selection offered is very limited in its character, regional and thematic representation. Whereas it cannot do justice to the wide range of themes and concerns with which conference participants struggled, it may still point to the wealth of contributions the *synaxeis* brought to the healing and reconciling experience of the Conference's daily life.

A list of all the titles of *synaxeis* offered at the conference follows.

During the conference the following synaxeis were offered:

Spiritual guidance, spiritual accompaniment. A workshop on spiritual guidance, using meditation, and a presentation of the Pearls of Life
Earthing liturgy in life – worship in a global community. Looking at healing liturgies as an integral part of Christian healing ministries in Britain and Germany
Come, Holy Spirit...the Holy Spirit and mission theology today
The Orthodox Church and the world mission
Mission and youth
Common witness in China
New ways of being church
Migrant churches
The extended community – a case study on the Pilsdon Community
The church of all and for all – case studies by the Ecumenical Disability Advocates Network (EDAN)
Turning hope into homes - a synaxis on mission and poverty
The missional church as a healing and reconciling community
Examples of inter-religious cooperation by the Urban Rural Mission Middle East and Africa networks
From strangers to friends
Christian faith and religious plurality – a study synaxis
Women's ministries of healing and reconciling mission
Healing the nations – diversity as a key for reconciliation, renewal and growth
Greater participation of people living with HIV/AIDS - a missiological challenge to the churches
"A journey to Argavia" - role-play on mission
Theological education as mission – mission in theological education
A Christian approach to HIV/AIDS prevention
Doing mission together – a dialogue process on church unity and mission in Germany
Multicultural ministries
"Called in Christ" – presented through Christian art
From Strangers to Friends – CEC and the South
Pastoral care: Christian counselling in situations of violence and abuse
Reconciliation and mission – a presentation of an exchange programme between Central America and the United States
Caring for caregivers: resources for mission and aid personnel
Film: "Roots of Violence", from Sierra Leone
Case studies on Canadian churches and First Nations people
Film: "Religion, Power and Violence"
The Church's healing ministry in the midst of war and conflict – a synaxis on healing and trauma
Healing ministry and the church – the role of Christian health institutions in the communities
Counselling with the terminally ill
"Lord that I might receive my sight"- a drama with narrative input

Healing the blind man – a synaxis on a life transforming tribal community in Myanmar
The healing congregation
Primary Health Care: a challenge in the context of the healing ministry – experiences from Congo and Sri Lanka
HIV/AIDS and ecumenical theological education
Why me? Learning to live in conflicts
Transforming churches to be HIV-AIDS competent – An Ecumenical HIV/AIDS Initiative in Africa
Equity and access in healing ministry : a challenge to the mission of the churches
Multi-dimensional healing - case studies from an evangelical perspective
Does being saved mean being healed? – a discussion panel
Healing cultural conflicts
Healing from the perspective of medical mission
Counselling for forgiveness, reconciliation and healing
Reconciling evangelism: Reconciliation and practices of evangelism
Reconciliation/healing of memories - conditions, successes and difficulties of reconciliation processes
Healing of memories and reconciliation – the case of South Africa
Victims' rights to truth, justice and reconciliation
Reconciliation and mission – Pentecostal and Orthodox perspectives
Reconciliation after violent conflicts
Pursuing truth and justice after violent conflicts. A missiological challenge
Reconciliation procedures in Indigenous communities
Towards a praxis of reconciliation – the Ecumenical Accompaniment Programme in Palestine and Israel (EAPPI)
Reconciliation between people; the story of Jacob and Esau – participation in dramatic story telling
Truth, justice, peace, mercy – group work on how the terms relate to reconciliation
Reconciliation among people in the process of reunification – the cases of Korea and Germany
Reconciliation in Rwanda – evaluation of reconciliation attempts in Rwanda, politically and within churches
Healing of the earth as reconciliation – an Indigenous People's approach to healing and reconciliation
Mary Ward – pioneer and prophet of reconciliation
Healing and reconciliation from the underside of communities (a Dalit perspective)
Empire and evangelism
Cultural issues in the language of exclusion
Churches seeking reconciliation and peace (DOV)
Disability, life and life in abundance
Christian witness in a world of destructive conflicts
The role of the church in providing integrated/holistic healing
Hope as healing – the Coptic Church's ministry for people living with HIV/AIDS
What do we mean by "healing" and "the healing ministry"?

| A new vineyard in Albania |
| Ministry of healing in Ireland |
| Healing the still open wounds of colonialism |

Come Holy Spirit ... The Holy Spirit and Mission Theology Today[1]

This well-attended synaxis (more than 100 people) enjoyed the presence of the two speakers from the morning, Dr Kirsteen Kim and Dr Wonsuk Ma, sitting on a panel with the moderator, Dr Christoffer H. Grundmann. After a brief introduction and orientation about the structure of the synaxis the moderator asked Dr Ma to comment on his statement that one of the basic convictions of Pentecostal mission work is the "prophethood of all believers", which would imply that mission is much more about prophetic existence sustained by the Holy Spirit than "making converts".

Dr Ma agreed to this, while at the same time pointing out that mission in the sense of calling people to Christ should be the overarching goal of all theological studies and that Pentecostals are much more interested in getting involved in such action than just reflecting on it.

Dr Kim, who defined mission as the "spiritual practice" of identifying, discerning, and affirming the workings of the Spirit, was asked about the place of proclamation in her concept to which she replied that she takes proclamation to be inherent in being a Christian and therefore need not to be addressed explicitly.

After this initial round the floor was opened for spontaneous reactions by participants, which resulted in a lively discussion. Numerous topics were touched upon, centring around three main areas:

(1) the very perception of healing (holistic approach; avoiding false alternatives; physical and spiritual healing; healing beyond the individual person considering the social and ecological dimensions);
(2) the necessity seriously to take up issues related to spirit worlds and the realm of the Spirit in general (experiences with spirit worlds; comprehending the spirit language of power; discernment of spirits; gifts of the Spirit);
(3) the theological challenge to develop a truly Trinitarian missiology by considering all persons of the Trinity accordingly (overcoming the Western subordination of the Spirit as fixed in the *filioque* by inviting an in-depth dialogue with Orthodox theology) and avoiding the pitfall of ignoring or unduly spiritualizing the Holy Spirit.

---

[1] *Editor's note:* This synaxis took place in the afternoon of 10 May 2005. Because of strict time limitations for the two thematic presentations in the opening plenary of that morning, it had been decided to provide an opportunity for both the speakers to elaborate on some of their affirmations and the participants to enter into a dialogue with them and with one another on pneumatology and mission.

The final part of the session was spent pondering questions of pneumatology and missiology. It was noted that in the past the *missio Dei* concept lacked reflection about its pneumatological implications. Today missiology is asked to unfold the Trinitarian richness and complexities of the *missio Dei*, which poses an intellectual challenge of no mean nature, especially in light of the abundance of indigenous churches surrounded by all sorts of spirit worlds as well as of the various Pentecostal and other charismatic traditions.

This also requires a heightened awareness of an adequate terminology, sensitive to the ambiguities of spirit worlds, which in the past tended simply to be condemned or ignored and left to cultural anthropologists for resolution.

In closing, the moderator shared his observation that during the entire session only once was the term "syncretism" used during the discussions; in previous world mission conferences, this concept was considered of decisive importance. This was not because the issues have become irrelevant or that syncretism is no longer considered important, but because it is possible today to address these issues frankly and try to come to terms with them even among such a broad variety of traditions, without foreclosing this discussion from the very start due to anxiety or fear of syncretism.

This he regarded as something genuinely new and a gift to this particular Conference as to all of missiology, for which to be grateful. Thus he encouraged participants to hold boldly to that faith to which Paul made reference in 1 Cor. 12:6 when declaring that all the different gifts "are activated by *one* and *the same* Spirit."

Christoffer H. Grundmann, Valparaiso, Indiana, USA.

Mission and Youth

Report on the Synaxis on "Mission and Youth"

Facilitators: Adèle Djomo Ngomedje (WCC), Elizabeth Tapia (Bossey), Garland Pierce (USA).

Methodology: The synaxis aimed at attracting youth, but many people turned out irrespective of age. They were led through informal discussions on the theme of the synaxis in the light of the preparatory document "Called to be Healers and Peacemakers Now!" Emphasis was on personal reflections and interaction amongst participants through prayer, meditation, brainstorming, discussion.

The following questions had been shared with young participants in preparation for the synaxis:

As you reflect on the document "Called to be Healers and Peacemakers Now!" and its relevance in your context, we ask you to consider the following questions:

1. What are the marks of the peacemaking community in your context?
2. What are the contributions of young people to healing in your communities?
3. Personal reflections.

Highlights

Future pattern of discipleship for youth in the West, emerging leadership from churches, motivation for youth in worldwide mission, other experiences of effective mission models for youth in an age of globalization – youth initiative, new alternatives to globalization – setting right perspectives in the age of globalization: how to act locally, local impact of globalization, role of adults and parents.

Called to be Healers and Peacemakers Now!

A Statement from the Seminar on Mission and Youth
in the Context of Globalization 17-23 August 2004,
World Council of Churches Ecumenical Institute at Bossey

We, 25 young people from various churches and youth organizations in Africa, Asia, Europe, North and South America, came together to reflect and seek deeper understanding of the role of young people and the church in carrying out mission in the context of globalization. Together, we prayed with and for one another; articulated our faith, experiences and reflections through Bible studies, singing, dancing and visual arts. We expressed our unity and solidarity through group work, cultural presentations and community building activities, and we celebrated the love of God through worship and joyful encounters.

We came from diverse geographical and cultural contexts. Recognizing that we ive and work in a broken world – a world in need of healing and reconciliation, we encouraged one another as we articulated our mission in the context of contemporary economic and socio-political concerns. We gathered to share our views and experiences in developing alternative paradigms for confronting the challenges of globalization.

Globalization: A Challenge to our Faith

Globalization challenges the basis of Christian faith and its vision of the oikoumene where there is fullness of life (John 10:10b) because it reduces human life to a mere business transaction. Globalization is a process which generates more victims and few beneficiaries worldwide. It facilitates communication, technological progress and gives the opportunity to know other cultures, yet access to these remains in the hands of a few.

Globalization imposes a culture of domination characterized by loss of identity and languages, spiritual oppression, loss of community life, erosion of Christian values and alienation. It systematically uses mass media (print and broadcast), educational institutions and, at times, even the church and its organizations, to propagate and justify its destructive and exploitative logic.

It has also taken its toll on Christian churches. Indifference and apathy to justice and peace-oriented ministries are more prevalent. Moreover, it has fueled religious fundamentalism and the proliferation of "prosperity theology".

The claws of globalization on the economic, political and social life have greatly affected the life and relationships of young people. War, particularly, has caused great damage in Asia and the Middle East in the name of the preservation of US world control. Globalization has aggravated the evils of class and caste systems. In Africa, economic injustice and political instability have deepened. In America and Europe, people migrating in search of jobs are perceived to pose economic and race problems while the massive migration causes brain and labour drain in the sending countries. The negative impacts of globalization are felt in all continents through intensified trafficking of women and children, poverty, unemployment, consumerism, immoral payment of foreign debts, economic injustices and other forms of exploitation and oppression. The HIV and AIDS pandemic has been exacerbated by the economic turmoil brought about by globalization. The logic of globalization has extended its reach to the point that young people have, consciously and unconsciously, become its agents.

Spirituality of Life: Our Mission

But globalization does not have the last word. More and more young people, at various levels, are becoming aware and are challenged to affirm their Christian faith through finding innovative alternatives and strategies in education and advocacy. Thus, the spirituality of death that globalization promotes is being overcome by the emergence of the spirituality of life, where the fullness of life is affirmed and valued.

As young people, we understand mission today as the announcement and realization of the fullness of life for all, which is the message of the Word of God. This is done through witnessing and action in the church and society. We need to discern the signs of our times and renew our commitment to resisting the powers and principalities that diminish life.

Mission needs to be rooted in the daily realities and shared views of all peoples, which require respect, love and the empowering of our different abilities. As Christians, we need to remember that we are all part of the body of Christ (1 Cor. 12:12) that should be united in working towards the realization of shalom – abundant life for all.

Mission is also faith in action (James 2:17) where we should "walk the talk" if we are to be true to our calling. It is in this principle that we are reminded that the power of prayer gives us strength to do our mission and that our collective actions confirm the foundations of our faith.

Life is Stronger than Death

Therefore, after prayerful reflection and analysis, we firmly and lovingly affirm that:

- the love of God and the vision of shalom for the oikoumene inspires us to breathe new life to a world where the forces of death continue to bring destruction in every dimension of our lives and relationships;
- in the grace of God, and the fruits of our unity reside the power to be co-creators with God in giving birth to a new and better world where life is experienced in its fullness; healing is not merely the absence of physical infirmities but also a process and state of spiritual, physical and social well-being;
- addressing the root causes of conflict and bringing about justice are paramount in peacemaking;
- the impetus of our analysis and response to the challenges of globalization is our Christian faith.
- The entire church, particularly the young people, is called to be a healing and peacemaking mission where we shall:
    - draw inspiration and strength from the richness of our faith resources and lessons of our faith journey;
    - use our creativity and the potential of our youthful vitality;
    - take recourse, principally, in strengthening our churches, sustaining education and pursuing actions of resistance and struggle, while we explore and develop new ones as conditions may require;
    - take steps to strengthen the capacities and empower the youth, children, women, indigenous peoples and persons with disabilities to defend themselves against the forces of death;
    - strive to develop alternative paradigms that uphold and preserve the peoples' values, interest and rights, ensure their sovereignty, guarantee economic justice and democracy, and respect their right to self-determination;
    - pray and work for the unity of the Body of Christ.

In view of the upcoming WCC Conference on World Mission and Evangelism, we offer this statement, our prayers and the youthfulness of our outlook. Furthermore, we invite the entire conference to reflect with us on the following:

- We hope for the full participation of the young people in all processes of the conference – where "spaces" are created for the articulation of youth perspectives on mission, where the voices of young people are included in decision-making, and where young people are well represented;
- We affirm that the meaning and paradigm of mission is rooted in Christian faith, in the spirit of ecumenism, and viewed from the perspectives of the indigenous peoples, women and persons with disabilities; and

- We expect that the process and results of the conference will be an inspiration and instruction as we advance our prophetic ministries with all believers.

May the Triune God empower us in our journey in faith and mission.
May we transcend barriers that separate us.
For we are called to be healers and peacemakers now !

New Ways of Being Church

This synaxis, facilitated by Council for World Mission staff and representatives (Desmond van der Water, Elizabeth Joy, Andrew Williams and Michael Heaney) offered the possibility to more than 50 participants to receive information on the Council for World Mission (CWM) through oral and video presentations, as well as on some of the projects supported or operated by its 31 member churches. Following is a summary of van der Water's paper which we publish here. There was group work as well as plenary discussion on the question of new ways of being church and comparisons between church life and witness in North and South.

'New Ways of Being Church' - A discussion paper

Desmond van der Water[1]

1. INTRODUCTION

More than 60 percent of the world's Christians today are in South, namely Africa, Latin America and Asia,[2] with current trends showing that the church in the two-thirds world continues to grow in stature and membership. In contrast, the church in the North struggles to survive, let alone grow, with a declining membership and influence decreasing as it becomes more and more marginal within society. Clearly there is something significant to learn from the branches of Christ's Body in the South, provided that the churches in North America and Europe have the desire and the will to reverse these negative trends. This brief paper seeks to reflect on a positive development that has emerged within the last five-to-ten years, namely the phenomenon which has become widely known as New Ways of Being Church.[3]

It is significant that even "secular" media, such as *Newsweek* magazine, have picked up and commented on this new trend, with *Newsweek* entitling its lead article, "The Changing face of the Church".[4] Although the phrase "New Ways of Being Church" seems to be the most widely used, other terms and phrases are also

---

[1] The Rev. Dr Desmond van der Water is the general secretary of the Council for World Mission.
[2] See Dana Robert, essay entitled, "Shifting Southward: Global Christianity Since 1945", *International Bulletin of Missionary Research 24* (2), pp50-58.
[3] As far as I am aware the term, "Ways of Being Church" was first formally used by Leonardo Boff in his ground-breaking and challenging book, *Ecclesiogenesis: The Base Communities Reinvent the Church*, (Orbis Books, Maryknoll, New York, 1997.

used to refer to the same phenomenon, such as New Forms of Church, Emerging Church, Fresh Expressions of Being Church etc. At the heart of these designations seems to be a strong and sincere desire to arrest the decay in the decline of the church and its witness within the post-modern era by responding more creatively to the new social realities, by coming to terms with shifting economic patterns, by repositioning itself in relation to a changing cultural milieu and by engaging constructively with the movements of New Age spirituality.

2. NEW WAYS OF BEING CHURCH - THE MISSIOLOGICAL CHALLENGE

The Council for World Mission (CWM) affirms and welcomes the emergence of the expressions, explorations and initiatives that give substance to New Ways of Being Church. In our assessment, this development represents an ecclesiological movement and direction that seeks to be faithful to a major challenge to the church and to Christianity, especially within the context of the northern hemisphere. However, CWM's particular interest and concern in relation to this new phenomenon is that the *mission agenda* should be what shapes and what drives the emerging of new churches, whatever name they may be given or by which they come to be called.

3. CHURCH PLANTING – A RELEVANT MODEL FOR TODAY?

There are those who argue that central to the creation of New Ways of Being Church is the ingredient of Church Planting, which has been defined as follows:

Church Planting is creating new communities of Christian faith as part of the Mission of God, to express his Kingdom in every geographic and cultural context.[5]

Other commentators, such as Stuart Murray and Anne Wilkinson-Hayes for example, suggest that the church-planting "boom has gone bust", advancing the following reasons for their finding:

- most churches which are able to plant another church early in the 1990s have not yet fully recovered sufficiently to do so again;
- few newly-planted churches have yet grown quickly enough to plant another church;
- the dominance of personnel-intensive models of church planting have discouraged smaller churches from becoming involved;
- a disturbing number of church plants have failed, have remained small and weak,or have attracted only those who were already Christians; and
- church planting has generally been restricted to areas where churches are already flourishing, leaving many urban and rural areas untouched.[6]

---

[4] *Newsweek*, April 2001, pp.46-52.
[5] Bob Hopkins, quoted in *Mission-Shaped Church: Church Planting and Fresh Expressions of Church in a Changing Context*, Church House, London, 2003, p 29.
[6] Stuart Murray and Anne Wilkinson-Hayes, *Hope from the Margins*, Cambridge, England, Grove, 2000, pp.4-5.

It is not difficult to see why the notion of church planting has been met with a degree of suspicion especially amongst the churches in the South, as it can be viewed as yet another form of neo-colonist expansionism, whereby what is really intended by church planting is *church transplanting* of the dominant North American and euro-centric model. The definition of church planting, quoted above, suggests that the contextual expression of the newly planted church is important, and right so. However, the question still remains as to which basic model inform and shape the new creation. Michael Frost and Alan Hirsh concludes that the heart of the problem with the notion of church planting, and with much of the church in the North is that of the planting and reproducing of "carbon copies of the already beleaguered, failing Christendom-style church" whereby the "'Christendom virus is passed on".[7]

4. NEW WAYS OF BEING CHURCH – NOT SO NEW AFTER ALL?

Church Planting aside, some would suggest that the phenomenon of New Ways of Being Church is not really a new development and that the movements in the latter part of the 20th century which produced the Small Christian Communities, Christian Grassroots Communities and Basic Christian Communities (or Basic Ecclesiastical Communities) are simply a variation of the same theme. It may also be argued that the phenomenon goes back even much further to the concept of House Church or the Cell Church which is derived especially from the book of Acts. Moreover, certain ecclesiastical traditions, like the Congregationalists for instance, would claim that they have attempted to be most true and faithful to the theology of the church as it is expressed in the writings of the New Testament. Be that as it may, the central question is whether we are simply seeing the recycling of old models, ideas and notions of church, giving them a semblance of contextual respectability, and calling them New Ways of Being Church? Or are we experiencing a movement that is an authentic resonance with the impulses and promptings of the Holy Spirit? In the final analysis, of course, it is the Holy Trinity who is the author and creator of renewal and transformation within the Body of Christ.

It would seem to me that there are certain marks or characteristics one should be looking for in discerning whether any of the expressions or formations of New Ways of Being Church is true and authentic to the letter and spirit of biblical teachings about the nature and role of church. I want to identify just a few of what I would consider to be the non-negotiable characteristics of being church, whether in the 21st century or beyond. For the purpose of this paper I will focus on the local church/parish/congregation.

5. NON-NEGOTIABLES OF BEING CHURCH, OLD OR NEW

1. The first mark is its contextual relevance to the needs, hopes and concerns of the local community life in which the local church is set. Its rootedness and relevance to the context must characterize the church's work, worship and witness. This is not to say that the church should therefore simply conform or

---

[7] Michael Frost & Alan Hirsh, *The Shaping of Things to Come: Innovation and Mission for the 21st Century Church*, Hendrickson, Peabody, Massachusetts and Strand. Erina, New South Wales, 2003, p.18.

at worst capitulate to values, norms and activities that contradict the gospel message. On the contrary, while being relevant, the church's presence should be transforming presence within the community, witnessing within its internal and external life to the values and standards of the Kingdom of God. In this regard the image that the church projects to the community is critical. With reference to the image of missionaries today, Sherron Kay George states that the following characteristics should be paramount: self-emptying, self-giving, other-receiving and other-empowering.[8] I would suggest that these should also be front-line traits of the local church today in whatever context it finds itself.

2. A second mark that I would identify is that the local church should have the understanding of its role as the *primary agent of Christian ministry and mission* within the community in which it is set. So much of what has gone wrong with the dominant church models arises from the fact that they have become overtly centralized, institutionalized, hierarchical and clericalized with disproportionate amounts of material and spiritual resources being poured into the creation, maintaining and perpetuating of the institution. It is no wonder that the local church has interpreted its role as that of being in support of denominational activity, instead of it being the other way round.

In many instances this pre-occupation with institutional development - and latterly with institutional survival - has been transmitted into the psyche of the local church community, with the multiplication of small institutional entities, most of whom simply hang on or struggle for local church institutional survival. One of the reasons why the African Instituted Churches (AICs) in South Africa,[9] for example, have grown so phenomenally in membership and influence is that their life, worship and witness is not dependent on buildings, bureaucracies, huge administrations and infrastructures. At the heart of the problem of ecclesiastical institutionalism is, in our view, the question of the dominant nature of the church. In other words, whether the church is first and foremost event, or is the dominant notion one of church as *institution*, a question which has its roots and its resolution within the teachings of the New Testament.[10] From a Roman Catholic perspective, Yves Congar argues that Jesus did in fact institute a structured community, but that the structure is subject to the calling of the community as a whole:

Jesus instituted a structured community, a community in its entirety holy, priestly, prophetic, missionary, and apostolic, with ministries at its interior: some freely aroused by the Spirit, others bound by the imposition of hands to the institution and mission of the Twelve...even those that are instituted and sacramental, take their position as services of precisely what the community is called to be and to do.[11]

In my view the very desire that has given birth to the seeking and creating of New Ways of Being Church is a reaction to and an attempt by ordinary Christians and

---

[8] Sherron K George, "The Quest for Images of Missionaries in a 'Post-Missionary' Era", *Missiology*, Vol. XXX, Number 1, January 2002, pp 62-63.
[9] Also known as the African Independent Churches.
[10] See, for example, E Schweitzer, *Church Order in the New Testament*, SCM Press, London, 1961, p.210.
[11] Congar, quoted in Leonardo Boff, *ibid*, p. 29.

church-people to break away from, amongst others, the shackles, encumbrances and the sheer weight of institutional maintenance. The burden of institutional maintenance has also, to a large extent, had the effect of, at best limiting, and at worst handicapping the church's missiological role and profile. Within the context of the United Kingdom, some of the expressions of these breakaway formations are identified and listed as follows by a working group of the Church of England's Mission and Public Affairs Council:

- alternative worship communities;
- base ecclesial communities;
- café church;
- cell church;
- churches arising out of community initiatives (both out of community projects, and the restructuring or refounding of an existing church to serve a community);
- multiple and midweek congregations;
- network-focused churches (churches connecting with specific networks);
- school-based and school-linked congregations and churches;
- seeker church;
- traditional church plants;
- traditional forms of church inspiring new interest (including new monastic communities); and
- youth congregations.[12]

3. The above list clearly shows that there can never be a blueprint or one-size-fits-all model. However, I would suggest that a third mark of authenticity would be the characteristic whereby the church is seen and experienced as a *welcoming community* as opposed to an exclusive community.

This task, namely the creation of a local church, parish or congregation that is welcoming, rather than exclusive, is a hugely challenging one. One of its assumptions, therefore, is that the nature and shape of the local religious community is that it is never a finished product, always open to the guidance of the Spirit through new ideas, influences and changes that challenge the settled, secure and comfortable establishments.

In many countries and contexts today the phenomena of multi-faith, multi-lingual and multi-cultural communities is growing, and if the church is to be true to its New Testament roots, it should embrace and not avoid this challenge.

4. A fourth mark, which not only gives authenticity and relevance but also indicates the incorporation of a sound theological basis, is that the new expressions of church will demonstrate its *connectedness to the world church and to the ecumenical community.*
The ecumenical commitment of a local church and its mission outreach are really two sides of the same coin. The quest for Christian unity is of course in tandem

---

[12] *Mission-Shaped Church: Church Planting and Fresh Expressions of Church in a Changing Context, p.44.*

with the church's task of pursuing and promoting the unity of all creation.

5. A fifth and final mark that I wish to list is the local church's willingness to be *committed to an engagement with the major global mission challenges of the age.*

Depending on the geography and context, of course, the focus will vary, but it is generally recognized that for our time the major global challenges are HIV and AIDS, poverty and economic deprivation, social justice, war and violence, global warming and the destruction of the environment.

The Extended Community – A Case Study on Pilsdon Community

Facilitator: Rev. Ruth Bottoms, Pilsdon, UK[1]

Number of participants: 22

Methodology: story-telling: introductory presentation, six photos passed around to groups of six people, chairs pre-arranged in small circles, a question to each group for discussion, feedback from participants which turn out to become the subject of the presenter's remarks.

Highlights: participants were impressed with the process and appreciated the interesting subject.

(excerpts from staff report)

Presentation of the Community (from Pilsdon leaflet)

A CHRISTIAN COMMUNITY
Pilsdon is a small community of 25-to-40 people (from age 18 up) dedicated to the ideals of the Christian gospel. It follows the example of the 17th-century Community at Little Gidding in Huntingdonshire that included families with children and was centred on a manor house, a small farm and a little church. The community lives a life of corporate simplicity set within the framework of daily prayers, meals, work and recreation.

A WORKING COMMUNITY
Pilsdon is a working community and everybody is expected to assist to the best of their ability with any work required. This can be with the farm animals (hand-milking cows, rearing pigs and sheep etc.), in the kitchen or jobs about the house, and usually involves about six hours work a day.

---

[1] The Rev. Ruth Bottoms is the moderator of CWME.

COLLABORATIVE COMMUNITY

The community cooperates closely with the local health and social service support services. We also arrange regular visits to AA and other alcohol and drug advisory services. We have close links with neighbouring communities.

A "DRY" COMMUNITY

Guests are asked to respect the life of the community. Alcohol and illicit drug consumption on or off the premises is not allowed. Anyone found intoxicated will be asked to leave immediately. Similarly, violent or threatening behaviour is not compatible with our shared community life.

Accommodation: Please note that you will be sharing sleeping accommodation in a room that has up to four beds.

Meals: We would like you to share meals with us as a family. Let us know if you have any special dietary needs (we always provide vegetarian alternatives) or if you will be out for a meal.

Chapel: Guests are always welcome to join us for times of prayer. We can also offer spiritual direction and preparation leading to baptism, confirmation, confession and reconciliation.

NEEDS IN COMMUNITY

Wellington boots, a torch and working clothes are useful to bring if you have them, as are warm clothes in the winter. We have a "boutique" of second hand clothes, as well as a laundry and drying facilities. We also have a small shop where stamps, toiletries, sweets, tobacco etc. can be bought. There is a shopping trip into Bridport or one of the other nearby towns once a week.

A CREATIVE COMMUNITY

We encourage guests to use our other facilities during recreation times (after tea, evenings and weekends). These include a pottery with a kiln, an art studio and craft room. There are opportunities for making music: choral and instrumental. There are also games rooms, with snooker, badminton, table tennis and occasional cricket and soccer teams. There is an extensive library and a fortnightly mobile county library, and opportunity for chess, cards and other board games. We have two TV rooms and a weekly DVD/video night. Also we have some of the finest Dorset countryside and coast for walks, swimming etc. on our doorstep as well as weekly visits to the Bridport pool and leisure centre.

DAILY TIMETABLE

07:25 am	Rising bell (8 am Sunday)
07:30 am	Eucharist or Morning prayer (Mon to Sat, 8 am Sun)

08-8:30 am	Breakfast (8:30-9 am Sunday)
11 am	Tea/coffee
11:15 am	Shop
12:15	Eucharist (Tuesday)
12:45	Midday prayers (Monday & Wednesday - Sunday)
01:00 pm	Lunch
04:30 pm	Tea
06:15 pm	Shop
06:30 pm	Evening prayers (with Eucharist on Sunday)
07:00 pm	Supper followed by tea/coffee (07:45 pm Sunday)
09:15 pm	Night prayers (chapel)

I dream of a community....

Where worship is central,
creative
simple and profound.

Which inhabits
sacred space,
holy ground
where hospitality is lavished.

Where everyone
works at life's chores,
where living is simple, ethical and joyful;
A community which knows how to party!

I dream of a community...
Where each is accepted and cherished,
loved and loving into being;
sending and sent
holding and held
embracing and embraced
in blessing.
Where women and men
are companions and helpmeets on the journey.
Where sexuality
is reverenced and celebrated
not demeaned, defiled or denied.

Which shuns patriarchy and hierarchy
which breaks down barriers
and is mutual, cooperative and collaborative;
where the possibilities for
the abuse of power
are minimized.

I dream of a community...
>   Ecumenically committed and open to the world,
>   which is still journeying
>   and does not think it has arrived
>   but is committed to the quest
>   and in the Spirit dances on.

I dream...

The Missional Church as a Healing and Reconciling Community[1]

Facilitators: Dr Tormod Engelsviken, Norway; Rev. Darrell Jackson, CEC, UK; Ms Vija Esenberga, Estonia; and Rev. Birger Nygaard, Norway.
21 participants, 4 speakers, and 2 staff

The Missional Church – A European Perspective

Rev. Darrell Jackson, researcher in European Mission and Evangelism, Conference of European Churches

(excerpts from the presentation made during the synaxis in Athens)

Describing the Missional Church

Mission-Shaped Church

- Alternative worship
"Alternative worship" emerged in the late 1980's; an early example was the "Nine o'clock service" or NOS, based in Sheffield in the UK. Many subsequent events owe much to that creative style, though distancing themselves from all forms of abusive leadership. They can provide a safety net for Christians who are moving out of charismatic or evangelical churches. They seek to be responsive to post-modern culture, expressing preferences for ambiguity and antiquity. Their inner sense of community is strong, the worship highly creative, but outward-facing mission is often weak, not least because their members are recovering from poor past experiences of church. They should not be thought of as simply youth churches because their age group is older and wider.

- Café church
A growing number of churches are engaging with café culture, developing a particular ambience where people meet for interaction and discussion around

---

[1] *Editor's note:* A very selective choice was made from the various texts presented during this synaxis. The purpose was to highlight examples of what can be meant by "missional churches" in a Western European context. At the synaxis itself, the presentations were followed by dialogue and discussion with the participants.

tables, rather than sitting in rows of church pews. Drinks and light snacks may be provided and careful attention is normally paid to the décor. Venues include youth clubs, cafés and pub rooms or a suitable room in an existing church building. Careful attention is paid to encouraging relationship and community through the interaction over the tables. A determined effort is made to avoid a consumer or spectator mentality. Café has been a useful way of easing entry into the wider Sunday church experience for those who have attended an Alpha course. The related notion of "table fellowship" looks back to Jesus and the disciples, with all the potential to create significant meeting between people and to encourage the exploration of life and of the gospel.

- Cell plants
Moves the focus of the church from the congregation to the small group. There are a number of models advocated but all insist that the major functions of church - worship, teaching, building community and engaging in mission - take place in a cell, not just in a congregation. Cells exist to multiply, but some argue they were not designed to stimulate growth but only to channel and develop it. Cell plants are not transitions of existing churches to cell-thinking but "fresh expressions of church" for non-churched people done from scratch with small teams. The other cell planting category is the creation of parallel cell churches to congregations. There is some evidence that cells makes church more effective in discipleship, lay ministry and evangelism, so some are changing existing churches to this model.

- Churches arising out of community development
The request from the wider community for a church to emerge from a community initiative, perhaps dealing with urban social deprivation, may be a surprise to the Christians engaged in such community development programmes. On other occasions the planting method may have been intentionally directed towards the particular social need or mission context. Commonly, such churches emerge in areas of social deprivation where existing forms of church are socially irrelevant. Christians involved in these initiatives find that community-building in partnership is the best way forward in working with the urban non-churched who are suspicious of all overt churchly approaches.

- Midweek church
The UK Church Census suggests that between nine and twelve percent of church attendance occurs midweek. Where these serve groups of people who make this their congregation, they are more helpfully thought of as ecclesial communities rather than just services. Increasing recognition is being given to midweek communions, provision of midweek church for the elderly, lunch time church for the business community and the creation of worship, tailored to children and accompanying adults, at the close of the school day. At times the attendance can be as large as on a Sunday and it offers the scope to widen the diversity created in a given community.

- Multiple congregations
Several denominations sharing one building for worship is still a feature of church life in the UK. The debate continues whether this is less difficult and divisive

than starting a new congregation in a fresh venue. Some experience in the early 1990's suggests that merely merging two or more congregational worship styles via administrative arrangements does not last. Elements that help give genuine identity to multiple congregations include: planned divergence of worship style, the provision of dedicated and recognized leadership, particularity in the chosen mission of differing congregations and the existence of discrete pastoral care structures for each congregation.

- Network-focused churches

These are a significant departure from inherited parochial patterns. Their commonality is their target group - people who find their identity in networks not territory - but diversity is apparent in the models of church and mission style employed to reach them. These may include cell church, seeker-sensitive churches, social engagement, and combinations of these with others. What clearly distinguishes them from previous eclectic churches is that, in the Anglican context of Britain, there is no parochial territory for which they are responsible. As such they raise sharp questions about the nature of Anglican existence and are a group of churches sparking great interest. Found within most denominations, they are most commonly located in large towns or cities where networks of people are most apparent and where, because the opportunities for mission are enormous, there is a greater desire to think creatively and commit resources to meeting the challenge.

- Traditional Resurgence

Forms of church inspiring new interest would include new congregations formed around services using the 1662 (Anglican) Book of Common Prayer, individuals preferring anonymous attendance at cathedrals, people converting to Orthodoxy and new monastic orders. Examples include the growth since the mid-1970's of the Northumbria Community and the recently launched Order of Mission based at St Thomas Crookes, Sheffield. Most expressions of this "new monasticism" have a dispersed rather than gathered or enclosed community. The timelessness of Christian doctrine is affirmed and ethics and liturgical practice are reinforced by welcome familiarity. At its best there is provision of stability in a vortex of change.

- Traditional or Conventional Church plants

Church plants are now regarded as "traditional" when they exist within a parish and serve a geographical subunit of it. Led by a curate or lay reader, they may take a small congregational team, find a secular building and offer informal services of a family service type. Some critics express the concern that too often this approach to planting has meant the cloning of churches that are failing or inappropriate.

- Youth congregations

These have weekly worship patterns, recognized leaders, pastoral structures and adopt mission goals. Although there are notable examples of youth congregations, in practice there are relatively few full-blown youth congregations that is possible to identify. Not included in this category are monthly, even quarterly, youth services. Increasing numbers of church leaders recognize the validity of youth congregation, as meeting a theological need, not just a strategic need. Some repudiate the concept as generationally ageist and unhelpfully homogenous. However cultural considerations suggest there is a case to consider and an examination of existing church - predominantly white, middle class and female – suggests that it constantly fails to recognize itself as homogenous, despite its criticism of other models.

Darrell Jackson

What is a Missional Church?

"Patterns of Missional Faithfulness"

Proclaims the Gospel

A community where all members are involved in learning to become disciples of Jesus

The Bible is normative in this church's life

Understands itself as different from the world because of its participation in the life, death and resurrection of its Lord

Seeks to discern God's specific missional vocation for the entire community and for all of its members

A missional community is indicated by how Christians behave toward one another

It is a community that practices reconciliation

People within the community hold themselves accountable to one another in love

Practices hospitality

Worship is the central act by which the community celebrates with joy and thanksgiving both, God's presence and God's promised future

The community has a vital public witness

There is a recognition that the church itself is an incomplete expression of the reign of God
Resources for further exploration:

Newbigin resources and studies: www.newbigin.net
North American Gospel and Our Culture Network: http://www.gocn.org/
    (includes bibliography of key missional church books)

British Gospel and Our Culture Network: http://www.gospel-culture.org.uk/
Miscellaneous literature lists, etc.: www.missionalchurch.org

Building the Circle, Community Building Through a Culture of Story-Telling

This Is at the Heart of URM (Urban Rural Mission)-CANADA

The critical role of the culture of story-telling is at the heart of URM and its practice of mission as accompaniment, in which the work is to "participate in the struggle of the exploited, marginalized and oppressed for justice and liberation". The URM vision recognizes that in order to fulfill its mission, the process "starts with people" and their context of struggle. And in order to make a difference, there must be a commitment to make a difference in the lives of people at the local level.

In the last 15 years, the Canadian URM Contact Group commitment has been to bring together community workers, and organizers who represent a microcosm of Canada's diverse society to engage in a process of community-building through its story-telling circles. It is a circle where women and men of different ages, people of different cultures, faiths and regions share their challenges and victories in providing and living a life of service in the communities. This is where they address issues such as Aboriginal People's land claims, racism, violence against women, poverty, sexuality, deforestation, depletion of fisheries, immigration, refugee and human rights.

Through a process of sharing and reflection in the circle, each person's experience is "given a voice" and space to be heard. Each story instructs, and each experience provides healing. As the process evolves, a community emerges that is based on acceptance, non-judgement, support, respect and love for self and others. The story-telling circle renews and empowers group members' passionate commitment to participate in finding solutions to common concerns at a local, regional or national level. It strengthens group members' trust and sense of belonging. Furthermore, it builds an analysis that links issues while nurturing solidarity, and facilitates the exchange of information, contacts and strategies.

The practice of story-telling is at the heart of URM-CANADA. And we live by telling it. Over the past year the Canadian Contact Group developed a resource for the URM family to share our practice of story-telling in a way that makes clear the benefit of a story circle process for the mission of URM in its work of solidarity, justice and community development.

URM-CANADA Story-Telling Guidelines

1.

URM-CANADA builds community through a culture of story-telling. We hold our Contact Group meetings by gathering in a story-circle that gives each of us time to tell the others of our lives and the current work and struggle of our community. These stories are normally recorded for our group minutes but it is possible to ask that all or part of your story not to be recorded.

2.

We do not set time limits on our story-telling but ask that the needs of the group are respected along with the limited time that is available. The story time is not a time of discussion and response but a time of listening and learning from one another about the realities in our communities and in our lives.

3.

We do not follow a particular order to go around the circle, instead each member volunteers to speak when they are ready. We refrain from commenting on the stories as they are told and we do not try to problem-solve or fix difficulties that are in them. There is no obligation to tell a story. You may speak until you are finished.

4.

The tradition is to present your life and circumstances so that as we work together we work from a knowledge of one another, and from some sense of our current struggles and circumstances. We have found that our circle is one place that our story can be told and heard. For some of our members it has been a vital place to give voice to their lives and to be heard. It can be a way of gathering support for our community work as our experience teaches us that it may provide some restoration of energy and hope through the sharing of stories.

5.

Following the stories we spend a few moments, led by our theological reflector considering the stories, their common themes and reflecting on the spiritual and theological significance of our lives and work.

Christian Faith and Religious Plurality

Presentation

This synaxis provided an opportunity for a discussion on the theme of preparatory paper No. 13 "Religious Plurality and Christian Self-Understanding". Klaus Schäfer presented the process which was behind the paper and the question. Three persons had prepared inputs for the debate; Christine Lienemann gave an overview over content and theses of the preparatory document, to which Veli-Matti Kärkkäinen reacted from a Pentecostal perspective and Hermen Shastri from an Asian perspective. A very lively and theologically relevant debate followed. The synaxis was so successful and well attended that it had to be repeated.

Introductory Remarks
Klaus Schäfer[1]

Dear friends,

I welcome you all to this synaxis on "Christian Faith and Religious Plurality".

As far as I can see this is the only synaxis where we explicitly take up a theological wrestling with the question of Christian identity in the midst of religious plurality. This issue is certainly a sensible one, and there are – I am sure – various facets one would need to discuss. There is, for example, the awareness of the world of religions and people of other faiths around us; there is the observation of increasing tensions around identity conflicts, not seldom with religious undercurrents; and we are sometimes also confronted with tensions related to mission or missionary activities. These and other issues raise a number of questions which we need to address: What is our contribution to reconciliation and healing in the field of religious plurality? How can we formulate a theological response to religious plurality? How should we responsibly define the relationship of Christian witness and interreligious dialogue?

In this synaxis we would like to address these issues on the basis of a process of fresh study and reflection that has emerged in the last couple of years within the WCC and led to the drafting of a study document entitled: "Religious Plurality and Christian Self-Understanding".

I would like to say a few things about the background and the status of the paper before we then come to a discussion of the thrust and content of the document. The initiative for a new conversation within the WCC on interreligious issues and a theological response to religious plurality came from the Moderator of the Central Committee, Aram I himself. In 2002, as he mentioned in his report to the Central Committee meeting in 2003:
In light of my report, the central committee in its last meeting recommended that Faith and Order, together with CWME and the Inter-Religious Relations and

---

[1] The Rev. Dr Klaus Schäfer is study secretary of the Association of Protestant Churches and Missions in Germany (EMW).

Dialogue office, study "the appropriate theological approaches on the relationship of Christianity and Other Religions".[2]

As a reaction to this challenging report of the Moderator, the Central Committee decided to lift up this issue as one of the topics for further study that should then also lead to some input to the WCC Assembly to be held in February 2006 in Porto Alegre, Brazil. The office of the WCC was assigned to take up the issue and find a way to bring this topic back to the Central Committee and, hopefully, finally into the agenda of the Assembly.

As a response it was decided to bring together a group of scholars and practitioners for a fresh discussion on these issues. How important the WCC itself regarded this exercise was underlined, for example, through the input of Sam Kobia, then designated General Secretary of the WCC, who attended the first meeting of the study group and gave some input to the discussion.

At the outset of this fresh discussion there were two guiding principles or ideas which set the framework for the discussion which was then taken up by the study group during their two meetings at Bossey in October 2003 and in October 2004, with a subgroup who did some drafting between meetings:

1. The first decision was related to the structural scope of the work. There was a strong feeling that a reappraisal of the situation of religious plurality and Christian self-understanding would require a common venture of the major programme areas of the WCC that are in some way or another engaged in these discussions. Therefore the group that was brought together consisted of representatives associated with the Dialogue Programme of the WCC, the Commission on World Mission and Evangelism and also persons associated with Faith and Order. People from each group were supposed to bring their specific perspectives to the reflection – the experience in dialogue with other living faiths, the mandate for mission and the theological work on the nature and identity of the Church. The group that finally came together consisted of 20 some people from various continents and denominations. Hans Ucko, Jacques Matthey and Alan Falconer had participated in the process as the concerned staff people of the WCC. And you may see that the Preparatory Paper before us has now the signature of staff people of these three WCC programmes – with Kerstin Storch instead of Alan Falconer who, meanwhile, had left the WCC to take up another ministry in Scotland. This collaboration between different programme units was something unique in the history of the WCC and turned out to be a very interesting and stimulating exercise.

2. The other reference point related more to the theological scope and content of the new conversation. It was decided to take two earlier WCC documents as the point of departure for the discussion. One document was the Section I report of the Conference on World Mission and Evangelism at San Antonio in 1989 with its relevant paragraphs on the relationship of Christian witness and dialogue. In this section it was said, among other statements relevant to our issues, that:

---

[2] *The Ecumenical Review*, vol. 55, 2003, p. 382

> "We cannot point to any other way of salvation than Jesus Christ; at the same time we cannot set limits to the saving power of God..."

While the "setting in life" of this San Antonio statement came from the circles engaged in mission, there was another document which was drafted in 1990 during a consultation of the Dialogue Programme of the WCC at Baar, Switzerland, and published in the WCC journal "*Current Dialogue*".[3] The major concern of this statement was to come to some kind of positive recognition of God's salvific work among people of other faiths. One of the central parts of this so-called "Baar Statement" reads as follows, partly with reference to San Antonio:

People have at all times and in all places responded to the presence and activity of God among them, and have given their witness to their encounters with the Living God. In this testimony they speak both of seeking and of having found salvation, or wholeness, or enlightenment, or divine guidance, or rest, or liberation.

We therefore take this witness with the utmost seriousness and acknowledge that among all the nations and peoples there has always been the saving presence of God. Though as Christians our testimony is always to the salvation we have experienced through Christ, we at the same time "cannot set limits to the saving power of God" (CWME, San Antonio 1989). Our own ministry of witness among our neighbours of other faiths must presuppose an "affirmation of what God has done and is doing among them" (CWME, San Antonio 1989).

While the formulation of San Antonio has for some people - particularly in mission circles - become almost a classical one, it is perhaps fair to say that the Baar Statement did not find a wide circulation at the time, even though it had become an important reference for the work of the Dialogue Programme within the WCC.

The work of the study group started with revisiting these earlier formulations and discussing their relevance today - in the light of new developments in the world as well as in the light of today's theological insights. Two of the guiding questions were whether there were – first of all -- already convergences between San Antonio and Baar and – secondly -- whether one could perhaps today even move ahead and come to some common statement that goes beyond the content and thrust of these two earlier documents. After having made such an assessment of these earlier formulations it was decided to engage in a process that would lead to the formulation of a new study document that would help the churches to find orientation in a world of religious plurality, to affirm this plurality and articulate Christian self-understanding with an awareness of the religious Other.

It is important to notice that the document in front of us must be regarded as a study paper; it is not an official document of the WCC. The conference here in Athens is the first opportunity to discuss this paper in public. Needless to say that the discussion will continue – for example in the Commission on World Mission and Evangelism and in other committees. They all will look at the study document and discuss whether this paper might be recommended as a helpful study document for the churches.

---

[3] No. 18, June 1990, pp. 3ff.

While engaging this afternoon in a discussion of the paper as well as of the issues expressed in the paper, we are invited to comment on questions such as these:
-        Does the paper help us to come to grips with a new exploration of religious plurality and Christian self-understanding?
-        Are the basic theological topics an adequate reflection of the situation we live in and the biblical faith we share?
-        How can we improve the paper or/and the issue?
In our preparation for this synaxis we thought the best way of starting off a conversation among us is to have, first of all, an introduction into the main content and thrust of the paper, and then to have two initial reactions by people who have carefully read and studied the paper before they came to Athens.

The first task is going to be taken up by Dr **Christine Lienemann**, Professor for Ecumenics and Missiology at the University of Basel, Switzerland. She was herself part of the team that drafted the paper and she has written many books and articles related to our topic. Christine will give us, on the background of her own participation in the drafting process and yet from her own reading, an introduction into, and an interpretation of, the study paper.

After her presentation we will listen to the reactions which have been prepared by Dr **Veli-Matti Kärkkäinen** and by Dr **Hermen Shastri**. Veli-Metti Kärkäinen is Finnish by birth and Pentecostal by denomination. He is currently teaching systematic theology in Fuller Theological Seminary in Pasadena, California. Veli-Matti is the author of many books and he has recently also published an introduction into the theology of religions from a Pentecostal perspective.
Dr Hermen Shastri is the general secretary of the Council of Churches in Malaysia and therefore very much exposed to a Christian-Muslim setting and engaged in Christian-Muslim encounter and dialogue, and he is going to respond to the paper from an Asian perspective and the experience of a minority church in an Islamic context.

After these presentations we will engage in a common discussion of the paper.

I also would finally like to mention that we have Jacques Matthey of the mission team in the WCC with us this afternoon. He has been part of the process of reflection, study and drafting the paper and he will intervene whenever he thinks it helpful or whenever we have a question which should be addressed to the WCC itself.

We regret that we do not have representatives from the dialogue programme of the WCC. Hans Ucko, who has been the responsible person of the dialogue stream of the WCC for accompanying and guiding the study process, was not able to join us but I am sure he will be most eager to learn what this esteemed audience at the World Mission Conference has to say and comment on the paper.

Christian Faith and Religious Plurality
Christine Lienemann

"Called in Christ to be reconciling and healing communities": What does that mean in the midst of competing groups in a global religious market? What can Christians do to overcome the clash of religions? And first of all: Can mission and evangelization become agents in interreligious encounter while they are criticized as a form of religious zeal creating hatred and suspicion between religions? The document I would like to present to you tries to answer some of these questions. It has been written by a group of Christians from different denominational backgrounds including Pentecostal, Roman Catholic, Orthodox and Protestant. People of other faiths – e.g., Muslims or Buddhists – have not been part of the drafting group. Therefore its claim is not to speak on behalf of people from different religions. It is rather a statement of Christians who came together out of deep interreligious experiences and discourse. They tried to give mutual account for the Christian faith in face of new challenges at the beginning of the 21st century. The document deals, first of all, with the Christian self-understanding in the context of new forms of religious plurality.

1. Contemporary Context: The Challenge of Plurality

Interreligious encounter is as old as the history of religions. Throughout its whole history, Christianity has never and nowhere been without any contact to other religions. But interreligious challenges have changed many times and answers to them have changed as well. The last thirty or forty years of intensified interreligious dialogue within the ecumenical movement have transformed not only Christianity but also other religions. Thanks to the interreligious dialogue and encounter religions have – at least in some regions of the world – mutated from fortresses with impregnable walls into houses with open windows and doors.

Today the religious world has become plural altogether. "Many Christians seek ways to be committed to their own faith and yet to be open to some others. Some use spiritual disciplines from other religious traditions to deepen their Christian faith and prayer life. Still others find in other religious traditions an additional spiritual home and speak of the possibility of 'double belonging'" (No. 10). In some parts of the world there is a trend to fluent transitions of believers from one religious community to another. The new religious behaviour is described some times as floating between two or even more communities, as conversion for a limited time or as religious mobility and migration. Indeed, "there is a pastoral need to equip Christians to live in a religiously plural world" (No. 10).

Religious communities as a whole are challenged, too, by a growing plurality within themselves. On their journey through history and moving from one culture to another, from one language to another, religions have transformed cultures and they have at the same time been transformed by them. Most of the major religious traditions as e.g. Judaism, Christianity, Islam, Hinduism, or Buddhism, "have had the experience of being cultural 'hosts' to other religious traditions and of being 'hosted' by cultures shaped by religious traditions other than their own. This means that the identities of religious communities and of individuals within them are never static, but fluid and dynamic" (No. 16). It is in this context that we need a theological response not only to the diversity of religions but also to the plurality within and between the religions (No. 15).

Religious plurality also raises for Christians the challenge to reflect afresh on the content, form and style of Christian witness and the whole concept of mission. To be sure, the situation of religious plurality does not make the witness to Christ obsolete, for there has always been religious plurality in the world. However, the tensions between religions, the violence associated sometimes with religions and the need for good neighbourhood in an increasingly globalized world with nevertheless partly estranged and fragmented communities urges us towards a re-appraisal of the very meaning and form of our Christian witness in the world.

2. Hospitality as a Metaphor for Christian Self-Understanding in the Midst of Religious Plurality

To cope with the described situation the study group introduces the metaphor of *hospitality* as the main hermeneutical key (No. 26). The document explores only some elements of that term; other meanings could easily be added. Hospitality not only mirrors the Christian way of interfaith encounter in a religious plural world; it also has deep biblical roots and therefore links our context with the gospel revealed to us in the Old and New Testament. Of course, hospitality, used as a metaphor, is polyvalent, e.g. it includes a variety of diverse meanings. These meanings have to be discerned carefully. Not all of them are helpful in every context; they do not all lead to a common interpretation of the Christian faith; the metaphor of hospitality – like any other metaphor – can even be misleading and confusing if it is used in an arbitrary way. But as we know, Jesus himself was teaching his disciples through metaphors; when he compares the Kingdom of God with a marriage feast he is speaking about hospitality.

Referring to Paul's letter to the Philippians, the document says: "This grace of God shown in Jesus Christ calls us to an attitude of hospitality in our relationship to others... Our hospitality involves self-emptying and in receiving others in unconditional love we participate in the pattern of God's redeeming love. Indeed our hospitality is not limited to those in our community; the gospel commands us to love even our enemies and to call for blessing upon them (Matt. 5:43-48; Rom. 12:14). As Christians, therefore, we need to search for the right balance between our identity in Christ and our openness to others in kenotic love that comes out of that very identity" (No. 29).

The multiple faces of hospitality are illustrated by four examples:

(1) Hospitality – a bridge between home and exile
Metaphor: Hospitality makes room for the encounter of those who are staying safe at their home with those who are – willingly or unwillingly – somewhere abroad. Hospitality is designed to balance an asymmetric relationship. Those who are privileged to own a house offer accommodation and shelter to others who

are in need of it. Situation: We are living today in a situation of global migration cutting people from their religious roots. Quite often they feel homeless in the host country. Probably for the first time in their life they suffer from belonging to a despised religious minority group. Strong Christian communities in the host land are called to welcome these religious others without misusing their weakness for the purposes of conversion. On the contrary, would it not be a Christian duty to help non-Christian immigrants enabling them to exercise their religion and have space for that (in terms of buildings, religious law etc.)? This is what we read in the letter to Hebrews: "Do not neglect to show hospitality to strangers, for by doing that some have entertained angels without knowing it (Heb. 13:2)". The study document remarks: "In today's context the 'stranger' includes not only the people unknown to us, the poor and the exploited but also those who are ethnically, culturally and religiously 'others' to us. ... Our willingness to accept others in their 'otherness' is the hallmark of true hospitality." (No. 36)

(2) Hospitality – a sign of respect for religious diversity
Metaphor: The differences between the host and the guest are a basic element of hospitality. Guests are supposed to share the family life only for a limited time. On the one hand, they enjoy specific privileges, on the other, they are excluded from some rights reserved to those who belong to the household. Hospitality is not aimed at inviting guests to stay forever and become members of the family. They are not blamed when they leave.
Situation: Christian communities quite often have difficulties to acknowledge the difference of people belonging to other religious communities. The notion of hospitality can probably help us to respect and even honour religious diversity – without losing our own Christian identity. Hospitality is the opposite of coercion to convert; it is an alternative to the well-intended but tiresome entreaties by which Christian missionaries and evangelists some times invite non-Christians to become member of a church. Of course, conversion should not be excluded as an option of the guest out of his or her own decision but this is definitely not in the focus of hospitality. Paul writes in Gal. 5:22-23 that love, joy, peace, patience, kindness, goodness, faithfulness, gentleness, self-control, wherever they are found, are the fruit of the Spirit. The study document makes a comment on that: "The person of the Holy Spirit moved and still moves over the face of the earth to create, nurture and sustain, to challenge, renew and transform. We confess that the activity of the Spirit passes beyond our definitions, descriptions, and limitations in the manner of the wind that 'blows where it wills' (John 3:8)" (No. 32; see also No. 45).

(3) Hospitality – an opportunity of mutual transformation
Metaphor: While conversion is not the focus of hospitality, mutual transformation of hosts and guests definitively is. Whoever invites strangers from outside will be transformed. And guests will not leave the house the same as they have been before because they have participated in the family's life and witnessed the spirit of welcome.
Situation: Religions as well as individuals are transformed by mutual encounter and dialogue. Not a complete change of identity is at stake when we speak about transformation but an extension or reorientation of our self-understanding. The

concept of what Christian faith is can be widened in the encounter with other religious communities and cultures. As a result of interfaith encounter, various forms of conversion and religious belongings are explored today; there is a growing variety of commitments among Christian communities worldwide. This creates a lot of debates about the difference between true Christian identity and syncretism, faithfulness and heresy or apostasy. But we are not the first to struggle with these questions. "Mutual transformation" is also seen in Luke's narrative of the encounter between Peter and Cornelius in the Acts of the Apostles. The Holy Spirit accomplished a transformation in Peter's self-understanding through his vision and subsequent interaction with Cornelius. This led him to confess that, "God shows no partiality, but in every nation anyone who fears him and does what is right is acceptable to him" (Acts 10:34-35). While this story is not primarily about interfaith relations, it sheds light on how God can lead us beyond the confines of our self-understanding in encounter with others (No. 41; see also 31 and 43).

(4) Hospitality – a risk
Metaphor: Hospitality can be a risky venture. It is not always peaceful and nice. To offer hospitality to others can turn into tension. It can end up in harmful conflicts due to different opinions or other incompatibilities. Hospitality is based on trust and confidence in persons whose identity remains partly hidden. Hosts can even be a danger if they are misusing the hospitality for their own purposes.
Situation: The document reads: "In situations of political or religious tension acts of hospitality may require great courage, especially when extended to those who deeply disagree with us or even consider us as their enemy... One may also at times feel obliged to question the deeply held beliefs of the very people whom one has offered hospitality to or received hospitality from, and to have one's own beliefs be challenged in return." (No. 38) Paul addresses a situation of conflict when he writes: "Welcome one another, therefore, as Christ has welcomed you, for the glory of God." (Rom. 15:7), and Jesus refers even to a situation of persecution when he says in the Sermon of the Mount: "Love your enemies and pray for those who persecute you, so that you may be sons of your Father who is in heaven." (Matt. 5:44)

3. Constants of Faith

Does the document question the identity of Christian faith all together? To my mind, the answer is '"No." It rather tries to balance commitment and openness and in doing so it is in continuity with former statements of WCC. Sure, the study group was exploring new ways of a theology of religions *beyond* the statements of former documents (e.g. a statement of the CWME in San Antonio, in 1989, or a statement written by a WCC consultation in Baar, Switzerland, in 1990). But the recent document is in fact *not more explicit* about God's self-revelation through other religions; it does not explain *how* exactly God is using other religions for the salvation of human beings. The wording of the document remains cautious and reluctant where the biblical records are silent themselves. In fact it affirms the position of the CWME in San Antonio, saying: "We cannot point to any other way of salvation than Jesus Christ; at the same time we cannot set limits to the saving power of God" (cf. No. 23).

Nevertheless, the document is indeed going beyond the previous statements of the WCC when it affirms *hospitality* as being a characteristic of the gracious God and the way God deals with humans. Hospitality in that sense is a witness to God. In a hermeneutics of hospitality theological approaches are combined with an anthropology of pilgrimage and mutual transformation.

The document says (No. 34): "We see the plurality of religious traditions as both the result of the manifold ways in which God has related to peoples and nations as well as a manifestation of the richness and diversity of human response to God's gracious gifts. It is our Christian faith in God, which challenges us to *take seriously* the whole realm of religious plurality, *always using the gift of discernment*. ... we must affirm our 'openness to the possibility that the God we know in Jesus Christ may encounter us also *in the lives* of our neighbours of other faiths' (CWME San Antonio 1989)".

My comments on this passage:
- Nothing is said here explicitly about the religious teachings and doctrines of them. It only mentions their lives. In my view, to remain silent about doctrines of other religions is an ambivalent, or even a weak, point in the document. Does it say that in non-Christian doctrines we may definitely not encounter Jesus Christ (unlike the lives of non-Christians)? Or is it silent out of fear that it may trigger a controversial debate among Christians?
- The document urges Christian communities to *take seriously* the realm of religious plurality; there is no word about *adopting* it uncritically. On the contrary: it remembers us to always use the gift of *discernment*. I would add that even criticism of religions including Christian self-criticism should be allowed in the dialogue. Of course to be constructive, criticism requires a spirit of basic mutual confidence and a basic feeling of togetherness and community.

The final section of the document is written in the spirit of *epoché* (abstention of a final judgement). "Salvation belongs to God", it says. "We need to acknowledge that human limitations and limitations of language make it impossible for any community to have exhausted the mystery of the salvation God offers to humankind." (No. 46) "It is this humility that enables us to say that salvation belongs to God, God only. We do not possess salvation; we participate in it. We do not offer salvation; we witness to it. We do not decide who would be saved; we leave it to the providence of God. For our own salvation is an everlasting 'hospitality' that God has extended to us." (No. 47)

Let us, on our part, extend God's hospitality to people of other faiths – not least because this is a very significant dimension of Christian witness. It is my hope that in doing so we may become reconciling and healing communities in Christ.

Response to the CWME Conference Preparatory Paper No. 13: "Religious Plurality and Christian Self-Understanding"
Veli-Matti Kärkkäinen

1. Introduction

The study paper "Religious Plurality and Christian Self-Understanding" is a significant paper in that it attempts to bring together various departments and approaches within the WCC that have dealt with the question of the theology of religions. The relation of Christianity to other faiths—i.e., the theology of religions question—is a textbook example of a challenge that naturally deals with various perspectives and vantage points from theology to pastoral practice to religious studies to missiology. Therefore, a joint project is needed to address the question.

I will divide my comments into three parts: First, I will give some preliminary comments on both the overall approach and some individual paragraphs. Second, I will identify problems and challenges having to do with the document. Third, I suggest some urgent tasks for further clarification and continuing reflection.

2. General Comments

I regard the title of the paper as significant and indicative of the direction to which the theology of religions reflection is currently moving, namely, the question of the "self-understanding of Christianity." I suggest that is one of the most significant tasks Christian theology and the church should take up when reflecting on its place in the midst of growing plurality of religions and religious pluralisms. In other words, the urgency of continuing reflection on the theology of religions' question does not only arise from the felt need of the contemporary context: namely, rapidly increasing communication between religions and alarming problems, even conflicts. Those are practical reasons speaking for the importance of the task and as such should not be dismissed. Yet the main impetus for drafting a document such as the one under discussion emerges out of the self-understanding of Christianity.

The document mentions both of these viewpoints as the impetus for undertaking the current project. Paragraph 5 speaks of the urgent need to continue conversation because of ". . . the context of increased polarization of communities, the prevalent climate of fear, and the culture of violence that has gripped our world. . . ." Paragraph 11, in turn, approaches the question of "Why" more from the vantage point of the self-understanding of Christian faith. I regard that paragraph to be extremely helpful and pointed:
As Christians we seek to build a new relationship with other religious traditions because we believe it to be intrinsic to the gospel message and inherent to our mission as co-workers with God in healing the world. Therefore the mystery of God's relationship to all God's people, and the many ways in which peoples have responded to this mystery, invite us to explore more fully the reality of other religious traditions and our own identity as Christians in a religiously plural world.(§ 11)

Paragraph 2 rightly speaks of the significance of "persistent plurality" of religions in the contemporary world. However—as Christine Lienemann notes —this is hardly a new phenomenon to either Christianity or other faiths who have always existed side by side. Yet there is something "new" in the contemporary situation, not only because the communication among religions is unprecedented globally and locally but also because, since the Enlightenment a number of vocal Christian theologians argue that a pluralistic approach to religions should be the "normative" stance. In other words, it is not only from "outside"—from other religions—that challenges originate but also from "inside", as it were. This is a topic the current document doesn't really discuss.

There is a healthy self-critical approach to Christian religion in the document, thus exemplifying the principle of hospitality towards others (§ 4), yet there is no naiveté about the weaknesses among other religions, too.

In general, I applaud the choice of hospitality as the main gateway to furthering interfaith encounters. As Lienemann outlines in a most helpful way, there are various facets to the metaphor of hospitality when applied to interfaith issues. Her presentation also reminds us of the obvious fact that metaphors are just that—metaphors and should be handled with care.

Many other praises could be added to the drafters of this working document, such as the acknowledgement of radical transformation of Christianity as it moves from North to South, adoption of the metaphor of journey as the way of speaking of religions, etc. I believe, from what I have said so far, it is evident how much I do appreciate the contribution of this study project to the theology of religions conversation.

3. Questions and Challenges

While I find the overall approach of the document—looking at the interfaith challenge through the lens of the metaphor of hospitality—helpful and fruitful, I also want to register my main concern with it. It has to do with the lack of careful theological reflection on the role of Christian witness and evangelization in relation to a hospitable attitude. For a study paper drafted for the Conference on World Mission and Evangelism, that is a pertinent and critical task. I wholeheartedly agree with the drafters that it is God only who saves and that the Christian churches—as other religions, too—have often failed to present our message in love and humility.

My insistence on the urgency of being more nuanced—and bolder—about witness and evangelization, even to the point of encouraging the followers of other faiths to join the church, may appear to work against the principle of hospitality. Indeed, it doesn't. I would like to argue, instead, that giving due credit to evangelistic outreach, which always has been part of the church's way of life in the world, reflects the idea of hospitality. What I mean is simply this: It belongs to the very idea of hospitality—as the document helpfully explains—to honour not only differences among religions but also to affirm their distinctive features based on their own self-understanding. Now the Christian faith, similar to Islam but unlike the Jewish faith, is missionary by nature. The church, therefore, not only does mission but—as the new ecumenical paradigm rightly emphasizes—exists as mission. The church is sent to the world to proclaim salvation in Christ and call people to submit their lives and destinies to the offer of the gospel. Affirming this—which I believe is the catholic consensus among all Christian churches—does not of course have to mean a blind exclusivity that either ignores the value of other religions or their revelations any more than a particularism that restricts the possibility of salvation to only those who have responded to the gospel. We need to hear again and again the reminder of paragraph 24: ". . . God's saving activity . . . [cannot] be confined to any one continent, cultural type, or group of people." God is bigger than us or particular religions (see §§ 46, 47). However, being tolerant—hospitable—to religions and honouring their self-understandings means nothing less than giving opportunity for trying to persuade the other of the supremacy of one's religion's view of salvation and God. When that is done in love and mutual respect, interfaith dialogue becomes much more dynamic and fruitful. Tolerance is not needed when everybody is either supposed to agree on everything or no one dares to challenge other views. Religions, by nature, deal with ultimate questions; in the name of hospitality and tolerance, and need to be given an authentic opportunity to argue for the truthfulness of their claims, otherwise we are stuck with the typical modernist pluralism which is hopelessly reductionist in denying the self-understandings of religions and their distinctive features.

Basically I agree with what Lienemann emphasizes, in relation to the story in Acts 10 concerning Peter's opening up to the gentile, Cornelius, namely, that "While conversion is not the focus of hospitality, mutual transformation of hosts and guests definitively is". Yet there is a more dynamic and complex relationship between conversion and mutual transformation, as chapter 10 of Acts tells us: having been transformed by the grace of God, Peter did call Cornelius and his household to put their faith in Christ, even baptized them into the Christian church! Therefore, hospitality not only "embraces the 'other' in their otherness" (§ 45) but also invites and confronts. It is of course true, as Lienemann helpfully explains, that "Hospitality is the opposite of coercion to convert". Yet I do not find very helpful the way the text continues: "[Hospitality] . . . is an alternative to the well-intended but tiresome entreaties by which Christian missionaries and evangelists sometimes invite non-Christians to become members of a church." More theological reflection is needed here to find the balance.

From this vantage point, I would like to encourage the study process to take another look at expressions such as the one found in paragraph 9: "The cultural and doctrinal differences among religious traditions, however, have always made interreligious dialogue difficult." Not only does this sentence state the obvious, but it also borders on absurdity: were there not differences among religions, no dialogue would be needed. I fear that behind clauses such as this there lurks the modernist idea of a "rough parity" of religions that tends to deny differences among religions as the way to resolve the question of dialogue. Neither dialogue nor tolerance would be needed if all agreed. Precisely because religions are different, dialogue and tolerance—as well as patient hospitality—are needed.

4. Tasks for Future Work

As with any fruitful study process, the current one, too, calls for some future work. In addition to the one I have explained above in more detail (the role of witness and evangelization in hospitality), let me mention briefly three more:

1) In the English-speaking world it is a commonplace to make a distinction between plurality (denoting the fact of existence of many religions) and pluralism (as an ideology or approach to the plurality of religions). The document focuses on plurality and I think that is the right choice. Yet reflection on religious pluralisms (we need to speak of pluralisms in the plural since there are various types of views here) is an urgent issue especially in relation to the role of mission and evangelization.

2) The document offers a number of helpful insights as to how hospitality helps us relate to the otherness of the other and thus affirm their identities and self-understandings, as well as our own. I wonder if help would be gained from the current interest within the theology of religions discourse in the importance of Trinity. The biblical idea of God as Love, the communion of Father, Son and Spirit, speaks both to unity and diversity, affirming uniqueness and embracing otherness. Communion is a dialogical and dynamic concept, thus urging Christians to embrace the other as well as find their own identity and self-understanding as a diverse community of followers of Christ.

3) As the Roman Catholic, Gavin D'Costa, among others, has strongly argued, Trinity calls the Christian church to "relational engagement with other religions", to discern the gifts of the Spirit among them. This discernment is two-fold, namely, to recognize on the one hand the various ways the Spirit is operative among religions and to discern on the other hand the falsehood and evil in religions, including our own. The present document helpfully speaks to the first task, but does not offer resources for the second task. I would urge the dialogue process to continue reflecting on the discernment of the Spirit and spirits among religions. Here again, hospitality means both affirming goodness and truth and confronting evil and falsehood. That task is too big for fallible human persons, the Spirit's sovereign wisdom is badly needed. Even when praying for that, let us not be too presumptuous that we got it all right!

Response to the CWME Conference Preparatory Paper No .13 "Religious Plurality and Christian Self-Understanding"
Hermen Shastri

1. Introduction

As I read and reflected on the study paper, "Religious Plurality and Christians Self-Understanding", I found the document to be a helpful appraisal of the experiences of minority churches, like those in Asia and many other parts of the world, who, on a daily basis, have to live out their Christian faith in relation to neighbours belonging to other living faiths.

The core theological issue, as I see it, is to see how a theocentric approach to the reality of living religions in the world, can help us move beyond the confines of our own faith and relate to others. It is to locate how God is at work in the world, and how Christians can participate in his work in the form of mission. The paper boldly declares (§ 34), "We see the plurality of religious traditions as both the result of the manifold ways in which God has related to peoples and nations as well as a manifestation of the riches and diversity of human response to God's gracious gifts. It is our Christian faith in God, which challenges us to take seriously the whole realm of religious plurality, always using the gift of discernment." Being recipients of God's generous and unconditional love in and through Christ, we are called in no less degree to love our neighbours and accept them in their otherness.

Asian theologians have for a long time insisted on a "continuity" and a "double belonging" as they live among neighbours of other faiths and seek to share in a common life within the ambit and what is perceived as "life in the fullness of God's purpose and will in the world". As Wesley Ariarajah succinctly puts it: "In the long run, what Asia needs is a "'wider ecumenism" or an "ecumenism of religious traditions that transcend and run parallel to Christian ecumenism – the destiny of the Christian people of Asia is no doubt tied up with the destiny of all its peoples. Building actual relationships across religious communities, which are recognized for who they are, is a necessary process on the road to a wider ecumenism" (as quoted in Ninan Koshy, *A History of the Ecumenical Movement in Asia*, Vol. II, p163).

2. Hospitality

Hospitality involves receiving one another as Christ has received us. The study makes the assertion that "hospitality" is a crucial "hermeneutical key" towards a theology of religions (§ 26). To what extent can the dictionary definition of the metaphor about hospitality go beyond its accepted meaning of "the reception of another"?

It is interesting to note here, that in the Malay language, the word for hospitality literally includes the aspect of "receiving" another. In fact, a whole theological resource can be built up, as we discern the meaning the word "hospitality" may communicate it in the many different languages around the world. Receiving one another should remain the hallmark of true hospitality, "our willingness to accept others in their 'otherness'". (§ 36).

3. Inclusive Spirituality

Practising and living a lifestyle of hospitality in a religiously plural context requires an appreciation of the spiritualities of reception that others may offer to Christians. In other words, "reception" is true reception when it nurtures an inclusive spirituality of reception. If hospitality, "requires Christians to accept others as created in the image of God, knowing that God may talk to us through others to teach and transform us, even as God may use us to transform others" (§ 42), then our approach to neighbours of other faiths, should be one that respects their dignity and their inviolable right to remain true to their faith beliefs. A

Christian spirituality of receiving others should not, in this case, degenerate into condemnation and belittling the religious heritage of others. We need to be careful about what we say and how we act when we speak to others.

WCC's Plenary Commission of Faith and Order that met for the first time in a Muslim-majority country (Kuala Lumpur, Malaysia, July 2004) spoke of the need of such a spirituality. Meeting under the theme: "Receive one another as Christ has received you, for the glory of God (Rom. 15:7); the commission issued a message to the churches, where it affirmed; "A spirituality of welcome, of reception, of hospitality, is central to the self-understanding of those who identify themselves as Christian".

Viewed from the other side, the Muslim Prime Minister of Malaysia in welcoming the delegates made a passionate plea when he said: "We cannot stand before a compassionate God while there is so much we have left undone because we are disunited. There is so much we could do, having received one another, to receive others." He went on to say, "For far too long, the various religious communities of the world have lived apart and these divisions have been sustained because of a narrow outlook that sees religious identity in exclusive terms."

A second recent event, the meeting of the 12th Assembly of the Christian Conference of Asia (Chiangmai, Thailand, March 2005), chose as its theme; "Building Communities of Peace for All". The Assembly emphasized that building communities of peace for a religiously diverse Asia cannot remain an exclusively Christian project. To succeed, it must harness the rich spiritual traditions of the living faiths of the Asian people in order to promote and sustain the theological perspective of one humanity under the providence of a loving God. The response to the tsunami tragedy revealed the spiritual potential that exists when people cross boundaries to reach out to those devastated by the disaster, out of love that seeks the well-being of all human beings regardless of religion or creed. People received each other in a common vocation to rebuild their shattered communities.

4. Dialogue

With religious pluralism a prevalent social reality in many parts of the world, interfaith dialogue has become priority as it is an indispensable path in nurturing peaceful co-existence.

There are unhelpful ways of approaching other faiths – either with an aggressive claim to exclusive possession of the truth or with a loss of confidence leading to a view that every religion is as good as another. The study document does point to this potential of conflict when it says: "On the one hand, religious traditions make universal truth claims. On the other hand, these claims by implication may be in conflict with the truth claims of others".

Dialogue begins by accepting the "otherness" of the other. It should never resort to putting one faith system against another. In perceiving reality together, partners in dialogue should appreciate that there are universal values that can hold communities together and when we act together for the sake of justice and peace in society, we are in fact, being in service to God in the most profound sense.

As interfaith dialogue takes into account, religious, cultural, political and social sensitivities, the act of showing hospitality, must always be sincere and honest, showing respect for traditions beyond our own.

These are the daily experiences of Christians living as minorities all over Asia.

The document does not adequately reflect the rich experiences of Christians in Asia, as on what it means to be "hosted" by other faiths in the country and what it means to show "hospitality" as a "minority" to other faiths.

5. Conversion and Competition

The issue of Christian proselytization remains a hotly debated theological issue related to the Gospel imperative of evangelization. The fact that Christian conversions are taking place especially in countries of the southern hemisphere, is well-attested by the vibrant growing churches found in many countries.

Although at the heart, conversion is an exercise of personal conscience undergirded by the principle of a universal human right, it does not necessary follow that the exercise of that right does not pose problem on the social and political levels.

People of other faiths feel threatened by the unbridled and competitive stance of churches when it comes to evangelism. They suspect a larger agenda of Christian groups to destabilize traditional communities with a religious culture open to varying churches and sects competing on an open-market for souls. Organized forms of evangelism may target whole nations and be sustained by funds coming from foreign mission agencies.

Presently, with a large segment of Muslims around the world, who share the view that "Islam is under siege", often react violently to foreign-sponsored evangelism missions in Muslim countries. In Malaysia, even Hindus, Buddhists and Sikhs are beginning to view their own communities as being under siege by an aggressive and impatient Christian evangelism.

The study paper affirms that hospitality is the acceptance of others in their "otherness". Surely there should never be room for triumphalism. The paper says such triumphalism does contribute to "religious animosity and violence that goes with it" (§ 42).

A theological understanding of religious plurality must challenge long held theological notions that one day the whole world will convert to Christ. That would not happen, not because God has failed, but because our theological perception of exclusion of others may need to be re-examined. "Condemnation theology" has no place in religiously plural societies.

If God is absent in the life of our neighbours, what do we make of our belief that God loves all people and that they live and move and have their being in God? Surely, God's hospitality is more embracing than our exclusive notions in our missionary practice.

Women's Ministries of Healing and Reconciling Mission

Facilitators: Elizabeth Tapia, Katja Heidemanns, Nilda Castro
Number of participants: 42
Flow of synaxis (from staff report):

Welcome and brief introduction,
Naming and stretching,
Ten-minute theological input on Women in Mission Process (Katja Heidemanns, Institute of Missiology, Aachen, Germany),
Three-minute stretching exercise,
Sharing of personal mission involvement at present,
Contextual Mission Perspective/Praxis by three women

- Elizabeth Joy, Council for World Mission (CWM), Orthodox, India
- Nilda Castro, Pontifical Council for the Pastoral Care of Migrants and Itinerant People, The Vatican
- Jacinta Maingi, Ecumenical HIV and AIDS Initiative in Africa (EHAIA), WCC, Kenya.

Highlights: Mission as healing and reconciliation becomes a reality only in an inclusive community of justice, forgiveness with its parameters as the family, church and the society. Women have always been self-empowered and the church, whether conscious or not, survives because of the support it gets from women. They also need support, recognition, opportunities, participation in decision-making in all church activities. There are some ministries in the world of human mobility that call specifically for women; for example the reintegration of battered or abused refugee or undocumented migrant women into the community.

Open Forum

Closing Prayer

(Following are the texts presented during the synaxis)

Women and Mission
Katja Heidemanns

Women and mission is a broad theme, broad enough to embrace all that women are doing within the framework of the mission of the church – in their own places and in their own church tradition. However, women's ministry has often been neglected. Though women bring untold life to the church, the ways in which women do mission are often not recognized as ministry for the sake of God's mission and the renewal of the church.

For some time now, an increase in relevant studies in mission history has opened our eyes to women's commitment to mission work, both in Roman Catholic and Protestant churches. Often the influential role of women missionaries as Gospel bearers and the various ways they have enacted vocation have been brought to light by women who themselves have begun exploring into the lives and witnesses of the women in their respective mission societies and churches searching for traces of gendered traditions of mission theory. Still US scholar Dana Robert is right when she asserts: "Despite their precedents in scripture, Christian tradition and their role in the expansion of Christianity over the last century, the issues around women in mission remain neglected and misunderstood in the churches today. In missiological reflection on such issues as church growth and contextualization, little attention is paid to the mission theories and contributions of women." Particularly missiological reflection from the perspective of women's theology or feminist theology has been hardly taken note of within the wider missiological community.

But not only in the academy, also among activists there seem to be quite a lot of ignorance and confusion regarding women's role in mission.

Some days ago I received an e-mail sent by one of the members of a missiology net group. It dealt with the "gender equality pressure" and its impacts on mission. The male author expressed his fear for the consequences that the struggle for gender equality would bring.

Consequences like: "...particularly low self-worth of female missionaries unless they have publicly recognized up-front roles that they often cannot cope with." According to the author, the pressures that women come to be under in mission environments seem to be responsible for many a crisis amongst mission personnel on the field. I felt rather shocked by this perception of women's missionary commitment. Why does it seem to be so difficult to treat women missionaries as competent, God-called adults?

Apart from that, the argument sounded all too familiar to a Roman Catholic woman. Like in last year's *Letter to the Bishops of the Catholic Church on the Collaboration of Men and Women in the Church and the World*, within the churches the call for gender equality is too often blamed for promoting an understanding of "sexual equality" that is in danger of obscuring the difference or duality of the sexes. The struggle for gender equality then is considered as an attempt to deny any differences and to view them as mere effects of historical and cultural conditioning. What a tragic misunderstanding. Surely for many women of faith but also for the entire church.

As a missiologist and someone who is working with a Roman Catholic Mission Society I understand it as my task to read the conflicts and crises of my own German context and ecclesial milieu as well as of the world as signs of God in history. I perceive them as challenges to prove the relevance of the gospel and our teaching in the world. This understanding results in priorities and real options. The decision to focus this conference on healing and reconciliation is one priority I cannot only identify with personally but one that could have been generated from a women's base of experience in ministry and mission. I am slightly reluctant to claim that women make better reconcilers in the light of their own experience of suffering and commitment to community or relationality (cf. Monica Melanchthon's article in *IRM*[1]). However, though the theme is essentially concerned with life, it evokes the need to contend with the forces of death and disparity that pervade our world. And women and their children are often the ones who are confronted most directly with the deadly consequences of these forces, feeling the need to push for reconciliation and healing literally with heart and soul. In other words, it doesn't matter so much if one is convinced of the women's natural gifts in healing and reconciliation or not. Alone, the fact that more and more women worldwide are forced to daily counteract the dehumanizing consequences of the global economic and political development (and, in many cases, do so very successfully) is reason enough to come together as women from diverse backgrounds and denominations in order to identify women's ministry of healing and reconciliation.

The WCC Study Process

Before we will have the opportunity to listen to some stories of women's involvement in healing and reconciling mission, I would like to share with you a few introductory thoughts on the subject of the study process "Women in Mission". Though it can't be more than a brief highlighting of the major themes and questions emerging out of the discussions these insights on mission from a women's perspective might be helpful to prepare the ground for our ongoing sharing and discussing at this workshop. After my presentation I will invite you to form buzz groups with neighbours in order to reflect on the results of the process against the background of your own experiences.

In 2002, Aruna Gnanadason from the WCC initiated an international and interdenominational study process on women and mission in order to provide an urgently needed forum of exchange and research for women missionaries and scholars, theologians and activists.

Part of the process was a seminar held at the Bossey Ecumenical Institute, 4-10 June 2003, which brought together more than 50 women from different contexts of the Southern and Northern hemispheres. Among the women were lay leaders, ordained clergy, and theologians. One of the intentions of this long-running study process was to prepare substantial contributions to this World Conference on Mission and Evangelism as well as to the Ninth Assembly of the WCC at Porto Alegre in 2006 by making women in mission and their contributions to justice, healing and reconciliation visible. This workshop in fact carries on the work of that meeting at Bossey very concretely. Some of the issues that were said to need further attention we will deal with today: among them the challenge to do mission in an HIV/AIDS context or the meaning of mission in the context of migration. First of all, what we discovered during the consultation in Bossey was that women

---

[1] Cf. Monica Melanchthon, "Reconciliation: Feminist Shadings", in *IRM*, Vol. 94, No 372, January 2005, pp. 117-132.

are engaged in a wide spectrum of ministries, often given in a voluntary capacity and often flourishing in areas where women are given space by male church authorities (education, health system, pastoral care for women and families, women's initiatives in overcoming violence etc.).

Bearing a strong witness to their faith and being highly identified with their churches and church traditions, the mission practice of women seems to offer a substantially different approach to the missionary tasks of the churches. However, often this difference is not so much the result of theological-missiological considerations but emerges from the particular kind of ministry which is accessible to women within their respective churches and communities.

Let me sketch two aspects emerging from the study process which I think are important for our subject:

1. Context Matters

Social, cultural, interreligious and ecclesial contexts influence the ministries women offer and impact the ways in which they do mission. This is not at all a new insight but worthy to be mentioned here, particularly as globalization obviously not only seeks to universalize economic norms but also cultural and doctrinal norms within the church. It is striking that there was no attempt to define mission in a single way but the women involved in the study process discussed a variety of ways of how witnessing can be done. The leading question was not "What is the meaning of mission today?" but "What is the urgent task to you as a woman of faith in your particular social and ecclesial context?" This observation leads us to the second.

2. Valuing our Differences and Seeking for Common Ground

When the context is that meaningful this also means that the diversity of our tradition and mission understanding has to be valued and maintained.

However, the urge to prevent and overcome homogenizing tendencies does not dispense with the need to seek common ground and to build sound relationships. In the context of aggressive identity politics, increasing fundamentalisms and denominationalism, the challenge is to transcend these divisions by a missionary practice that doesn't promote uniformity but is relational, informed by mutuality, and oriented toward transformation. For many women obviously a common ground can be found in their consciousness of the brokenness and suffering of the world and the awareness of God's longing for all people of the world to experience a "new heaven and a new earth." It is this awareness of God's longing that motivates them to engage in mission in various contexts and in diverse ways.

Mission from this angle cannot but be an encounter which lives in and, by reciprocal relationship, between human beings. An encounter which becomes an existential and ultimately transforming experience for everybody involved. This understanding resonates with a relational concept of the Divine Spirit as source of both creative and transformative energy among all living beings and the whole creation, as powerful and redemptive presence of God which overcomes duality and separation, heals our broken bonds and sustains diversity in *koinonia*. Mission then also implies to empower people to re-imagine and recognize the trajectories of the Spirit in order to go beyond their isolation and to reach out to each. The challenge is to understand mission in a way that opens up liberating spaces by enabling people to recognize our global interdependence and responsibility for our common past and present.

Let me summarize the results of the process: is there any distinctiveness of women's way of doing mission? The results of the study process give reason to believe that women follow a more cooperative way of working. They seem to be more likely to be participatory, to affirm diversity, to model partnership, to be aware of the relevance of social contexts, to challenge hierarchical social structures that oppress, to question the abuse of power, to see greater fluidity between practical situations and theoretical discussions, to view tension as leading to creativity. This distinctiveness of women's approach, however, might not be due to innate differences with men but shaped by women's varied cultures, histories, social and ecclesial contexts. Unmasking and deconstructing patriarchal practices that exist in these contexts, within ecclesial communities, cultures, and societies is a task that must be taken on by women in partnership with men. Therefore, what is urgently needed today is an approach to mission that aims at empowering women and men to participate together and work in ways that are life affirming within particular social and ecclesial contexts.

To put it in more theoretical terms: mission needs to be redefined and conducted in ways that challenge colonialism, racism and sexism. In the study process the concern has been expressed by many women that the church itself needs to be missionized.

This, however, requires that the missionary practice of women comes into the view as participation in the mission of the church, that is to receive, celebrate, proclaim and work for the fullness of life in Christ in a time of globalization, increasing violence, fragmentation and exclusion.

Women's Ministry of Healing and Reconciling Mission
Elizabeth Joy

Introduction

I am Elizabeth Joy. My late mother, Sheela Sujaya Kantha, was a schoolteacher and my father, Jesupatham John Anderson, is a retired pastor. I have five sisters and two brothers who are all married having their own families. I was a member of the India Evangelical Church. By marriage, I have joined the Indian Orthodox Church. My husband, Niravil George Joy, is a priest of this church. We have two children – our son, Sudarshan Joy, is 16-years-old and our daughter, Deepthi Joy, is 14. My late father-in-law was an agriculturalist and my mother-in-law is a housewife (in my understanding, an environmentalist).

As a child, I fancied preaching, as a teenager I started teaching in Sunday school and Vacation Bible School (VBS) when the teachers were absent. My late grandfather, who was also my pastor, encouraged me to take classes and admired my attempt to teach on the spot when I was requested to do so. My father trained me to be a teacher in the Sunday school and VBS. These gave me an impetus to pursue my theological studies after graduation, even though my church at that time never even recognized women as voting members of the church!

After completing my basic theological education, the church did not employ me and even my offer to do voluntary work was turned down. Since one of my teachers at the Theological College was the chairperson of the Student Christian Movement of India (SCMI), he advised me to go there and seek a temporary part-time job as a programme assistant. Thus I began my career with SCMI in 1986. Later I had the privilege of serving this institution both as the women's desk co-ordinator and its first woman general secretary (2000-2002). Prior to this, I worked with the Christian Institute for the Study of Religion and Society (1993-2000), which opened my eyes further to the realities in life and the struggles of women at the grassroots both for their survival and to experience total human liberation. This institution sponsored my education in doing a Masters in Theology and formed me for mission with women. My brief tenure at the Bible Society of India (1987) as the editorial officer where I began my full-time career, gave me the identity of a whole person beyond the barriers of age and gender. From the end of 2002, I am with the Council for World Mission as the executive secretary for mission education. A person, who was rejected by the local church, simply on account of being a woman, is now working with a global community of churches! Today I am here, to share with you my experiences of doing mission as healing and reconciliation.

Stories to Support Mission as Healing and Reconciliation

1. Family

I was born in a traditional Christian family, which affirmed the patriarchal structures and its way of life as God-given. Though we used to read the Bible regularly and have our family prayers in the mornings and evenings without fail, everything was done within the patriarchal framework. Therefore, I was socialized from childhood to perpetuate this patriarchal structure. I was given to understand that I have to be subordinate to my husband and do all things for him at all times. However, one incident on the day after my wedding changed me, as well as my attitude.

It was the day after our wedding. We were getting ready to go out. I got ready and as my husband was getting ready, I ran and took his shoes and socks and faithfully brought it and kept it near his feet. He shouted at me, saying, "What are you doing?" I was very nervous and thought that I probably made a terrible mistake – maybe I brought the wrong pair of shoes or socks without getting his opinion or just left it at his feet without helping him to put it on. Before I could decide what to do next, he shouted again saying, "Go and put it back in its place. This will be the first and the last time that you will be doing this for me unless I become an invalid. I did not marry you to do all these for me. You are my partner and we will always do things together, understand?" This was indeed a moment in my life, which I can never forget. The whole process of socialization, preparing me to lead a secondary position in family life crumbled down to the ground. I felt elevated, recognized as a full human being to begin my married life with a man who was different. Of course, we still have reasons to quarrel or express our dissent in different matters. However, this person, ever since has made a lot of sacrifices to see that I can continue to be in God's mission to bring about healing and reconciliation in many ways among women and men in their relationships to impart what I believe in. How do we spread this message of equal partnership within the family to experience mission as healing and reconciliation?

2. Church

In the Council for World Mission, we have a programme called Building a Community of Women and Men in Mission (CWMM). As part of this, we have a team visits programme on the theme: "All God's People Enabled". We have had six team visits in six different churches with the aim of increasing capacity-building of the CWMM through mutual learning and sharing working methods in building such a community. The visits show that though the churches have grown in recognizing the importance of the role of women in the church, we still have women lacking in the higher levels and decision-making bodies. There were also churches, which have journeyed beyond the token representation of women, by having a visible representation. At the same time, there are also churches where men are disappearing in large numbers where women are into leadership but perpetuating the same patriarchal structure and models. For a successful mission of healing and reconciliation, we need new models. We cannot pour the new wine into the old wine skins. New models that recognize the importance of the role of both women and men will bring about healing and reconciliation.

3. Society

Recently, on a journey with my friend and colleague Mr Humphry Joseph in South Africa, who was actively involved in the anti-apartheid struggle (presently one of the coordinators of the Training in Mission Programme of CWM), I heard this story:

He was narrating to us his experience of torture and his undivided commitment to wipe out racial segregation. He had been in and out of prison several times, tried in different courts and released. Nothing could ever prevent him from his mission. He went on organizing people whether he was in prison or outside to fight apartheid and was totally involved in the struggle until it was abolished.
Last year, he and his sister arranged a surprise party for his mother who celebrated her 80th birthday. They had invited over a hundred of their mother's friends. When he was asked to speak at this celebration, he said, "For a minute, I was wondering what I could speak on? What new information could I share with her friends? Then I realized that indeed I had something to tell them and I was sure they would not know about it." So he began saying, "Today, I am going to tell you something about my mother, which many of you are not aware of". There was a

silence and people wondered what it could be. Humphry went on to unravel the stories of the past – the struggle against the apartheid and shared with them how his mother participated in this struggle. She was supportive of her son and his activities though it was very painful to see him suffering so often. Of course the family too was not spared and had their share on account of his activities. Among the many things she did, she used to hide all the banned literature in her white friend's house as the police would not go and search there! She used to bring them during midnight to let her son read and be equipped for his mission.

Friends, it is not just this mother, many would have done similar daring acts. See how the white woman and the coloured or black woman came together to struggle for a right and just cause. Isn't this a true mission that gave birth to healing and reconciliation in the South African context? Yes, we need to work as women and men and cross the boundaries of class, caste, age, region, religion and gender to carry out mission as healing and reconciliation. How can we promote such a mission today?

Strategies for Doing Mission as Healing and Reconciliation

1. Doing mission as healing and reconciliation requires us to look into the three arenas of our life – the family, the church and the society, all of which are equally important for us as followers of Christ. Even if one of the above three is neglected, our mission will be in vain.
2. For mission to be successful in bringing about healing and reconciliation, we need to work as a Community of Women and Men in Mission (CWMM) or rather an "Inclusive Community in Mission" (ICIM), which will include children, youth, women and men of all ages. All people should participate in God's mission and the mission should be directed to all people as well as the environment. No complete healing and reconciliation can be achieved either by leaving a section of the population or the world around us.
3. No healing and reconciliation will be adequate if it is limited to our denomination, religion, region or culture. All these boundaries are to be crossed essentially. However, mission as healing and reconciliation begins with the family.

Conclusion

Mission as healing and reconciliation will become a reality only when we work together as an inclusive community in mission. Acts of justice and forgiveness are the pillars of such a mission. Mission as healing and reconciliation from gender perspective includes within its parameters the family, church and society. It addresses every issue that supports or silently promotes inequality, oppression or domination. May God guide us to be actively involved in such a mission to bring glory and honour to God always.

The Mission and Ministry of the Pontifical Council for the Pastoral Care of Migrants and Itinerant People
Nilda M. Castro

It is not easy to describe in ten minutes the mission of my office and its ministry among migrants and itinerant people but I shall try.

The Challenges That We Face

The people that we reach out to are all those who have left their homelands or have none, either temporarily, permanently or periodically. They are migrants, refugees, international students, nomads, gypsies, circus, fair and travelling show people, seafarers, airport and airline workers and travellers, people on the road and in railroad stations, tourists and pilgrims.

They are a great variety of people but they have one thing in common: human mobility.

Even the most voluntary human mobility implies a certain degree of uprooting: a person leaves his or her usual environment and enters a new one -- where people may speak a different language, where things are done differently, where customs, traditions, culture, mentality, food are different, where the unspoken language is new and probably unknown to the newcomer, so that he or she runs the risk of not understanding and being misunderstood.

Quite a lot of human mobility, however, is forced. People would have stayed in their own countries if conditions had been different but wars, violence, persecution, hunger and natural calamities have driven them out.

Even without reaching these extremes, people leave their countries because they and their families can no longer live with dignity, well-being and security in their homeland due to poverty, violation of human rights, unequal opportunities, concentration of wealth in the hands of a few and so on. They look for better opportunities and a better future elsewhere.

However, we know how difficult it is to enter another country, especially if one comes from the third world. For this reason many fall into the hands of unscrupulous criminals who smuggle and traffic people across borders, with false documents or without any at all.

Foreigners are often at a disadvantage in a foreign country. Migrant workers, for example, are often paid less and enjoy fewer rights than local workers. Seafarers from third world countries often get lower salaries than their counterparts elsewhere. Foreign workers may suffer discrimination, xenophobia and even racism.

When foreigners do not have proper documents, they are even more vulnerable. They can fall victims of indentured labour or forced into prostitution, and they cannot ask for the protection of the law. They are condemned to keep silent at the mercy of their employers or exploiters.

What is more, in many cultures, women's rights are not recognized. Thus a woman migrant suffers a double vulnerability. Sadly, a large proportion of people in human mobility are women. Also, a significant number are minors.

Our Mission*

It is part of our mission to heal the wounds of physical and moral suffering among these people "on the move" and for healing to be complete, very often it is necessary to offer the gift of reconciliation, which begins with the ordinarily difficult act of forgiving. Our Pontifical Council encourages the particular churches in the different countries in the world to carry out this task.

The first form of healing that we want to provide is in response to the most basic human needs. A migrant, a refugee or other people involved in human mobility may find themselves in situations where they literally need food, clothing and shelter. They may need medicine and medical care. We try to afford them welcome, through the proper channels, as we try to create a culture of welcome in our communities and give them our solidarity *(cf. EMCC 39-43)*.

When their rights are trampled on, we defend them. Additional effort is made where women and children are concerned because they are more vulnerable. When human dignity is not respected and human rights are violated, the result is a moral suffering that causes a brokenness in the human family. As the *Universal Declaration of Human Rights* (art. 1) affirms, "all human beings are born free and equal in dignity and rights". Any inequality in this sense, therefore, needs to be healed. We make use of "advocacy", when necessary *(cf. EMCC 6)*.

With the easy access to transportation and modern-day globalization, human mobility has greatly caused an intermingling of cultures, religions and beliefs. While this could be an enrichment, it has certainly caused tension in the past, which has persisted, and considerably so in some cases. The antidote to this tension is dialogue – at all levels: ecumenical dialogue between Christian churches and ecclesial communities, inter-religious dialogue and dialogue with those who do not have a religious creed or inter-cultural dialogue. This is a process that leads to the recognition of values that are in common and an attitude of respect for differences, a first step towards reconciliation *(cf. EMCC 34-36; 56-59; 69)*.

The late Pope John Paul II, in his Message for the World Day of Migrants and Refugees (no. 3), affirmed the need "for a dialogue between people of different cultures in a context of pluralism that goes beyond mere tolerance and reaches sympathy." He continued: "We should encourage … a mutual fecundation of cultures. This implies reciprocal knowledge and openness between cultures, in a

---

* For those wishing to know more about the mission of the Pontifical Council, references are made to its document Erga migrantes caritas Christi – "The Love of Christ towards Migrants" (EMCC).

context of true understanding and benevolence."

Of course, "there is nothing more beautiful than to be surprised by the Gospel, by the encounter with Christ", as Pope Benedict XVI recently said. "There is nothing more beautiful than to know Him and to speak to others of our friendship with Him." Fundamental to our mission is giving witness to Jesus Christ and to His Gospel of love and peace, through our lives and our words *(cf. EMCC 100)*.

A Little Secret

In trying to achieve what I mentioned above, I use a little secret that I find quite effective. There is only one thing that can really bring about healing and reconciliation: love, but not just any kind of love, but love that is a reflection of God, who is Love (1 John 4:8). Not just maternal love or brotherly love, not just friendship nor even nuptial love. It is a love that goes beyond any human measure. As St Paul wrote to the Romans (5: 6-8, 10) "When we were still helpless, at the appointed time, Christ died for the godless. You could hardly find anyone ready to die even for someone upright ... So it is a proof of God's own love for us, that Christ died for us while we were still sinners... We were reconciled to God through the death of his Son." It is a love that is ready to face utmost sacrifice.

Christ taught us how to love. He said: "No one can have greater love than to lay down his life for his friends" (John 15, 13); and "You must love one another just as I have loved you" (John 13:34). We know how Christ loved us: through his suffering and death on the cross. There, he drew everything to himself and healed all brokenness and reconciled all divisions. In him every suffering acquires meaning because they are a participation in his work of redemption, a share in his love.

We are all called to participate in this mission of love, but somehow, women are more apt for this mission. Allow me to explain. God prepared women for childbearing and motherhood by endowing them with a greater capacity to bear pain and suffering, and not only in the physical sense. Because of this, in general, women have a greater capacity to love because love is also sacrifice.

This is probably the reason why, in the world of human mobility, there are some ministries that call specifically for the involvement of women. Let me cite, for example, ministry in the reintegration of battered or abused refugees or undocumented migrant women into the community, in caring for and bringing up orphaned refugee or undocumented children, in forming a community in refugee or detention camps. They are in fact good catechists and prayer leaders and even distribute food rations more fairly. Women are more effective because, in general, they are more patient and understanding, they are more inclined to listen and more altruistic. Their propensity to sacrifice and motherly instinct make it more spontaneous for them to think of others rather than of themselves.

Conclusion

To bring the healing and reconciling power of Christ in the world of human mobility, we in the Pontifical Council for Migrants and Itinerant People try to help each and everyone involved in the phenomenon of human mobility to be reconciled with God and with one another, whatever way may be necessary, so that we all may become one people of God, a single family united in his love *(cf. EMCC 37)*.

HIV and AIDS, WOMEN and CHURCH MINISTRY
Jacinta Mwikali Maingi

How I Got Started in HIV/AIDS Work

In 1983, I was working in the US with a Christian NGO that was providing counseling and family therapy. At that time, HIV and AIDS was a very new and scary issue globally. We got a few cases referred to us for counseling because either the client was HIV positive or a relative or friend of someone infected with HIV. Due to the sensitivity of the issue, nobody in the whole organization wanted to be given any client associated with HIV. I took a bold move and agreed to take all the HIV related cases (those days it was basically the gay community, hemophiliacs or drug users). It was the best thing I have ever done because even when I came back to Kenya in 1987, I started introducing HIV and AIDS into every initiative I have been involved in. That is why, 22 years later, I am still working in the HIV and AIDS programme. A few years later, I lost several family members to AIDS and this strengthened my commitment to work in HIV and AIDS, not as a job but as a ministry.

Who is Affected by HIV and AIDS?

1. Nations, communities, churches, families, children, women

Although the HIV and AIDS pandemic has become the most devastating disease humankind has ever experienced and has destroyed without mercy the lives of men, women and children, it is women who bear the brunt of the consequences. In spite of massive campaigns by women for their rights legally, culturally and religiously, their issues have not been addressed adequately. Consequently, most women infected with HIV have been silent, believing that their sero-status is considered something dirty, shameful, immoral and unusual. Most of this perception is derived from the fact that over the years most of those courageous men and women who went public about their HIV status have been treated with contempt, stigmatization, blame, discrimination and, at times, even rejection by their family circles. With the problem of HIV and AIDS bringing more burdens to women, it is a matter of urgency that religious leaders should pay attention to the plight of women, orphans and vulnerable children. Remember the words of Agnes Aboum in describing the woman who works with people living with HIV and AIDS...

Who is This Woman?[2]

The woman I want to introduce to you lives in Africa and other parts of the world:
- she is your mother, sister, daughter, grandmother, aunt, wife, mother-in-law or friend;
- although she is created in the image of God, she is seen only through the eyes of a man;
- she is part of a society but not supposed to be seen and definitely, not heard;
- though she is a pillar of the family she is considered the weaker sex;
- yes, she is constantly reminded that she is not the head. But at times I fail to understand to which part of the body she belongs because the abuses she endures should never be subjected to any part of the body;
- she is central to productivity but not a key beneficiary;
- she is the embodiment of life but she is almost lifeless and full of sacrifices, at times a substitute for cheap means of transport and domestic labour force;
- she forms the majority of society only as an object of development but not a decision-maker;
- she is only seen and heard through the eyes and names of her husband, son, brother or father;
- she is the major resource needed for development in the society but not on her terms, condition or strength;
- although she deserves her own identity and dignity, she usually remains a number – a mere statistic in a proposal for development inventions to which she has no say;
- in spite of being a reservoir of life and hope, a bank for future sustainability of the family name, her children are hers only if they are failures in life. If they are successful or famous, they obviously belong to the father; and
- she is the one who takes care of others even when she too needs care even when suffering from HIV and AIDS.

Jesus' View of a Woman

We need to look critically at the examples set by Jesus Christ:
- he **healed women** who otherwise nobody wanted to touch (Matt. 9:20-22);
- he **raised** the son of a widow (Luke 7:2);
- he encouraged women to **leave their culturally assigned roles** and pursue their interest (Luke 10:38-41) and the Samaritan woman who left her jar for fetching water and went back home to tell the people about Jesus (John 4:1-30);
- he **interacted even with prostitutes** and allowed Mary Magdalene to wipe his feet in spite of tremendous protest from his disciples; and
- he chose to **appear** to two women after crucifixion, when he rose from the dead.

This clearly indicates that Jesus recognized and acknowledged the importance and value of women and the support that should be accorded to them.

---

[2] Original text from Dr Agnes Abuom's presentation.

Women in Church Ministry and Leadership

We can talk endlessly about women's empowerment, but in my view women have always been self-empowered. The church, whether conscious or not, survives because of the support it gets from women. They are the majority in terms of attendance and are usually more organized as a group than men. So what they need is not really empowerment but support, recognition, opportunities, participation in decision-making and appreciated as being able to play a supplementary and complementary role in all church activities. It is unfortunate that in most cases the church has not been eager to appreciate the resourcefulness of women. On the contrary, women have had to assert themselves to be given a chance to share in the church leadership and this has not been widely accepted – and where it has been accepted, it has been done quite sparingly.

Conclusion

Since Christianity's teaching is compounded and glued with messages of love, it would not be far fetched to add that compassion, forgiveness, acceptance, support and understanding bring power. Power for the church to make life worth living for those infected and affected. The establishment of Africa Network of Religious Leaders Infected and Affected by HIV and AIDS (ANERELA+) has clearly demonstrated that the church in Africa is recognizing that HIV and AIDS is in the church and is posing a great threat to its evangelistic ministry and growth. We have to remember that being HIV positive does not make one less a person or unable to contribute. However, the atmosphere that we set will determine the productivity of one's life after HIV infection. Peer counseling is highly recommended; i.e., peer counseling among people living with AIDS, youth, men, church leaders, orphans etc.

One thing I have realized is that working in the field of HIV and AIDS especially in Africa, with all the other accompanying and pre-existing problems, is a call. It is a vocation and a mission and if one gets involved in the field of HIV and AIDS as a job, they will not last even a day. However, it can be also rewarding if someone may die with a smile on their face because they knew that someone else cared and stood in the gap as Christ's ambassador.

Healing the Nations:
Becoming a Multicultural Church

Facilitator: Rev. Raafat Girgis, the Presbyterian Church (U.S.A.) (PCUSA)

Presentation

Girgis presents the proposal of multicultural churches as a way to respond to the present reality of many societies in the world as well as to the reality of the churches.

Recalling the changes in the composition of the US population and PCUSA membership, Girgis highlighted two possibilities of responding to the new challenges: the model which tries to respond to the requirements of each ethnic, racial, cultural group and the unified model, the one he advocates, recognizing both are necessary.

The unified model is expressed in a multicultural church, that is, a church which intentionally recognizes, incorporates and celebrates the gifts of the diverse membership. It does so in worship, in evangelism and mission and in sharing power with the different ethnic, racial and cultural groups that conform the church, and reflect the make up of the diverse society. It is through the becoming together of people of every "nation, tribe and language" that healing and wholeness take place. In a multicultural church issues of injustices, racism, sexism, ageism and xenophobia will be addressed and dealt with in much more effective ways than if they were dealt with in a segregated and isolated setting.

Why multicultural churches? Because of:
- God's intention (cf. Gen. 1:2,31; Acts 17: 26; 10:34-36; Rom. 2, 11; Matt. 25)
- Jesus' example (cf. John 4; Luke 19; Matt. 23:13-14)
- Leadership of the Holy Spirit (cf. Acts 2:6; 15)

Different texts of the New Testament reveal the basis of multicultural churches, e.g.: Acts 2:1; Gal. 3:28; Is. 56:7b; Rev. 7:9; Gal. 3:8; Matt. 28:9; Rev. 22:2b.

Participants in their interventions showed examples and lessons learned from multicultural churches in Kenya (Coptic Orthodox Church); Australia (Uniting Church) and Canada. Another one recalled that stressing culture should not forget the centrality of the pursuit of justice.

Girgis closed the synaxis, thanking participants for their presence and interventions which helped to clarify some points of his presentation.

During the presentation different kinds of materials were distributed. The following are reproduced below: ideas for building an inclusive church; and principles of multicultural evangelism.

Ideas for Building an Inclusive Church

What is a multicultural church?
- a church which affirms and lives out its faith in God as it is revealed through Jesus Christ;
- a church which acknowledges interconnectedness with people of all races, ethnicities and cultures;
- a church which embodies and rejoices in those diversities as gifts to humanity;
- a church which welcomes all people into the community of faith without discrimination;
- a church which formally recognizes and utilizes the diversity of gifts in the Christian family

- a church which takes a stand in solidarity with those who seek a genuine embrace of the races, ethnicities and cultures in the church;
- a church which makes multiracial and multicultural inclusiveness a key organizing force; and
- a church which works for justice and peace in the global community.

What Can You Do?

- pray for the Holy Spirit to liberate you to be open to God's call for the church to become a church of many races and cultures;
- if you are a counselor in your church, learn about the uniqueness of other cultures so that you can minister effectively to them.
- build relationships with people who are of a different race or culture;
- practice hospitality by being the first to welcome racial and ethnic newcomers to your church;
- participate in a variety of racial and ethnic worship experiences;
- become functionally fluent in a second language; teach English as a second language;
- self-examine your feelings and attitudes toward other races;
- recognize that everyone has a cultural heritage that may be different from your own;
- contact your representative whenever you discern that pending public policy will adversely affect persons of other cultures;
- join others from different backgrounds to do team counselling about your community needs;
- create an organization that provides food, clothing, and job counselling to unemployed men and women;
- sign up with a student exchange programme in which you allow a child from another culture to stay with you and your family;
- seek ways to bring diversity to your private organization, church and association;
- coordinate volunteers from different churches to visit hospitals and nursing homes;
- encourage lawyers and accountants in one church to offer legal services to members of another church who could not otherwise afford professional help;
- partner with other churches to develop programmes for the elderly of another culture; and
- gather members who are willing to nurture and care for children after school until parents get home from work.

What Can the Local Church Do?

- form cell groups to biblically explore God's call for inclusiveness in church and community;
- establish partnerships with churches of other racial and ethnic backgrounds;
- sponsor anti-racism workshops so that people will understand and work to alleviate the root causes of racism;

- research and write articles for the church newsletter highlighting the contributions of other groups to the human family;
- explore creative ways to make Martin Luther King's birthday meaningful;
- conduct community and church self-study to discern new initiatives for ministry in partnerships with other cultures;
- plan a variety of worship experiences that draws upon the style and practice of other ethnic groups;
- set up a minority business loan partnership with a local bank, with churches serving as business incubator centres;
- network with other churches so that the business skills of members of one church are shared with another church in joint business seminars;
- partner with a compassionate ministry centre that works toward church and community development;
- work with other churches to create a partnership with governments to help find housing for the homeless;
- develop a mentoring programme with another church; start mentor teams: one white mentor and an ethnic mentor with one or two children;
- take youth to churches where they can experience other worship styles and discuss the differences;
- churches can develop "church exchanges," where the pastor and choir from one congregation exchange Sunday morning services with another;
- churches can help establish new church buildings in their community for ethnically diverse people; and
- churches can integrate their staffs to help promote racial diversity in the congregation.

Self-Assessment

- How do you feel about whites and people of colour building strong relationships? If your child told you that they were seriously dating an African, Asian, Hispanic, Middle Easterner or Indigenous person, would you immediately give them your full support?
- Do you perceive most people of colour as lazy, dangerous or violent?
- Have you been in an environment where you had the opportunity to start a conversation with or witness to an African-American but you chose not to for fear of rejection by other whites that may have been watching?
- Has there been anything done at church, work, or among your Anglo friends that you know would have been blatantly offensive to a person of colour, but you kept quiet about it?
- Does it rub you the wrong way to have a man or woman of colour in authority over you (e.g., the pastor of your church)? Could you honestly honour and respect their leadership?
- Do you believe that people of colour do not learn as well as others because you perceive them as being less intelligent than whites?
- Were you against the Martin Luther King national holiday? Was your reason because he was an African-American and therefore not worthy of such an honour?
- Do you automatically assume that when blacks move into your neighbourhood the community is being devalued?

- Would you be willing to live in a majority Black or Hispanic neighbourhood that was comparable to the area in which you now live?
- When your Anglo friends begin telling racial jokes, do you correct them, or remain silent?

Principles of Multicultural Evangelism

1. Multicultural evangelism involves a call to faith and witness of individuals whose background includes at least two cultures and who communicate because they share language, time and space.
   This sharing is an essential element of culture and may be unstated assumptions, beliefs, norms, values or behavioural patterns.
2. Multicultural evangelism takes place when all parts of the church are involved in sharing the gospel of God's love and salvation in Jesus Christ to people of all races and cultures.
3. Multicultural evangelism operates at a level where there might be crucial transition: periods of radical transformation, cultural conflict, loss and change such as shifts in rural and semi-rural people living or moving to urban or suburban areas.
4. Christians when acting individually or in unorganized groups are not only free but encouraged, lovingly, sensitively, faithfully, and responsibly to make friends with persons who are not disciples of Christ, to learn about them, to care for them, to enter into dialogue with them and to share the gospel with them, finding ways of relating them to the church.
5. When any group, functioning as or under a governing body of the church decides to engage in concern and possible mission among particular persons who are not followers of Christ, a different dynamic comes into focus. Because we live in a world of people with multiple links to others, and because we are members of a church with connections all over the nation and in the world, we need to take care to work in close cooperation with the whole church, for all are affected by the actions of others. In this way we express our unity in Christ and develop a more effective witness.
6. We should engage in friendship that is sincere and lasting. It is not helpful to pretend friendship merely for the sake of delivering a message. Think and act with the intention of welcoming people into a circle of life-long friends, with mutual appreciation and respect. Begin with simple things - hospitality, companionship in work or recreation, mutual assistance, sharing of needs, talking about joys and sorrows.
7. Good communication requires understanding and speaking the language of the heart. Wherever possible, some members of the group must learn the language of the people with whom they are doing evangelism. In fact, language learning (and teaching) can be one of the best ways of making friends and ultimately of sharing in dialogue.
8. Praying for people and for ourselves in relation to them is as important for us, as it was for Jesus. In prayer we seek the mind of Christ - the love and understanding of Christ for the particular persons with whom we are concerned. We also seek the direction of God in ministering with the persons and the work of the Holy Spirit in all concerned.

9. How can the witness to the Good News and evangelism take place? Because most of the non-Christian people of the world are followers of other religions or ideologies, Christians are called to special sensitivity in witnessing to their faith. That sensitivity includes careful attempts to understand and respect the other person's religion, culture, and faith journey, as noted above. Beyond that, however, the Christian is called "to give account for the hope that is in you" (1 Pet. 3:15). Numerous ways may be used. Here are a few options:

   a. After listening to another person's story, finding points of similar experience and telling one's own faith journey, relating how the grace of God in Jesus Christ has been active in one's life—in the attitude of "one beggar telling another where to find bread" (D.T. Niles).

   b. Inviting people to participate in Bible study around various subjects or issues—from the context of their respective lives.

For more information, please, visit www.pcusa.org/diversity and www.presbyte rianmulticulturalchurch.net You may also order a free copy of Living the Vision: Becoming a Multicultural Church by emailing rgirgis@ctr.pcsua.org .

A Journey to Argavia
A Role Play on Mission in Unity

Offered by: the Mission in Unity Project[1]
Contact: Jet den Hollander, Executive Secretary

Aims

1. To enable participants' reflection on mission and unity, how these relate in their own church and context and what might be ways to overcome present stumbling blocks to reconciliation and joint witness.
2. To use the method of role play in order to allow for a critical assessment in a way that is:
   a. non-threatening (looking at your own church in the mirror of the churches in Argavia);
   b. concrete (the discussions bring out both theological and non-theological realities and factors at stake);
   c. humourous (the positions are overstated which invites participants to exaggerate their roles as well); and
   d. broadening one's perspective (dividing the roles helps to look at one's own church through the eyes of others, and looking anew at others by trying to walk in their shoes for a while).

---

[1] The Mission in Unity project was common to the World Alliance of Reformed Churches (WARC) and the John Knox International Reformed Center (Grand-Saconnex, Geneva, Switzerland).

Contribution to the Theme of the Athens Conference

The synaxis brings to life the reality of divided churches in a particular context. It identifies different factors at play (historical and current dynamics) and how this impacts on the witness of the churches in that context. It then stimulates participants to reflect theologically and missiologically on vision and reality, both in the fictional country, Argavia, and in their own context, to discuss concrete ways of overcoming (some of) the hurts implied in the divisions and engage in common mission. In this way the CWME focus on healing and reconciliation is explored in terms of: what exactly it is that needs to be healed or reconciled, why, how, what ways forward might there be? It seeks to avoid any suggestion of "easy solutions" or cheap reconciliation in the complex realities we live in today.

Outline of Synaxis

1. Introduction (10 minutes) to the synaxeis and the main concern of the Mission in Unity Project of the World Alliance of Reformed Churches.

2. Journey to Argavia (10 minutes). Participants are led into the fictional country Argavia.

3. Role play (40 minutes). In groups they identify with a particular church (context, history, doctrines, mission engagement, current dilemmas and vision for the future) and clarify their position concerning different issues. They then come together for a joint mission consultation, moderated by the synaxis leader, where specific mission and unity challenges are discussed in plenary from the four different perspectives. Spokes persons from each group argue the positions of that church. If the groups are small, all participants can share in the discussion.

4. Back to who we are (30 minutes). Plenary discussion of the Argavia experience in relation to participants' own churches and contexts as well as the Athens theme.

A Journey to Argavia

Group: Church of Argavia

1. Imagine you are a citizen of Argavia. You are also a church leader (youth leader, elder, women's guild secretary, choir director or pastor) in the Church of Argavia (CA). Today you are attending the monthly board meeting. Read the background information below. Then turn to your neighbour and discuss how you feel about being an Argavian and a leader in the CA, starting with: "I am .... and what I like about our country / our church is ..."

Argavia is a small but beautiful country.

It has high mountains, dense forests and two winding rivers which ensure that there is much fertile soil. Our country would indeed be able to feed its entire population but for the fact that well over a century ago the neighbouring country Imposia did, true to its name and through all kinds of wicked trade agreements, impose on it a monoculture of sunflowers. While this gives Argavia a decidedly sunny look during the flowering season, it has also led to poverty in much of the country.

Now it so happens that there are four Christian churches in Argavia. The *Church of Argavia (CA)* is the oldest church in the country. It was established in the year 450 AD by the mountain peoples after they heard the Good News from travelling preachers. These missionaries had stayed for just two years and then left the Christian heritage in the capable hands of the mountain tribes. So the Church of Argavia developed in truly Argavian ways and looks back on a long history of Christian presence among the Argavians.

Then there is the *Sunflower Church of Argavia (SCA)*, a church of the Reformation tradition that was founded some hundred years ago by sunflower planters who settled in the lowlands and on the slopes of the mountains. The SCA has developed a strong emphasis on predestination. Eight years ago, however, the church split, not over this deep and difficult piece of doctrine but over language and liturgy issues: the majority in the church wanted to change to worship in Argavian while the minority, including many of the older generation, wished to hang on to the traditional Sunnish liturgies, even if Sunnish was no longer spoken by anyone in society at large.

And so ... in a somewhat mistaken attempt to be faithful to the old Reformed adage ecclesia *reformata semper reformanda, the third church, the Reformed Sunflower Church of Argavia (RSCA)*, was founded with a strong commitment to contemporary language and liturgy. Within months a new hymnary was produced. Today, the old church's doctrines and confessions are playing a less important role and, if truth be told, the invigorating worship services, youth empowerment days and "look after your community" campaigns are already bearing much fruit.

The fourth church in our country is the *Zidonia Evangelical Church in Argavia (ZECA)*. It was established just ten years ago by missionaries from Zidonia, a rich country on the other side of the world. The Zidonian missionaries focus in particular on the poor lowlanders. And notwithstanding culture clashes and rather undemocratic power structures, the evangelical spirituality of the missionaries connects well with that of the lowlanders. As do, of course, the development projects and schools that the missionaries are setting up with funds from Zidonia.

2. Today, the main item on the board's agenda of is a letter of invitation. It has come from the Bishop's office of the Church of Argavia. Discuss this letter in your board.

To sisters and brothers of all Christian churches in Argavia.

Peace be to you!

With this letter we, the Bishop's Conference of the Church of Argavia, would like to invite you most warmly for a joint mission consultation. We believe it is high time that we have a serious discussion about the missiological challenges that our country and our churches are facing. To name just a few:

- *the ever-increasing gap between rich and poor Argavians.*
- *the inadequate housing and educational provisions for the seasonal workers at the sunflower plantations.*
- *the problem of decreasing church membership, shortage of young people and shortage of pastors*
- *confusion over the nature of our missionary calling today, including how to understand our calling vis-à-vis neighbours of other faiths.*
- *our isolation from the world church.*
- *the burdensome legacy of no less than three theological colleges in our tiny country: one owned and run by the CA; the second by the SCA but since the split faced with a shortage of students and staff; and then the ZECA seminary which is funded and staffed from Zidonia. N.B.: As you are aware, the RSCA mostly sends its students abroad to a college with a strong emphasis on liturgical renewal - but alas, quite a number has not returned upon completion.*

In view of these and many other issues, we believe it is time to engage in an in-depth analysis of the issues at stake, and in fact, we hope that we can do so as the entire Christian family in Argavia. We therefore invite you to a mission consultation at the CA Conference Centre in October 2005. details ....

3. In view of the Joint Mission Consultation, prepare to argue the position of your church, the Church of Argavia, in the following matters:

- As a church developed by Argavians themselves, you strongly believe that a contextual understanding of mission needs to be developed in Argavia. Why? How will you go about it?

- You think that joint ministerial training will help the churches to engage in mission more effectively. Why, how, what?

You also believe that it's time to work towards church union in Argavia, but are aware that the other churches fear to be taken over. What kind of communion could be a way forward?

4. Choose someone to be the spokesperson for your church at the joint mission consultation.

A Journey to Argavia

Group: Reformed Sunflower Church of Argavia

1. Imagine you are a citizen of Argavia. You are also a church leader (youth leader, elder, women's guild secretary, choir director or pastor) in the Reformed Sunflower Church of Argavia (RSCA). Today you are attending the monthly board meeting. Read the background information below. Then turn to your neighbour and discuss how you feel about being an Argavian and a leader in the RSCA, starting with: "*I am … and what I like about our country / our church is …*"

Here, all the sheets have the same text, cf. the sheet of the "Church of Argavia Group".

2. Today, the main item on the agenda of the board is a letter of invitation. It has come from the Bishop's office of the Church of Argavia. Discuss this letter in your board.

All the sheets have the same letter as the one reproduced of the "Church of Argavia Group".

3. In view of the Joint Mission Consultation, prepare to argue the position of your church, the Reformed Sunflower Church of Argavia, in the following matters

- You want to rethink further the ministry and mission of the church. The renewal of the RSCA, especially the liturgical renewal, of the past years has produced very good results. Has it changed your understanding of mission?

- But you wish you could break down the walls between yourself and the old church, the SCA, and share with them something of your new found joy and energy of being church in Argavia. Would the mission consultation present an opportunity for reconciliation? What are the obstacles to the SCA and the RSCA working together? What is your theological vision here?

- You see the need to begin training your ministerial students at home. The human and financial cost of doing this overseas is too high. But you do not want to send them to the SCA college because it's understaffed and you find the teaching not always relevant. What to do?

4. Choose someone to be the spokesperson for your church at the joint mission consultation.

Healing Cultural Conflicts

Presentation

Seongja and Colville Crowe from Australia, both leading members of the International Network Forum on Multicultural Ministry (INFORM) were at the Conference to lead home groups as well as one of the workshops –"Healing cultural conflicts within multicultural churches". Each person who came to this synaxis received a booklet of nine stories from personal experiences of reconciliation – between Aboriginal and non-Aboriginal Australians, between first and second-generation immigrants and in building multiracial communities. And each person had their own stories to add to the discussion.

That was one of three workshops sponsored by INFORM. The programme was arranged so that these were in different session times, so that someone who chose this field of concern could take part also in our colleagues' programmes. Rev. Richard Chung-Sik Choe from Canada led a PowerPoint and Panel presentation on "Multicultural Ministries – ministries of healing and reconciliation". Rev. Raafat Girgis from the US led a discussion on "Healing the Nations: diversity as a key for reconciliation, renewal and growth".

There was a workshop on "Healing and Reconciliation in the Process of Reunification in Korea and Germany". This included three moving personal accounts: Hong Sung-Dam, a Minjung Artist from South Korea, spoke with a video presentation about "State Violence and Process of Healing"; Bishop Axel Noack spoke on "Nonviolent Revolution and Reunification: an Eastern German Perspective"; Ms Yoo Hye Ran, an Exiled North Korean living in South Korea, was interviewed.

In the following pages, we reproduce the introduction to the synaxis as distributed to the participants, containing the programme and method, as well as sample of stories.

The stories are reproduced here (with permission) from the following book:

Signposts. Stories of Personal Journeys towards Healing and Reconciliation amid Cultural Conflicts. Colville and Seongja Crowe, eds. Sydney, 2005. Published by INFORM in cooperation with the Mission and Ecumenical Formation Team of the WCC

Healing Cultural Conflicts within Multicultural Churches

1. Contribution to Conference Theme

Centuries of colonialism and enslavement, world wars, massive migration and racial displacement, along with modern technology and the global market system in the latter half of the 20th century, have brought many cultures, many religions and new value systems into most countries. As countries become diverse in culture, race, language and religion, churches have also become multicultural and multiracial. Each church and each community seems to form a microcosm of the world.

In this workshop, the discussion points will focus on healing from cultural conflicts which arise between different cultural groups - indigenous members, newly arrived immigrant members and mainstream members - when they serve together in one church within the pluralistic community.

Many churches have been founded by immigrants according to their own denominations, worshipping in their own languages. At the same time many immigrants, both individuals and groups, have joined established churches in the country they come to, making those churches multicultural or multiracial.

The changes are huge. The adjustments are difficult. We all suffer. Indigenous members always carry in their hearts the anguish of invasion, dispossession and the destruction of their culture. Their pain makes them withdraw from the common life of the whole church. Mainstream church members experience fear of loss, being threatened by the presence of new immigrants. Often they refuse to accept the changes happening in our church life. It seems natural for them to express the feeling of superiority as a cloak for their fear. New immigrants, like severely pruned trees transplanted into foreign soil, also experience a lot of hardship as a marginalized group. Their enthusiasm to maintain their own culture for self-protection may develop into nationalistic attitudes.

Often we experience conflicts created by different cultural value systems within one church or one community. Sometimes distinctive cultural value systems are difficult to accept. Some immigrant churches are building high cultural walls around themselves, isolating themselves from the rest of the community. Some immigrant churches govern their church by their home church rules; meanwhile the established churches expect them to follow the established church order as it has been constituted.

How can the Aboriginal members be healed from their accumulated despair? How can they become active in church life with other members? How can the mainstream members accept the responsibility of apology and open their hearts to the changes? How can the newly arrived immigrant members overcome their fear of losing their traditions? How can the whole church with its various cultural value systems govern all members in unity based on love, respect and humility? How does the Holy Spirit come to heal and reconcile in this situation?

Diversity calls for respect of each cultural value system. Unity in Christ, we believe, transcends racial, cultural, economic and national boundaries. Where is the balance? To what extent can each cultural group maintain its cultural freedom, yet build unity in Christ?

Is the culture which surrounds us static? It is not! While we are struggling with various cultural value systems in our church and community, further changes are constantly happening, bringing new features into the common relationship. A new culture is being created, absorbing every aspect of our present common lives. The fact that a new culture is being created through the common life of all culturally different members in each church and in each community is an opportunity for transformation of our life. What kind of culture are we called in Christ to become? The kind of culture that is being created depends on the attitudes of each member and each cultural group within it, and their response to the leading of the Holy Spirit.

In this workshop, we will gather suggestions from participants about how to build reconciling and healing communities - ways for indigenous members to find healing for their pains; ways for minorities to come forward and take full part; ways for mainstream members to open their hearts to changes; ways for immigrant members to break down their thick cultural walls... All of these will be sought in order to repair relationships and to become signs of "Unity in Christ".

This workshop will try not to touch directly the area of interfaith dialogue or of struggles in relationships with other faiths in the pluralistic community.

2. Aims

The workshop will try to analyze the present situation of the multicultural churches, in terms of their experience of cultural conflicts between culturally different people. It will seek ways for all culturally different groups – indigenous, immigrant and mainstream church members – to build and share in the common life of peace, harmony, justice, acceptance and co-operation under the guidance of the healing and reconciling Holy Spirit.

3. Activity

3.1	Welcome and Introductions:	5 minutes
3.2.	Introduction of Resource book:	5 minutes

Nine Stories about healing and reconciliation as they have been experienced by culturally different members are introduced in three categories. They are printed in a booklet entitled SIGNPOSTS – Stories of Personal Journeys Towards Healing and Reconciliation amid Cultural Conflicts:

- First, stories focusing on the process of healing and reconciliation between indigenous members and mainstream/white members;
- Secondly, stories focusing on struggles of immigrant members in maintaining their own culture and in adjusting to new systems;
- Thirdly, stories focusing on building a community which transcends racial, economic and cultural boundaries.
  Look at the 3 categories in the Contents, page 3.
  Which category most interests you?
  We form 3 working groups

3.3   Reading time   10-15 minutes
            In your group, choose one story in your category.
            Read the story.

3.4.   Group discussion   30 minutes

3.4.1   Analyze the situation as shown in the story in terms of these questions:

- **What sort of cultural conflicts were experienced?**
- **How were the conflicts solved?**
- **How was the Holy Spirit involved?**

3.4.2   (Each group is asked to appoint a reporter to present their findings in answer to the following question.)

- **What will we do?**

> (group 1)   Towards healing and reconciliation between Indigenous and mainstream members in the church.
>
> (group 2   Towards helping immigrant members.
>
> (group 3)   Towards building a community which transcends racial, economic and cultural boundaries.

3.5   Presentation of findings   15 minutes
         (3 groups x 5 minutes each)

3.6   Concluding remarks   5 minutes

3.7.   Concluding Prayer

4. Facilitators

Mrs. Katalina Tahaafe-Williams (United Reformed Church in UK)
Rev. Magdalena Zimmermann (Protestant Church of Switzerland)
Rev. Colville Crowe (Uniting Church in Australia)
Mrs. Seongja Crowe (Uniting Church in Australia)

5. Inform

The Facilitators have met and worked together in the meetings and networking of the International Network Forum on Multicultural Ministry.

The proposal for this Synaxis was submitted to the Conference by Colville and Seongja Crowe.

MONUMENT TO A MASSACRE
John P. Brown

The Myall Creek Memorial was erected and dedicated on 10 June 2000, in memory of a group of Aboriginal women and children and old men who were massacred there on 10 June 1838. It all started in 1998, when the Uniting Church, planning a regional conference on reconciliation with Aboriginal people, was invited by descendants of those who were murdered to hold the conference near the site of the massacre.

The massacre was notorious because of its callousness and brutality. About twelve stockmen rode into Myall Creek late one afternoon. They herded together about thirty local Wirrayaraay people who had been living peacefully for some weeks alongside the Myall Creek Station huts, tied them up and dragged them away a few hundred yards, shot one or two and hacked the rest to death. They then piled up the bodies and burned them. The Aboriginal men were away working on another property.

Such massacres were common enough in the fighting that erupted as pastoralists seized Aboriginal lands in the early 19th century. This one was unique because for the first time the perpetrators were brought to trial for the crime. In the first trial, the men were found not guilty. But they were immediately re-arrested and some of them turned Crown witnesses. In a second trial, seven of the men were found guilty of murder and were hanged for the crime. This was the first and perhaps the only time in Australian history when white people were found guilty of the murder of Aboriginal people. It was not the end of the massacres but it did mark a significant moment in the history of relations between Indigenous and non-Indigenous people in Australia.

Five years ago, after two years of planning and painstaking negotiations a number of Aboriginal and non-Indigenous people, some local and some from other places erected a beautiful memorial to the people who died in the massacre. The Memorial stands on a knoll overlooking the site of the massacre and the Myall Creek Station. It was opened in the presence of a gathering of about fifteen hundred people from near and far. About half were Aboriginal people, and half were non-Indigenous. For several years prior to that a few people had gathered nearby each year to commemorate the history.

Each year since then, on the Saturday nearest the event, a memorial service has been held at the site.

The Memorial was erected because people believed that a frank acknowledgment of the truth of our shared history is a necessary step in reconciliation.

About three weeks before the opening of the memorial, I was approached by a person who said she was a descendant of one of the murderers. She asked if the Aboriginal people would mind if she came to the opening because she had always worn the shame of being a descendant of one of those who participated in the massacre. I invited her to come to the next meeting of the organizing group. She was welcomed with open arms and embraces by the descendants of those who were murdered. On the day of the dedication, three people who were descended from the murderers and a number of people who were descendants of the victims came together in an emotion-filled act of personal reconciliation.

But this event was not just about personal reconciliation between descendants of the murderers and those who were murdered. This was a representative group of people from the six States and Territories of Australia acknowledging the truth of our shared history as part of our commitment to work together for a just reconciliation.

Some of the wording of that initial service is recorded below.

Perhaps equally significant for the reconciliation movement was the fact that later that afternoon three local Myall Creek families with little children walked down the path to the Memorial Rock and, respectfully laying flowers at the base of the rock, one of the children was heard to say, "We are going to look after this place forever."

Because of its notoriety, this massacre is representative of all the massacres that occurred across Australia. For that reason, those who planned the memorial invited those who came to the dedication ceremony to bring with them a large stone from their place. These stones from all over New South Wales and some from other states were then set in a circle around the edge of the white gravel surrounding the Rock. They symbolize the fact that this memorial commemorates the shared history of all of us.

Transcript of Part of the Dedication Service:

<u>We remember:</u>

Beaulah Adams and Des Blake:
We are descendants of, and represent, all those who carried out murder and mayhem on the slopes below.

Sue Blacklock and Lyall Munro:
We are descendants of those who survived the massacres.

Sue, Lyall, Beaulah and Des:
We acknowledge this our shared history;
We seek reconciliation between our peoples,
And healing of the wounds of the past.

All: (as the four embrace)
This is the history of every one of us;
We are all heirs and survivors, beneficiaries and victims
Of its injustices and misunderstandings.
We too want reconciliation and healing.
<u>We acknowledge our shared history</u>

John Brown:
(As an Aboriginal and a non-Aboriginal young person together light the red candle)

We light this candle in memory of those who died on the slopes below,
needlessly, brutally, wrongly. Their spirits are with us here.
They are glad that we are remembering them today.

We also honour those who died all over the country, courageously defending
their land, or because they spoke the truth in the face of violent power and
aggression.

And we honour those good people who reported the massacre, William Hobbs,
the manager, and Frederick Foot who rode to Maitland and on to Sydney to report
the massacre; Edward Denny Day, the magistrate who rode up here to investigate
the reports under instructions from Governor Gipps; those who prosecuted and
brought the criminals to justice.

We honour all those people who throughout our history have reached
 out to one another across the racial divisions, and dreamed of more just,
 respectful and caring ways of sharing the land.

We acknowledge
- that violence continued at places all over the country for 140 years;
- that it was all part of the taking of the land without negotiation or payment;
- that Aboriginal people rightly defended their land, families, culture and heritage;
- that there was a war between laws, cultures and belief systems.

We grieve
- this lack of respect and negotiation in the taking of the land;
- the destruction of language and culture;
- the breaking up of the families and their dispersal to lands
  that belonged to other people with different stories;
- the forced separation of many children.

We acknowledge
- that this destruction and evil continues to affect the lives of people now;
- to cause confusion fear and violence;
- that some people direct the violence at themselves, their families and loved ones;
- or direct it randomly, and go to gaol.

We acknowledge that oppression continues in the present
- in racist discrimination in employment, healthcare, schools and shops;
- in the inequity in access to, or use of the land;
- in the disrespect for Aboriginal culture and traditional custodians;
- in a history still told largely from the viewpoint of non-Aboriginal people.
We commit ourselves to a just reconciliation

(As Rebekah and Benjamin light the second candle and the music sticks begin softly)

And we light another candle – a candle of hope, healing, acceptance.
For we have gathered today to honour both perspectives on the history,
and to renew our commitment to tell the truth to our children and grandchildren.
We commit ourselves to the continuing search for more respectful, equitable and just ways of living together in the land.
- when a person's lot will no longer be determined on the basis of their ancestry or skin-colour;
- when young people will no longer bear a grudge against the society because it treats
  their people and history and culture unjustly;
- when the history of 60,000 years is honoured together with the history of the last two
  centuries;
- when the glorious parts of the history are celebrated with pride, and the dishonourable parts are acknowledged with shame.

(As the bull-roarer sounds)
And we pray that the Creator Spirit will reward and bless our efforts, and grant healing and peace in the land.

Unveiling the Plaque:

Sue Blacklock and Beaulah Adams:

We dedicate this monument to the telling of the truth of our shared
 history, and to the reconciliation of our peoples.

All (joining hands):

We will walk together
And find more respectful and just ways
Of living together in this land.

22 March 2005

John P Brown

Rev. Dr John P. Brown was Uniting Aboriginal and Islander Christian Congress Covenanting Coordinator, 1993-1998. The Covenanting Report to the National Assembly of the Uniting Church in Australia in 2000 began with this paragraph:
Since the establishment of the Covenant between the UAICC and the rest of the UCA in 1994, the Covenanting process has become an important and life-giving movement in the church. The relationships forming between the

> *Congress and the non-indigenous members of the church will, given the grace of God, create a truly Australian church which sees its identity as discipleship communities in the context of the repairing of relationships between Indigenous and non-indigenous Australians. It is an ongoing journey which promises to liberate Indigenous and non-indigenous Australians from the nightmare of our terra nullius history which affects our lives today.*

WHATEVER IT TAKES
Robin Yang

Introduction

My name is Robin Yang and I am a second generation Korean-Australian. My parents immigrated to Australia from Korea in the early 1970s and they worked hard to establish a new life in their new country. Church became an important part of their life early on. For my parents and many first generation Koreans, church was not only a place to worship but it also was a place to network with other Koreans and gain acceptance in a way that could not be found in the white Australian community.

Personal Journey

I began attending Sunday school at church from a young age and whilst I looked Korean, I felt like a stranger. Having been born in Australia, my understanding of Korean was limited at best and I found it difficult to comprehend worship songs, prayers, sermons and even the announcements. I remember always nudging my friend next to me to interpret what was being said.

In my later high school years many students like myself and their parents expressed the need to address the issue of language. Many attempts were made in the high school ministry to cater for English and Korean speaking youth. Attempts included bilingual services where the sermon was translated into English and hymns were sung in both English and Korean.

Despite the best efforts of teachers and ministry leaders, things did not work. Young people were leaving the church and either attending other churches or leaving altogether. To prevent this, the church eldership created an English-speaking worship service. They called an Australian youth worker, Fuzz Kitto, to pastor to this fledgling group of people.

The English Service

The early days of the service were difficult. Despite the best efforts of its supporters and members, the service was not seen as an important priority by the whole leadership in the overall vision of the church. Consequently, the service was held at inconvenient times, after all morning worship services and activities were finished. It was held in a small room close to the dining hall where people were having lunch and often the service would be interrupted with people walking into the room looking for a place to eat, unaware that the service was in progress. The service was always seen as a sub-group of the young adult ministry, one that catered for only a small minority and not important.

The value of this ministry in its vision to share the gospel with other Korean-Australians was completely lost on the first generation. For them, the need to maintain language and proper church/cultural protocols surpassed all others, including the spiritual needs of young adults. Conflict between members and supporters of the English service and the first generation leadership was ongoing. I remember one time when the eldership decided to terminate the service without consultation with us and the ensuing conflict resulted in almost all of the members leaving the church and Christian faith. The first generation had unknowingly caused the very thing they were trying to prevent by establishing the English service – a mass exodus of English-speaking "Generation X'ers" from the Korean church.

Aftermath

Despite the difficulties, God used this experience to call me into ministry and today, 15 years on, I look at the aftermath of this turbulent time and I stand torn between a profound sense of hope contrasted with deep despair. My heart breaks with grief over the souls who tasted the kingdom of God in all its fullness for a short time through the English service but now live with bitterness and disillusionment at the treatment received from the church. Save an outpouring of grace by a good measure of the Holy Spirit, these brothers and sisters will spend an eternity apart from God. At the same time, I look at where this ministry is now and my heart beats with hope that a new generation is encountering Christ and deepening their roots in God.

I am currently a youth minister, serving God as a pastor to a Uniting Church congregation in Adelaide. I have not served in a Korean context for over five years, yet my heart remains totally sold and committed to sharing faith with second and third generation Korean-Australians in God's time. I frequently look from the outside into the Korean church and ministry with Korean second generation young people.

A New Paradigm

A paradigm shift in understanding mission needs to happen within the Korean Christian community. The current paradigm emphasizes the importance of speaking the mother language, keeping and respecting first generation traditions and being together as the whole family of God in a congregation. Vision and leadership of the church continues to lie in the hands of the minister and eldership who are generally all males over 60 years old. It is interesting to note, that young adults in their mid 30s are given tasks like helping in the kitchen, cleaning the church on weekends or teaching Sunday school (not that there is anything wrong with that) but during the week professionally work for multi-national corporations and are responsible for multi-million dollar projects. Why does the church not trust these people with leadership? Furthermore, ministry with second and increasingly third generation young people continues to be seen as a sub-ministry of the church similar to a children's ministry or young adult ministry.

My hope lies in a new paradigm being born where everyone will catch anew the vision of introducing people to Jesus and transforming them into His committed and passionate disciples – no matter the cost! A vision that places the eternal destiny of every second and third generation child, youth and adult above buildings and programmes. I dream of a church where people are bold for the sake of the gospel and willing to step outside of their comfort zones to reach lost people for Christ whatever it takes. I long for a church where people are placed in leadership, not because of their status, age or achievements but by the spiritual giftings God has given them. My heart yearns for the day when a radical Acts 2 church will be born to proclaim Jesus Christ to Korean-Australians who for too long have been ignored, neglected and shamed by a generation unwilling to leave their comfort zones, and be prepared to sacrifice everything for the sake of the gospel.

5 April 2005

Robin Yang

NO LONGER KOREAN OR AFRICAN
Story of a Disabled Baby
Sook Ja Chung

About a year ago, a Nigerian pastor called to meet me. He wanted me to visit his congregation to speak about the regulation of Korean Employment Permit for Nigerian and some other African congregations. We made an appointment, and several weeks later I visited them. After I finished the speech, he took me to a room where an African lady was waiting for me. The speech was an excuse to invite me, but the real reason was to make me meet this lady.

She was an unmarried pregnant woman. The pastor wanted me to take care of the woman because she was afraid that the community would criticize her pregnancy, not knowing her partner. He also wanted me to take care of the woman because the pastor himself was a man who did not know what to do about the pregnancy. Because he was a Nigerian, he did not know where this woman should go for a check-up. So I took her to a hospital and also introduced her to a "medical counselor" of our Centre. Her name is Ms Lee, Ok Dong, who started to help migrant workers around her house because she has been living in the area where a lot of migrant workers have been working since ten years ago.

When we started the Women's Center for Migrant Workers eight years ago, she helped us to visit migrant workers' working places and living houses. Then she became the "medical counselor" for our Centre. When we call her "medical counselor", it means that she helps take migrant workers to hospital and helps them register or pay medical fees and also she helps to get medicine for them. She is not a doctor to check the sick but she is an ordinary housewife with one daughter, living with her husband and mother-in-law.

She started to take care of this pregnant woman. After six months of pregnancy, this African woman lost her job. This means that she did not have any way to live. So Ms Lee found a family for her to stay with by teaching English to the children of the family, so that she could survive until she gave birth to a girl. She delivered successfully and her condition was all right but unfortunately her baby's health condition was not good. So the baby had to remain in the hospital and the African mother was discharged from the hospital. But she did not have any place to go because the family where she worked before could not take care of her and her baby any more. So Ms Lee took the woman to her own house for the woman's after-delivery health care. Ms Lee's house has three bedrooms which are occupied by all the family members. One room is the couple's room, another is her mother-in-law's room and the other is her husband's study room. Ms Lee vacated her own bedroom for the woman to help recover her health.

The baby girl was born disabled. When the mother was pregnant, she did not want to show her pregnancy to her friends and so she tightly bound her body. And when she went to see a doctor, the doctor said she should loose her body from the strong tie for her baby's sake. Anyway, the baby's brain was not working normally and the baby could not move the lower part of her body. The baby had to have an operation to take out a large quantity of liquid flowing from her brain. Even after the operation, the lower half of the body was not functioning normally, so she needed another operation.

We had to find some source of financing her hospital fees. Fortunately an NGO medical supporting group helped us and the baby safely came back home to her mother's breast. Ms Lee now had to take care of the baby too. When I visited her house, I was so surprised that I could not express my thanks with words to Ms Lee. The African woman and her baby were using the couple's own bedroom, Mr. Lee was using his study room, and Ms Lee and her daughter were using the living room for sleeping. All the family members were treating the African lady as an important guest of the family.

They are deacons of a Christian church in Korea. I noticed that they are living to practise the love of God through their real lives. As Paul said, there is no longer Jew or Greek, there is no longer slave or free, there is no longer male and female; for all of you are one in Christ Jesus (Gal. 3:28). This verse came alive to me through this event. Yes, there is no longer Korean or African. There is no longer migrant worker or officer. There is no longer Korean hierarchical man or unmarried pregnant woman. For all of us are one in Christ Jesus. Their lives were the living confession of this faith.

We found a good Korean Care House for the Disabled to adopt the baby at the request of the baby's mother because she has to work for her living and that is impossible with her sick baby. And she was afraid that her friends would find out the baby's story, so we had to do all this in secret.
When I was invited to write a story, this story came to my mind because it was an unforgettable story which I experienced in my own life. I hope this will become a blessing to the mother and the baby.

Rev. Dr. Sook Ja Chung, a Minister of the Presbyterian Church in the Republic of Korea, is Director of the Women's Centre for Migrant Workers in Kyeonggi-do, South Korea.

Caring for Caregivers:
Resources for Mission and Aid Workers
Kelly O'Donnell[1]

The purpose of our synaxis is to orient participants to the international and multi-disciplinary field of member care. We will define member care, and identify some basic principles of staff development. We will then overview some current trends, research on the adjustment of mission/aid personnel workers and future directions for member care. Finally, we will highlight several key resources and ways to further connect with, and contribute to, this growing field.

Member care can be defined as the ongoing investment of resources by sending groups, service organizations and workers themselves, for the nurture and development of personnel. It focuses on every member of the organization, including children and home office staff. It seeks to implement an adequate flow of care from recruitment through retirement. The goal is to develop resilience, skills and virtue, which are key to helping personnel stay healthy and effective in their work. Member care is thus as much about developing inner resources (e.g., perseverance, stress tolerance) as it is about providing external resources (e.g., team building, logistical support, skills training).

Core Readings:
- Doing Member Care Well: *Perspectives and Practices from Around the World* (2002). Pasadena, CA: USA, William Carey Library. Edited by Kelly O'Donnell (referred to as DMCW).
- Sharing the Front Line and the Back Hills: *Peacekeepers, Humanitarian Aid Workers, and the Media in the Midst of Crisis* (2002). New York USA: Baywood Pub. Edited by Yael Danieli.
- Global Member Care Briefing (free e-mail newsletter from MemCa, sent three-times a year with updates, resources, analyses; contact *102172.170@compuserve.com*; archived issues at www.membercare.org

---

[1]Dr Kelly O'Donnell is a consulting psychologist based in Europe. He chairs Global Member Care Resources (MemCa) which is part of the World Evangelical Alliance's mission commission. He has also been on staff with Youth With A Mission for over 20 years. Kelly studied clinical psychology and theology at Rosemead School of Psychology, Biola University, in the United States. Specialties include personnel development, setting up member care affiliations, team building and crisis care. Together with his wife, Michèle (also a psychologist), he has published several articles in the member care field.

Some Historical Perspectives on Member Care

Over the last 20 years, a special ministry, really a movement, has developed around the world which is called member care. At the core of member care is a commitment to provide ongoing, supportive resources to further develop mission/aid personnel. Sending organizations and churches, colleagues and friends, and specialist providers are key sources of such care. Several conferences and special training symposia, for example, have taken place over the last 10 years in countries like India, Singapore, Malaysia, Indonesia, Hong Kong, The Philippines, South Korea, Cote d'Ivoire, Cameroon, Nigeria, Cyprus, Germany, The Netherlands, Brazil, El Salvador, Canada, US, New Zealand and Australia. Member care has truly become international, plus a core part of mission/aid strategy!

The member care ministry and movement did not develop easily. It was often through crises, mistakes and failure that we began to realize that Christian workers needed quality support in order to help them in their challenging tasks. At first many of us thought that we were being unspiritual or weak, and not trusting the Lord enough. But we were overlooking our own humanness, sometimes trying to be something that we were not created or called to be. We began to realize our biblical need for one another—as seen in the dozens of "one another" verses in the New Testament (e.g., Hebrews 3:13; 1 John 4:7,8). We began to understand that the issue was not so much our having a lack of faith but rather our need to clearly see God's plan and his provision of care.

I remember how much I myself needed better training and support during my first cross-cultural ministry trip (thirty years ago). I was a young, enthusiastic believer of 19. What joy I felt when I heard that I could join a short-term team to work with a tribal group in the mountains of southern Mexico. It was a mixed experience for me, as are many mission experiences for people. Not surprisingly I got sick with stomach problems (unclean water), confused by the language (a different dialect of Spanish was used) and was often cold (did not bring the right jacket), tired (from the high altitude and reduced oxygen), and hungry (little food available in this poor area). By the time I returned to my home country, I was not very excited about doing mission work again. God used me nonetheless. But some of my struggles, as I think about it now, could have been easily prevented.

Member care, I have learned, is not about creating a comfortable lifestyle. Nor is it about trusting people instead of trusting the Lord. Rather, it is about further developing the resiliency and godliness to do our work well. We want to balance the realistic demands of suffering and sacrifice with the realistic needs for support and nurture in our lives. We can pray for stronger backs to endure, yet at times we must also find ways to lighten the load of ourselves and our colleagues. The call to take up our cross daily is also understood in light of the fact that we are to support each other as we bear our crosses together. And in light of the reminder from the Lord to come to him for refreshment, as his yoke is easy and his burden is light.

Finally, let me say that the same discipline that Paul said is needed to "run to win"(1 Cor. 9:24-27) is also needed so that we can "rest to win" (Matt. 11:25-30).

Think of member care then, as a type of discipline. It is a personal, community and biblical practice—an intentional practice—to help renew us and remain resilient. May the Lord help all of us as we both run to win and rest to win!

Struggles for Mission/Aid Workers

The following accounts illustrate the realities of stress in overseas postings. These excerpts are from letters written by mature, committed personnel.[2]

A single medical worker in Asia working with refugees: During times of stress this year I find myself struggling to maintain a balanced eating pattern. It seems we are always on call and it is hard to turn away such needy people. There are days when I go to the refrigerator and look for things to eat and yet I am aware that I am not even hungry. This really bothers me because I hate to see myself falling into the trap of eating to cope with stress. I wish our base had a person with a pastor's heart who was willing to listen to our concerns and offer advice and encouragement.

An organizational leader in India coaching first-term staff: Culture shock is the biggest struggle as our new staff pursue learning a different language and culture. This usually is hard on their sense of identity and sifts out those who can stay on long-term from those who cannot. Loneliness and isolation are two words to describe the first year. Depression is frequently a part of the stress they feel as they try to cope with their new and demanding work.

A couple teaching in the Middle East: As westerners, we must fight the fear of being unfairly labelled as politically subversive or as enemies of the established religion, and consequently be deported from the country. Paranoia is something that can keep one from sharing and helping. We often feel forced to lead divided and overly busy lives. Our "free time" is spent making visits, doing studies and housing visitors. Faith compels us to be people-oriented and compassionate, willing to "waste time" on individuals. The problem is there just isn't enough time.

A middle-aged administrator in Europe: What are the issues that led my wife and me to resign? First, I had laboured here for more than three years without having the slightest contact from other leaders from our organization in this country. No one asked how I was doing, what I was doing – or why. The isolation from full-time workers, from fellowship and from avenues of dealing with the problems here, were the primary factors. Oddly, in discussing these issues with another leader, he seemed perplexed that they would even be issues. Such mentality prompted a letter to our international director in which I expressed my concern for more in-depth and comprehensive pastoral oversight of staff and leaders. It seems that too little is understood and too much is presumed.

---

[2] *Missionary Care: Counting the Cost for World Evangelization*, Pasadena, CA, USA, William Carey Library, 1992, from chapter eight.

Departing in Peace or Pieces?
Research on Attrition for Mission Personnel

Let's look at the recent 14-nation attrition study sponsored by the World Evangelical Alliance (WEA) for some updates.[3]

The three Percent of Attrition

Basically, the WEA study found the overall annual attrition rate to be 5.1 percent for the 453 sending societies that were surveyed. When items such as normal retirement and possible transfer to another agency were ferreted out, the bottom line figure becomes 3.1 percent attrition that is "undesirable" because it is premature, preventable and likely permanent. Think of this as the 3Ps of the three percent, to help remember the findings.

In real person terms, this may mean that more than 12,000 staff are lost each year out of the global pool estimated to be over 425,000, both Catholic and Protestant.[4] That is more staff than are in many sending organizations combined. Such undesirable attrition also spills onto others, negatively impacting thousands of family members and friends in the home and host communities.

More Results

So why do staff leave the field? According to the WEA study the main reasons given were, in order, normal retirement (9.4 %), children's issues, change of jobs, health problems, lack of home support, problems with peers, personal concerns, disagreement with agency, lack of commitment and lack of call (4.1 %). Note that those surveyed in this study were mission administrators such as personnel directors, rather than the actual workers themselves.

Several important comparisons were also made between different groups of staff.

- Staff from the Newer Sending Countries (NSCs--e.g., Korea, Brazil, Nigeria) were a bit more at risk for "preventable" attrition than those from the older sending countries (OSCs--e.g., the UK, US, Australia).
- Reasons for overall annual attrition between NSCs and OSCs were very different: for NSCs the top reasons were reported to be lack of home support (8.1 %), lack of call (8 %), inadequate commitment (7.3 %), disagreement with agency (6.1 %), problems with peers (5.7 %), health problems (5.1 %); for OSCs, the top reasons were normal retirement (13.2 %), children (10.1 %), change of job (8.9 %), health problems (8.4 %), problems with peers (6 %), personal concerns (5. 2 %).
- In general the larger and older the sending society, the lower the preventable attrition rate.
- Those working in the same culture as opposed to cross-culturally had about the same preventable attrition rates.
- Workers in pioneer/church planting settings had lower preventable attrition rates than those in relief and development settings.

---

[3] This study is found in the 1997 book *Too Valuable to Lose: Exploring the Causes and Cures of Missionary Attrition*, Bill Taylor, ed. It includes chapters from mission and member care leaders from all around the world.
[4] Barrett, *International Bulletin of Missionary Research*, 2005.

To continue, the most important factor in preventing attrition was reported to be the worker having a clear call. This was then followed by having a supportive family, healthy spirituality, cultural adaptation, good relationships, pastoral care, and financial provision. Interestingly, a key component of pastoral care was the "regular communication" that occurred for field workers, which was rated even higher than pastoral visits or pre-field training (which are also very important).

Transience
Contact with so many cultures and people is so enriching. Yet transition, even planned transition, usually destabilizes. For some it creates a pervasive sense of loss while others experience a chronic low-grade sense of mourning. Others seem relatively unfazed, possibly because they have learned to form and sustain selective friendships, a practice encouraged in chapter six of Ecclesiasticus.

We can also develop a "quick release button", to use the words of Dave Pollock of Interaction. We only get so close to colleagues, and when transition is imminent, we jettison the "relationship" to minimize the separation pain. Newcomers can likewise be jettisoned, since we are already quite involved with our current friendships and our usual workloads to make time for them. They in turn can inherit and pass on this technique, for better or worse.

Some Suggestions
How do we reduce our attrition rates? There's no way around it: We, in missions must commit ourselves to more comprehensive, culturally sensitive approaches to sustain and nurture our personnel over the long-haul. Who will do all this? Caring leaders (church and mission) who make time for their people. People like personnel development specialists, pastors, strategy coaches and cross-cultural trainers, who are available to support and further equip our workers. And finally colleagues and friends--you and me--whose mutual encouragement provide the backbone for effective member care programmes.

- Let's also use the findings from the WEA study to help our people to: clarify and grow in their sense of call; prepare realistically through good pre-field selection and training approaches; cultivate their walks with the Lord;
- stay connected with supportive friends and family;
- care for their children's educational and developmental needs;
- improve interpersonal, conflict resolution and ministry-related skills;
- raise finances for long-term involvement;
- maintain good communication with leaders and peers;
- understand various service opportunities and career development possibilities;
- connect with leaders and mentors who can help them negotiate the cross-cultural world;
- receive helpful member care resources throughout the course of their lives; and
- go through exit interviews with follow-up for greater closure on their experience.

Final Thoughts

Attrition, historically, has been part of the cost the church has paid for reaching people in need of the gospel. People in conflict settings are vulnerable, and inevitably get hurt. Our weaknesses as people and as sending agencies also make us vulnerable. So let's put attrition in perspective. Whether it be considered preventable or unpreventable, desirable or undesirable, worker attrition happens as we work together following the One who underwent deepest attrition for the salvation of the world.

CHOPS Stress Inventory

Kelly and Michèle O'Donnell

In Matthew 10:16 Jesus sent his disciples out as "sheep in the midst of wolves". This exercise explores ten "wolves" – which we refer to as stressors – that cross-cultural workers frequently encounter. We use the acronym CHOPS as a way to help identify and deal with these stress-producing "wolves".

Directions: Using a separate piece of paper, write down some of the stressors that you have experienced over the past several months. Refer to the ten stressors and some of the examples mentioned below. Put these under a column labelled "Struggles". In a second column, "Successes", list some of the helpful ways you have dealt with stress during the past several months. Next, under a "Strategies" column, jot down some of your ideas for better managing stress in the future. You may also want to do the same for some of the important people in your life, such as individuals and groups found at the bottom of this page (use additional paper). Discuss your responses with a close friend or a counsellor. Note that each stressor can be both a source of stress or a symptom of stress.

The ten "stressors" for the column labelled "**struggles**" (potential examples in brackets):

Cultural (getting needs met in unfamiliar ways: language learning, culture shock, re-entry);

Crises (potentially traumatic events, natural disasters, wars, accidents, political instability);

Historical (unresolved past areas of personal struggle: family of origin issues, personal weaknesses);

Human (relationships with family members, colleagues, nationals: raising children, couple conflict, struggles with team members, social opposition);

Occupational (job-specific challenges and pressures: work load, travel schedule, exposure to people with problems, job satisfaction, more training, government "red tape");

Organizational (incongruence between one's background and the organizational ethos: differing with company policies, work style, expectations);

Physical (overall health and factors that affect it: nutrition, climate, illness, ageing, environment);

Psychological (overall emotional stability and self-esteem: loneliness, frustration, depression, unwanted habits, developmental issues, stage of life issues)

Support (resources to sustain one's work: finances, housing, clerical and technical help, donor contact);

Spiritual (relationship with the Lord: devotional life, subtle temptations, time with other believers, spiritual warfare).

Columns:
Struggles _____ **Successes** _____ **Strategies**

Answers apply to (circle): self, spouse, child, friend, department, team, company, other

Questions About Stress

- How do you know when you are experiencing stress? How does it affect you physically, spiritually, emotionally, relationally, mentally?

- When was the last time that you went through a significant period of stress? What was it like?

- How did Jesus deal with stress? There are 25 or more things he did to manage his levels of stress.

- What things do you do to deal with stress? What helps? What does not help?

Good Practice Principles

Good practice is a term used by many human service organizations. It refers to recognized principles and performance standards for the management and support of staff. These principles are written, public statements which are formed, adopted, distributed and reviewed by several organizations. Each organization voluntarily signs and holds itself accountable to these principles. Organizations can further adjust the principles according to their settings and ethos. "Key indicators" are also identified which are criteria to measure how each principle is put into practice.

Good practice has emerged from the felt need for agreed-upon guidelines to raise the work quality. For humanitarian aid organizations, for example, this meant establishing guidelines for providing relief services, relating to other agencies and caring for their staff — often in stressful or dangerous situations. Good practice also arose within the national and international health care communities where guidelines for providing health care services were needed, based on research and expert consensus.

Good practice is a relatively new term within evangelical mission, although the underlying emphasis on the quality of care has been part of evangelical missions thinking and practice for some time. I see best practice as being rooted in the example of the loving care offered by Christ, the "Best Practitioner". Our Lord's model of relationship with us serves as a foundation for our interaction with others and for the best practice principles that we develop for member care. The middle two dimensions of being comforted and challenged are normative for us, and reflect many of his encounters with disciples in the New Testament. The extremes on the continuum represent "worst practice" and do not reflect Christ's relationship with us. Likewise, they should not reflect our helping relationships with mission personnel—that is, overly protecting them and not sufficiently challenging them (coddling), or blaming them for having needs/frailties (condemning).

Jesus Christ as Best Practitioner:
His Love Relationship with Us is a Foundation for Best Practice

Coddler	**Comforter**	**Challenger**	Condemner
Placater	**Peace-giver**	**Provoker**	Punisher
worst practice	best practice	best practice	worst practice

Within the secular humanitarian aid world, good practice is increasingly being addressed. One of the many organizations helping to lead the way is the UK-based "People In Aid". This organization connects with an international network of development and humanitarian assistance agencies. It helps organizations whose goal is the relief of poverty and suffering to enhance the impact they make through better people management and support. Their "Code of Good Practice" was born out of research into the stressful situations in which humanitarian aid workers find themselves. It is a quality assessment tool which International Non-Governmental Organizations (INGOs), and others, can use to assure themselves that their human resources policies and practices, along with the organization's budgets and plans, lead to effective fulfilment of their mission. www.peopleinaid.org

Future Directions for Member Care[5]

Developing member care well is a process. We cannot expect, for example, younger sending groups to develop in just a few years what has taken other sending groups several years to achieve. It will take time and toil to "knit the net": the net of care givers, the net of concepts, the net of organizational culture, the net of communication, the net of centres, the net of consultations and, above all, the net of cooperation. But it is happening!

I believe that there must be an intentional and Spirit-led direction as to how this global member care net is developed. Here are five such directions which will help us to work

---

[5] Excerpts from *Doing Member Care Well: Perspectives and Practices from Around the World (DMCW)*, Kelly O'Donnell, ed., Pasadena, CA, USA; William Carey Library, 2002, pp. 8,9.

together and further provide and develop member care. They involve forming close relationships with colleagues as pursuing cooperative tasks with each other.

Pioneering: Is it time to break out of some member care and sector bubbles? Yes indeed. We must go to places with relatively few member care resources. Prioritize those working among the least evangelized peoples—many of these peoples are often the poorest of the poor. Innovate. Stretch. Help set up interagency member care teams for instance, in Central Asia, India or Africa. Sure it would be challenging but why not? Or how about helping to connect culturally sensitive member care workers with the many interagency partnerships ministering in those regions?

Affiliations: Bring together member care workers for mutual projects, mutual support and mutual consultation. Purposefully affiliate. Set up regional or organizational networks of care givers. Specialists can likewise band together for personal and professional support—physicians in travel and tropical medicine, personnel directors in human resource management, crisis caregivers etc. Form short-term teams with members from different agencies or service groups. Encourage their members to track with personnel over time. In addition, convene and attend strategic consultations of personnel and member care workers to discuss ways to further coordinate services. These can be small and informal or larger and more formal. Prioritize these for regions of the world where coordination is still really needed. Finally, consider forming a national or regional member care task force within your organization or interagency.

Continuing Growth and Care: Member care is an interdisciplinary field, requiring considerable effort to keep on top of new developments and to maintain one's skills. Prioritize time to read, attend seminars and upgrade. Grow. It would be helpful for some to link with a few of the secular umbrella agencies like the World Health Organization and United Nations High Commissioner for Refugees, and also smaller agencies like People in Aid or the Humanitarian Practice Network in the United Kingdom. Such linking will help us keep abreast of current trends too. I believe it is so important at this time to build connections and bridge gaps between the "faith-based" and "non-faith-based" organizations involved in international health, exchanging information on the management and support of personnel. Some examples would be attending conferences, reading journals and reviewing the peer support network and psychosocial support programme for staff offered by humanitarian aid organizations. Do not isolate ourselves by interacting solely with the evangelical community. Also, member care can be a burnout profession. So we must maintain accountability with others, pace ourselves, find ways to emotionally "refuel", seek God and practice what we preach!

Training: Resource staff and member care workers alike via workshops at conferences. Impart both your skills and your life (1 Thess. 2:8)! Include member care tracks at major conferences. Teach member care courses, seminars and modules at key graduate schools and seminaries, including the Bible Colleges in Africa and India, and the ministry training centres in Asia and Latin America. Training in peer counselling, marriage enrichment, family life, team building, spiritual warfare and crisis intervention are especially important. Further, help mission personnel from both the New and Old Sending Countries develop member care skills and member care programmes which are culturally relevant. There could be opportunities to join with groups in various places who offer counselling courses in different locations to train their personnel in helping skills. On-line courses are also especially relevant.

Special Projects: Based on strategic needs and common interests, pursue some short-term and longer-term projects together. Fill in member care gaps. Some current projects that are being done include maintaining and updating a global referral base of member care organizations along with a global member care web site (www.membercare.org); supporting the efforts of groups like Trans World Radio's "Member Care Radio" which broadcasts encouraging programmes for field workers; doing joint research/articles; setting up member care hubs and groups in needed areas (e.g., Chiang Mai, Thailand, Cyprus, India, Africa). Let us be sure to pursue some projects together where we get a bit "dirty"—and take some risks. A cutting edge example would be to provide supportive services— critical incident debriefing, counselling, reconciliation seminars—to people who have been traumatized by war and natural disasters. In short: be proactive; do not reinvent the wheel; pursue God's heart for the unreached peoples; and finally, prioritize time to work on strategic, do-able, field-related projects.

Decade to Overcome Violence (DOV)–Churches Seeking Reconciliation and Peace

Number of participants: 33

Flow of synaxis

Welcome

Introduction to the DOV (background, focus) by power-point
(Hansueli Gerber, DOV staff person at WCC)

Theological reflections on DOV (below)
Fernando Enns, Mennonite Church, Germany

Open Forum: contributions and discussions by participants.

Theological Reflections on DOV
Fernando Enns

1. The "Decade to Overcome Violence – Churches seeking Reconciliation and Peace. 2001-2010" (DOV) was inspired by the ecumenical campaign "Peace to the City": seven cities – as centres of major concentrations of different forms of violence - from around the world had been chosen to present "successful" examples of overcoming violence by non-violent means: Boston (US), Belfast (Northern

Ireland), Colombo (Sri Lanka), Durban (South Africa), Kingston (Jamaica), Rio de Janiero (Brazil) and Suva (Fiji). In all these cities overcoming violence was started by overcoming anonymity, isolation and separation through building relations. For the churches involved, this has had a two-sided effect:

First, building relations to others meant becoming public, being in relation to non-church organizations and governmental institutions, finding allies in the efforts for overcoming violence outside the church-walls.

Second, a strong spiritual growing within the community took place, strengthening its own identity as a local congregation. This has reduced violence, has changed and in fact has saved lives. Here we find communities of hope in the midst of some of the most violent places in the world.

2. Since the initiation of the DOV in 2001 the ecumenical community has followed this active approach. The call to be healing and reconciling communities is asking for a response. It is necessary for the churches to discern, reflect and pray together,but that is not enough. This call is a call for discipleship. Discipleship is not primarily "doing good works" as a means in itself but it is a call to participate in the life and the work of Jesus Christ. Therefore, the call to discipleship is an encouraging and empowering call: God trusts the church ecumenical, has confidence in his church. Why should the church have doubts in its own strength?

The implications of this call are manifold: the church cannot remain within its own walls but needs to go beyond, to get involved in the surrounding society. The church will become active in the local context and the larger community. The church will become a confessing church, a witnessing church or it is not faithful to the call to discipleship.

3. The confession of the church implies both reconciliation and healing. This is at the heart of any Christian theology. The church truly believes that in Jesus Christ, God has reconciled the world with Godself, a restoration of the relation between God and creation. The cross is the most powerful metaphor for God's way to reconciliation: a non-violent way of confronting violence, dismantling it and thereby overcoming violence. The community of believers is, by definition, a healing community because it is the reconciled community in Christ. Overcoming violence is at the centre, at the heart of the Christian confession, the witness of the church, visible in discipleship.

4. What is violence? I suggest we speak of violence whenever a person's dignity is injured or neglected or destroyed, physically or mentally, because this is a destruction of the personhood of a person. Second, whenever right relations are destroyed or denied, violence is a destruction of right relations. Thus violence neglects both person and relation. As Christians we know that both, person and relation is created and sustained by God's justice, i.e. grace. We are all created in the image of God. That makes us persons. And God has healed and restored relations by his grace in Jesus Christ. This enables us to live in reconciled, right relations. It is a gift of the Holy Spirit.

5. In the ecumenical movement, we have re-discovered the dialectical link between person and relation within the framework of a trinitarian approach to theology:

There is no person without relation, the person is constituted by relation (The Son is the Son because of the relation to the Father, etc.). In addition, there is no relation without individual persons. Relation is constituted by person.

This approach provides us with a systematic view that helps us understand the dynamic of overcoming violence. Respecting the individual personhood as being a constitutive part of a larger community *(koinonia)* is an essential starting point from the church's perspective to overcome violence. The high priestly prayer (John 17): "that they all may be one" is an expression of this truth. It does not speak of uniformity and exclusion of those who are different but of reconciled diversity – a community with a distinct character. Building such a koinonia – participating in this divine koinonia is peace building (overcoming violence). The church ecumenical becomes the gifted model for a reconciled and healed community, empowered to reconcile and heal by giving an example. The church is a sign, a foretaste of the new creation, where violence is overcome.

6. What are the implications for the mission of the church? The church is, by definition, a community of peace, since it is a community that respects the individual person, living in right relations. It is itself a witness to the world. As the community of right relations, it is :
  - a confessing church
  - a relating church, far beyond its own boundaries
  - it is not an end in itself
  - an ecumenical church
  - a healing community, fulfilling its ministry of reconciliation
  - a part of the missio Dei, the work of the Holy Spirit through the love of Christ
  - as such it is the "salt of the earth", "the city on the hill" (Matt. 5)

7. DOV is an instrument in the hands of the churches of the ecumenical family, helping the churches to be faithful to the call and to become what they are called to be.
  DOV is :
  - a call to become part of a movement that believes overcoming violence, restoring relations and respecting the individual personhood are external marks of the church.
  - an opportunity to discover each others' gifts of the Holy Spirit in the common journey to overcome violence, to strengthen each other and to grow in ecumenical fellowship, as a vivid example of right relations.
  - a challenge for critical self-reflection in order to explore the church's own infliction in the vicious-circles of violence.
  - a vision to become peace-churches through living and building a culture of non-violence, reconciliation and healing, as identity-markers of Christians and churches.

Healing Ministry in War

Description

The synaxis was led by Harriet Hill and Jean-Pierre Popaud (Wycliffe International).

The group read and reflected on the story of John Mba (and the questions).

Dr Hill and Mr Popaud presented a PowerPoint dealing with their ministry in Africa of helping local church leaders help their people heal from the trauma they have experienced as a result of wars and other events.

He also shared his testimony of a healed trauma.

Finally there was an open forum.

The Story of John Mba[1]

John Mba and his wife Mary lived in a small village in Bingola. They had two children living at home, and one older son who was in the nearby town working as a teacher. One night some rebel soldiers invaded the village and started setting fire to the houses. John, Mary and their children ran out of their house as the roof caught fire. Two soldiers grabbed John, though Mary and the children managed to run away. As they ran, Mary looked behind and saw a soldier cutting off John's arm with a machete.

Not long after, they heard some trucks arriving, and the rebels quickly got into them and left the village. Mary ran back to John and was able to stop the bleeding from the stump of his arm. They went to the local hospital where the wound was treated and stitched. When their son in the town heard this news, he was horrified. After a little while John's wound healed. The rebels were chased out of the area, so life came back to normal for most people.

John began to learn to farm with only one arm. Although he did his best, he was angry with everyone. He started beating his wife and children and quarrelling with all the neighbours. Mary was not angry with people but she felt very sad inside. She wasn't interested in eating very much and often wanted to die. Sometimes when she was alone in the house, she became very frightened for no particular reason. Both she and John had trouble sleeping and often had nightmares.

The older son in the town, who had been a very good teacher, now started losing interest in his job. He drank a lot with his friends at night and was often late arriving at the school in the morning. He had a lot of headaches and stomach aches but the clinic couldn't find anything wrong with him.

---

[1] Reproduced with permission from: Margaret Hill, Harriet Hill, Richard Bagge, Pat Miersma, eds, *Healing the Wounds of Trauma. How the church can help*, Nairobi, Paulines Publications Africa, copyright Wycliffe Africa, 2004.

All three of these people were Christians and went to church regularly. Every Sunday the pastor told them what God wanted them to do, how they should give money and how they should work on the pastor's farm. One day, Mary began telling the pastor's wife how miserable and frightened she felt but the pastor's wife told her that Christians should not have those kind of feelings. This made her feel ashamed of her feelings, so she never tried to talk to people again.

John's friends never talked about his missing arm. They just pretended nothing had happened. For John, his whole life had changed and he could not pretend that nothing had happened. John himself believed that men shouldn't talk about their problems and he kept his feelings inside. The pastor knew that some people in his church had changed their behaviour for the worse since the troubles. He thought the solution was to preach more about God's laws.

Discussion Questions

1. What wounds are John, Mary, and their son carrying, in addition to John's physical wound?
2. How could the community or church help John and his family recover from the wounds of their hearts?
3. How would it affect a community or church if many of its members suffered from wounds of the heart?

(or:

2. In our area, what are some ways in which people's hearts have been wounded?
3. What does our culture teach us to do with our emotions when we are suffering inside?)

Counselling People Facing a Terminal Illness

Facilitators: Reena George, Usha Jesudasan, Sara Bhattacharji (India)

Methodology: presentation, handbook, role play, testimony and discussion

A. Summary-Palliative Care: In Dying We Are Born…

Dr George is professor and head of the palliative care unit in the
department of radiation oncology at the Christian Medical College, Vellore, India

In Him we live and move and have our being.

We live our lives in the womb of God – our understanding is incomplete, our growth unbidden, our busy-ness irrelevant. And when we face death, the apparent end of the only life we know, it can be disruptive and terrifying, a time of great pain and uncertainty, especially when it comes prematurely and unexpectedly. We are not able to fathom that this precipitous journey takes us into the arms of God, the mother who loved us and birthed us into life.

In the Garden of Gethsemane we see how Jesus identifies and suffers with those who face their own deaths. He experienced fear, sorrow and vulnerability, common human responses to loss. He prayed desperately for the death sentence to be taken away. Like many sufferers he alternated between fear and hope, travelling the spiral road from struggle to acceptance and then again at Calvary through despair to surrender and new hope.

From his friends he asked only that they watch and pray -- the service of attentive presence. As we seek to accompany the dying we need to be mindful that we tread on holy ground -- the journey of a soul being drawn to God, a road that Christ has travelled, and on which he is the source of light and strength for sufferer and companion.

Jesus strove to understand God's will, to find meaning in his suffering and to find courage. The answers to these profound and important questions came from God, not from the mindless prattle of human friends, from our clumsy efforts to provide answers or simplistic solutions. It takes a deeper faith and love to be willing to stay, and to understand that the emotions of fear and pain, loss and doubt, need to be expressed and heard sensitively. Well-meaning comments to be strong and not worry can prevent the expression of painful emotions or force a veneer of courage and acceptance on a person who is waiting for strength and hope from a higher source.

What then is the role for practical service and care? Relief of severe pain or distressing physical symptoms is, for many, an urgent need. Assisting in alleviating this pain can allow patients to attend more easily to important familial and spiritual concerns. Jesus, himself, cried "I thirst". Cicely Saunders, the founder of the modern hospice movement speaks about the "sacrament of the cup of cold water and the foot-washing." Pressing physical needs should not be ignored (and the skills to assist with these can be easily learned) but neither should they become the sole focus of our time and effort.

Palliative care services recognize that suffering has physical, emotional social and spiritual aspects. While the physical might, in many instances, be urgent, the others are often more important. There is great potential here for the church and community to work with professional palliative care services to support dying people and their families. In this ministry there should not be tension or dichotomy between the healing ministry and professional health care. There is little reason for medical specialization to dominate where hope and healing are unlikely to be found in the physical domain.

Paradoxically the weeks and months of a terminal incurable illness can be, for some, a period of profound intra- and inter-personal healing; the finding of wholeness in brokenness, a final chapter that sheds new light on the life that has been lived.

In these last weeks and months there is often a pressing felt need for reconciliation. When life is short, the divisions and prejudices of the past can be viewed very differently, prompting reconciliation with God and neighbour. There are rich resources and routes to healing, reconciliation and transcendence such as in:

- Relationships with God, self and neighbour;

- Reconciliation, both interpersonal or sacramental;

- Rituals and resources of religion such as eucharist, healing prayer, anointing, confession and scripture;

- Renewal through solitary retreats and readings, communal celebrations and such creative pursuits as art, music, embroidery and writing; and

- Reminiscence, by finding meaning in life experience through various means like photographs, journaling and letters.

Yet we must remain humbly mindful that transcendence cannot be commanded or predicted. There were two thieves on Calvary facing death in the company of Christ. One was overwhelmed by the immediate unbearable distress and finality of death and screamed in anger for short-term relief; the other sought healing of the past and hope for the future. And so ultimately it remains a personal encounter between God's initiative and a dying person's response.

As sojourners we are grateful for the times we see new life and hope in the face of death, and we surrender to God's mercy all that is imperfect and incomplete in ourselves and in those we serve.

B. Handbook for Synaxis Participants
IN DYING WE ARE BORN

Introduction

Facing death takes people to profoundly intimate places which contain fears for most people and may ring alarm bells of vulnerability for professionals. However, being present when people express their intimate thoughts and feelings provides the opportunity for affirmation and acceptance, challenges the isolation of suffering and creates space for meaning and growth.[1]

"To face death is to face life and to come to terms with one is to learn much about the other.[2]"

"God revealed in Christ shares and shared in the darkness, suffering and dying and has transformed the reality of death."[3]
"Jesus died of something he didn't deserve. Jesus who always did good, suffered

---

[1] Barnard D, 1995, "The promise of intimacy and the fear of our own undoing", *Journal of Palliative Care*, 11(4): 22-6.
[2] Saunders C, 2003, *Watch with me*, Mortal Press, Sheffield.
[3] Ibid.

terribly too, without painkillers, and was lonely and afraid at the end, just like me so he really understands what I've been through and what I am about to go through too."[4]

Trial and Testing -- Struggling Within

Facing death: With Jesus in Gethsemane and Calvary

Emotion	Jesus' words	Words or actions to be AVOIDED by the companion
Fear and sorrow	My soul is sorrowful	Don't worry- trivializing
Struggle	Take this cup away from me	You must accept God's will -- forcing acceptance in answer to the question 'Why me?'
Vulnerability	The flesh is weak	Don't cry
Acceptance	Your will be done	You must not lose faith that you will be cured
Struggle	My God, my God why have you abandoned me?	Don't question God
Physical need	I thirst	Ignoring or over-emphasizing the practical
Acceptance	Into your hands I commend my spirit	You must not lose faith that you will be cured
Transcendence	Today you will be with me in paradise	There is no hope now

---

[4] Jesudason U, 1998, *I will lie down in peace*, East West Publishers, Chennai.

Facing Death: Other Difficult Emotions

Denial	The diagnosis is wrong. I don't have any illness	Conspiracy of lies or forcing the truth
Anger	I am angry at God and the world	Don't get angry

"We do not know why God allows this, but we do know that he will share it; and as he does so he will redeem and transform it."[5]

Trial and Testing -- Searching and Seeking

Stay with me
Remain here with me
Watch and pray
Watch and pray...
                    Taize
Be present
Be attentive
Be prayerful

	Mistake	**Stemming from**
Stay	Avoidance	Helplessness, fear, reluctance
Watch	Busy-ness, talking	Superficiality
Pray	Professional pride	Self-sufficiency

Watch with me...

Those words did not mean 'understand what is happening' when they were first spoken. Still less did they mean 'explain' or 'take away'.

However much we can ease distress, however much we can help (people) find a new meaning in what is happening, there will always be the place where we will have to stop and know that we are really helpless... Even when we feel we can do absolutely nothing we still have to be prepared to stay. 'Watch with me' means above all, just 'be there.'[6]

---

[5] Saunders C, *Watch with me*, op.cit.
[6] Saunders C, op.cit.

"How to be silent, how to listen and how just to be there. As we learn this we will also learn that the real work is not ours at all."[7]

Pray

"The sacred nature of life finds an unequalled focus in its conclusion which is why for many people, dying and death are holy ground, because of the intensity they bring to what is precious and meaningful."[8]

"It is care which moves beyond the conventional approach dependent on expertise and into an encounter between two vulnerable people alert to the creative possibilities of transcendence despite being grounded in life's fragility."[9]

"As we watch with them we know that he has been here, that he is still here and that his presence is redemptive..."[10]

Being with – Ilustrated Through a Role Play

Listen

Follow the suffering person's agenda

Respect silence

Allow expression of emotion

Give time

Be non-judgmental

Avoid closed questions

Respect confidentiality

Allow the person to find his or her own answers in their own time

'... to relate, to accept, to listen. In this way (you) will be able to diagnose some of the fears uppermost in the (person's) mind.

(You) will pay far more attention to feelings rather than words, watching with gentleness and listening with attention and respect.

(You) can ask yourself such questions as: Who is this person to whom I am ministering? How is he or she responding to this present predicament? What are some of the special spiritual needs at this time?

---

[7] Ibid.
[8] Cobb M, 2001, The Dying Soul: Spiritual Care at the End of Life, Open University Press, Buckingham.
[9] Ibid.
[10] Saunders C, op.cit.

The (companion) in recognizing some of the feelings and demands of the patient, can then help him to absorb, interpret and transcend them, so that the temporal eventually becomes transformed into the eternal.[11]

Transcendence

Not everyone makes the journey to transcendence. The two thieves on Calvary responded differently to suffering.

A discussion with Usha Jesudasan, author of "I Will Lie Down in Peace" (testimony)

Paths to Transcendence

In you we live and move and have our being

Relationships
> *God*
> *Neighbour*
> *Self*

Reconciliation
> *Interpersonal*
> *Ritualized*

Rituals and religion
> *Anointing*
> *Healing prayer*
> *Confession*
> *Eucharist*

Renewal
> *Solitary: retreat, reading*
> *Communal: celebration, holidays*
> *Creative: writing, music, art, embroidery*

Reminiscence
> *Looking back: memoirs, photographs, art, memory boxes*
> *Looking into the future: letters for children for birthdays and celebrations to come*

Rebirth
> *We live our lives on this earth in the womb of God -- unbidden growth, irrelevant busy-ness, incomplete understanding. Our dying, like the pain of labour could be unbearably painful, even untimely. Yet through this dying we are born into a greater life -- to beholdGod -- the mother who has nourished us and given us life.*

> **Jesus remember me when you come into your kingdom**

---

[11] Autton N, 1975, "Pastoral Care" in RW Raven, ed., *The Dying Patient*, Pitman, Kent.

References

Barnard D 1995 The promise of intimacy and the fear of our own undoing, *Journal of Palliative Care*, 11(4):22-6.

Saunders C 2003 *Watch with Me*, Mortal Press, Sheffield.

Jesudasan U 1998 *I will Lie Down in Peace*, East West Publishers, Chennai.

Cobb M 2001 The Dying Soul: Spiritual Care at the End of Life, Open University Press, Buckingham.

Autton N 1975 Pastoral Care in RW Raven, ed. *The Dying Patient*, Pitman, Kent.

A bridge
Can enable a crossing
Because it is present
Rooted in the depths
And interlinked yet apart
But the traveller
Journeys on...

The Healing Congregation

Facilitator: Dr, Anthony Allen and other members of the team

Methodology: the synaxis was very well attended with about 50 people present. There was dynamic interaction between the facilitator and participants who were able to ask and clarify issues as the presentation moved along.

Highlights: the holistic approach can be applied to any size congregation. It is based on the 'four Rs' concept:
- Regular exercise
- Relaxation
- Recreation and hobbies
- Reaching out to God, relatives and friends.

Health and nutrition, compliance to medication and the power of small groups was stressed as an agent of healing. A critical remark concerning the need to include sexuality as one of the essential components in life in the holistic approach was shared, although it was not part of the presentation (from staff report).

Becoming Whole Together: a Caribbean Perspective on Healing and Reconciliation

E. Anthony Allen, MRCPsych, MDiv.[1]

Only in the Caribbean were societies brought into being by the destruction of an Indigenous population and the violent mass relocation of an ethnic group from its native land - all for the purpose of slavery.[2] Systematic efforts to eradicate family systems and cultural norms began a process of social disintegration.[3] Today, in spite of many strides towards progress, countries are still struggling to overcome poverty and underdevelopment. Evidence of family decay includes fatherless homes, multiple partners and teenage pregnancies. Domestic violence, street children, child abuse and neglect are on the increase. HIV and AIDS prevalence rates are second only to Sub-Saharan Africa.[4] In Jamaica our 2004 murder rate of 44 per 10,000,[5] one of the highest worldwide, is largely gang-related, driven by drugs, extortion, reprisals and party politics. Injury-care and lifestyle-related diseases overburden our hospital expenditures.

The negative forces of both past and present have created spiritual, psychological and social barriers to health and development, which have been cause for theological reflection and innovative practices. As Caribbean Protestants, we wrestle with the need for healing and reconciliation through a paradigm of liberation theology and seeking to understand and promote whole-person wellness in Christ.

Theological Formulation For and From Action

The Caribbean liberation theology movement, according to Lewin Williams, asserts that an understanding of oppression as the unifying factor among Caribbean voices provides the focus for "the task of indigenous theology to attempt the creation of a mindset in the local people towards liberation".[6]

The congregation-based Whole Person Healing Ministry paradigm and model[7] focuses on a rediscovery, from biblical and practical theology, of wholeness and healing (from all forms of oppression) as a context of faith and the "abundant life" in Christ. By integrating faith and science, many congregations are becoming channels of healing through faith and prayer in combination with medicine, counselling and community outreach services. They are accepting the challenge to adopt a paradigm shift through a rediscovery of the true meaning of health and salvation as shared below.

A dualistic Cartesian philosophy, traditionally influencing both Western medicine and Protestant mainline Christianity, claims that the mind and the body are

---

[1] E. Anthony Allen is consultant in Whole Person Health and Church-sponsored Health Ministries, past director of the Bethel Baptist Healing Ministry, director of the Whole Person Resource Centre, Jamaica.
[2] Orlando Patterson, *The Sociology of Slavery*, Great Britain, MacGibbon & Kee, 196, p.9
[3] Anthony E. Allen, "West Indians" in Comas-Dias, Lilian & Griffith, Ezra, eds, *Clinical Guidelines in Cross Cultural Mental health*, John Wiley & Sons, 1988, p. 327.
[4] "AIDS Seminar Stresses Prevention Through Change", *The Gleaner*, February 25, 2000. p. C11.
[5] Ministry of National Security and Justice, Kingston, Informal Communication, 2005.
[6] Lewin L. Williams, *Caribbean Theology*, New York, Peter Lang, 1994, pp.217-218.
[7] E. Anthony Allen, *Caring for the Whole Person*, Kingston, Whole Person Resource Centre, 1995.

completely independent entities. Also, Western scientific materialism seeks to negate the reality of a human spirit existing in relationship with a divine spirit. Thus physical, emotional and spiritual well-being and care have been separated both in understanding and practice. Yet in Thessalonians 5:23, Paul prays: "May God himself, the God of peace, sanctify you through and through. May your whole spirit, soul and body be kept blameless at the coming of our Lord Jesus Christ" (TEV). In our rediscovered Biblical paradigm, health is understood as *wholeness or harmony between body, mind and spirit, between the individual and the human environment, between the individual and the natural environment and between the individual and God as centre. Health is also a development issue, seeking liberation of the socially and economically marginalized.*

Jesus also called his disciples both to "preach the kingdom" and to "heal the sick" (Luke 9:2 TEV). Healing, therefore, is central to evangelism and is a sign to point persons to God's Kingdom, which brings the greatest good.

We read in Genesis 3:9 that, influenced by the devil's direct activity, our basic problem of sin or alienation from God leaves us unprotected and thus vulnerable to a disintegration of self. This leads to disease of the body, mind and spirit and disharmony with others. Alienation from one another, from our selves, and from God essentially comes through some form of "missing the mark" or erring, which is what "sin" is. Though not all suffering or disease is due to the ill person "missing the mark", reconciliation with God and others, through forgiveness, is the most frequent path to healing. Hence there is the need for Christ's double work on the cross of forgiving, reconciling and redeeming, on the one hand, and healing or re-integration on the other. Indeed "*by his wounds we are healed*" (Isa. 53:5, NIV). Guilt is met by forgiveness as well as healing of its consequences, as in the case of the paralytic (Mark 2:5-12). The psalmist, in declaring "Praise the Lord, O my soul; and forget not all his benefits – who forgives all your sins and heals all your diseases" (Psalm 103: 2-3), is affirming that salvation, therefore, is related both to moral forgiveness and transformation and to the destruction of sickness and suffering. In other words, *salvation is healing of the whole person through Christ.*

As we grapple with our Caribbean realities of mistrust and alienation, our biblical reflection has been informing us of the critical role in healing of reconciliation through confession and forgiveness -- from God to us and from us to each other. Thus Christ teaches, "if you forgive others the wrongs they have done you, your father in heaven will forgive you" (Matt. 6:14). According to Christ, *true forgiving means not to take revenge* (Matt. 5: 39), but rather than hate, we need to "love your enemies, do good to those who hate you, bless those who curse you and pray for those who mistreat you" (Luke 6:27, 32 TEV).

Seeking forgiveness, and thus reconciliation and healing, involves *confession.* Firstly, we confess to God who will "forgive us our sins and purify us from all our wrong-doing" (1 John 1:9 TEV). We then confess to the other person. Thus Christ exhorts that before seeking to do service to God, or to seek atonement from him, we should first look about our relationship with anyone with whom we have 'missed the mark' by making peace through confession (Matt. 5:23-24 TEV). The apostle James encourages us to "confess your sins to one another" and to "pray for one another" while assuring us that "... prayer made in faith will heal the sick; the Lord will restore them to health; and the sins they have committed will be forgiven" (James 5: 16, 15 TEV). Reconciliation sometimes involves reparation. So Zacchaeus said to Christ "If I have cheated anyone I will pay back four times as much" (Luke 19:9 TEV).

Counselling and Prayer for Healing and Reconciliation: Perspectives on Practices

In the area of counselling, ministers provide pastoral counselling, while some churches are able to provide services through professionals in the multi-disciplinary team such as counsellors, physicians and nurses. Most activities, however, are informal, using lay counsellors and lay health and community workers. This involves *being with* persons and families *where they are* in the home, on the streets, in hospitals and prisons and as part of local church activities. This informality is an answer to the "trust divide" and the reluctance of many of our people to open up and to be seen in areas where formal counselling is provided. In both settings, persons in a confidential atmosphere will have the opportunity of admitting to shortcomings, sharing forgiveness as well as seeking God's forgiveness and intervention for human reconciliation. Small group sharing is also encouraged in the various ministries. In community counselling, the church has a critical role in healing and reconciliation. A process is beginning to take shape where this is seen as an integral part of a community-based approach to serving and witnessing.

Violence creates a vicious cycle of attack and reprisal, which can only be healed by reconciliation and restorative justice. Here, Christians aim to seek, love, justice and the dignity of each person beyond considerations of political party, money, class, colour, gender, status or family role. Thus they are encouraged to become involved in designated and informal ways as conflict mediators and to act as models and mentors. Community counselling mainly occurs informally in direct practice with community groups and organizations. Here church workers functioning as animators seek to facilitate and to ensure the sustainability of peace and development initiatives. Referrals are made where professional and outside social development help are needed.

Above all, prayers of confession and for forgiveness, healing and reconciliation are facilitated in all settings. Prayers are also made, recognizing that not all disease and suffering are due to "missing the mark". Some churches have special prayer counsellors as well as integrating prayer in the functioning of the multi-disciplinary healing ministry team. In the congregation, as a healing and reconciling community, worship services can be a time where persons could go to the altar and confess their shortcomings before God and ask for the church's prayers.

While nearly all lay and professional counsellors are trained in western paradigms of counselling, all are aware of sub-cultural diversities, that persons might be of other spiritual orientations and that some are open to occult or other traditional healing practices. Listening skills are highlighted to enable persons to "tell their own story" for purposes of understanding, self-disclosure and ventilation. Efforts are made to point to possibilities of empowerment for healing and reconciliation by integrating the proclamation of the gospel into our counselling, from the individual to community levels. As Burchell Taylor, a Caribbean theologian, states, "when the quest for freedom from social and political oppression is met by an experience of the redemptive power of the gospel, it becomes an extraordinary event of great moment".[8]

We are discovering that we can best receive and rejoin persons by being with them whoever and wherever they are and at their moment of need so as to truly contextualize the healing and reconciling gospel. Given the frequent absence of much of a sacramental or formally developed approach to confession, forgiveness, reconciliation and healing, we are seeking to discover "spaces" and "flashes of opportunity" in time, location and situation for this "being with" one another so that God can enable the process.

The following case study and vignettes will seek to demonstrate some of these efforts.

Case Study: The Bethel Baptist Church Healing Ministry

The congregation-based Whole Person Healing Ministry paradigm and model had one of its early beginnings in the Bethel Baptist Church in Kingston, Jamaica, in 1974. Services that are whole person in nature, comprehensive, (being promotive, preventative, curative and rehabilitative) and community based, serving underserved communities, the community surrounding the "crossroads" church, as well as the local congregation. Personnel are largely volunteers, mostly non-health professionals.

Health Promotion activities include education in healthy lifestyles, family planning, care for the elderly, HIV and AIDS, women's and men's health. Exercise, sports, table games and other forms of recreation are provided. The weekly church bulletin is a regular source of health education as well as a "Health Corner" in a weekday cafeteria. The family life programme within the congregation involves lay leaders who offer counselling on preparation for marriage, a marriage enrichment group and parenting education and follow-up support for persons having their children dedicated in the church. "Family Month" presentations deal with a variety of topics related to healthy family living. Special support and counselling are provided to common-law couples where at least one member is seeking church membership. These health promotion activities offer opportunities for confession and healing of missing the mark in caring for self and each other in our lifestyles.

Preventive Services include maternity monitoring, child immunization, and dental,

---

[8] Burchell Taylor, "Daily Bible Study 1: Onesimus - The voiceless, powerless, initiator of the liberating process" in Howard Gregory, ed., *Caribbean Theology: Preparing for the Challenges Ahead*, Kingston, Canoe Press, 1995. p.21.

vision and medical screening. Counselling, prayer and referral are provided for persons with newly detected illnesses. Special "Health Fairs" and a "Health Week" offer screening and health education for the public. A mentorship programme provides for the total development of youth at risk. In the area of crisis intervention a bereavement group supports persons experiencing the traumatic death of loved ones. Lay training has been provided for support in death and suffering.

Curative services at the Healing Centre are provided on a multi-disciplinary basis. Waiting patients participate in a morning prayer service. New clients are screened by the counsellor who notes mental, spiritual, social and physiological concerns, frequently with the aid of a "wholistic assessment questionnaire". They are then referred as is appropriate, to the Healing Centre's medical doctors, psychological counsellors, prayer counsellors and the church's social worker. Outside the Healing Centre a first aid kit is available for all who use the church's several facilities. Training in first aid and lay counselling is provided for use in the home, church and community. The church also runs a pharmacy.

> The counsellor at the Bethel Baptist Healing Centre shares that "forgiveness of self and others is an issue that several clients have to grapple with. I have had clients who have returned to report that the prayer of forgiveness works, they feel more focused and can move on with their lives". She shares that in a post-slavery culture of role deprivation "self-esteem keeps coming up again and again. Reconciliation is one of the biggest struggles... Many make the breakthrough with self-esteem."

Rehabilitative services include a volunteer "care team" led by a community nurse and a church staff member. There are outreach services for the elderly, shut-in, mentally ill and persons and their families with HIV and AIDS. This includes holistic care as well as referrals to and advice from mental health and other specialists from within the church and elsewhere. "Health care assistants" training for rehabilitation is also provided to members by the Baptist denomination.

Several lay persons receive training in counselling, basic health care provision and ministering support of persons with HIV and AIDS. A special AIDS policy stresses a commitment to complete inclusiveness in all aspects of church life (e.g. baptism and holy communion), non-discrimination, the best possible church-wide information, direct services and ensured participation of persons living with HIV in the life of the church.

Community outreach services are offered to three nearby low-income communities and certain rural villages. These include a Participatory Learning and Action (PLA) approach for problem-solving and the promotion of self-help development efforts. Such activities include basic (kindergarten) school, "kids club", swimming classes, youth homework centre, drug rehabilitation drive, adult literacy skills training, health care assistant training, environmental programmes and community advocacy. A bakery provides employment and dignity for members of a rural community. Through conflict mediation efforts and joint dialogue, the church attempts to bring together two rival communities with a history of violence.

A summer employment programme including our inner city youth provides for jobs and life skills training as well as employment and opening the door for future work opportunities. Health promotion and screening include the church's "Health Fairs", "Health Week" and "Healing Sunday".

A Sunday school, services and evangelism programme provide for spiritual aspects of our Whole Person Ministry.

Prayer ministry for divine healing is carried out within the congregation and its related communities. Here recoveries from an illness, which is outside medical understanding, may occur. In our worship services there is intercession for healing. A group meets weekly to pray for the sick. There is a deacon's prayer group, house prayer groups, emergency telephone prayer chains, hospital visits and home visitation to pray for the sick, individuals with personal problems and the elderly shut-ins. "Healing Sundays" are held to emphasize divine healing for the whole person as part of the church's ministry and worship. Church members are divided into birth month "caring groups" who support each other in times of distress and celebrate in times of joy. Laying on of hands can take place spontaneously as the Spirit leads in our prayer. Weekly groups meet to pray for the ministry and our intercessory prayer ministry is one of the cornerstones of the church:

> Marion (not her real name) states, church brothers and sisters share with me. Hands were laid on me during prayer. It took a few weeks for their prayers to be answered, during which time I had major surgery. Yet I had no doubt that I would receive God's healing. I remember feeling thankful and happy when the prayers were answered. Surprisingly, I can now speak fluently and I have no problems with movement. The neuro-surgeon said that my degree of recovery is a miracle. "Indeed", states Marion, "God still heals today!"

The church seeks to be an inclusive and reconciling community. Besides our 17 paid staff there are over 50 volunteers involved directly in the healing ministry. Many more are involved from other auxiliaries of the congregation.

Other "Spaces" and "Flashes of Opportunity"

- The Medhaven Minister's Fraternal, in Kingston, Jamaica, initiated a "Forgiveness Campaign" consisting of television education, a newspaper website page and a national forgiveness service involving representatives of both political parties. They have a developed "Seven Steps in Forgiving" brochure for use in communities and special church "forgiveness" services.[9]

- The Mel Nathan Institute of the United Church in Kingston has developed a mass dialogue process in community counselling. This event commences with a thematic cultural package put on by groups of children, teens, parents,

---

[9] Devon Dick, Pastor, Boulevard Baptist Church, Kingston, Jamaica, Informal Communication, 2005.

the elderly and economic cooperative partners. A short presentation on a critical theme (determined by prior consensus) leads into a group based dialogue. From dialogue sessions the community groups commit to action, which is followed by team evaluation.[10]

- In the Methodist's Operation Friendship in the violent inner-city of Kingston Webster Edwards supervises skill training to more than 200 young men. "While teaching skills you are a big brother, father and elder. Hardened criminals, once they discover a desire for dialogue, they soften up. We do conflict mediation every day. In my drawer, the amount of ratchet knives! Yet you can reason with each other."[11]

During Bible studies and evangelistic crusades in some churches, the use of certain scripture passages prompt members to share testimonies of confession, forgiveness and reconciliation.

In one church, during an evangelistic crusade a gunman who, under the threat of death was on his way to kill himself, came in to confess to an elder, not knowing that the elder was a policeman. Yet he was led to reconcile to Christ. The Minister says, "Nobody can convince me that people don't have consciences.[12]

Several churches in most denominations in Jamaica have developed similar programmes to Bethel, several with other innovative activities. Initiatives have also begun in territories such as Trinidad and Tobago, Barbados and the Leeward Islands. Methodist community medical work is also prominent in Haiti.[13] The Caribbean Conference of Churches runs training programmes across the region for HIV and AIDS education, counselling and care.

Conclusion

All of us who are healers have our national, personal and family histories of some pain and alienation. Yet we have a common Christ who heals us and reconciles us to him and to each other. He challenges us to be his agents of healing and reconciliation. Some forms of suffering are not due to alienation from one another. They also are met with the *dunamis* or healing power of Christ through ministry in missions. We need to be in the "spaces" and "flashes of opportunities" that present themselves in unintended moments and then call on us to be more intentional in our being with others whoever and wherever they are.

---

[10] Maitland Evans, *Counselling for Community Change*, unpublished thesis, University of Birmingham, UK, 1999.
[11] Webster Edwards, Director, Operation Friendship, Kingston, Jamaica, Informal Communication, 2005.
[12] Catherine Gayle, Pastor, Providence Methodist Church, Kingston, Jamaica, Informal Communication, 2005.
[13] Rachel Vernon, Sub-Regional Coordinator, Caribbean Conference of Churches, Kingston, Informal Communication, 2000.

"What Do We Mean By 'Healing' and the 'Healing Ministry'?

Presenter and facilitator: *Christoffer H. Grundmann, Valparaiso, IN, USA*

This synaxis came about as the result of listening attentively to the various presentations in the plenary and elsewhere and noting a bewildering, fairly indifferent use of the terms 'healing' and 'healing ministry'. There was a tendency for a constant broadening of the concepts by means of spiritualizing them to such an extent that they lose their meaning. However, no attempt was made to press for a strict definition. Rather the point was to comprehend the specifics of the terms in question by scrutinizing them critically.

To facilitate this process the audience was presented the following set of statements. They stimulated a very intensive discussion, which was just the declared purpose of this synaxis.

1. Since healing is not a Christian prerogative (see e.g. DNA repair; different cultural systems) the point is not healing as such but the way in which it gets interpreted within the framework of the Christian faith.

2. Explaining healing within the categories of the power paradigm is not typically Christian; it is archaic.

3. A Christian perception of healing is possible when fully availing ourselves of the richness of a genuine trinitarian theology: naming God the creator and sustainer of life (natural life), Jesus Christ as God incarnate (actively healing people, individuals, as well as communities and finally the cosmos; representing the confluence of restitutio ad integrum and restitutio ad integritatem in a unique way once and for all) and the Holy Spirit as the appropriation of the presence of God here and now (discernment, affirmation and engagement, criteria also important for exercising medicine, diagnosis and treatment). But this potential becomes noticeable only by the explicit proclamation of the gospel.

4. Since healing can be interpreted and fully comprehended in such a genuinely Christian way every healing becomes a potential encounter with salvation.

5. The specificity of healing is its corporeal dimension. If physical betterment is not arrived at, what is achieved, despite the lack of physical restoration, should not be called 'healing' but more appropriately 'coping', save if people directly affected declare themselves as being healed, which of course has to be honoured as a statement of personal conviction.

6. The 'healing ministry' constantly reminds the church of the corporeality of salvation. It, however, has to again and again sober-mindedly acknowledge that healing happens only occasionally if it happens at all. This, however, does not mean a failure of the ministry, which actually has to consciously bear the tension between promise and fulfilment. This is its very task by which it powerfully reminds the church of its eschatological reality like no other.

WRITTEN RESULT

World Council of Churches
Conseil œcuménique des Eglises
Consejo Mundial de Iglesias
Ökumenischer Rat der Kirchen

CWME Conference Office

Postal address: P.O. Box 2100
                   CH-1211 Geneva 2
                   Switzerland
Visiting address: 150 route de Ferney
Phone: (+41-22) 791 61 11
Fax: (+41-22) 791 03 61
General e-mail: infowcc@wcc-coe.org
Website: www.wcc-coe.org

A LETTER FROM ATHENS TO THE CHRISTIAN CHURCHES, NETWORKS AND COMMUNITIES

Come Holy Spirit, Heal and Reconcile:
Called in Christ to be Reconciling and Healing Communities
Version adopted by the CWME Commission (edited May 19, 2005)

Dear Sisters and Brothers in Christ,

Greetings from Athens, Greece. We write to you during the holy time between Easter and Pentecost, when the risen Christ prepared his followers for the gift of the Holy Spirit and called them to carry the good news to "the ends of the earth" (Acts 1:8), promising to be with them until "the end of the age" (Matt. 28:20). Here, on the shores of the Aegean Sea, 600 of us have gathered, from 105 countries, hosted by the Church of Greece and other churches in Greece and called together by the World Council of Churches for the 13th international Conference on World Mission and Evangelism, meeting from 9-16 May 2005. And as the sun rose on the conference, a small boat sailed out of the dawn, carrying a huge olive-wood cross: a gift from the churches in Jerusalem, a sign of both suffering and hope, made from the fragments of the trees uprooted during the building of the wall separating Palestinians from Palestinians and from Israelis. We pray that this cross become a sign of reconciliation.

For the first time, this CWME conference has taken place in a predominantly

KOMM, HEILIGER GEIST,   VEN, ESPÍRITU SANTO,   VIENS, ESPRIT SAINT,   ΕΛΘΕ, ΠΝΕΥΜΑ ΑΓΙΟ,
HEILE UND VERSÖHNE!   SANA Y RECONCILIA!   GUERIS ET RECONCILIE!   ΘΕΡΑΠΕΥΣΕΣ ΚΑΙ ΣΥΜΦΙΛΙΩΣΕ ΜΑΣ:

Orthodox context. Young people, though far fewer than planned, have played an important part. For the first time the meeting included a significant number of fully participating delegates from non- WCC member churches, that is the Roman Catholic Church and some Pentecostal and Evangelical churches and networks. "We", therefore, are a diverse group, from every corner of the world and many ethnic and cultural backgrounds, speaking many languages, and representing the major Christian traditions. Our theme is a prayer: "Come Holy Spirit, Heal and Reconcile".

This letter is an attempt to share with you some of the week's insights and challenges, as well as the experiences of joy and pain it has brought us. In these days, we have journeyed together, although we have not always agreed. We are in mission, all of us, because we participate in the mission of God who has sent us into a fragmented and broken world. We are united in the belief that we are "called together in Christ to be reconciling and healing communities". We have prayed together. We have been particularly helped by readings of Scripture as we struggled, together, to discern where the reconciling, healing Spirit is leading us, in our own contexts, two thousand years after St Paul arrived on these shores carrying the good news of the Gospel of Jesus Christ. We want to share that journey with you and to invite you to make it your own.

We stand now at a particular moment in the history of mission. While the centres of power are still predominantly in the global North, it is in the South and the East that the churches are growing most rapidly, as a result of faithful Christian mission and witness. The missional character of the Church is experienced in greater diversity than ever, as the Christian communities continue the search for distinctive responses to the Gospel. This diversity is challenging, and it can sometimes make us uneasy. Nevertheless, within it we have discovered opportunities for a deepening understanding of the Holy Spirit's creative, life-sustaining, healing and reconciling work. For the power of the Holy Spirit touches us in many ways: in gentleness and truth, comfort and creativity, worship and action, wisdom and innocence, communion and sanctification, liberation and holy contemplation. But there are evil spirits too, active in the world and sadly even in many of our histories and communities. These are spirits of violence, oppression, exclusion, division, corruption, self-seeking, ignorance, failure to live up to our beliefs and of fearful silence in the face of injustice. In discerning the work of the Holy Spirit, we have experienced the need to return constantly to the roots of our faith, confessing the Triune God, revealed to us in Jesus Christ, the Word-made-flesh.

In Athens we were deeply aware of the new challenges that come from the need for reconciliation between East and West, North and South, and between Christians and people of other faiths. We have become painfully aware of the mistakes of the past, and pray that we may learn from them. We have become conscious

COME HOLY SPIRIT, HEAL AND RECONCILE !

| KOMM, HEILIGER GEIST, | VEN, ESPÍRITU SANTO, | VIENS, ESPRIT SAINT, | ΕΛΘΕ, ΠΝΕΥΜΑ ΑΓΙΟ, |
| HEILE UND VERSÖHNE! | SANA Y RECONCILIA! | GUERIS ET RECONCILIE! | ΘΕΡΑΠΕΥΣΕ ΚΑΙ ΣΥΜΦΙΛΙΩΣΕ ΜΑΣ: |

of our own tendency to reinforce barriers by excluding and marginalizing on grounds such as race, caste, gender, disability or by tolerating the continuation of oppressive practices within our own societies and our own churches. Halfway through the Decade to Overcome Violence, we realize anew that the call to non-violence and reconciliation stands at the heart of the Gospel message. As a global gathering, we are challenged by the violence inflicted by the forces of economic globalization, militarism, and by the plight of the marginalized people, especially the indigenous communities and peoples uprooted by migration.

St Paul speaks of the new creation heralded by Christ and enabled by the Holy Spirit. "In Christ", he says, "God was reconciling the world to himself, not counting their trespasses against them, and entrusting the message of reconciliation to us. So we are ambassadors for Christ, since God is making his appeal through us; we entreat you on behalf of Christ, be reconciled to God." (2 Cor. 5:19-20) It is this "new creation" that we hold to be the goal of our missionary endeavour. With Paul, we believe that reconciliation and healing are pivotal to the process by which that goal is to be reached. Reconciliation, as the restoration of right relations with God, is the source of reconciliation with oneself, with other people and with the whole of creation.

But the road to reconciliation and healing is not an easy one. It involves listening, truth-telling, repentance, forgiveness and a sincere commitment to Christ and his justice. For this reason, we have explored a range of ways by which the healing power of God is made available to us. These include the healing that takes place through prayer, ascetical practices and the charisms of healing, through sacraments and healing services, through a combination of medical and spiritual, social and systemic approaches and through sensing the sustaining presence of the Holy Spirit, even when we accept and continue to struggle with illness and traumas. We celebrated healing services and were moved by the stories of Christian health and counselling professionals and their struggle for more holistic approaches. We were inspired by the stories of people living with HIV and AIDS and were challenged to counter stigma and discrimination and to promote wholeness for those living with HIV and AIDS. We heard testimonies of people healed by the power of the Holy Spirit, as well as those who have not been healed, or have encountered corrupt or exploitative healing practices. We also heard stories of healing in the midst of struggles for social, economic and ecological justice. All true healing comes from God. It includes physical, mental, emotional and spiritual healing and it shares the tension of the coming of God's reign as "already here" and "yet to come". We therefore celebrate true healing as a living sign of God's new creation.

Living in the Holy Spirit, anticipating the reign of God, called to be children of

KOMM, HEILIGER GEIST, VEN, ESPÍRITU SANTO, VIENS, ESPRIT SAINT, ΕΛΘΕ, ΠΝΕΥΜΑ ΑΓΙΟ,
HEILE UND VERSÖHNE! SANA Y RECONCILIA! GUERIS ET RECONCILIE! ΘΕΡΑΠΕΥΣΕ ΚΑΙ ΣΥΜΦΙΛΙΩΣΕ ΜΑΣ;

COME HOLY SPIRIT, HEAL AND RECONCILE!

God's new Creation, we have also to acknowledge the troubled and confusing present. It is a source of pain to us to recognize that God's mission is distorted by the divisions and lack of understanding that persists in and among the churches. In our longing for a fuller and more authentic participation in God's mission, we continue to carry the pain of our inability to overcome the barriers that prevent us from celebrating together the most healing and reconciling of sacraments, the Eucharist – the Lord's Supper. The conference theme, therefore, has been a call to a humble acceptance of our own need for healing and reconciliation.

But God calls us to be a community of hope. "Called in Christ to be healing and reconciling communities", we have continued here in Athens the task of defining the kind of community God desires us to become, a community that bears witness to the Gospel in word and deed; that is alive in worship and learning; proclaims the Gospel of Jesus Christ to all; that offers young people leadership roles; that opens its doors to strangers and welcomes the marginalized within its own body; that engages with those who suffer, and with those who struggle for justice and peace; that provides services to all who are in need; that recognizes its own vulnerability and need for healing; and that is faithful in its commitment to the wider Creation. We pray that the Holy Spirit will breathe healing power into our lives and that together we may move forward into the blessed peace of the new creation.

In conclusion, we wish to express our deep gratitude to all those who made this conference possible. From the country in which St Paul proclaimed the Gospel of God's reconciling love in Jesus Christ, we pray that the grace of our Lord Jesus Christ and the love of God the Father and the communion of the Holy Spirit be with all.

Athens, May 18, 2005

Rev. Ruth Bottoms
CWME moderator

Dr. George Mathew Nalunnakkal
CWME Vice-moderator

Rev. Jacques Matthey
CWME officer

| KOMM, HEILIGER GEIST, | VEN, ESPÍRITU SANTO, | VIENS, ESPRIT SAINT, | ΕΛΘΕ, ΠΝΕΥΜΑ ΑΓΙΟ, |
| HEILE UND VERSÖHNE! | SANA Y RECONCILIA! | GUÉRIS ET RECONCILIE! | ΘΕΡΑΠΕΥΣΕ ΚΑΙ ΣΥΜΦΙΛΙΩΣΕ ΜΑΣ! |

THE SIGNIFICANCE OF ATHENS

Some Reflections on the Significance of Athens 2005

Two-and-a-half years after the world mission conference in Athens, one may ask the question of its significance in the light of traditional emphases and themes of CWME conferences since 1963. There is no one answer to such a question, and that is why, shortly after the event, the *International Review of Mission* published a dozen papers by missiologists and theologians from very different denominational and cultural backgrounds. As the conference had opened up space for dialogue among a broad variety of Christians, so should the interpretation of its meaning. Written within a few weeks of the event, the issue of *IRM* featuring these papers is reproduced on the CD ROM accompanying this book.[1]

The purpose of these reflections is not to give an official interpretation, but to suggest directions and potential lines of research in missiology from the point of view of one of the main organizers and conceivers of the conference. In that sense it is a biased reading of Athens and should be received as such.[2]

1. Towards a Wider Ecumenical Dialogue on Mission and Evangelism

One of the main characteristics of the Conference on World Mission and Evangelism (CWME) held in Athens in 2005 was to create a space for a dialogue on mission which would include representatives of growing parts of world Christianity not always involved in ecumenical discussions and reflections on mission. The presence of the so-called "wider constituency" in CWME conferences was not new, since one of the specificities of the WCC mission network is to allow for such participation. The Commission on World Mission and Evangelism has Roman Catholic, evangelical and Pentecostal representatives as members with full rights.

We had taken care to include representatives of such churches in significant ways in the preparation and in the leadership of the conference. We planned the agenda in a way to allow the great variety of Christians to feel secure and at home by having a conference which was not task-oriented but dialogue-oriented.

---

[1] *IRM* Vol. 94, No 374, July 2005, "Athens 2005 – Listeners' Reports".
[2] I owe much to all those who helped prepare for Athens, who presented papers and who offered inspired interpretations. In order not to overload it and since it doesn't pretend to have academic character, this text does not give all references in footnotes, but I want to acknowledge that I am deeply indebted to those who shaped the content of the conference and its preparatory documents.

In that sense, it was an imperfect, but real, foretaste of what a "Global Christian Forum" with specific emphasis on mission could be. As the organizer of that ecumenical space, the CWME appeared more as a "space provider" for an open discussion on mission, and less as a body with its own programmatic and ideological identity, planning new options and concrete steps in world mission. As such, the CWME illustrated one of the potential roles the WCC could play in the future worldwide ecumenical movement.[3]

We live at a real turning point for Christianity and in consequence for the ecumenical movement. Either the WCC, as one of its main instruments at the global level, is able to renew its vision, methods and theological approaches to take the reality of the changing landscape of Christianity seriously into consideration or it will miss the opportunity to continue to play a leading role in the search for visible unity, and consequently could lose its credibility. The major significance of Athens may well have been its successful attempt at opening up the dialogue on mission by including a good number of the major contemporary players in witness and church: Roman Catholics, Pentecostals, evangelicals, Orthodox, Anglicans and classical Protestants. Ecumenism includes all those or it is not ecumenism. That is true today; it will be even more so in the future.

In the present configuration and time, there is a certain price to pay for the planning of such a wide forum: some significant issues in mission and ecumenism were not highlighted during the five days of the relatively brief Athens conference. Nor was it possible to envisage common formulations or decisions on priorities in witness and methods. In the present period of opening up the dialogue to new and important partners, such a limitation appeared to be realistic and necessary. In the long run, however, one could not justify it. The ultimate goal of ecumenism remains visible unity and not just practical cooperation. On the way towards this goal, forms of visible church fellowship are needed, not just occasional meetings: authentic ecumenism means debate on all matters which hinder the progress toward visible church unity and credible witness in, and to, the world; it implies cooperation with long-term involvement and mutual accountability between churches; it means a struggle to find ways to overcome theological and ecclesiological positions which are divisive; it requests the willingness to move towards full recognition of Christ's church in other churches, and much more. The journey toward full visible unity needs structures of fellowship and communion (though they may be imperfect) which allow for common decisions and partnership as churches move toward the aforementioned goals. As important as it was, the Athens conference had its limits, and these limits must be acknowledged.

2. Shift from "Messianic" to "Pastoral" Missiology

Mission theology shared in the preparatory process for the conference and in Athens was mainly characterized by a more humble approach to what Christians and churches can accomplish in the world today than seemed to have been the approaches in earlier CWME meetings. The formulation of the theme in two

---

[3] On the roles of WCC, cf. *Towards a Common Understanding and Vision of the World Council of Churches. A Policy Statement*. Geneva, WCC, 1997.

sentences was a confession that full healing and reconciliation are not the result of our struggle and capacity but of God's eschatological presence, intervention and gifts. Humanity cannot "heal the world" nor create "shalom". We have to acknowledge our limitations and thus we call on God: "Come Holy Spirit, heal and reconcile!" We continue to believe that the present reality and future fulfilment of the kingdom of God is the global and holistic content and horizon of *missio Dei*. But we do not pretend that this new creation, this life with divine quality, will be the result of our transforming actions and political wisdom, however important and essential these are.

The role of churches and Christians within *missio Dei* is central, yet nevertheless it is limited limited: to give witness to God's healing and reconciling identity and to build, renew and multiply communities where something of this new life can be experienced (in the sense of "first fruits"). Some have qualified this attempt as a move from a "prophetic" to a more "priestly" mission. I prefer to speak of a move from a "messianic" to a "pastoral" approach to mission.

Let me try to explain what this means. In my use of the term, a "messianic" formulation of Christian involvement affirms a constant and direct link between human words and actions and the advancement of the kingdom of God within a certain understanding of historical progress. It can easily fall into a "God-with-us" spirituality leading to crusades in mission and/or politics and so domesticate God within a dogmatic approach to Christianity and world history.

A "pastoral" missiology, as I understand it, tries to link:
- the *holistic purpose* of God for creation and humanity;
- the *community life* of the local church (which includes worship, sacraments, sharing and witness) as the expression of the church universal in its socio-political context; and
- the transforming power of the Spirit in people's communal *and personal lives.*

A "pastoral" approach also acknowledges a potential discontinuity between these three levels and puts an emphasis on the quality of community life and on the attention to personal needs, without pretending to know the mind of God and history's final end.

Such a "pastoral" approach will bear prophetic features when a community authentically witnesses to the kingdom of God in its specific socio-political context. To move away from a "messianic" approach does not mean to renounce standing for justice and advocating for those who are the victims of oppressive people, processes, communities, structures or spiritual forces. Prophecy is a vital element of mission, as ecumenical missiology has rightly affirmed and well practiced.

The programme of Athens reflected such an emphasis on the "pastoral" approach in the way the days were structured and the significant opportunities provided for common prayer, Bible meditation and personal sharing, in addition to theological debates. We don't pretend that Athens was an exception among ecumenical conferences because we built on earlier experiences. What was new, perhaps, was the CWME commission's decision to refrain from adding any other objective to that of enabling participants to experience a healing and reconciling community, at least partially, during the five days passed in Aghios Andreas.

3. Reconcile a *Missio Dei* Approach with *Missio Ecclesiae*

The double title chosen by the CWME commission was, and is, an indicator of the intention to keep the two approaches in creative tension. Since the International Missionary Council (IMC) Conference in Willingen in 1952, the wide *missio Dei* perspective gained in importance in the ecumenical movement, in reaction to narrower or exclusively ecclesiocentric formulations of the missionary task. It was essential indeed to liberate Christian witness from narrow perspectives, as if the triune God's presence in, and availability to, the world was manifested only inside the visible frontiers of existing church life. The whole "oikoumene" as inhabited world, and ultimately the whole creation, was to become the horizon and space for God's challenging and life-enabling presence. Ecumenical missiology widened its scope to include social, political and religious movements or institutions in its vision of history moving towards the accomplishment of God's promises of peace and justice. It did so in some extreme formulations by neglecting the specific purpose and mission of the church, disregarding the spiritual needs of persons and communities, and uncritically referring to a linear Western perspective on time and history, considered as "progress".

Post-modern approaches then started to challenge all the so-called "grand narratives" and the question had to be raised whether any concept of *missio Dei* linked with an interpretation of history was not such a "grand narrative", the legitimacy of which has been challenged by philosophers. Reflections shared by the CWME's affiliated bodies and related networks or theological institutions[4] led the commission to make that choice. We decided to keep the reference to *missio Dei* as expressing our conviction that God has a holistic and global vision and purpose for humanity and creation. "Come, Holy Spirit, heal and reconcile" thus became the slogan and the text of our much cherished conference hymn. Much has been said about the importance of hymns in Christian spirituality. Athens remains intensely present in my own emotional life when I sing or hear the hymn.

The second part of the title contains what we understand as the mandate, the *missio ecclesiae*: "Called in Christ to be reconciling and healing communities". For the 2005 mission conference, we decided to concentrate our attention on the specific importance of the edification of missional churches as healing and reconciling communities. The limitation may be criticized, but since Athens came shortly before the Ninth WCC assembly of February 2006, in which the full width of ecumenical theology and action responding to God's transforming will and power was to be highlighted,[5] there was justification for a more focused approach.

---

[4] Cf. the proceedings of a significant theological consultation held 50 years after the Willingen mission conference, held again in Willingen, Germany in 2002, *IRM* Vol. XCII No 367, October 2003, "Missio Dei Revisited, Willingen 1952-2002". The CWME position had already been formulated indirectly in the statement adopted by the commission in 2000, entitled "Mission and Evangelism in Unity Today", in: *You are the light of the world. Statements on Mission by the WCC 1980-2005*. Geneva, WCC, 2005.

[5] the theme of the 2006 Porto Alegre assembly was: "God, in your grace, transform the world".

A wide mission agenda has marked ecumenical theology since the integration of the IMC and the WCC in 1961. Every world mission conference, however, included in at least one of its sections ecclesiological reflections or other work on church partnerships or the sharing of personnel. Even some of the most radical conferences, such as Bangkok or Melbourne, have produced significant documents on the role of the church in mission. Section III of the 1980 Melbourne conference may be counted as one of the best -- but least highlighted -- examples of such an emphasis. Much of Melbourne's section III report influenced the famous Ecumenical Affirmation of 1982.[6] The specificity of the Athens conference was to have put more theological weight on *missio ecclesiae*, in a conscious attempt to find a better balance between the wide and the specifically church-related approaches to mission. In recent years, the Faith and Order Commission increasingly included a missional perspective in its ecclesiological studies and texts.[7] CWME's "Athenian emphasis" allows for a certain convergence in ecumenical theology.

Any follow-up must keep this indispensable link between *missio Dei* and *missio ecclesiae*. Pursuing what it means for the church to be missional as healing and reconciling community will allow us to revisit in a most creative way the best of the insights gained in earlier decades,[8] but it also will open our minds and hearts to the new challenges and opportunities brought to the ecumenical movement by the growth and increasing importance of Pentecostal and charismatic missions. The potentiality of a "rapprochement" between missiology and pastoral theology should allow for an authentic consideration of the necessarily spiritual grounding of a community that presumes to offer healing and reconciliation, as well as of the religious nature of human beings.

4. "Reconciling" Missiology - Opportunities and Challenges

Reconciliation has again become one of the main themes of ecumenical thinking and practice, clearly reflecting social and political realities and experiences. In earlier times, reconciliation appeared in dogmatic theologies in parallel to the treatment of justification and related doctrines but in rather theoretical and often abstract language. Often in ecumenical mission conferences it was referred to as the content of the gospel,[9] but the concept not explored in detail nor in its consequences. Drawing on recent worldwide experiences and reflections (in particular in South Africa and Latin America), the study process in and around Athens attempted to clarify the link between the three dynamics of reconciliation and our mission:

The *vertical* dynamic of reconciliation is offered and realized by God, in favour of humans. It is the re-establishment of just and healed relations between God and humanity, both as individuals and as a collective. This has a specifically religious

---

[6] The section III report even included a chapter on "healing communities", not taken up in the 1982 document, but to which one could refer again today with profit. Cf. *Your Kingdom Come – Mission perspectives. Report on the Conference on World Mission and Evangelism, Melbourne, Australia, 12-25 May 1980.* Geneva, WCC, 1980, pp.193-207 (199-200).

[7] Cf. *The Nature and Mission of the Church. A Stage on the Way to a Common Statement.* Geneva, WCC, 2005, Faith and Order Paper No 198.

[8] Such as the intentions of the "missionary structure of the congregation" study process of the sixties.

[9] The 1952 Willingen IMC conference highlighted reconciliation in its approach, which led to the development of the *missio Dei* theology.

or spiritual characteristic embodied in the message, its proclamation within and outside the church and in the sacraments.

The *horizontal* dynamic of reconciliation between human collectivities (ethnic, social or national) is made possible through Christ's death on the cross. In theology, we affirm that the struggle for healing and reconciliation has become possible because the most fundamental division between humans lost its inevitable character as a consequence of Christ's dying on the cross (as clearly emphasized by Paul in Galatians and in the hymns of Ephesians and Colossians).

The *circular* or cosmic dynamic of reconciliation points to the modified relationship between God, humans and the creation in general, as the new creation is both already present yet still expected.

The emphasis of the CWME's work and documents was mainly on the second aspect of reconciliation, whereas the liturgical setting of the programme of Athens was an attempt to provide space for an experience of, and response to, the first aspect.

I see at least four main challenges ahead of us:

(1) We must strive to understand and work out what it means that God's mission has an ecological purpose, i.e. to *renew the whole creation.* Whereas the reconciliation of creation is not as such humanity's agenda, but that of *missio Dei,* it has immeasurable consequences on the definition of the priorities for *missio ecclesiae,* if the church's witness is to reflect God's identity and purpose. Athens did not deal sufficiently with this topic. It must be taken up urgently in the following three dimensions:

- the cosmic horizon of *missio Dei* must find an expression in communitarian liturgy and personal spirituality or mysticism. Our spirituality must express our sharing in the joy of the new creation made possible in Christ and our participation in the suffering of creation, alienated as a consequence of the power of sin and abuse by humanity;
- our theological task is to move away from an anthropocentric approach to God's mission and to history, yet without falling into a divinization of creation. Such new missiology will have to relate to intercultural and interreligious dialogues;
- Christian ethics, both personal and community oriented, is to be redefined to grasp the urgency of the revolution in culture and society which is required and now scientifically undergirded. Whereas Christianity has contributed to the present domination of creation by humanity, it could draw on its own traditions (ascetism, mystics) to redefine creation-friendly ethics; and
- none of these makes sense without a clear prophetic stance when addressing global or local destructive and alienating policies and practices. The present emphasis on short-term profits and efficiency on the financial markets, as well as on political ideologies, must be denounced and long-term sustainable policies proposed and supported.[10]

---

[10] The most recent work on mission and creation in ecumenical circles took place at a consultation organized in September 2006 at the John Knox Centre near Geneva. Cf. Lukas Vischer (ed): *Witnessing in the Midst of a Suffering Creation.* Report and Papers from an international Consultation at the John Knox Centre, Geneva, from 17-21 Septembre, 2006. Geneva, 2007, 234p.

(2) We must interpret how the church's mediating role links with its prophetic calling. This must attempt to balance two essential missiological functions within a theology of reconciliation -- the role of mediator and the advocate for the victims.

Referring to the understanding of the Holy Spirit as "go-between God" (John V. Taylor) and to experiences such as the election-monitoring groups in South Africa, the preparatory document on mission as reconciliation urges churches to assume their mission as "go-between", to overcome violence by engaging in the delicate and often dangerous role of mediation between partners to conflicts.[11] Churches, peace groups or (cross-cultural) ecumenical workers in mission should be encouraged (and trained) to invent with creativity invent or seize opportunities for dialogue as means to live out conflicts and diminish violence. This requires an ability to gain the confidence of most, if not all, involved parties to conflicts and the courage to stand in the dangerous middle when requested to do so.

The other function grows out of a particular solidarity for the victims of violence, abuse, injustice, threats, war, racism and other forms of discrimination. The Athens preparatory paper sees the church's reconciliation ministry as witnessing to God's preference for the victims. By stressing the necessity of giving priority to the victims, Athens recaptures the earlier theological language of "God's preferential option for the poor". It may well be that in contemporary terms, the most urgent advocacy for the poor is to take care of and advocate for the victims of conflicts, political, economic, cultural or family violence; more precisely, to offer a space where the victims themselves can speak and tell their stories. It is one of the best contributions of the Urban Rural Mission (URM) movement to such a ministry that it insisted on letting the poor tell their stories and that it developed or reinterpreted techniques for enabling them to do so. In reconciliation theology, "story telling" receives its place and significance as a means to witness to God's preferential option for the victims.[12] As Athens has shown, this role is also being played by churches of the Pentecostal or the evangelical traditions, to name but those who are not members of the WCC.[13]

A future reflection should ponder whether such views could be creatively linked with earlier insights formulated by one of the former WCC evangelism secretaries, Raymond Fung, who showed that humans are both sinners and victims of sin. Following Christ's way, we may understand that mission can and should manifest its concern for both sinners and the victims of sin. Reconciliation processes enable us to address both facts – provided these processes are guided with wisdom and given enough time to mature.

---

[11] Ref: Mission as ministry of reconciliation. CWME Preparatory Paper No 10, in this book.

[12] Cf URM – positions of people in struggle. CWME Preparatory Paper No 9 and URM Synaxis – both in this book. As all work on reconciliation stresses, the precise definition of who is perpetrator and victim may be easy in some cases, but overlapping in others.

[13] One of the best papers worked out in an international consultation on reconciliation was produced in a group born out of the 2004 Forum on World Evangelization, organized in Pattaya, Thailand by the Lausanne Committee for World Evangelization. Cf. *Reconciliation as the Mission of God. Christian Witness in a World of Destructive Conflicts.* A 2005 paper from 47 Christian leaders across the world. www. reconciliationnetwork.com

In trying to answer under what conditions and in what contexts the mediating and prophetic (advocacy) roles are compatible and how they may be related, we might well be inspired to interpret again how and why the prophetic and wisdom traditions overlap in the Old Testament. At the same time, we must remain aware that this question will not be solved in theory alone, but by learning from case studies.

(3) We need to recapture the *link between reconciliation and evangelism*. Paul understands the ministry of reconciliation as including an urgent call to humans to accept being reconciled with God (2 Cor. 5: 19 – 6:2). In other words, in Pauline theology there is no reconciliation without a qualified response to an evangelistic call. The search for an ecumenically responsible evangelism was not at the centre of the preparatory process nor of the Athens conference, and this lack of emphasis has been rightly criticized, in particular from European mission circles and by Pentecostals and evangelicals. There is a tendency in ecumenical and "mainline" networks to stick to a primarily socially oriented theology of witness, in which holistic mission is understood as *diakonia* with the added value of worship or prayer, the whole re-baptized as the "ministry of reconciliation". Such a combined approach of *diakonia* or solidarity plus liturgy makes much sense as a form of Christian witness in a religiously plural world, in two conditions. One is to gain clarity as to the intimate link between solidarity and the gospel, the ground on which Christians stand, and the content of their faith and hope; the other is to take care not to use diaconal or solidarity work to cover purposes of religious conquest and proselytism.[14]

The 1996 world mission conference in Salvador da Bahía, Brazil, offered some reflections on culture-sensitive evangelism which could be helpful in this search. The report of section I referred to the link between preaching and healing in Isa. 61:1, the gentleness and caring love of the messenger in 1 Thess. 1:7-8, the love of Christ as motive in 2 Cor. 5:14, the humility of the evangelist in Phil. 2:5-8 and the Emmaus story near the end of Luke's gospel. In Salvador's exploration of culture-sensitive evangelism, dialogue and cooperation in community development were seen as socially and culturally appropriate forms of witness, so long as dialogue was not seen as displacing proclamation. Another form of respectful evangelism referred to in 1996 was "presence", that is, an effort to get to know and understand people in a community, listen and learn, followed by a sharing of interests, questions, objectives and priorities. "At the right time people could be invited to participate in the story of the gospel."[15] In some cases, the conference added, "silent solidarity may be the most appropriate form of Christian witness. Others insist that there is no substitute for preaching the word. While acknowledging that Christian presence within communities is important, they also see the need for witnessing to the signs of the dynamic movement of the Spirit and actively voicing the gospel. ...In contexts where the dominant

---

[14] Since the Athens conference, a common international study process was launched between the WCC and the Pontifical Council for Interreligious Dialogue to elaborate a common "code of conduct on conversion" addressing potential misuse of emergency aid and development for evangelistic purposes.
[15] All references to and quotes from Salvador are taken from: Christopher Duraisingh (ed.): *Called to One Hope. The Gospel in Diverse Cultures.* Geneva, WCC, 1998, pp.37-39, in the chapter "Voicing the Gospel: Evangelism today", part of the report of section I "Authentic Witness within Each Culture".

culture is hostile to the proclamation of the gospel message, some suggest the need to provide a 'safe space' for spirituality to germinate, where the Jesus story can be revealed." In line with earlier mission conferences, Salvador reaffirmed the necessary link between words and works, between evangelism and solidarity. It insisted on the importance of the "integrity of all involved: the person offering the witness, the congregation or faith community to which the witness or the messenger belongs" and the respect of the integrity of the community "to which witness is being offered".

The above-mentioned reflections may help us in pursuing the meaning behind the Pauline understanding of the ministry of reconciliation that includes proclamation and an insistent call to accept God's reconciling offer. We must continue to find a way to link the concern for overcoming conflicts and violence, for building a society in which former enemies cooperate in justice and the clear witness pointing to the one Jesus Christ through whom reconciliation became possible. Moreover, evangelism not only points to Jesus Christ, but includes the call to be reconciled with God through him (2 Cor. 5:20 b and 6:1). Indeed, in the New Testament there is an intimate, but not dogmatically fixed, relation between "objective" reconciliation through Christ and its effect or concrete realization in one's personal life, mind, heart and body. To be reconciled is the result of a mysteriously combined dynamic of personal decision and acceptance (which can take the form of a dramatic conversion or of a slow change on a long journey) with the initiative of the Holy Spirit to come and inhabit the most intimate core of our being as persons and communities and to radiate from there in all our words and acts ("Come, Holy Spirit...").[16]

(4) *Visible church unity* is again high on the agenda of ecumenical missiology. There is no way for churches to pretend to have any competence to offer regarding reconciliation processes in the secular or religious world, if they are unable to prove their passion for the healing of memories and the reconciliation of divided churches in Christianity itself. Mission and unity are two cornerstones of ecclesiology.

Mission conceived separately from the search for visible unity misses a key element of the gospel: such an understanding implies that the calling together of a community of disciples of various cultural and social origins, the constitution of an alternative community as an embodiment and signpost of the coming kingdom, was not an integral part of Jesus' message. It also falls short of witnessing to the imperfect, but real, correspondence between the visible *koinonia* of the worshipping church and the confessed *koinonia* of the triune God. It fails to point to the final aim of God's mission, which is to unite everything that exists with God on earth and in heaven. The ultimate end is not judgment or separation but unity. How both relate, we do not know, but our witness must not bypass the latter.

---

[16] For a reflection on reconciliation and evangelism, we could also draw on insights shared in the 1987 Stuttgart Declaration which resulted from a common consultation between representatives of the WCC /CWME and of the Lausanne Committee for World Evangelization, and the seminar on evangelism from an ecumenical perspective held at the Ecumenical Institute, Bossey, Switzerland, in June 2006. Papers from the latter will be published in *IRM* July/October 2007.

The passion for unity, for which our Lord prayed at the time of his trial and death and on which he insisted as his testament, corresponds with the aim that the whole world may understand and believe who God is, the Trinity of love. In John 17, the reason why Jesus prays that the disciples may be one is so that the world may believe that the Father sent the Son to offer salvation to all. The search for unity without relating it to mission misses that essential role of the church in God's plan as well as the sending dynamics of the Son's and his disciples' lives (John 20). And if the church is to be in this time and world the "body" of Christ, the community assembled around his eucharistic table, unity must become visible.

However, at Athens we experienced once more how difficult and painful we find the way toward the real manifestation of that given and promised visible unity. Because of its strong emphasis on group sharing, healing and community-building, the 2005 mission conference increased the sense of frustration with church divisions for quite a number of participants, due to the impossibility of celebrating the eucharist together despite the deep spiritual communion that was being experienced.

To resume working on mission and unity, focusing respectively on ecclesiology and mission, thus seems a logical consequence of Athens and may explain why the WCC has decided to include both concerns and the related work of the Commission on Faith and Order and the CWME, in one new programme on "Unity, Mission, Evangelism and Spirituality".

5. Christian Theologies of Healing

Around Athens, we attempted to recapture the indispensable link between the mission of the church and its healing ministry and so to unite two main traditional networks of the WCC, the mission movement and the Christian Medical Commission. For years, the ministry of healing had been considered mainly as pertaining to the diaconal and development services of the church, following the Western logic of division of tasks between spiritual and material, soul, mind and body. We must heal our theologies from the divisions and shortcomings of radical Enlightenment or secular approaches and from denominational protectionism.

One could probably affirm that work around the healing ministry had some prominence at the Athens conference, in its various aspects, from prayer for healing and healing services to pastoral care, from listening to people living with HIV and AIDS to testimonies of representatives of the Ecumenical Disability Advocates Network (EDAN). I see the following tasks ahead and would hope that they could be undertaken on the basis of, or in dialogue with, the Athens preparatory paper on the healing mission of the church (No. 11) and the results of the consultation held in Breklum, Germany, in September, 2005 as a follow-up on the mission conference[17]:

[17] *IRM* Vol. 95, Nos 376/77, Jan/April 2006 «The global health situation and the mission of the church in the 21st century».

- Revisit the denominational theologies of *charisms*, the gifts of the Spirit, and proceed with an ecumenical dialogue on their importance, variety and distribution in church and world, with particular attention to those pertaining to the healing ministry, to the edification of a reconciling community and to the search for visible unity[18];

- Deepen existing reflections on *ecclesiology and mission* or on the missional character of the church by viewing them in relation with acknowledged characteristics of a healing community;

- Pursue the promising theological *dialogue between Pentecostals and Christians living with disabilities*, which started in Athens with high visibility and was deepened in the aforementioned Breklum consultation between two senior African theologians.[19] This could lead to a balanced understanding of the relationship between faith, cure and healing, of the role of the Holy Spirit and medical cures, and lead to a holistic and respectful pastoral approach to people who suffer from illness, injury, disability, oppression, violence or other evils;

- Encourage churches to take up the challenge put to them by the World Health Organization that *mental health* issues affect important segments of the population in both the global North and South, and expect religious communities to show their competence and importance on that matter. Addressing this issue will contribute to a revised and non-dogmatic theology of healing and to the distinction between witness and proselytism; and

- Future dialogues on the healing ministry and mission should relate to the essential role of *worldviews and cultures* on the perception of what health, healing, suffering and evil are, what it means to be whole and safe. There is no one single worldwide understanding of anthropology in the context of society, creation and the divine. Both spiritual and medical approaches to illness and sickness are culture-bound and not universal or "neutral", even if elements of universality cannot be denied. Discernment is required for a renewed intercultural dialogue on the healing ministry. In this way, the ecumenical movement could resume the work on gospel and cultures, somewhat neglected after the world mission conference in Salvador da Bahía.

6. The Role of World Religions in God's Purpose and the Mission of the Church

Since the famous consensus formulation found at the world mission conference of San Antonio 1989, no real theological progress has been made in the CWME,

---

[18] Much remarkable ecumenical work has been done on ministry and sacraments, but one misses an emphasis on dialogue between churches and church traditions on *charisms*, a dialogue which could rely on some excellent existing material.
[19] See the remarkable dialogue between Samuel Kabue and Opoku Onyinah in *IRM*, Jan/April 2006, *op.cit.*, pp.112-127.

nor in the WCC, on the question. The preparatory document No 13 for the Athens conference carried the results of a two-year reflection process by scholars linked to the WCC's networks on Faith and Order, Mission and Dialogue. That process was an attempt to reopen the question of the relation between Christians and people of other religions at a theological level. The reactions during the workshops dedicated to that document in Athens showed that much more study and intra-Christian dialogue is needed to come to minimal forms of common understanding and vision on this question within the mission networks of the WCC.[20]

Where do we stand on this question? The document emphasizes hospitality as a key concept for a reconciling mission, and links it with a reference to a holistic understanding of *missio Dei* but with an "apophatic" touch – there is much we don't know about God and God's priorities, as well as about subjects like final salvation. This option of emphasizing hospitality is only understandable when linked with the vision that all humans are on a life-long pilgrimage, within which they meet, share, enter into conflict and may experience solidarity. It makes sense only when linked with an insistence on mission in humility and vulnerability and the hope that encounters may lead to mutual transformation. In that context, the document affirms the right and necessity of Christian witness to neighbours of other faiths. On the "ministry of reconciliation", the document says:

> "(The ministry of reconciliation) presupposes both our witness to the 'other'" about God in Christ and our openness to allow God to speak to us through the 'other'. Mission when understood in this light has no room for triumphalism; it contributes to removing the causes for religious animosity and the violence that often goes with it. Hospitality requires Christians to accept others as created in the image of God, knowing that God may talk to us through others to teach and transform us, even as God may use us to transform others." (§ 42)

The participants who dealt with this theme were divided as to the theological wisdom of the approach. One group welcomed the text as one of the best they had received from the WCC in many years, while the majority criticized it for not taking sufficient consideration of the difference between the general revelation of God and the special revelation in Christ's incarnation leading to the cross. According to the critiques, the paper fails to explain how hospitality is articulated with the evangelistic mandate. Some also found that the document neglected the fundamental salvific role of Christ.

We have to revisit the matter. It seems to me that we can use the frame outlined above, i.e. the clustering of hospitality, *missio Dei*, apophatic theology, pilgrimage and mutual transformation because essential elements of the biblical witness are taken care of. We may need to connect those considerations with an exegesis of Paul's manner of addressing the Athenians when meeting them at the Areopagus (Acts 17). His well- edited speech combines various approaches. He draws on the religious and

---

[20] The preparatory document No 13 as well as the introductions and prepared contributions to the workshop (synaxis) held in Athens are reproduced in this book.

philosophical tradition of his audience first, affirming its adequacy as an expression of truth because it recognizes God's presence and proximity (v. 22-28). Drawing on the same religious traditions, however, he indicates how they lead to criticism of the inadequacies of the popular forms of religion he has encountered (v. 22-29). These two approaches to the "high" and "low" philosophy or religion of the Athenians, in form of dialogue and content, are then followed by a third form of communication, the reference to Christ's role within God's mission and a call to conversion (v. 30-31). In Acts 17, the precise theological link between the three "strategies of communication" is not evident and it is the last part, the call to conversion, which is least detailed and elaborated in the text. Referring to preparatory document No 13, one could say that participants at the Athens conference found that the final lacked any reflection of the last communication form of Acts 17.

The New Testament itself gives only a few examples of direct evangelistic communication to non-Christians.[21] A clear parallel to the last part of Paul's missionary addresses to gentiles in Acts (14 and 17) is found in his first letter, I Thessalonians, at the end of chapter 1. Other classical and relevant texts which may give an indication as to how to witness to those "outside" the community, and the Jewish tradition, are Colossians 4: 5-6 with its remarkable balance between grace and challenge and I Peter 3:13-17 where we are encouraged to give testimony to the hope we have in Christ.

We may try in future to work on revising the document on Christian identity and religious plurality by elaborating on the "last" part of Paul's speech to the Athenians, drawing also on these other texts which allude to what one could call an inviting and respectful witness. And we may find ways to link such reflections with a draft discernment of the role of Christ and the Spirit in God's mission and the consequences this may have for our understanding of the place and role of other religions. But we will be well advised to take care to leave an "uncertainty factor" in our theological search. That "uncertainty factor" has to do with what we described earlier as the mysterious link between personal acceptance of the gospel and the Holy Spirit's indwelling presence and, ultimately, with our limited knowledge of God's inner-trinitarian relationships and God's mission of salvation in and for the world[22].

7. A Missional Pneumatology Leads to a Trinitarian Missiology

Athens provided the opportunity to reopen an ecumenical debate on pneumatology, essential indeed both for a relevant missiology in a world of many religions, as well as in a context in which humanity must find a new self-understanding as part of creation. As Kirsteen Kim has shown extensively in various articles and recent or forthcoming books,[23] reflection on pneumatology was an unfinished task since

---

[21] If we except Jesus' own preaching (mainly) to the Jews in Jerusalem and Palestine.

[22] In that sense, the so-called consensus formulation of San Antonio still carries much wisdom, affirming in substance "'We cannot point to any other way of salvation than Jesus Christ; at the same time we cannot set limits to the saving power of God.' There is a tension between these two statements, a tension which has not yet been resolved" (as referred to in the document "Mission and Evangelism in Unity Today", in: *You are the light of the world, op.cit.* p. 81)

[23] *The Holy Spirit in the World. A global conversation.* Maryknoll, NY, Orbis, 2007.

the intense debates at the 1991 Canberra assembly of the WCC. The preparatory process for Athens intended to reopen the question of the relevance of a renewed pneumatology for mission and the conference built on important contributions from Orthodox and Pentecostal theologians as well as from Kirsteen Kim herself; she has succeeded in synthesizing new and traditional perspectives, suggesting a pattern for the development of a pneumatological missiology within a trinitarian framework. In addition to the theological tasks hinted at in the earlier chapters, two more seem essential now:

- The tentative, but promising *dialogue on the Holy Spirit between Orthodox and Pentecostal* theologians, which started in Athens, must continue and be broadened for the benefit of both traditions, and of the ecumenical movement as a whole; and

- dealing with pneumatology obliges us to face a difficult intercultural question, the one of the *world-view* which does or should influence our theology. Is reality made of one spirit or do we have to deal with a reality made up of various and perhaps conflicting spirits? In other words, do we base our theology on a "non-spirit" cosmology (a fully secular approach), a "one-spirit" cosmology (every spiritual phenomenon is related to God) or a "many-spirits" cosmology (in which there is something like a conflict between various spiritual realms or forces)? We encountered this type of question very clearly in the preparatory work on the healing ministry, especially in dialogues with Pentecostals in Africa.[24] That form of the dialogue of world-views has not surfaced often in the North-South debates and may well be one of the most difficult ecumenical and intercultural tasks ahead of us. The question can be seen as a cultural issue, each region of the world having its own world-view, or as a theological question, having to do with biblical hermeneutics, or as a subtle combination of both. The answer to the question of the reality and role of the spirit(s) has immense consequences on mission strategy and on pastoral theology.

One must conclude these provisional reflections on Athens. The move to a much more pneumatologically oriented approach to mission has been welcomed by Orthodox and Pentecostal participants and could indeed – at least I strongly hope so – bring new missional dynamics in our anthropology and ecclesiology, as well as in our creation theology. The risk, however, lies in disregarding a warning coming from the New Testament itself. As many exegetes have discerned, there is practically no passage in the New Testament clearly affirming a universal presence of the Holy Spirit in humanity and creation. Of course, the basis of Christian theology has its roots in the Old Testament where God's Spirit, Word and Wisdom are confessed as both transcendent and immanent with regard to creation and there is a clear affirmation of such presence and action outside God's chosen people. One can thus argue that it doesn't have to be reaffirmed. Still, we need a clarification regarding the Holy Spirit, in particular because there are texts in the New Testament which mention the universal presence of God in humanity

---

[24] Cf. IRM Vol. 93, Nos 370/71, July/October 2004, "Divine Healing, Pentecostalisms and Mission" and also the CWME Preparatory Document No 11 on the Healing Mission of the Church.

and creation. They refer, however, to the worldwide potential presence of Christ (cf. Matt. 25:31-45; Col. 1:12-20) and not to the worldwide action of the Spirit. One might want to discern an indirect hint for the interpreting community: the worldwide presence of God cannot be separated from the person of Christ.

The following observations may help us not to over-emphasize the matter. First, in Paul's letters, the functions of God, Christ and the Spirit are not fixed once for ever (1 Cor. 12:4-5). Second, there is the hint in Romans 8 of the potential parallel between the yearning of the Spirit within Christians and the Spirit's yearning with the suffering creation. Third, in John 3:8, Jesus uses the parable of the wind which can be interpreted as referring directly to an attribution of the Spirit.[25] Fourth, the ethical fruit of the Spirit does not seem to be restricted to Christians.

We must try to find a balanced way forward and this is the reason for the title of this last part of my paper. Definitely, a missiology which starts with the Holy Spirit will lead us to a renewed dynamic spirituality and missional life, both as persons and as communities, inspired by the incredibly radical content of the Spirit's influence (see Luke 4:18 ff, which is a kind of pneumatological manifesto), its non-violent approach to reality but also its challenge to the world as it is (John 16:7 ff). Missiology rooted in the Spirit will be able to keep together, in a holistic way, bold but pastorally responsible evangelism, healing and reconciling community, challenging prophecy (both within and outside the church), kingdom ethics, love and community edification, as well as openness to the Spirit's blowing where it wills.

What should be avoided, however, is to de-link that dynamic from Christ's incarnation and Jesus' death and resurrection and so fall into a general or generous religious philosophy of encompassing love and reconciliation in a nice and sinless world. The New Testament doesn't allow us to bypass the fact that Christ had to die for our salvation, for reconciliation. Mission must move from a pneumatological point of departure to a fully trinitarian faithfulness. "Come Holy Spirit, heal and reconcile" was the first theme of Athens. But it could not have produced such fruitful spirituality without the second: "Called in Christ to be reconciling and healing communities". The reference to Christ and to the specific mission of the church are key also for the future of ecumenical missiology. A missional pneumatology must lead to a trinitarian missiology.

Jacques Matthey

---

[25] Another interpretation considers it a meteorological parable for how difficult it is to understand how a person can have been baptized by the Spirit: one can't discern his/her origin or final end without the help of the Spirit.

APPENDICES

1. Participants List

Title	First Name	Last Name	Country	Organisation	Capacity
Rev.	Kjetil	Aano	Norway	Church of Norway / Council on Ecumenical & International Relations	Delegate from a WCC member church
Ms	Inger	Aasa-Marklund	Sweden	Church of Sweden	Adviser/Consultant
Rev.	Goergios	Adam	Greece	Greek Evangelical Church	Delegate from a WCC member church
Rev.	Subodh	Adhikary	Bangladesh	National Council of Churches, Bangladesh	Delegate from a CWME affiliated body
Pfarrer	Dezso Zoutan	Adorjani	Romania	Evangelical Church of the Augsburg Confession in Romania	Delegate from a WCC member church
Bishop		Agathangelos	Greece	Church of Greece	Member of the Athens Local Arrangements Committee
Sister	Maria Aranzazu	Aguado	United States of America	Roman Catholic Church	Delegate from the Roman Catholic church
Rev. Dr	Risto	Ahonen	Finland	Finnish Evangelical Lutheran Mission	Delegate from an Evangelical church/body
Reverend Dr	Athanasius Amos	Akunda	South Africa	Greek Archdiocese of Johannesburg and Pretoria	Delegate from a WCC member church
Mr.	Stefanos	Alexopoulos	Greece	Church of Greece	Delegate from a WCC member church
Dr	E. Antony	Allen	Jamaica	Whole Person Resource Centre, Jamaica	Adviser/Consultant
Sra	Gabriela	Amaya	Argentina	Evangelical Methodist Church of Argentina	Delegate from a WCC member church
Rev. Dr	Allan	Anderson	United Kingdom	Research Unit for Pentecostal Studies, University of Birmingham	Adviser/Consultant
Madame	Magalie	Andral	France	French Evangelical Department for Apostolic Action	Delegate from an Evangelical church/body
Rev.	Barbara	Andrews	Canada	Anglican Church of Canada	Delegate from a WCC member church
Revda	Dora	Arce	Cuba	Presbyterian Reformed Church in Cuba	Delegate from a WCC member church
Mr	Gérald	Arci	Switzerland	World Council of Churches	WCC staff
Ms.	Susanna	Argyri	Greece	World Council of Churches	Co-opted staff
Pastor	Washington Miguel	Armas Benavides	Ecuador	Latin American Council of Churches	Delegate from wider constituency - other
Mr	Arsenios	Arsenakis	Greece	Church of Greece	Steward
Reverend Dr	Johnson	Asamoah-Gyadu	Ghana	African Theological Fellowship	Delegate from wider constituency - other
Rev.	Peter	Ashton	Israel	Franciscan Custody of the Holy Land	Delegate from the Roman Catholic church
Dr	Jesudas	Athyal	India	Mar Thoma Syrian Church of Malabar	Adviser/Consultant
Ms	Marta	Axner	Sweden	Church of Sweden	Delegate from a WCC member church
Mr	Vahagn	Azizyan	Armenia	Armenian Apostolic Church (Holy See of Etchmiadzin)	Steward
Mr	Christos	Balaskas	Greece	Church of Greece	Steward
Rev.	Tevita	Banivanua	Fiji	South Pacific Association of Theological Schools	Delegate from wider constituency - other
Father	John	Banoub	Zambia	Coptic Orthodox Church	Delegate from a WCC member church
Fr	Issak	Barakat	Lebanon	Orthodox Church of Antioch	Delegate from a WCC member church
Mr	Elter Nehemias Santos	Barbosa	Brazil		Steward
Revda	Ana Maria	Barolin Siboldi	Uruguay	Methodist Church in Uruguay	Delegate from a WCC member church
Rev.	Simon	Barrow	United Kingdom	Churches' Commission on Mission	Delegate from a CWME affiliated body
Pastor	Guenter	Baum	Germany	Association of Protestant Churches and Missions in Germany	Delegate from a CWME affiliated body
M.	Jean-Nicolas	Bazin	Switzerland	World Council of Churches	WCC staff
Herrn Prof. Dr	Dieter	Becker	Germany	International Association for mission Studies	Adviser/Consultant
Mrs	June	Beckx Liem	Netherlands	Samen Kerk In Nederland (SKIN)	Adviser/Consultant
Pfarrerin	Jutta	Beldermann	Germany	United Evangelical Mission	Delegate from a WCC member church
Rev.	Andrew	Bell	New Zealand-Aotearoa	Presbyterian Church of Aotearoa New Zealand	Delegate from a WCC member church
Mr	Alexander	Belopopsky	Switzerland	World Council of Churches	WCC staff
Mr	Kenneth	Ben	Cook Islands	Cook Islands Christian Church	Delegate from a WCC member church
Madame	Eva	Berberian	Greece	Armenian Apostolic Church (Holy See of Cilicia)	Delegate from a WCC member church
Pastor	Katharine	Bergbusch	Canada	Evangelical Lutheran Church in Canada	Delegate from a WCC member church
Dr	Sara	Bhattacharji	India	Church of South India	Delegate from a WCC member church
Ms	Moumita	Biswas	India	National Council of Churches in India	Delegate from a CWME affiliated body
Mr	Gustavo Alberto	Bonato	Switzerland	World Council of Churches	WCC staff
Rev. Dr	Hyacinth Ione	Boothe	Jamaica	United Theological College of the West Indies (UTCWI)	Delegate from wider constituency - other
Mrs	Bethany	Borak	United States of America	Presbyterian Church (USA)	Delegate from a WCC member church
Rev.	Ruth Anne	Bottoms	United Kingdom	Baptist Union of Great Britain	Delegate from a WCC member church
Mr	Sotirios-Ange	Boukis	Greece	Greek Evangelical Church	Steward
Mrs	Lorraine	Boukis-Kefalas	Greece	Greek Evangelical Church	Steward
Rev.	Avedis	Boynerian	United States of America	Union of the Armenian Evangelical Churches in the Near East	Delegate from a WCC member church
Rev.Canon	Malcolm	Bradshaw	Greece	Church of England	Member of the Athens Local Arrangements Committee
Rev. Dr	Tobias	Brandner	Hong Kong	Church in Prisons of Hong Kong	Adviser/Consultant
Frau	Ulrike	Brodbeck	Germany	Association of Protestant Churches and Missions in Germany	Delegate from a WCC member church
Rev. Canon	Kathleen	Brown	Ireland	Church of Ireland	Delegate from a WCC member church
Mr	Stephen	Brown	France	Ecumenical News International	Spouse of participant
Dr	Humberto Fernando	Bullon Campos	Costa Rica	Fraternidad Teologica Latinoamericana	Delegate from wider constituency - other
Pasteur	Théo	Buss	Switzerland	Pain pour le Prochain	Interpreter

CWME - Athens, 09 - 16 May 2005
Participants List

Title	First Name	Last Name	Country	Organisation	Capacity
Dr	Gosbert	Byamungu	Switzerland	Bossey Ecumenical Institute	Delegate from the Roman Catholic church
Father	Alkiviadis	Calivas	United States of America	Ecumenical Patriarchate	Adviser/Consultant
Rev.	Phaedon	Cambouropoulos	Greece	Greek Evangelical Church	Member of the Athens Local Arrangements Committee
Reverend Dr	Jim	Campbell	United Kingdom	Irish Council of Churches	Delegate from a CWME affiliated body
Rev. (Ms)	Shengjie	Cao	China	China Christian Council	Guest
Brother	David	Carroll, FSC	United States of America	Roman Catholic Church	Delegate from the Roman Catholic church
Ms	Nilda	Castro	Vatican City	Pontifical Council for the Pastoral Care of Migrant & Itinerant People	Delegate from the Roman Catholic church
Ms	Alina Mosebo	Chabane	Lesotho	Lesotho Evangelical Church	Delegate from a WCC member church
Rev. Mrs	Heawon	Chae	Korea, Republic of	Presbyterian Church in the Republic of Korea	Delegate from a WCC member church
Rev. Prof. Dr	Sooil	Chai	Korea, Republic of	Presbyterian Church in the Republic of Korea	Delegate from a WCC member church
Dr	Sung-Bae	Chang	Korea, Republic of	Korean Methodist Church	Delegate from a WCC member church
Ms	Catherine	Chang	United States of America	Presbyterian Church (USA)	Delegate from a WCC member church
Mrs.	Heather	Chappel	Switzerland	World Council of Churches	Co-opted staff
Sister	Agnes	Charles	Italy	Roman Catholic Church	Delegate from the Roman Catholic church
Mr	Michael	Chatziyannis	Greece	United Bible Societies	Delegate from wider constituency - other
Ms	Meilin	Chen	China	China Christian Council	Delegate from a WCC member church
Rev. Dr	Nan-Jou	Chen	Taiwan	Presbyterian Church in Taiwan	Delegate from a WCC member church
Dr	Puunnoose Mathew	Cherical	India	Church of South India	Adviser/Consultant
Ms	Yeukai	Chikwizo	Zimbabwe	Africa University	Steward
Pasteure	Felicidade Naume	Chirinda	Mozambique	Presbyterian Church of Mozambique	Delegate from a CWME affiliated body
Rev.	Richard Chung-Sik	Choe	Canada	International Network Forum on Multicultural Ministry	Adviser/Consultant
Rev.	Vicken	Cholakian	Greece	Union of the Armenian Evangelical Churches in the Near East	Member of the Athens Local Arrangements Committee
Mr	Kaare Scheide	Christensen	Denmark	Evangelical Lutheran Church in Denmark	Delegate from a WCC member church
Rev.	Berit	Christensen	Denmark	Evangelical Lutheran Church in Denmark	Delegate from a WCC member church
Mr.	Christakis	Christophorou	Cyprus	Church of Cyprus	Delegate from a WCC member church
Rev. Dr	Keith	Clements	Switzerland	Conference of European Churches	Guest
Rt Rev. Dr	David	Coles	New Zealand-Aotearoa	Anglican Church in Aotearoa, New Zealand and Polynesia	Delegate from a WCC member church
Mrs	Joy	Coles	New Zealand-Aotearoa	Anglican Church in Aotearoa, New Zealand and Polynesia	Spouse of participant
Ms	Monica	Coll González	Cuba	Presbyterian Reformed Church in Cuba	Steward
Rev. Dr	Gianni	Colzani	Vatican City	Roman Catholic Church	Delegate from the Roman Catholic church
Dr	David Martin	Conway	United Kingdom	World Council of Churches	Interpreter
Prof. Rev. Dr	Omar	Cortés - Gaibur	Chile	Latin American Theological Fraternity	Delegate from wider constituency - other
Rt Rev. Bishop	Graham	Cray	United Kingdom	Church of England	Delegate from a WCC member church
Dr	James A.	Cress	United States of America	Seventh-day Adventist Church World Headquarters	Delegate from wider constituency - other
Rev.	Didier	Crouzet	France	Reformed Church of France	Delegate from a WCC member church
Mrs	Seongja	Crowe	Australia	International Network Forum on Multicultural Ministry	Adviser/Consultant
Rev.	Norman Colville	Crowe	Australia	International Network Forum on Multicultural Ministry	Adviser/Consultant
Rev.	Brent	Dahlseng	United States of America	Evangelical Lutheran Church in America	Accredited press
Canon	Tim	Dakin	United Kingdom	Church Mission Society	Delegate from a CWME affiliated body
Rev.	Boonsong	Dangruan	Thailand	Church of Christ in Thailand	Delegate from a CWME affiliated body
Dr	Richard	Daulay	Indonesia	Communion of Churches in Indonesia (PGI)	Delegate from a CWME affiliated body
Rev.	Mendelson Marcelino	Davila Amaya	Nicaragua	European Evangelical Alliance	Adviser/Consultant
Rev.	R. Randy	Day	United States of America	Presbyterian Church (USA)	Delegate from a WCC member church
Rev.	Niroshan	De Mel	Sri Lanka	Church of Ceylon	Delegate from a WCC member church
Pasteur	Félicité	Debat	France	Community of Churches in Mission	Delegate from a CWME affiliated body
Pasteur	Komla Edoh	Degbovi	Togo	Evangelical Presbyterian Church of Togo	Delegate from a WCC member church
Mr	Friedrich	Degenhardt	Switzerland	World Council of Churches	WCC staff
Prof.	Konstantinos	Delikostantis	Greece	Ecumenical Patriarchate	Adviser/Consultant
Ms	Jet	Den Hollander	Switzerland	World Alliance of Reformed Churches	Delegate from a WCC member church
Fr	Paula	Derec	Zambia	Coptic Orthodox Church	Delegate from a WCC member church
Mrs	Paula	Devejian	Armenia	Armenian Apostolic Church (Holy See of Etchmiadzin)	Delegate from a WCC member church
Mrs	Nynke	Dijkstra-Algra	Netherlands	European Evangelical Alliance	Delegate from an Evangelical church/body
Mr	Nikolaos	Dimitriadis	Greece	Church of Greece	Adviser/Consultant
Rev.	Bernard	Dinkelaker	Germany	Association of Protestant Churches and Missions in Germany	Delegate from a WCC member church
Ms	Adele	Djomo Ngomedje	Switzerland	World Council of Churches	WCC staff
H.B. Archbishop	Khoren	Doghramajian	Greece	Armenian Apostolic Church (Holy See of Cilicia)	Delegate from a CWME affiliated body
Ms	Panagiota	Dogka	Greece	Church of Greece	Steward
Mr	Frans	Dokman	Netherlands	International Association for mission Studies	Delegate from the Roman Catholic church

CWME - Athens, 09 - 16 May 2005
Participants List

Title	First Name	Last Name	Country	Organisation	Capacity
Mrs	Janneke	Doornebal	Netherlands	Netherlands Missionary Council	Delegate from a CWME affiliated body
Ms	Fleur	Dorrell	United Kingdom	Church of England	Delegate from a WCC member church
Rev. Dr	Rodney Dean	Drayton	Australia	Uniting Church in Australia	Delegate from a WCC member church
Frau	Annegret	Druke	Germany	Association of Protestant Churches and Missions in Germany	Delegate from wider constituency - other
Dr	Julia	Duany	United States of America	Global Reconciliation Network	Delegate from wider constituency - other
Rev. Dr	Cheryl	Dudley	United States of America	American Baptist Churches in the USA	Delegate from a WCC member church
Mr	Michael William (Mike)	Dumont	Canada	United Church of Canada	Steward
Dr	Annemarie	Dupré	Italy	Federation of Protestant Churches in Italy	Adviser/Consultant
Rev.	Sean	Dwan	Ireland	Missionary Society of St Columban	Delegate from the Roman Catholic church
Sister	Maureen Theresa	Dwan	New Zealand-Aotearoa	Roman Catholic Church	Delegate from the Roman Catholic church
Pastor	Jan	Edström	Finland	Finnish Ecumenical Council	Delegate from a CWME affiliated body
Ms	Anna	Edvardsson	Sweden	Mission Covenant Church of Sweden	Steward
Rt Rev.	Riah Abu	El Assal	Israel	Episcopal Church in Jerusalem and the Middle East	Delegate from a WCC member church
Rev. Dr	Nancy Nelson	Eisenheimer	United States of America	United Church of Christ	Delegate from a WCC member church
Mrs	Grace Mejang	Eneme	Cameroon	Presbyterian Church in Cameroon	Delegate from a CWME affiliated body
Professor Dr	Tormod	Engelsviken	Norway	Church of Norway	Delegate from an Evangelical church/body
Rev. Dr	Fernando	Enns	Germany	Mennonite Church in Germany	Adviser/Consultant
Mrs	Simone	Ergas	Switzerland	World Council of Churches	WCC staff
Ms	Vija	Esenberga	Norway	Evangelical Lutheran Church of Latvia	Adviser/Consultant
Pasteur	Jean - François	Faba	France	French Evangelical Department for Apostolic Action	Delegate from a CWME affiliated body
Ms	Beate	Fagerli	Switzerland	World Council of Churches	WCC staff
Rev.	Tofinga	Falani	Tuvalu	Tuvalu Christian Church	Delegate from a WCC member church
Bishop	Brian	Farrell	Vatican City	Pontifical Council for Promoting Christian Unity	Delegate from the Roman Catholic church
Rev.	Christopher	Ferguson	Canada	United Church of Canada	Co-opted staff
Ms	Diana	Fernandes dos Santos	Brazil	Methodist Church in Brazil	Steward
Ms	Christina	Fertis Ioannou	Switzerland	World Council of Churches	Interpreter
Pasteure	Laurence	Flachon	Belgium	United Protestant Church of Belgium	Delegate from a WCC member church
Mr	Vaclav	Flasar	Czech Republic	World Council of Churches	Co-opted staff
Bishop	Petru	Florea	Romania	Romanian Orthodox Church	Delegate from a WCC member church
Mrs	Linda	Ford	Switzerland	World Council of Churches	WCC staff
Dr	Andreas	Franz	Germany	Association of Protestant Churches and Missions in Germany	Delegate from a Pentecostal church/body
Rev. Dr	Arne	Fritzson	Sweden	Church of Sweden	Delegate from a WCC member church
Mrs	Astrid	Fylling	Norway	Church of Norway / Council on Ecumenical & International Relations	Delegate from a WCC member church
Prof.	George	Galitis	Greece	Church of Greece	Member of the Athens Local Arrangements Committee
Sister	Ana	Garrigues	Italy	Roman Catholic Church	Delegate from the Roman Catholic church
Rev.	Juan	Gattinoni	Argentina	Evangelical Methodist Church of Argentina	Adviser/Consultant
Dr	Reena Mary	George	India	Christian Medical College	Adviser/Consultant
Rev.	Hansulrich	Gerber	Switzerland	World Council of Churches	WCC staff
H.E. Metropolitan	Alexander-George	Gianniris	Nigeria	Greek Orthodox Patriarchate of Alexandria and All Africa	Delegate from a WCC member church
Reverend	John	Gichimu	Kenya	Organization of African Instituted Churches	Delegate from an Evangelical church/body
Rev.	Theodore	Gill	Switzerland	World Council of Churches	WCC staff
Ms	Zoi	Giovani	Greece	Church of Greece	Steward
Rev.	Raafat Shehata	Girgis	United States of America	International Network Forum on Multicultural Ministry	Adviser/Consultant
Mr	Giovanni	Giuranna	Vatican City	Roman Catholic Church	Delegate from the Roman Catholic church
Mrs	Anastasia	Gkitsi	Greece	Church of Greece	Steward
Rev. Dr	Christopher	Gnanakan	United Kingdom		Adviser/Consultant
Pfarrer Mag.	Manfred	Golda	Austria	Austrian Missionary Council	Delegate from a WCC member church
Dr	Gerard	Goldman	Australia	Roman Catholic Church	Delegate from the Roman Catholic church
Rev.	Laszlo	Gonda	Hungary	Reformed Church in Hungary	Delegate from a WCC member church
Sister	Victoria	González de Castejon	Italy	Roman Catholic Church	Delegate from the Roman Catholic church
Sra	Rhode	González Zorilla	Cuba	Council of Churches of Cuba	Delegate from a CWME affiliated body
Archpriest	Mikhail	Goundiaev	Russian Federation	Moscow Patriarchate	Delegate from a WCC member church
Mr	Rinalds	Grants	Latvia	Evangelical Lutheran Church of Latvia	Delegate from a WCC member church
Prof. Rev. Dr	Christoffer	Grundmann	United States of America	Zentrum für Gesundheitsethik, Evangelischen Akademie Loccum	Adviser/Consultant
Mr	Bogdan	Gumenyuk	Greece	Moscow Patriarchate	Steward
Ms	Viki	Guzauskas	Switzerland	World Council of Churches	Spouse of participant
Rev. Ms	Matild	Gyori	Slovakia	Reformed Christian Church in Slovakia	Delegate from a WCC member church

CWME - Athens, 09 - 16 May 2005
Participants List

Title	First Name	Last Name	Country	Organisation	Capacity
Mr	Panayiotis	Hadjipandelis	Cyprus	Church of Cyprus	Adviser/Consultant
Rev. Dr	Carlos	Ham	Switzerland	World Council of Churches	WCC staff
Ms	Natalie	Hanna	United States of America	American Baptist Churches in the USA	Steward
Ms	Judith	Harke	United States of America	Moravian Church in America - Southern Province	Delegate from a WCC member church
Mr	Jyrki	Härkönen	Finland	Finnish Orthodox Aid	Co-opted staff
Sister	Anne Elizabeth	Hartigan	Ireland	Roman Catholic Church	Delegate from the Roman Catholic church
Herrn Pfarrer	Philipp	Hauenstein	Germany	EKD-Evangelical Lutheran Church in Bavaria	Adviser/Consultant
Pastor	Danielle	Hauss-Berthelin	France	French Evangelical Department for Apostolic Action	Delegate from a CWME affiliated body
Rev.	Michael	Heaney	United Kingdom	Congretional Federation	Delegate from a CWME affiliated body
Father	Johannes Petrus (Jape)	Heath	South Africa	African Network of Religious Leaders Living with or Personally Affected by HIV or AID	Adviser/Consultant
Ms	Katja	Heidemanns	Germany	Roman Catholic Church	Delegate from the Roman Catholic church
Ms	Martina	Helmer-Pham Xuan	Germany	Kirchenamt der EKD, Kirchlicher Entwicklungsdienst	Delegate from a WCC member church
Dr	Harriet	Hill	United States of America	Wycliffe Bible Translators/SIL	Delegate from wider constituency - other
Pasteur	Sylvan	Hinds	Jamaica	United Church in Jamaica and the Cayman Islands	Delegate from a WCC member church
Pasteur	Martin Max	Hoegger	Switzerland	Federation of Swiss Protestant Churches	Delegate from a WCC member church
Mr	Holger	Holtz	Germany	Association of Protestant Churches and Missions in Germany	Delegate from a WCC member church
Rev. Dr	Young-gi	Hong	Korea, Republic of	Institute for Church Growth	Adviser/Consultant
Rev.	Sung Dam	Hong	Korea, Republic of	Presbyterian Church in the Republic of Korea	Adviser/Consultant
Rev.	Vebjorn L.	Horsfjord	Norway	Church of Norway / Council on Ecumenical & International Relations	Accredited press
Rev. Dr	Gordon	How	Canada	United Church of Canada	Co-opted staff
Rev. Dr	Eugene	Hsu	United States of America	Seventh-day Adventist Church World Headquarters	Delegate from wider constituency - other
Rev. Fr	Heikki	Huttunen	Finland	Orthodox Church of Finland	Adviser/Consultant
Ms	Christina Josefien	Hutubessy	Indonesia	Protestant Church in South-East Sulawesi	Steward
Rev.	Merlyn	Hyde-Riley	Jamaica	Jamaica Baptist Union	Delegate from a WCC member church
Bishop		Ieronymos	Tanzania	Greek Orthodox Patriarchate of Alexandria and All Africa	Delegate from a WCC member church
H.E. Metropolitan		Ignatios	Greece	Church of Greece	Adviser/Consultant
Rev.	Hyang Ja	Im	Korea, Republic of	Korean Methodist Church	Delegate from a WCC member church
Mrs	Catherine	Inoubli	Switzerland	World Council of Churches	WCC staff
Obispo	Carlos	Intipampa Aliaga	Bolivia	Evangelical Methodist Church in Bolivia	Adviser/Consultant
Monsignor	Chidi Denis	Isizoh	Italy	Pontifical Council for Interreligious Dialogue	Delegate from the Roman Catholic church
Mr	Sigbjoern	Jaarvik	Norway	Church of Norway	Delegate from a WCC member church
Rev.	Hawea Albert Reed	Jackson	Niue	Church of Niue	Delegate from a WCC member church
Rev.	Darrell Richard	Jackson	Hungary	Conference of European Churches	Delegate from wider constituency - other
Mr	Jean Paul Victor	Jacky	Senegal	World Alliance of YMCAs	Delegate from wider constituency - other
Fr	Deepa	Jacob	India	Syrian Orthodox Patriarchate of Antioch and All the East	Delegate from a WCC member church
Ms	Beate	Jakob	Germany	German Institute for Medical Mission	Adviser/Consultant
Ms	Anita	Jakobsone	Latvia	Evangelical Lutheran Church of Latvia	Delegate from a WCC member church
Ms	Usha	Jesudasan	India	Church of South India	Adviser/Consultant
Rt Rev. Dr	Swamidawson	Jeyapaul David	India	National Council of Churches in India	Delegate from a CWME affiliated body
Reverend	Ole	Joergensen	Denmark	Danish Missionary Council	Delegate from a CWME affiliated body
Rev.	Tore	Johnsen	Norway	Church of Norway	Delegate from a WCC member church
Dr	Eleonor J.	Johnson	Canada	Anglican Church of Canada	Delegate from a WCC member church
Mrs	Elizabeth T.	Joy	United Kingdom	Council for World Mission	Adviser/Consultant
Ms	Doris	Juliano	Germany	Mennonite Church in Germany	Steward
Ms	Julie Amanda	Justus	United States of America	American Baptist Churches in the USA	Steward
Rt Rev.	Lunga Lungile Magqwaqwa	ka Siboto	South Africa	Ethiopian Episcopal Church	Adviser/Consultant
Mr	Samuel N.	KABUE	Kenya	Ecumenical Disability Advocates Network	Adviser/Consultant
Mr	Itonde Abraham	Kakoma	Switzerland	Lutheran World Federation	Adviser/Consultant
Rev.	Baoping	Kan	China	China Christian Council	Delegate from a WCC member church
Prof.	Nam-Soon	Kang	Korea, Republic of	World Conference of Associations of Theological Institutions	Delegate from wider constituency - other
H.C. Bishop	André	Karamaga	Switzerland	World Council of Churches	WCC staff
Ms	Dr Vasilios	Karayiannis	Cyprus	Church of Cyprus	Delegate from a WCC member church
Ms	Zacharoula	Karkafiri	Greece	Church of Greece	Steward
Dr	Veli-Matti	Kärkkäinen	United States of America	Finnish Pentecostal Movement	Adviser/Consultant
Mr	Rifat Odeh	Kassis	Switzerland	World Council of Churches	WCC staff
Mr	Marinos	Katsanos	Greece	Church of Greece	Steward
Ms	Tina	Kaufmann	Germany	EKD-Churches	Steward
Mr	Mathew	Kavunkal	India	Assemblies of God	Delegate from a Pentecostal church/body

CWME - Athens, 09 - 16 May 2005
Participants List

Title	First Name	Last Name	Country	Organization	Capacity
Sister	Mary Jane	Kenney	Italy	Roman Catholic Church	Delegate from the Roman Catholic church
Rev.	Nono	Kepatou	Cameroon	Evangelical Church of Cameroon	Delegate from a WCC member church
Mr	Guillermo	Kerber Mas	Switzerland	World Council of Churches	WCC staff
Ms	Monda	Kercyku	Albania	Orthodox Autocephalous Church of Albania	Steward
Ms	Mary	Khalaf	Syria	Evangelical Synod of Syria and Lebanon	Delegate from a WCC member church
Dr	Kirsteen	Kim	United Kingdom	United College of the Ascension	Adviser/Consultant
Rev.	Kyung In	Kim	Korea, Republic of	Presbyterian Church of Korea	Delegate from a WCC member church
Rev. Dr	Michael	Kinnamon	United States of America	Eden Theological Seminary	Adviser/Consultant
Dr	Antonios	Kireopoulos	United States of America	National Council of the Churches of Christ in the USA	Delegate from a CWME affiliated body
The Rev. Dr	Philip	Knights	United Kingdom	Roman Catholic Church	Delegate from the Roman Catholic church
Rev. Dr	Samuel	Kobia	Switzerland	World Council of Churches	WCC staff
Mrs	Judith	Kocher	Switzerland	World Council of Churches	WCC staff
Rev.	Fepai Fiu	Koila	Samoa	Samoa Council of Churches	Delegate from a WCC member church
Bishop	John	Kongi	Sudan	Africa Inland Church - Sudan	Delegate from a WCC member church
Mr	Nikolaos	Konstantinidis	Greece	Church of Greece	Steward
Rev.	Theodore	Kontidis	Greece	Roman Catholic Church	Delegate from the Roman Catholic church
Prof. Dr	Dimitra	Koukoura	Greece	Theology Dept. of Thessaloniki Univ.	Delegate from a WCC member church
Rev. Dr	Khamphone	Kounthapanya	Laos	Lao Evangelical Church	Delegate from an Evangelical church/body
Ms	Maria	Koutatzi	Hungary	Roman Catholic Church	Delegate from the Roman Catholic church
Mr	Sergey	Kozlov	Greece	Moscow Patriarchate	Steward
Sra	Laura Mabel	Krenz Erlig	Uruguay	Federation of Evangelical Churches in Uruguay	Delegate from a CWME affiliated body
Dr	Manoj	Kurian	Switzerland	World Council of Churches	WCC staff
Archimandrite	Isaias	Kykkotis	Cyprus	Church of Cyprus	Delegate from a WCC member church
Mr	Theodosis	Kyriakidis	Greece	Church of Greece	Steward
Very Rev.	Kwame Joseph	Labi	Switzerland	World Council of Churches	WCC staff
Commissioner		Laikiamlova	India	Salvation Army	Delegate from wider constituency - other
Mrs	Catherine	Lambert	Australia	Uniting Church in Australia	Delegate from a WCC member church
Mr	Stéphane	Lauzet	France	Alliance Evangélique Française	Delegate from an Evangelical church/body
Rev. Dr	Hong-Jung	Lee	China	Presbyterian Church of Korea	Delegate from a WCC member church
Reverend Dr	S. Unzu	Lee	United States of America	Presbyterian Church (USA)	Delegate from a WCC member church
Mr	Georges	Lemopoulos	Switzerland	World Council of Churches	WCC staff
Ms	Puleng	LenkaBula	South Africa	University of South Africa	Adviser/Consultant
Rev. Fr	Jan	Lenssen	Kenya	Pontifical Council for Promoting Christian Unity	Delegate from the Roman Catholic church
Rev.		Leung	China	Hong Kong Christian Council	Delegate from a CWME affiliated body
Sister	Maria Josefa	Leyva Almedros	Spain	Roman Catholic Church	Delegate from the Roman Catholic church
Prof. Dr	Christine	Lienemann	Switzerland	Swiss Reformed Church	Adviser/Consultant
Metropolitan Prof.	Nikolaos	Limouris (Gennadios of Sassima)	Turkey	Ecumenical Patriarchate	Adviser/Consultant
Mrs	Hilda	Lind	Sweden	Church of Sweden	Delegate from a WCC member church
Rev.	Anna	Ljung	Sweden	Swedish Mission Council	Delegate from a WCC member church
Rev.	Julio César	Lopez	Argentina	Iglesia Presbiteriana San Andrés	Adviser/Consultant
Rev.	Hartmut	Lucke	Switzerland	World Council of Churches	Interpreter
Ms	Elizabeth Ann	Lyall	United Kingdom	Church of Scotland	Co-opted staff
Rev.	Wonsuk	Ma	Philippines	Asian Pentecostal Society	Delegate from a Pentecostal church/body
Dr	Julie (Jungja)	Ma	Philippines	Asian Pentecostal Society	Delegate from a Pentecostal church/body
Commissioner	Christine	Mac Millan	Canada	Salvation Army	Delegate from wider constituency - other
Presidente	Luis Reinaldo	Macchi	Argentina	Church of the Disciples of Christ	Delegate from a WCC member church
Mr.	Gérald	Machabert	France	World Council of Churches	Co-opted staff
Rev. Dr	Daisy L.	Machado	United States of America	Christian Church (Disciples of Christ)	Delegate from a WCC member church
Rev.	Lawson	Mafaute	Marshall Islands	United Church of Christ-Congregational in the Marshall Islands	Delegate from a Pentecostal church/body
Frau	Stefanie	Magin	Germany	Evang. Missionswerk in Südwestdeutschland e.V. Indonesia Liaison Desk	Delegate from a WCC member church
Ms	Jacinta	Maingi	Kenya	Norwegian Church Aid	Delegate from a CWME affiliated body
Ms	Kirsti	Malmi	Estonia	Estonian Evangelical Lutheran Church	Adviser/Consultant
Prof.	Tinyiko Sam	Maluleke	South Africa	University of South Africa	Adviser/Consultant
Dr	Philip	Mamalakis	United States of America	Greek Orthodox Archdiocese	Delegate from a WCC member church
Ms	Ginny	Man	China	Hong Kong Christian Council	Delegate from a CWME affiliated body
Miss	Leelavathi	Manasseh	India	Evangelical Fellowship of Asia	Delegate from an Evangelical church/body
Rev. Dr	Deenabandhu	Manchala	Switzerland	World Council of Churches	WCC staff
Dr	Christoph	Mann	Switzerland	World Council of Churches	WCC staff

CWME - Athens, 09 - 16 May 2005
Participants List

Title	First Name	Last Name	Country	Organisation	Capacity
Ms	Anna	Marshall	United States of America	United Methodist Church	Delegate from a WCC member church
Rev.	Chandran Paul	Martin	India	United Evangelical Lutheran Church in India	Delegate from a WCC member church
Mrs	Demina	Massoula	Greece	Church of Greece	Member of the Athens Local Arrangements Committee
Pastora	Norma Beatriz	Mastropierro	Argentina	Christian Biblical Church	Delegate from a WCC member church
Rev. Dr	George	Mathew Nalunnakkal	India	Malankara Orthodox Syrian Church	Delegate from a WCC member church
Rev.	Jacques	Matthey	Switzerland	World Council of Churches	WCC staff
Stadtpfarrer	Attila	Mátyás	Romania	Evangelical - Lutheran Church from Romania	Delegate from a WCC member church
Ms	Natalie Kim	MAXSON	Switzerland	World Council of Churches	WCC staff
Rev. Dr	Marian	McClure	United States of America	Worldwide Ministries Division, Presbyterian Church (USA)	Delegate from a WCC member church
Rev. Dr	Clinton	McCoy	United States of America	Presbyterian Church (USA)	Delegate from a WCC member church
Rev.	Stanley	McKay	Canada	United Church of Canada	Delegate from a WCC member church
Rev.	A. Roy	Medley	United States of America	American Baptist Churches in the USA	Delegate from a WCC member church
Rev.	Herbert	Meissner	Germany	Association of Protestant Churches and Missions in Germany	Delegate from a CWME affiliated body
Dr	Monica J.	Melanchthon	India	Andhra Evangelical Lutheran Church	Adviser/Consultant
Rev. Sister	Camille Rosette	Melezan	Jordan	Roman Catholic Church	Delegate from the Roman Catholic church
Sra	Patricia	Menutti	Argentina	Evangelical Methodist Church of Argentina	Spouse of participant
Rev. Fr	Andon	Merdani	Albania	Orthodox Autocephalous Church of Albania	Delegate from a WCC member church
Mr	Juan	Michel	Switzerland	World Council of Churches	WCC staff
Frau	Peggy	Mihan	Germany	Association of Protestant Churches and Missions in Germany	Delegate from a WCC member church
Rev. Prof. Dr	Vasile	Mihoc	Romania	Romanian Orthodox Church	Adviser/Consultant
Mr	Medhat	Mikhail	Egypt	Coptic Orthodox Church	Steward
Rev.	Charles	Mock	United States of America	National Baptist Convention USA, Inc.	Delegate from a WCC member church
Mrs	Simei	Monteiro	Switzerland	World Council of Churches	WCC staff
Revd	Emilio N.	Monti	Argentina	Argentine Federation of Evangelical Churches	Delegate from a CWME affiliated body
Sra	Catarina Elena	Morales de León	Guatemala	Fraternidad de Presbiteriales Mayas	Adviser/Consultant
Sister	Elizabeth	Moran	Switzerland	World Council of Churches	WCC staff
Rev.	Charles	Mororod	Vatican City	Roman Catholic Church	Delegate from the Roman Catholic church
Mrs	Sita Susi	Morgan de Monti	Argentina	Argentine Federation of Evangelical Churches	Spouse of participant
Prof. Rev. Dr	Nicolae Viorel	Mosoiu	Romania	Romanian Orthodox Church	Delegate from a WCC member church
Major	Jackson	Muasa	Kenya	Salvation Army	Delegate from wider constituency - other
Pastor	Iara	Mueller	Brazil	Ecumenical Disability Advocates Network	Delegate from wider constituency - other
Mr	Lian Sian	Mung	Philippines	Asian Pentecostal Society	Delegate from a Pentecostal church/body
Bishop	Ulises	Muñoz Moraga	Chile	Pentecostal Church of Chile	Delegate from a Pentecostal church/body
Pasteur	Elisée	Musemakweli	Rwanda	Presbyterian Church of Rwanda	Delegate from a WCC member church
Dr	Rommie	Nauta	Netherlands	Uniting Protestant Churches in the Netherlands	Delegate from a WCC member church
Ms	Anna	Navrozidou	Greece	Church of Greece	Member of the Athens Local Arrangements Committee
Fr	Constantin	Necula	Romania	Romanian Orthodox Church	Adviser/Consultant
Ms	Abagail	Nelson	United States of America	Episcopal Church in the USA	Delegate from a WCC member church
Ms	Aino	Nenola	Finland	Orthodox Church of Finland	Adviser/Consultant
Rev.	Winfried	Neusel	Germany	Association of Protestant Churches and Missions in Germany	Delegate from a WCC member church
Mrs	Sarah	Newland-Martin	Jamaica	Bethel Baptist Church	Delegate from wider constituency - other
Mrs	Riina	Nguyen	Finland	Suomen Ekumeenisen Kasvakutsen; Yhdistys rv (SEKY)	Delegate from a WCC member church
Rev. Msgr	Barnaba Phuong	Nguyen Van	Vatican City	Roman Catholic Church	Delegate from the Roman Catholic church
Rev. Dr	Patricia	Nickson	United Kingdom	Church Mission Society	Adviser/Consultant
Ms	Catherine	Nkosi	Malawi	Malawi Council of Churches	Delegate from a CWME affiliated body
Bischof	Axel	Noack	Germany	EKD-Evangelical Church of the Province of Saxony	Delegate from a WCC member church
Dr	Gerritt	Noort	Netherlands	Uniting Protestant Churches in the Netherlands	Delegate from a WCC member church
Pasteur	Jacques	Noumon-Kpessou	Benin	Protestant Methodist Church of Benin	Delegate from a WCC member church
Rev.		Nyansako-ni-NKU	Cameroon	Presbyterian Church in Cameroon	Delegate from a WCC member church
Mr	Birger	Nygaard	Denmark	Areopagos	Adviser/Consultant
Dr	Beatrice	Odonga Mwaka	United Kingdom	Global Reconciliation Network	Delegate from wider constituency - other
Dr	Kelly	O'Donnell	France	World Evangelical Alliance	Adviser/Consultant
Ms	Anjeline	Okola Charles	Kenya	Ecumenical Disability Advocates Network	Other
Deaconess	Oluyinka	Olatunbosun	Nigeria	Methodist Church Nigeria	Delegate from a WCC member church
Sr	Horacio Rubén	Olthoff	Argentina	Reformed Church in Argentina	Delegate from wider constituency - other
Rev. Dr	Opoku	Onyinah	Ghana	Pentecost Bible College	Adviser/Consultant
Archbishop	Fidelia	Onyuku-Opukiri	United Kingdom	Council of Christian Communities of African Approach in Europe	Delegate from wider constituency - other
Dr	John Cherian	Oommen	India	Christian Hospital, Bissamcuttack	Adviser/Consultant

CWME - Athens, 09 - 16 May 2005
Participants List

Title	First Name	Last Name	Organisation	Country	Capacity
Mme	Samia	Ouraied	World Council of Churches	Switzerland	WCC staff
Rev.	Evert	Overeem	Protestant Church in the Netherlands	Netherlands	Delegate from a WCC member church
Rev.	Simon	Oxley	World Council of Churches	Switzerland	WCC staff
Rev.	Judith Marianne Therese	Paas	United Protestant Church	Netherlands	Delegate from a WCC member church
Rev. Dr	Lalsangkima	Pachuau	International Association for mission Studies	United States of America	Adviser/Consultant
Reverend	Gonzalo	Paiz Sabino	Moravian Church in Nicaragua	Nicaragua	Delegate from a WCC member church
Dr	Wing N	Pang	Chinese Coordination Centre of World Evangelism	United States of America	Delegate from an Evangelical church/body
Mr	Ioannis	Pantelidis	Church of Greece	Greece	Steward
Mr	Jorgo	Papadhopuli	Orthodox Autocephalous Church of Albania	Albania	Delegate from a WCC member church
Dr	Athanasios N.	Papathanasiou		Greece	Member of the Athens Local Arrangements Committee
Rev. (Ms)	Sartje	Papoeling	Evangelical Christian Church in Halmahera	Indonesia	Delegate from a WCC member church
Dr	Tito	Paredes	Centro Evangélico de Misiología Andino Amazónica	Peru	Delegate from an Evangelical church/body
Rev. Dr	Soo-Kil	Park	Korean Christian Church in Japan	Japan	Delegate from a WCC member church
Mr	Dimitris C.	Passakos	Church of Greece	Greece	Member of the Athens Local Arrangements Committee
Mrs	Katerina	Pasvanti	Church of Greece	Greece	Steward
Ms	Margaret Ann	Pater	World Council of Churches	Switzerland	Interpreter
Ms	Gillian	Paterson	Roman Catholic Church	United Kingdom	Adviser/Consultant
Ms	Annie priya	Patta	United Evangelical Lutheran Church in India	India	Steward
Ms	Soili	Penttonen	Orthodox Church of Finland	Finland	Delegate from a WCC member church
Reverend Dr	Iosua	Pepine	Tangintebu Theological College	Kiribati	Adviser/Consultant
Archbishop	Aristarchos	Peristeris	Greek Orthodox Patriarchate of Jerusalem	Israel	Delegate from a WCC member church
Dr	Emmanuel P.	PERSELIS	University of Athens School of Theology	Greece	Other
Pastor	Héctor Osvaldo	Petrecca	Christian Biblical Church	Argentina	Delegate from a WCC member church
Ms	Rut	Petrecca	Christian Biblical Church	Argentina	Delegate from a WCC member church
Sra	Linda Elizabeth	Petrecca	Christian Biblical Church	Argentina	Other
Sra	Silvina Graciela	Petti	Evangelical Methodist Church of Argentina	Argentina	Delegate from a WCC member church
Fr.	Bijesh	Philip	Malankara Orthodox Syrian Church	India	Delegate from a WCC member church
Rev. Dr	Larry D.	Pickens	United Methodist Church	United States of America	Delegate from a WCC member church
Rev.	Garland	Pierce	National Council of the Churches of Christ in the USA	United States of America	Delegate from a WCC member church
Rev.	François	Pihaatae	The Maohi Protestant Church	French Polynesia	Delegate from a WCC member church
Rev. Mrs	Janet	Plenert	Mennonite World Conference	Canada	Delegate from wider constituency - other
Dr	James Newton	Poling	Presbyterian Church (USA)	United States of America	Adviser/Consultant
Ms	Alexandra	Pomezny	World Council of Churches	Switzerland	WCC staff
Rev.	Tevaraji	Ponnu	Methodist Church in Malaysia	Malaysia	Delegate from a WCC member church
Monsieur	Jean-Pierre	Popaud	Wycliffe Bible Translators/SIL	Congo, People's Republic of	Delegate from wider constituency - other
Dr	Donald	Posterski	World Vision International	Canada	Delegate from wider constituency - other
Fr	Leonid	Psarianos	Church of Greece	Greece	Member of the Athens Local Arrangements Committee
Mr	Stefanos	Psarras	Church of Greece	Greece	Co-opted staff
Mr	Jean Charles	Puippe	Raptim Travel S.A.	Switzerland	Co-opted staff
Ms	Marina	Punnilathil	Malankara Orthodox Syrian Church	India	Delegate from a WCC member church
Sra	Carla Andrea	Quila Reyes	Free Pentecostal Mission Church of Chile	Chile	Delegate from a WCC member church
Señor	Manuel	Quintero Perez	Frontier Internships in Mission	Switzerland	Delegate from wider constituency - other
Ms	Viola	Raheb	International Centre of Bethlehem	Israel	Adviser/Consultant
Dr	Krishnasamy	Rajendran	India Missions Association	India	Adviser/Consultant
Archdeacon	Radomir	Rakic	Serbian Orthodox Church	Yugoslavia	Delegate from a WCC member church
Madame	Mbolatiana	Ramamonjy-Ratrimo née Rajaonah Raholimanana	Reformed Church of French Guyana	Madagascar	Delegate from wider constituency - other
Bishop	Donald J.	Reece	Pontifical Council for Promoting Christian Unity	Antigua and Barbuda	Delegate from the Roman Catholic church
Ms	Myriam	Reidy Prost	World Council of Churches	Switzerland	WCC staff
Ms	Regina	Reuschle Schaepers	World Council of Churches	Switzerland	Interpreter
Rev.	Alain	Rey	Evangelical Community for Apostolic Action	France	Delegate from a CWME affiliated body
Rev.	Helen	Richmond	Uniting Church in Australia	Australia	Delegate from a WCC member church
Rev. Dr	Seppo Tapani	Rissanen	Finnish Evangelical Lutheran Mission	Finland	Delegate from an Evangelical church/body
Father	Martin	Ritsi	Ecumenical Patriarchate	United States of America	Delegate from a WCC member church
Rev.	Irving	Rivera	Reformed Church in America	United States of America	Delegate from a WCC member church
Mr	Samuel	Rizk		Lebanon	Adviser/Consultant
Rev. Fr	Carlos	Rodríguez Linera	Roman Catholic Church	Vatican City	Delegate from the Roman Catholic Church
Mr	Eugeniu	Rogoti	Romanian Orthodox Church	Romania	Delegate from a WCC member church
Ms	Gracia Violeta	Ross Quiroga	Christian Evangelical Church in Bolivia	Bolivia	Adviser/Consultant

CWME - Athens, 09 - 16 May 2005
Participants List

Title	First Name	Last Name	Organisation	Country	Capacity
Pastor	David Dagoberto	Ruiz Molina	Great Commission Round Table /Cooperación Misionera de Iberoamérica	Guatemala	Delegate from wider constituency - other
Prof.	Brenda Consuelo	Ruiz Perez	Baptist Convention of Nicaragua	Nicaragua	Adviser/Consultant
Dr	Samuel Mwenda	Rukunga	Christian Health Association of Kenya	Kenya	Adviser/Consultant
Dr	Vida	Rus	Roman Catholic Church	Romania	Delegate from the Roman Catholic church
Rev.	Tuula	Sääksi	Evangelical Lutheran Church of Finland	Finland	Delegate from a WCC member church
Dr	Minna	Saarelma-Maunumaa	Evangelical Lutheran Church of Finland	Finland	Delegate from a WCC member church
Bishop	Ioannis	Sakellariou	Church of Greece	Greece	Member of the Athens Local Arrangements Committee
Mr	Mats	Sandelin		Sweden	Other
Dr Ms	Pauline	Sathiamurthy	Church of South India	India	Delegate from a WCC member church
Fr Dr	Ioan	Sauca	Romanian Orthodox Church	Switzerland	WCC staff
Mrs	Renate	Sbeghen	World Council of Churches	Switzerland	Adviser/Consultant
Rev. Dr	Klaus	Schafer	Association of Protestant Churches and Missions in Germany	Germany	Adviser/Consultant
Prof.	Ruth Norma	Schneider	Evangelical Methodist Church of Argentina	Argentina	Spouse of participant
Pasteur	Olivier	Schopfer	World Council of Churches	Switzerland	WCC staff
Rev. Dr	Robert	Schreiter	Roman Catholic Church	United States of America	Delegate from the Roman Catholic church
Prof. Dr	Erika	Schuchardt	Association of Protestant Churches and Missions in Germany	Germany	Adviser/Consultant
Ms	Marilia	Schüller	World Council of Churches	Switzerland	WCC staff
Sr	Hugo Waldemar	Schultheis	Evangelical Church of the River Plate	Argentina	Delegate from a WCC member church
Ms	Bibiana Nalwindi	SEABORN	URM Canada	Canada	Adviser/Consultant
Mr	Rethabile Isaac	Semethe	Lesotho Evangelical Church	Lesotho	Delegate from a WCC member church
Dr	Erlinda	Senturias	Southern Christian College	Philippines	Adviser/Consultant
Fr	Fr. Moses	Shafik	Coptic Orthodox Church	Kenya	Delegate from a WCC member church
Rev. Dr	Hermen	Shastri	Council of Churches of Malaysia	Malaysia	Delegate from a CWME affiliated body
Soeur	Bedour Antoun (Sister Irini)	Shenouda	Sisters of Our Lady of the Apostles	Italy	Delegate from a CWME affiliated body
Rev.	Batara	Sihombing	Indonesian Christian Church (HKI)	Indonesia	Delegate from a WCC member church
Rev.	Derek	Silwenga	United Church of Zambia	Zambia	Delegate from a WCC member church
Reverend	Erord	Simae	Provinces of the Moravian Church in Tanzania	Tanzania	Delegate from a WCC member church
Sister	Gemma	Simmonds	Roman Catholic Church	United Kingdom	Delegate from the Roman Catholic church
Mr	Higumen Filipp	Simonov	Russian Orthodox Church	Russian Federation	Delegate from a WCC member church
Mr	Carlos	Sintado	World Council of Churches	Switzerland	Interpreter
Ms	Pohathai	Sittiyot		Thailand	Steward
Mr	Lambert Chirtranjan Devadasen	Solomon	Ecumenical Coalition on Tourism (ECOT)	Hong Kong	Adviser/Consultant
Msgr	Antonio	Soto Guerrero	Roman Catholic Church	Vatican City	Delegate from the Roman Catholic church
Mr	Vasileos	Stamatelatos	Church of Greece	United Kingdom	Steward
Fr	Brian	Starken	Roman Catholic Church	Ireland	Delegate from the Roman Catholic church
Mr	Libor	Stava	World Council of Churches	Czech Republic	Co-opted staff
Pasteure	Claire Antoinette	Steiner	Swiss Missionary Council	Switzerland	Delegate from a CWME affiliated body
Dr	Valdir	Steuernagel	World Vision International	Switzerland	Delegate from wider constituency - other
Rt Rev.	Seraphim	Storheim	Orthodox Church in America	Canada	Adviser/Consultant
Rev.	Jane	Stranz	World Council of Churches	Switzerland	WCC staff
Mrs	Annegreth	Struempfel	World Council of Churches	Germany	Co-opted staff
Rev.	Göran	Sturve	Swedish Mission Council	Sweden	Delegate from a CWME affiliated body
Rev. Dr	Joseph	Suico	Asia Pacific Theological Seminary	Philippines	Delegate from a Pentecostal church/body
Rev.	Bertil	Svensson	Mission Covenant Church of Sweden	Sweden	Delegate from a WCC member church
Mr	Ondrej	Svora	World Council of Churches	Czech Republic	Co-opted staff
Rev.	Bertram Granville	Swartz	United Congregational Church of Southern Africa	South Africa	Steward
Rev.	Cesar	Taguba	Ecumenical Ministry for Filipinos Abroad (EMFA)	Netherlands	Adviser/Consultant
Mrs	Katalina	Tahaafe-Williams	United Reformed Church	United Kingdom	Delegate from a WCC member church
Rev.	Tiina Marja	Talvitie	Evangelical Lutheran Church of Finland	Finland	Adviser/Consultant
Mrs	Eleni	Tamaresi - Papathanasiou	Church of Greece	Greece	Spouse of participant
Monsieur	Serge	Tankeu Keusseu	Evangelical Church of Cameroon	Cameroon	Steward
Rev. Dr	Elisabeth S.	Tapia	World Council of Churches	Switzerland	WCC staff
Ms	Lizette Pearl	Tapia-Raquel	National Council of Churches in the Philippines	Philippines	Delegate from a CWME affiliated body
Ms	Evelyne	Tatu		Switzerland	Interpreter
Ms	Tara	Tautari	World Council of Churches	Switzerland	WCC staff
Ms	Dalena Ivandie	Taylor Pondler	Moravian Church in Nicaragua	Nicaragua	Steward
Madame	Marie Noelle	Tchouya Njayang	Evangelical Church of Cameroon	Cameroon	Delegate from a WCC member church
Fr		Thomas	Coptic Orthodox Church	Kenya	Delegate from a WCC member church

CWME - Athens, 09 - 16 May 2005
Participants List

Title	First Name	Last Name	Country	Organisation	Capacity
Mr	Fridthjofur - Fiffi	Thorsteinsson	Iceland	Evangelical Lutheran Church of Iceland	Steward
Rev.	Samuel	Tialevea	Samoa	Congregational Christian Church in Samoa	Delegate from a WCC member church
Mme	Madeleine Sara	Tiki-Koum (Soppo)	Cameroon	Evangelical Church of Cameroon	Delegate from a WCC member church
Sra	Ester	Titosse	Portugal	Evangelical Presbyterian Church of Portugal	Delegate from a WCC member church
Ms	Gunilla	Togan	Sweden	Swedish Mission Council	Delegate from a CWME affiliated body
Rev.	Angharad Malama	Toma	Fiji	Congregational Christian Church in Samoa	Steward
Ms	Monica	Tompkins	Argentina	Anglican Church of the Southern Cone of America	Delegate from a WCC member church
Ms	Idan	Topno	India	Gossner Evangelical Lutheran Church in Chotanagpur	Adviser/Consultant
Rev.	Timoteo Luis Antonio	Torres Esquivel	Cuba	Ecumenical Patriarchate	Delegate from a WCC member church
Rev.	Hans Alfred	Trein	Brazil	Evangelical Church of Lutheran Confession in Brazil	Delegate from a WCC member church
Pr.	Patricia M.	Tucker	United States of America	Christian Church (Disciples of Christ)	Delegate from a WCC member church
Rev.	Pieter C.	Tuit	United States of America	Reformed Ecumenical Council	Delegate from a CWME affiliated body
Rev.	Peseti Latu	Tukutau	Tonga	Free Wesleyan Church of Tonga (Methodist Church in Tonga)	Delegate from a WCC member church
Mr	Mathews	Tulombolombo	Malawi	Malawi Council of Churches	Delegate from a CWME affiliated body
Mr	Mats	Tunehag	Sweden		Adviser/Consultant
Mr	Bernard	Ugeux	France	Roman Catholic Church	Delegate from the Roman Catholic church
Ms	Nance	Upham	France	AIDS-bells.org	Adviser/Consultant
Rev.	Gerard S.	Valdivia	United States of America	Pentecostal Church of Chile	Delegate from a Pentecostal church/body
Prof.	Mammen Varkki	Valiyaparayidam	India	People's Reporter	Accredited press
Commissioner	Netty	van der Harst	Netherlands	Salvation Army	Delegate from wider constituency - other
Rev.	Sybout	van der Meer	Netherlands	Habitat for Humanity International	Adviser/Consultant
Rev. Dr	Desmond Peter	van der Water	United Kingdom	Council for World Mission	Delegate from a CWME affiliated body
Rev. Drs	Wout	van Laar	Netherlands	Netherlands Missionary Council	Delegate from a CWME affiliated body
Dr	George	Vandervelde	Canada	World Evangelical Alliance	Delegate from an Evangelical church/body
Herrn Prof. Dr	Christos	Vantsos	Greece	Ecumenical Patriarchate	Delegate from a WCC member church
Rev.	David	Vargas	United States of America	Christian Church (Disciples of Christ)	Delegate from a WCC member church
Rev.	Nirmala	Vasanthakumar	India	Church of South India	Delegate from a WCC member church
Dr	Petros	Vassiliadis	Greece	Society for Ecumenical Studies and Inter-Orthodox Relations	Adviser/Consultant
Ms	Anastasia	Vassiliadou	Greece	Church of Greece	Delegate from a WCC member church
Deacon	Alexander	Vasyutin	Russian Federation	Russian Orthodox Church	Adviser/Consultant
Mr	Dmytro	Verlanov	Greece	Church of Greece	Steward
Ms	Elizabeth Anne	Visinand	Switzerland	World Council of Churches	WCC staff
Prof.	Horacio Rubén	Vivares	Argentina	Evangelical Methodist Church of Argentina	Adviser/Consultant
Ms	Denise	Von Arx	Switzerland	World Council of Churches	WCC staff
Mr.	Thomas Emmanuel Orlando Philippe Gregorius	von Sandnaes	Switzerland	World Council of Churches	Spouse of participant
Rev. Dr	Klaus Peter	Voss	Germany	Arbeitsgemeinschaft Christlicher Kirchen in Deutschland e.V. Ökumenische Centrale	Adviser/Consultant
Mr	George	Voucanos	Greece	Church of Greece	Member of the Athens Local Arrangements Committee
Ms	Carol Spicher	Waggy	United States of America	Church of the Brethren	Delegate from a WCC member church
Rev.	Ron	Wallace	Canada	Presbyterian Church in Canada	Delegate from a WCC member church
Mr	Aleksander	Wasyluk	Switzerland	World Council of Churches	WCC staff
Dr	Dietrich	Werner	Germany	Missionsakademie an der Universität Hamburg	Adviser/Consultant
Reverend Dr	Andrew Price	Williams	United Kingdom	Council for World Mission	Delegate from a CWME affiliated body
Rev. Mrs	Omatsola	Williams	Nigeria	Church of the Lord (Aladura) Worldwide	Delegate from a WCC member church
Miss	Eirwen Ann	Williams	United Kingdom	Union of Welsh Independents	Delegate from a WCC member church
Dr	Kathleen	Williams	Australia	World Conference of Associations of Theological Institutions	Delegate from wider constituency - other
Mr	Peter	Williams	Switzerland	World Council of Churches	WCC staff
Mr	Michael	Xekardaxis	Greece	Church of Greece	Steward
Mr	Dimitris	Xygalatas	Greece	World Council of Churches	Translator
Frau	Hye Ran	Yoo	Korea, Republic of	Presbyterian Church in the Republic of Korea	Adviser/Consultant
Prof.	Hae Yong	You	Korea, Republic of	Presbyterian Church in the Republic of Korea	Adviser/Consultant
Bishop		Youakim	Kenya	Coptic Orthodox Church	Delegate from a WCC member church
Rev. Dr	Hesdie	Zamuel	Suriname	Moravian Church in Suriname	Delegate from a WCC member church
Mrs	Tatjana	Zarraga	Switzerland	World Council of Churches	WCC staff
Rev.	Magdalena	Zimmermann	Switzerland	Basel Mission	Delegate from a WCC member church
Very Rev. Archimai (Aristotle) Ambrose		Zographos	Korea, Republic of	Ecumenical Patriarchate	Delegate from a WCC member church
Mrs	Maria	Zorba	Greece	Church of Greece	Steward
Fr	Milan	Zust	Italy	Roman Catholic Church	Delegate from the Roman Catholic church
Frau	Dita	Zwafelfink	Germany	EKD	Delegate from a WCC member church

2. List of Affiliated Bodies

Argentine Federation of Evangelical Churches
National Council of Churches in Australia
Austrian Missionary Council
Bahamas Christian Council
National Council of Churches, Bangladesh
Missionary Commission of the United Protestant Church
Canadian Council of Churches
Hong Kong Christian Council
Council of Churches of Cuba
Middle East Council of Churches
Church of Jesus Christ on Earth by his Messenger Simon Kimbangu
Danish Missionary Council
Finnish Ecumenical Council
French Evangelical Department for Apostolic Action
Evangelical Community for Apostolic Action
Association of Protestant Churches and Missions in Germany
National Council of Churches in India
Communion of Churches in Indonesia
Society of the Divine Word
Sisters of Our Lady of the Apostles
Missionaries of Africa
Marist Missionary Sisters
Jamaica Council of Churches
Nippon Christian Academy Tokyo Center
Federation of the Protestant Churches in Madagascar
Malawi Council of Churches
Council of Churches of Malaysia
Evangelical Federation of Mexico
Myanmar Council of Churches
Netherlands Missionary Council
Conference of Churches in Aotearoa New Zealand
National Council of Churches in Pakistan
National Council of Churches in the Philippines
Portuguese Council of Christian Churches
Council of Churches of Puerto Rico
National Council of Churches in Korea
Council of Churches in Sierra Leone
National Council of Churches of Singapore
South African Council of Churches
National Christian Council of Sri Lanka
Swedish Mission Council
Frontier Internships in Mission
Swiss Missionary Council
Church of Christ in Thailand
Christian Council of Trinidad and Tobago
Churches' Commission on Mission
Irish Council of Churches

Council for World Mission
Federation of Evangelical Churches in Uruguay
National Council of the Churches of Christ in the USA
Reformed Ecumenical Council
Christian Council of Zambia
Zimbabwe Council of Churches

3. CWME Officers
The officers of the Commisison on World Mission and Evangelism are
Rev. Ruth Bottoms, moderator
Rev. Dr. Geroge Mathew Nalunnakkal, vice-moderator
Rev. Jacques Matthey, staff

4. List of Commissioners
Rev. Dr Athanasius Amos Akunda, South Africa (Kenya)
Ms Deborah E. Bass, USA
Dr Christoph Benn, Switzerland (Germany)
Dr Sara Bhattacharji, India
Rev. Ruth Bottoms, UK
Rev. Avedis Boynerian, USA (Syria)
Rev. Boonsong Dangruan, Thailand
Dr Tormod Engelsviken, Norway
Rev. Arne Fritzson, Sweden
Fr Mikhail Goundiaev, Switzerland (Russia)
Rev. Michael Heaney, UK
Dr Eleanor J. Johnson, Canada
Pasteur Joseph Nono Kepatou, Cameroon
Deaconess Linda I. Koroma, Sierra Leone
Ms Maria Koutatzi, Hungary (Greece)
Rev. Dr Lee, Hong-Jung, Hong Kong (Korea)
Fr Jan Lenssen M. Afr., Kenya (Belgium)
Rev. Anna Ljung, Sweden
Dr George Mathew Nalunnakkal, India
Rev. Dr Marian McClure, USA
Rev. Herbert Meissner, Germany
Sister Celine Monteiro, fmm, Vatican (India)
Prof. Rev. Dr Nicolae Viorel Mosoiu, Romania
Mr Obadiah Moyo, Zimbabwe
Dr Rubén E. Paredes Alfaro, Peru
Bishop Paul, Kenya (Egypt)
Pastor Héctor O. Petrecca, Argentina
Rev. Garland Pierce, USA
Pastor François Pihaatae, Tahiti, French Polynesia
Father Martin Ritsi, USA
Profesor Violeta Rocha, Costa Rica (Nicaragua)
Dr George Vandervelde, Canada
Dr Petros Vassiliadis, Greece
Rev. Dr Hesdie Zamuel, Suriname

5. The Conference Planning Committee
Rev. Ruth Bottoms, UK
Dr. George Mathew Nalunnakkal, India
Dr. Sara Bhattacharji, India
Ms. Linda Koroma, Sierra Leone
Ms. Maria Koutatzi, Greece
Rev. Anna Ljung Hansson, Sweden
Rev. Herbert Meissner, Germany
Dr. Tito Paredes, Peru
Rev. Héctor Petrecca, Argentina
Dr. Petros Vassiliadis, Greece
Rev. Avedis Boynerian, Lebanon
Rev. Dr Lee, Hong Jung, Korea
Rev. Patricia Tucker, USA

6. The Spiritual Life Committee
Father Alkiviadis Calivas, Ecumenical Patriarchate, USA (Co-moderator)
Rev. Anna Ljung, Mission Covenant Church, Sweden (Co-moderator)
Rev. Juan Gattinoni, Methodist Church, Argentina
Father Heikki Huttunen, Finnish Orthodox Church, Finland
Ms. Martha Kumwenda, Pentecostal Church, Zambia
Dr. C. Poonnoose Mathew, Christian Medical College, India
Ms. Brenda Ruiz, Baptist Church, Nicaragua
Dr. You, Hae-Yong, Presbyterian Church, Korea
Sr. Honorine Yamba, Roman Catholic, Congo - Nigeria
Rev. Garland Pierce, African Methodist Episcopal Church, USA

7. Members of the Athens Local Arrangements Committee
Bishop Ioannis of Thermopylae, Church of Greece
Fr. Theordore Koutidis, Roman Catholic Church
Rev. Phaedon Camboropoulos, Evangelical Church of Greece
Archbishop Khoren Togharamadjian, Armenian Orthodox Church
Rev. Vicken Cholakian, Armenian Evangelical Church
Revd. Malcolm Bradshaw, Anglican Church in Greece
Co-opted staff:
Bishop Agathangelos, Director of Apostoliki Diakonia
Fr. Leonid Psarianos, Apostoliki Diakonia, Church of Greece
Mr. George Voucanos, Church of Greece
Prof. Dr. George Galitis, Church of Greece
Ms. Demina Masoula, Church of Greece
Mr. Michael Chatziyannis, Greek Bible Society
Mr. Athanasios Papathanasiou, Church of Greece
Dr. Dimitrios Passakos, Local organiser

COMMISSION ON WORLD MISSION AND EVANGELISM
AND
CONFERENCE ON WORLD MISSION AND EVANGELISM
BY-LAWS

1. INTRODUCTION

In 1961, the International Missionary Council (IMC) – which traces its history to the Edinburgh conference of 1910 – was merged with the World Council of Churches on the understanding that concerns for mission and evangelism would have a structured place at the heart of the WCC. This finds expression in the Conference and the Commission on World Mission and Evangelism.

2. MEANINGS in These By-Laws:

2.1   **The Conference** means the Conference on World Mission and Evangelism.
2.2   **The Commission** means the Commission on World Mission and Evangelism.
2.3   **The Officers** shall be the Moderator and Vice-Moderator of the Commission and the Coordinator of the Mission and Evangelism Team.
2.4   **The Staff** means the staff members of the WCC assigned to work on world mission and evangelism.

3. THE COMMISSION

3.1 Aim
In continuity with the functions formerly carried out by the International Missionary Council and articulated in the Common Understanding and Vision of the WCC, the aims of the Commission are:
3.1.1   To carry out the aim of the Conference: "to assist the Christian community in the proclamation of the gospel of Jesus Christ, by word and deed, to the whole world to the end that all may believe in him and be saved" (cf 4.1).
3.1.2   To facilitate the common witness of the churches in each place and in all places and to help them support each other in their local, national and worldwide work of mission and evangelism.

3.2 Specific Functions of the Commission
The specific functions of the Commission in collaboration with staff members assigned to the Mission and Evangelism Team, are:
3.2.1   To advise the Central Committee of the World Council of Churches through the Programme Committee on matters relating to mission and

evangelism, including issues relating to health and healing, community and justice, and assist in the evaluation and review of programmes as appropriate.

3.2.2 To assist the churches and councils and other bodies in common exploration of the truth and content of the gospel in relation to culture and the manner of its public proclamation.

3.2.3 To promote biblical and theological studies on the nature of Christian witness, as demand arises from the life of the churches in their encounters with the contemporary world, and from the concerns of the various expressions of the ecumenical movement in mission.

3.2.4 To provoke the churches, mission agencies and other bodies to discern the opportunities and priorities for holistic mission, including issues relating to health and healing, community and justice, in various cultures and power structures, locally and worldwide.

3.2.5 To encourage common, unequivocal yet sensitive "witness in Christ's way" so as to promote the fellowship of the church in mission.

3.2.6 To promote mutual dialogue on mission understanding, practice and relationships with churches as well as with other bodies not presently related to the Conference.

3.2.7 To communicate the ongoing concerns of mission and evangelism through publications and other instruments such as the *International Review of Mission* and the World Wide Web.

3.2.8 To recommend to the Central Committee the holding of and to facilitate meetings of the Conference.

3.2.9 To seek the enlargement, where appropriate, of the circle of formal affiliation and informal association with the Conference.

3.2.10 To set up *ad hoc* task groups from time to time to address specific issues related to mission and evangelism, subject to availability of funds and the approval of the Programme Committee of the Central Committee.

3.2.11 To raise funds for specific work arising from the Conference, subject to the approval of the Central Committee.

3.3 Structure of the Commission

3.3.1 The Commission shall consist of not more than thirty persons appointed by the Central Committee. The outgoing Commission on World Mission and Evangelism shall submit nominations at the appropriate time, to the Central Committee, for membership of the Commission, according to the following categories:

a) the majority should be drawn from the member churches of the World Council of Churches;

b) about 25% should be chosen from those nominated by the Affiliated Bodies of the Conference;

c) the remaining members should be drawn from a wider constituency. In choosing members of the Commission consideration shall be given, *inter alia*, to proven ability and commitment to reflect on mission, and to confessional, gender and regional balances consistent with WCC policies.

3.3.2 Members of the Commission shall be appointed after each WCC Assembly and shall hold office until the following Assembly. They shall be eligible for a further term. If a member of the Commission ceases effectively to hold office during the term of his or her appointment, a replacement will be appointed by the Central Committee to serve until the next Assembly.

3.3.3 The Commission shall have a Moderator elected by the Central Committee and a Vice-Moderator elected by the Commission. The Moderator normally represents the Commission and the Conference on the WCC's Programme Committee.

3.3.4 The Commission shall report to the Central Committee and shall work with staff of the WCC under the direction of the General Secretary.

3.3.5 The Commission shall keep the member churches and the affiliated bodies of the Conference informed of its work.

3.3.6 The Commission may appoint a small Executive Group to act on its behalf between meetings of the Commission. Such an Executive Group would include the Officers.

3.3.7 The Commission shall meet normally every 18 months.

3.3.8 The staff of the Commission shall be the members of the Mission and Evangelism Team as assigned by the General Secretary. Staff shall report to the Commission but are accountable to the General Secretary on behalf of the Executive and Central Committees.

3.3.9 Finance
    a) The budget for the activities of the Commission shall be prepared and submitted to the Finance Committee as part of the unified budget of the Council.
    b) Within the overall budget and policies agreed by the Central Committee, the Commission will oversee the funding and costs of activities and projects.
    c) The Commission shall assist in developing financial resources for the work of mission and evangelism.

4. THE CONFERENCE

4.1 Aim
The aim of the Conference is to assist the Christian community in the proclamation of the gospel of Jesus Christ, by word and deed, to the whole world to the end that all may believe in him and be saved.

4.2 Governing Principles
4.2.1 The main task of the Conference is to provide opportunities for churches, mission agencies, groups and national and regional councils concerned with Christian mission to meet together for reflection and consultation leading to common witness.

4.2.2 The Conference shall normally meet once between Assemblies. This Conference Meeting shall be convened by the Commission with the approval of the Central Committee. The Moderator and vice-Moderator of this Conference Meeting shall be the Moderator and Vice-Moderator of the Commission together with the Coordinator of the Mission and Evangelism Team.

4.2.3　The results of the Conference Meeting shall be communicated to the constituency of the Conference by the Commission and shall also be reported to the Assembly and the Central Committee through the Commission.

4.2.4　Administrative and executive responsibilities of the Conference shall be carried out by the Commission and staff.

4.3 Membership of the Conference

4.3.1　Subject to the approval of the Central Committee the Commission shall determine the size, membership and programme of the World Conference, with due attention to regional, confessional, gender and age diversity within the overall norms set by the WCC. Due care will be taken to provide for substantial representation of WCC member churches and CWME Affiliated Bodies from names submitted by these member churches and bodies, along with a number of other persons involved at the frontiers of Christian mission.

4.3.2　The Commission shall take care to maintain an ongoing communication with member churches and members of the Conference following the Conference Meeting itself, in order that this body of people may assist in following-up decisions made by the Conference Meeting and may serve as interpreters of developments related to Conference follow-up.

4.3.3　Members of the Conference shall seek to promote in their councils and churches the aims and findings of the Conference Meeting and the work of the Mission and Evangelism Team. Members of the Conference shall draw to the attention of the Commission matters with which they feel it should be concerned. They shall seek to promote support, including financial support, for the work of the Mission and Evangelism Team.

4.3.4　Consultants and observers may be invited to meetings of the Conference. They shall have the right to speak but not to vote.

4.3.5　*Quorum of the Conference*
One third of the members of the Conference shall constitute a quorum at any given session, provided that
a)　among them there are members of the Conference from each continent, and
b)　among the members present at least one third of the Affiliated Bodies are represented.

4.4 Affiliation and Consultative Relations

4.4.1　National councils or regional conferences which accept the aim of the Conference may become affiliated to the Conference. All Councils affiliated to the CWME under the previous Constitution shall be regarded as affiliated to the Conference under these by-laws, unless they notify to the contrary.

4.4.2　Churches in countries where there is no affiliated national council may apply for affiliation to the Conference.

4.4.3　A group of churches organized for joint action for mission in a country where there is an affiliated national council or such an international or intercontinental group of churches, may also apply for affiliation.

4.4.4　Applications for affiliation shall be considered by the Commission. If the application is supported by a two-thirds majority of the Commission present and voting, this action shall be communicated to the affiliated members of the Conference and, unless objection is received from more than one third of them within six months, the applicant shall be declared affiliated. There shall be consultation with the member churches of the WCC in the area concerned, except in the case of councils already in association with the WCC.

4.4.5   National and regional Christian councils and churches and other groupings, may – while not desiring affiliation – request a consultative relation with the Conference. In such cases, those requesting such a consultative relationship must accept the aims of the Conference. Action on such requests shall be taken by the Commission. Councils and other groupings in consultative relation may send consultants to meetings of the Conference, who shall be entitled to speak but not vote.

5. AMENDMENTS

5.1   The Central Committee may make amendments on the recommendation of, or in consultation with, the Commission.

5.2   Amendments may be proposed by the Conference, the Affiliated Bodies of the Conference or the Commission.

5.3   Notice of any proposed amendment must be sent to the Affiliated Bodies of the Conference not less than six months prior to its consideration by the Commission.

5.4   The Commission may recommend a proposed amendment to the Central Committee unless one-third of the Affiliated Bodies of the Conference have indicated in writing prior to the Commission meeting that they oppose the amendment.

Version as adopted at the 1999 session of the WCC Central Committee and at the April/May 2000 session of the CWME Commission.

MAP OF AGIOS ANDREAS

1. Main building

2. Plenary tent

3. Worship tent

4. Synaxis tent 1-2

5. Synaxis tent 3-4

6. Synaxis tent 5-6

7. Glass house

8. Outdoor chapel

9. Clinic

10. Shop

11. Cafeteria

12. Seaside taverna